PUNISHMENT AND

Punishment and Freedom

A Liberal Theory of Penal Justice

ALAN BRUDNER

OXFORD
UNIVERSITY PRESS

Great Clarendon Street, Oxford OX2 6DP

Oxford University Press is a department of the University of Oxford.
It furthers the University's objective of excellence in research, scholarship,
and education by publishing worldwide in

Oxford New York

Auckland Cape Town Dar es Salaam Hong Kong Karachi
Kuala Lumpur Madrid Melbourne Mexico City Nairobi
New Delhi Shanghai Taipei Toronto

With offices in

Argentina Austria Brazil Chile Czech Republic France Greece
Guatemala Hungary Italy Japan Poland Portugal Singapore
South Korea Switzerland Thailand Turkey Ukraine Vietnam

Oxford is a registered trade mark of Oxford University Press
in the UK and in certain other countries

Published in the United States
by Oxford University Press Inc., New York

© Alan Brudner, 2009

The moral rights of the author have been asserted

Crown copyright material is reproduced under Class Licence
Number C01P0000148 with the permission of OPSI
and the Queen's Printer for Scotland

Database right Oxford University Press (maker)

First published 2009
First published in paperback 2012

All rights reserved. No part of this publication may be reproduced,
stored in a retrieval system, or transmitted, in any form or by any means,
without the prior permission in writing of Oxford University Press,
or as expressly permitted by law, or under terms agreed with the appropriate
reprographics rights organization. Enquiries concerning reproduction
outside the scope of the above should be sent to the Rights Department,
Oxford University Press, at the address above

You must not circulate this book in any other binding or cover
and you must impose the same condition on any acquirer

British Library Cataloguing in Publication Data
Data available

Library of Congress Cataloging in Publication Data
Data available

Typeset by Newgen Imaging Systems (P) Ltd., Chennai, India
Printed in Great Britain
on acid-free paper by
CPI Group (UK) Ltd., Croydon, CR0 4YY

ISBN 978–0–19–920725–1

ISBN 978–0–19–965233–4 (pbk.)

1 3 5 7 9 10 8 6 4 2

For Fern

General Editor's Preface

In presenting this volume on *Punishment and Freedom: A Liberal Theory of Penal Justice*, the Oxford Monographs series welcomes a major contribution to the theory of penal law, focusing on the rationale for punishment and on the theoretical underpinnings of the general part of criminal law. Situating the debate within constitutional and political theory rather than moral philosophy, the author draws on Hegelian insights in developing his conception of deserved punishment and the concepts of 'formal agency' and 'real autonomy' that underpin his analysis of fundamental elements of criminal liability such as *actus reus* and *mens rea*, justification and excuse. The author concedes the complexity of his depiction of the criminal law and of the interacting paradigms that shape the general part of a liberal penal law, but argues that they can and should be seen as a kind of unity. The argument embodies not only a direct rejection of the challenge of some critical writers, but also a radical revision of what may be regarded as prevailing orthodoxies in liberal criminal law theory. Professor Brudner has written a stimulating and insightful work, which it is a pleasure to welcome into the series.

Andrew Ashworth

Preface

This book sets out an understanding of the general part of the penal law of a liberal legal order. By a liberal legal order I mean one based on a fundamental belief common to all denominations of philosophical liberalism: that the individual agent is, by virtue of its capacity to set ends for itself, a locus of inviolable worth. Of the many implications of this belief, two are foundational for what follows: that it is wrong for any private person to force a competent, adult human being to serve ends not actually its own; and that it is wrong for anyone acting in the name of a public authority to force a human being to serve the private ends of others.

How the general part of a liberal legal order's penal law differs from its special part may be understood in various ways, but I believe the following ground of distinction is the most basic. Whereas the special part limits the liberty of the subjects of a political authority, the general part limits the liberty of officials who exercise that authority's penal power.[1] Whereas the special part announces what conduct is proscribed for the subjects of a particular legal regime, the general part sets forth the conditions under which, given a factual breach of any legal command, penal force against the lawbreaker is justified. Thus a theory of the general part of a liberal legal order's penal law is a liberal theory of penal justice.

Contrary to a common belief, a liberal theory of penal justice is not necessarily one that conceives the individual as an abstract subject or person uprooted from its social and ethical environment. Certainly, that is not what I mean by such a theory. Rather, by a liberal theory of penal justice I mean one that derives legal constraints on punishment from an idea of what reconciles penal force with the freedom and inviolable worth of the individual agent. To be sure, part of the story about these constraints will presume the abstract subject as protagonist, but not all of it will. On the contrary, the full story rests on a highly contextualized picture of the individual agent, of which the abstract subject is only a part.

Broadly stated, my thesis is that the full story about how official penal force can be reconciled with the freedom and inviolability of the individual agent provides the most integrative and ethically satisfying view of the penal law of liberal legal systems—or rather of their general part. Penal law theory, on this view, is a branch of political and constitutional rather than of moral theory; for it is primarily a theory about when it is permissible to restrain and confine a free agent, not a theory about when it is appropriate to blame and make suffer an individuated moral will or character.

I say "primarily" because the constitutional theory about when it is permissible to restrain a free agent will admit, on terms compatible with it, a moral

---

[1] This distinction corresponds roughly to Meir Dan-Cohen's distinction between decision rules and conduct rules; see 'Decision Rules and Conduct Rules: On Acoustic Separation in Criminal Law,' (1984) 97 *Harvard Law Review* 625.

supplement within the narrow confines of excuse, which I distinguish (as the positive law does) not simply from justification but from exculpation more generally.[2] Of course, qualifiers such as "primarily" as well as talk about supplements will raise a red flag among critical theorists, for whom qualifiers indicate stress lines in a theory and for whom supplements are always sleeping insurgents. However, the final chapter's burden is to show how, notwithstanding its complexity, the penal law can be conceived as a unified whole of which both primary and supplemental frameworks are subordinate parts. Within this whole, the supplement is no longer an ad hoc addition and so no longer potentially subversive.

Though the founders of modern penal law theory saw their study as part of a political theory of rightful coercion rather than as part of a moral theory of justified blame and censure, few now do.[3] The critique of a once-dominant utilitarianism in the name of desert and responsibility has triumphed, but the victor has been a moral understanding of criminal desert and responsibility. Thus the ascendant view in penal law theory today is that the general part is best understood from the standpoint of a theory concerning when it is fair to blame and censure someone for engaging in proscribed conduct and (if at all) for the results of that conduct.[4] The moral theory of the penal law takes various forms, but all espouse the view that moral blameworthiness for wrongful conduct and consequences is a suitable basis for liability to judicial punishment. The account of criminal liability offered here challenges that understanding and offers a distinctively legal account of criminal desert free, I believe, of its problems.[5]

One might think that understanding the penal law through a justification for coercing free agents rather than through one for censuring moral characters hitches penal law theory to a particular and historically contingent form of punishment, namely, incarceration. Of course, confining human beings in state prisons is only one of several sentencing options available to judges nowadays. Noncustodial punishments involving home detention, community service,

---

[2] Anglo-American law treats excuses as affirmative defences presupposing the elements of criminal wrongdoing; defences that negate an element are exculpatory. For citations, see Introduction, n. 10.

[3] Cesare Beccaria, *Of Crimes and Punishments*, trans. Jane Grigson (Oxford: Oxford University Press, 1964); Jeremy Bentham, *An Introduction to the Principles of Morals and Legislation* (Darien, Conn: Hafner, 1970); Immanuel Kant, *The Metaphysics of Morals*, trans. Mary Gregor (Cambridge: Cambridge University Press, 1991); GWF Hegel, *Philosophy of Right*, trans. TM Knox (Oxford: Oxford University Press, 1967). I use the term "coercion" to cover both the physical application of force to a person and the giving of a command backed by a threat of physical force.

[4] See, for example, Michael Moore, *Placing Blame* (Oxford: Clarendon Press, 1997); RA Duff, *Punishment, Communication, and Community* (Oxford: Oxford University Press, 2001); William Wilson, *Central Issues in Criminal Theory* (Oxford: Hart, 2002), 61–5; Jeremy Horder, *Excusing Crime* (Oxford: Oxford University Press, 2004); Victor Tadros, *Criminal Responsibility* (Oxford: Oxford University Press, 2005); Andrew von Hirsch and Andrew Ashworth, *Proportionate Sentencing* (Oxford: Oxford University Press, 2005), 12–34, 134–7; John Gardner, *Offences and Defences* (Oxford: Oxford University Press, 2007).

[5] It is perhaps unnecessary to add that by a "legal account" I do not mean a simple description of the liability conditions found in the positive penal law of Western jurisdictions. I mean a theory of penal liability that foregrounds the legitimacy conditions of the state's applying penal force to free agents *and* that, in doing so, resonates powerfully with the positive penal law of liberal jurisdictions.

probation conditions, and monetary fines also exist; and there is a growing movement toward using incarceration sparingly for the most serious offences or for the most incorrigible offenders. It might therefore seem that the idea of censuring a moral character captures this range and historical reality better than the idea of coercing a free agent.

The simple response is that all forms of judicial punishment are coercive. Community service orders force convicts to work for ends not necessarily their own; and that is surely a classic form of incursion into the sanctum of an agent's liberty. Home detention and probation orders restrict freedom of choice and movement, while monetary punishments involve actions which, were they performed by private actors, would be considered interferences with the liberty to dispose of one's property as one chooses. And no softening of punishments will alter the hard coercive reality of arrest and pre-trial detention. So, the claim that penal law theory is part of a political theory of legitimate coercion by the state rather than part of a moral theory of appropriate censure by the offender's community in no way assumes an equation between judicial punishment and incarceration.

Several chapters of this book are revised versions of, or contain material from, essays previously published in scholarly journals. The articles from which I have borrowed are: 'Excusing Necessity and Terror: What Criminal Law Can Teach Constitutional Law,' (2009) 3 *Criminal Law and Philosophy*, 147–66; 'Subjective Fault for Crime: A Reinterpretation,' (2008) 14 *Legal Theory*, 1–38; 'Insane Automatism: A Proposal for Reform,' (2000) 45 *McGill Law Journal* 65–85; 'Owning Outcomes: On Intervening Causes, Thin Skulls, and Fault-Undifferentiated Crimes,' (1998) 11 *Canadian Journal of Law and Jurisprudence* 89–114; 'Imprisonment and Strict Liability,' (1990) 40 *University of Toronto Law Journal* 738–74; 'A Theory of Necessity,' (1987) 7 (3) OJLS 339–68.

This book brings to fruition 25 years of studying penal justice in the company of several distinguished colleagues and challenging students. I am particularly grateful to those who read and commented on parts of the manuscript: Bruce Chapman, Markus Dubber, Antony Duff, David Dyzenhaus, George Fletcher, Miriam Gur-Arye, Alon Harel, Mireille Hildebrandt, Tatjana Hörnle, Youngjae Lee, Jeff McMahan, Mayo Moran, Arthur Ripstein, Re'em Segev, Hamish Stewart, Robert Sullivan, Malcolm Thorburn, and Ernest Weinrib. Thanks also for many helpful corrections and suggestions to two anonymous reviewers for Oxford University Press.

I must also acknowledge a debt of gratitude to the participants in the law and philosophy reading group of the Faculty of Law, University of Toronto. By making the strongest possible case for Kant's theory of justice, they contributed to my appreciation of the unsurpassed power of Hegel's.

Inexpressible, however, is the gratitude I owe my wife, to whom this book is dedicated—at last.

A.B.
Spring, 2009

Summary Contents

List of Terms Used	xvii
Introduction	1
1. Punishment	21
2. Culpable Mind	59
3. Culpable Action	99
4. Responsibility for Harm	131
5. Liability for Public Welfare Offences	169
6. Justification	189
7. Excuse	233
8. Detention after Acquittal	273
9. The Unity of the Penal Law	295
Conclusion	321
Bibliography	329
Index	333

Contents

List of Terms Used	xvii
Introduction	1
1. Punishment	21
1. The Concept of Public Reason	21
2. Public Reason as Formal Agency	23
3. The Features of the Formalist Paradigm	28
4. Formalist Right and Wrong	35
5. Culpable Wrong and Formalist Punishment	37
6. A Response to Critics of Retributivism	48
7. The Limits of Formalism	55
2. Culpable Mind	59
1. The Two Roles of *Mens Rea*	60
2. Character, Choice, and Opportunity	63
3. A Legal Account of *Mens Rea*	75
4. A Response to Objections	85
5. Conclusion	96
3. Culpable Action	99
1. The Austinian View of the *Actus*	100
2. The Moral Account of the *Actus*	108
3. A Legal Account of the *Actus*	115
4. Inchoate Crime	120
5. Epilogue	130
4. Responsibility for Harm	131
1. Public Reason as Real Autonomy	131
2. The Features of the Real Autonomy Paradigm	137
3. What Does the Right to Author One's Moral Fate Entail?	141
4. Fault-Undifferentiated Crimes	150
5. The *Novus Actus Interveniens*	158
6. Conclusion	165
5. Liability for Public Welfare Offences	169
1. What is a Public Welfare Offence?	169
2. Why is Subjective Fault Not Required for Public Welfare Offences?	173

3. What Principles of Penal Justice Apply to Public Welfare Offences?	178
4. Ignorance of the Law	184
5. Conclusion	188

6. Justification
	189
1. Introduction	189
2. The Lesser Evil	193
3. Double Effect	197
4. Justification against Wrongdoers	205
5. Justification against Innocents	223

7. Excuse
	233
1. The German Constitutional Court and the *Luftsicherheitsgesetz*	233
2. Exculpation and Exonerating Excuse	235
3. Why Should Excusing Necessity and Duress Exonerate?	240
4. Excuse as Moral Analogue of Legal Exculpation	254
5. Excuse as Staying the State's Sword	262
6. Partial Excuse as Moral Analogue of Partial Exculpation	267

8. Detention after Acquittal
	273
1. Requiem for a Defence	273
2. Why is Detention of the Innocent Insane Permissible?	277
3. Divergence of the Criteria for Insane Automatism and Diminished Respect	286
4. Toward a New Legal Definition of Disease of the Mind	290
5. Conclusion	293

9. The Unity of the Penal Law
	295
1. Introduction	295
2. The Interdependence of Formal Agency and Real Autonomy	297
3. Public Reason as Dialogic Community	305
4. Dialogic Community in the Paradigms	313
5. Epilogue	319

Conclusion 321

Bibliography 329
Index 333

List of Terms Used

actus	Any externalization of a culpable choice.
actus reus	The kind of externalization necessary and sufficient for criminal liability.
agency goods	The things necessary to *real autonomy*.
basic responsibility	The possibility of attributing bodily motion to a free choice.
coercive action	Either the communication of a command backed by a believable threat of unacceptable harm if the addressee fails to comply; or the use of physical force upon a person to carry out a threat or to pre-empt, confine, or direct his or her bodily movements whether or not there was an antecedent threat.
criminal law	The legal rules pertaining to *true crimes*.
culpable wrong	A *transgression* committed with any of the mental orientations toward conduct to which a right denial is imputable.
desert	The connection between a *culpable wrong* and liability to coercion.
dialogic community	The mutual recognition of distinct agencies as having final worth.
exculpate	Either negate a *transgression* or preclude the inference of a right denial from a transgression.
excuse	Remove the moral blameworthiness of a *culpable wrong*.
exonerate	Fully release from the burden of punishment.
fault-undifferentiated crime	One that conflates different degrees (intention, *recklessness, negligence*) of *outcome responsibility*.
formal agency	A capacity to have chosen otherwise than one did.
inchoate crime	One in which the defendant's criminal aim is unrealized; not one in which the defendant has not committed a complete crime.
innocents	Those who cross a boundary involuntarily or with consent, or who cross a boundary in justified defence against a *transgression*, or who do not cross a boundary at all.
judicial punishment	A *penal force* reaction by the political sovereign to an antecedent *culpable wrong*.
negligence	Neither the proscribed result nor the risk thereof were chosen but the result was avoidable had the agent chosen to exercise the foresight of which human agents (including this one) are capable.

List of Terms Used

noncontradiction proviso	The public good of autonomy cannot coherently be pursued by penal means that secure autonomy for some by denying it to others.
outcome responsibility	The degree to which a deed or its consequence is connected to the agent's free choice as distinct from being ascribable to chance.
penal force	An official's interference with an agent's liberty, whether by administering *judicial punishment* or by imposing a *penalty*, for a *culpable wrong* or a *public welfare offence*.
penal law	Comprises both the sphere of *true crimes* and the sphere of *public welfare offences*.
penalty	A *penal force* reaction, not attached to a *culpable wrong*, directed towards the achievement of a public goal.
presumptive criminality	Also called "unequivocality"; actions in context, such that, absent other evidence, a reasonable observer would infer the defendant has publicly manifested a culpable choice.
private interest	One that is possessed by one or some of the subjects of a political authority and not by others.
public interest	One that is contingently or necessarily shared by all subjects of a political authority.
public reason	A *public interest* necessarily shared by all subjects of a political authority; the fundamental purpose of collective action by people organized in a political society.
public welfare offences	Contraventions of statutes regulating the pursuit of satisfactions or protecting *agency goods*.
real autonomy	Consists not simply in the capacity for undetermined choice, but in the realized potential for self-determined choice.
recklessness	Only the risk of the proscribed outcome was chosen and the risk materialized; chance has played a role in the happening of the proscribed result in the degree to which the result is underdetermined by the agent's choice.
strict penal liability for results	Liability to *judicial punishment* for the harmful result of a *culpable wrong* in the absence of any degree (intention, *recklessness*, or *negligence*) of connection between the result and the agent's choice.

transgression (wrong, right infringement)	A voluntary crossing without consent, not justified by self-defence or defence of others, of the boundary of an agent's rightful liberty.
true crimes	Offences against the person, property, the administration of justice, and the safety of the state.

Introduction

Punishment and violence

Much of the criminal law descended from the common law of Great Britain consists of answers to the question: when is it permissible for the state to do to the individual under the rubric of "punishment" what in ordinary circumstances would amount to a criminal assault, robbery, forcible confinement, or murder? To the outward eye, after all, nothing distinguishes an arrest, a fine, an incarceration, or an execution from their criminal counterparts except an elaborate set of formalities and rituals under which any criminal syndicate with imagination and resources could cloak its misdeeds. Obviously, the ritual surrounding punishment is not what essentially distinguishes it from naked violence; rather, the ritual must symbolize an intellectual distinction marked by the fulfilment of liability conditions (and the absence of justificatory and excusing ones) that are generated from an idea of what justifies applying force to a human being. The liability conditions form the surface doctrine of the criminal law—its furniture, so to speak; but the idea that generates these conditions lies murkily in the background of the legal practice of punishment, like a lamp shaded by a curtain. Lawyers and judges typically busy themselves in the half-lit anteroom—arranging the furniture, tidying it, discussing its antique pedigree. Seldom, however, do they draw back the curtain to allow the lamp to shed its full light on the room. As a result, they arrange the furniture instinctively and with much groping in the dark.

Because the idea of punishment is not explicitly investigated by lawyers, the criteria laid down by the positive law for distinguishing a recipient of punishment from a victim of unjustified violence are rarely clear or univocal. For example, though it is generally agreed that someone is justly punished by a public authority only if he or she has at least engaged in conduct proscribed by a just law, judicial opinions differ as to what sort of inward or mental orientation to their conduct persons must have had before they may justly be punished for it. Must they have engaged in the conduct intentionally—that is, either purposely or knowingly? With conscious indifference as to whether or not they were engaging in it? Or is it enough that they engaged in the conduct thoughtlessly and without taking reasonable care to avoid it? Even on the outward side, disagreement is rife as to what sort of conduct warrants punishment. Are failures to act justly punished, and if so, when? Can being something (drunk, a member of a terrorist group, in possession) be rightly punished? And at what point do efforts or plots to produce proscribed outcomes themselves become rightly punishable as criminal "attempts" or "conspiracies?"

Nor is there agreement on whether or when proscribed conduct engaged in purposely or knowingly can ever be justified or excused so as to remove the justification for punishing the actor. Is one ever justified in taking life to save another life? Can one ever be excused for doing so even though the act is admittedly wrong and unjustifiable? If yes, on what basis? Because there was no *real* choice? Because the threat of punishment would not have been effective to deter? Because the conduct evidenced no blameworthy character trait? Even assuming the conditions exist for an excuse, does excuse remove the right to punish or does it merely give a reason for the state's forbearing from exercising the right?

In this book I offer an answer to the question as to what distinguishes penal force by state officials (in particular, physical restraint, confinement, extraction of property, coerced service) from the wrongful force of criminals, and try to show how this answer integrates enough of the penal law's general part to deserve the title of that law's underlying theory. Broadly speaking, the answer offered in the following pages is this: penal action by public officials is permissible force rather than unjust violence only if it could be accepted by the sufferer, considered as a free and independent person, as being consistent with his or her freedom. We will see that this general formulation must be specified differently depending on whether penal force is punishment for an antecedent wrong (violation of a right) or the execution of a threat of disadvantage in the service of public goals. So, penal force by public officials is just *punishment* rather than unjust violence only if it can be conceived as self-imposed by the sufferer by virtue of his choice to do what he did. Penal force by public officials that executes a threat of disadvantage in the service of public goals is a just *penalty* only if it respects the individual's control over his vulnerability to sanctions as an absolute constraint on the promotion of the public welfare.

Consensual coercion?

The claim that penal force is justified only if it could be accepted by a free person as being consistent with its freedom might seem to heap oxymoron upon paradox. The claim might seem oxymoronic, for if the force is consented to by the sufferer, in what sense is it any longer coercive and in need of a justification? Force that is consented to is neither justified nor unjustified; it is simply not "force." The claim seems paradoxical, for if punishment is indeed coercive, how can it be consistent with freedom?

Resolving the paradox of a punishment that is consistent with freedom is the burden of the book as a whole. But the apparent absurdity of a consented-to act of coercion needs to be dispelled at the outset, for it rests on a misconception about who is doing the consenting. Forcing an agent to do X is to make it do X against its free choice, and we must assume that no convict actually chooses to have his or her liberty radically curtailed even though some on occasion may. Indeed, this is just why force applied to the convict needs a justification; if there were no interference with free choice, there would be nothing to justify, no real or apparent wrong to put in a rectifying light.

That punishment is coercive is a juridical postulate rather than a juridical presumption. It is not simply that we presume nonconsent from what we know about typical human preferences; for in that case the public authority would do no wrong in acceding to an exceptional request for incarceration while dispensing with the usual justificatory reasons and probative procedures. It is rather that the criminal law could not even give effect to a consent to a deprivation of liberty so as to remove the need for justification, any more than it can give effect to a consent to have death or slavery inflicted on oneself. It could not do so because the criminal law postulates subjects who are free and who cannot (normatively speaking) do anything or consent to anything inconsistent with their freedom. It is true, of course, that "no wrong can be done to the willing"; but this maxim applies only up to a limit, that of the abiding free subject, whose foundational status explains the maxim—explains, that is, why consented-to harms or risks consistent with an abiding freedom are not injustices.

So, when we say that just penal force is distinguished from unjust violence by its acceptability to the free person, we must put out of mind any image of a real individual empirically consenting to punishment after persuading himself of the good reasons for it. As far as the law is concerned, empirical individuals are not consenting whatever their observable behaviour. Even if the accused begs for punishment before trial to placate a raging conscience, officials will ignore his entreaties until he has pleaded guilty to an indictment in open court and been sentenced by a judge according to law.

But if the law cannot accept the actual consent of individuals as authorizing their punishment, whose consent can count? What we need is a form of consent that assumes empirical nonconsent and whose effect is thus not to remove the need for a justification but rather to justify an admitted act of coercion. Moreover, if it is really "consent" we are talking about and not an imposition on the individual dressed up as consensual, then the consent must come from someone the empirical individual could accept as a representative consenting on its behalf. Of course, the qualifications of such a representative must be stringently defined with a view to the intercessory role it must perform. In particular, they must ensure a thoroughgoing identity of interests between representative and principal such as to leave no doubt that the proxy's consent counts as the principal's, yet without thereby collapsing the proxy's consent into the principal's empirical consent so as to eliminate the proxy as an intermediary.

The qualifications of the representative, accordingly, are as follows. First, the representative must have no ends or interests of its own distinct from its principal's. This is possible only if the representative is either a clone of its principal or bereft of subjective ends. Since a clone would give its principal's empirical consent (would not be an intermediary), the representative must be conceived as having no subjective ends. Second, like Rawls's veiled representative, the intercessor must be ignorant of its principal's subjective ends, for if it consents pursuant to those ends, it gives its principal's empirical consent, which, as we have seen, cannot count before law. Third, the representative must be constrained to act solely for the sake of its principal's freedom to pursue ends of its own choice. Meeting the first two qualifications is meeting the third, for if the representative has no material ends of its own and is ignorant of its principal's material ends, then it has no interest to act on except the freedom to choose and pursue material ends. Fourth, the representative must possess, like the principal in whose shoes it stands, the epistemic powers of a finite, thinking being. That is, it must have the power to grasp logical connections as well as a limited power to know the circumstances and foresee the consequences of its principal's actions. However, as an intercessor between its principal and the penal law, the representative must possess these powers to a relative perfection, without the idiosyncratic frailties of its principal. By a relative perfection I mean the perfection of which a finite being, situated in a particular place and time, is capable. The representative would not be an intercessor if it replicated its principal's peculiar failings; but the intercessor would not be representative if it did not share its principal's human condition. Thus, the representative's knowledge of circumstances and foresight of consequences are limited by its principal's location here and now.

Clearly, this representative is not itself an empirical person. It is a notional person to whom we ascribe choices based on what a person concerned *only* with the preservation of its independence would necessarily choose and to whom we ascribe the finite powers of knowledge and foresight belonging to the situated agent's capacity for thought. The representative agent can thus be characterized in two ways. Considered as grasping the logical entailments of a commitment to freedom, the representative agent is the thinking agent in its principal's shoes; considered as interpreting facts, assessing probabilities, and making judgments under conditions of uncertainty, the representative agent is the reasonable agent in its principal's shoes. Inasmuch as the representative possesses no interest other than an interest in independence that all agents *qua* agents possess and chooses nothing but what all agents *qua* agents would choose as serving independence, we can call it simply the Agent; and we can inquire into (1) the conditions under which the Agent, based on its exclusive concern for its independence, would endorse on its behalf the coercion of an actual agent, and into (2) the exceptional conditions under which, despite the conditions under (1) being met, the endorsement would be withdrawn.

The reason for disallowing the empirical agent's consent to punishment does not apply to the notional one. The empirical agent cannot consent to a deprivation of liberty, because its freedom is the fundamental norm of a liberal legal order and so not its own to dispose of according to its subjective ends. But the notional agent has no ends that are subjective. Its only end is the freedom by which subjective ends are chosen and acted upon; and so it can hypothetically accept or reject on their behalf the coercion of empirical agents as being necessary to, or inconsistent with, freedom. What we have, then, is a twofold deeming that reconciles the coerciveness of punishment with its being consented to by the recipient. Because the notional agent is a fiduciary of the real one, constrained to act solely in the interests of the latter's freedom, its consent to punishment may be *imputed* to the real agent it represents even as the real agent is deemed not to consent empirically.

Formal agency, real autonomy, communal belonging

If the claim that coercion is justified only if it could be accepted by a free person is not the oxymoron it might appear to be, neither is it the oversimplification it might seem to be. This is so because there are different conceptions of what it means to be a free person, and each will generate its own set of justificatory conditions for applying force to the individual.

For example, one view of freedom sees it as consisting in a bare capacity to have chosen otherwise than one did. This is a capacity to resist the impulse caused by an object by rejecting as a motive for action the end—pleasure—relative to which the object appears desirable or repugnant. If a being *can* renounce a gratification for the sake of a rational conception of its good, then satisfying an appetite or aversion is something it does freely rather than necessarily. According to this conception, then, one is free simply by virtue of one's motion being uncaused by the force of an external mover in accordance with unalterable natural laws. It is not essential to this conception that the agent's ends actually be self-determined after deliberation and reflection on reasons pro and con. As long as they are not forced upon the agent, they may be given by appetitive impulse, custom, or the unexamined opinions of others. Nor does it matter to this conception whether the consequences of the choice for which the law holds an agent responsible were within its power to control or the result of unforeseeable accident; as long as the individual could have chosen otherwise than he did, the legal bed he sleeps in need not have been entirely made by him. I shall call this conception of freedom the formal agency conception. Liability to punishment will be consistent with freedom in this sense just in case it can be conceived as chosen by the agent (rather than simply as overpowering it with physical force) as the necessary implication of its actual choice to pre-empt the free choice of another.

Another conception of freedom views it as consisting not simply in the capacity for undetermined choice, but in the actuality of self-determined choice. In the possibility of rejecting ends given by impulse lies a potential for acting from ends the agent deliberatively sets for itself. These ends are not given by instinct or by immediate biological need; rather, they are generated from the agent's own purposiveness—from its capacity to form and realize a life plan reflecting a self-conscious conception of its good. Freedom, on this view, consists in actualizing the agent's potential for self-determination. Thus, an agent is free only if it acts from ends that are self-authored and only if the vulnerability of its life plans to adversity is limited by law to a vulnerability to accidents it could have foreseen and avoided. I shall call this conception of freedom real autonomy. Whereas formal agency distinguishes agents from things, real autonomy distinguishes agents who actively form ends and whose life by and large reflects those ends from agents who passively receive their ends and whose lives are mostly shaped by external influences. Punishment will be consistent with an agent's real autonomy only if it is a fate within the agent's power to avoid and only if it is tied to outcomes of its action the reasonable agent could have foreseen.

A third conception of freedom is the freedom of the citizen. According to this conception, freedom consists in belonging to a political community dependent for its vitality and reproduction on the spontaneous commitment of its members. The citizen is free in willingly conforming his or her conduct to the moral expectations the community has of someone occupying various social roles, such as spouse, parent, job holder, and citizen. These expectations are not burdensome impositions, for they resonate with the ends the virtuous character sets for itself for the sake of a life well lived. Penal law is consistent with freedom in this sense to the extent that, addressing the citizen as a reasoning being, it communicates shared norms of conduct all can reflectively endorse, while calling citizens to answer to their fellows collectively for alleged wrongdoing—through exculpatory explanation if innocent and through re-integrative penance if guilty.[1] Call this communal solidarity.

Now, when confronted with diverse conceptions of an abstract concept they regard as normatively fundamental to law, legal theorists typically choose from among three argumentative strategies. One is to defend one of the conceptions against its rivals and then to construct an ideal picture of the law around the favoured conception, rejecting doctrines inconsistent with that conception as mistakes. Call this the monist strategy. Its fatal flaw is its partisanship. Because his preferred conception excludes others, the monist's interpretation of the law will be one given from a particular perspective asserted against opposing ones. No doubt, good reasons will be offered for preferring one conception to others, but the very one-sidedness of the conception entails that allegiance to it must spring ultimately from an arbitrary choice; for the good reasons will point to values the favoured conception contains that its rivals lack, and that is just the sort of argument its rivals will also be entitled to make. How one weighs up the pros and cons of the mutually exclusive conceptions must be a matter of personal judgment. Of course, the monist might deny any value at all in opposing conceptions and so refuse to acknowledge the incompleteness of his own. However, those who persist in valuing those conceptions may likewise denigrate what the monist values; and since there is no shared ground to which the foes can appeal in argument (the dispute is over fundamental norms), the monist cannot escape partiality and arbitrariness.

---

[1] RA Duff, *Punishment, Communication, and Community* (Oxford: Oxford University Press, 2001), 75–130; *Answering for Crime* (Oxford: Hart Publishing, 2007), 49–56, 191–3; John Gardner, *Offences and Defences* (Oxford: Oxford University Press, 2007), 80.

A second strategy is to abstain from committing to any particular conception and instead to deduce the minimum, abstract, and uncontroversial content of principles that any plausible version of the concept must require, leaving the specific meaning of the principles to be filled in politically or by judicial discretion. Call this the minimalist strategy. For example, one might confidently assert that, whatever else a commitment to freedom might entail, it certainly entails adherence to the principle that the innocent ought not to be punished. But of course the publicly enforced meaning of "innocent" is the prize for which rival conceptions of freedom compete. Does innocent mean "not a volitional cause of the proscribed event" or "not a negligent cause" or "not an intentional cause"? The minimalist will say that law is mute here, that these are political questions rightly decided by a democratic legislature, and that judges must either enforce the political decision or, where the legislature has not spoken, legislate themselves. But therein lies the fatal flaw of the minimalist strategy. By ceding the substance of legal concepts to extra-legal determination, it leaves the rule of law with hardly any domain over which to rule. All the important questions regarding the meaning and requirements of penal justice are now left to the vagaries of power. While ruling elites may consider this absence of restraint all to the good, free subjects are entitled to think otherwise.

A third option draws the logical conclusion from the minimalist one. It abstains both from committing to a conception and from deducing neutral but near-vacuous principles of just punishment and instead interprets what masquerades as nonideological law as a patchwork of truce lines between sectarian interpretations of fundamental concepts. Call this the debunking stategy. Its favourite words are "contradiction," "conflict," and "ambivalence"; and it is happiest when it can show how a one-sided conception requires supplementing from what it excludes and how admission of the repressed threatens to disrupt the conception's complacent rule.[2] Now, this critical method has enduring worth and is indeed incorporated as an element of the positive reconstruction of the penal law undertaken here. But in stopping at "dialectical critique", the debunking strategy reveals a fatal flaw of its own: laziness of thought. From the fact that there exist latent interdependencies between conceptions held in dichotomous opposition, the debunker concludes that law is insolubly conflicted. However, this is a *non sequitur,* for the latent interdependencies intimate an inclusive whole within which the interdependencies are explicit and acknowledged; and so it is at least theoretically possible that the several conceptions form parts of a comprehensive conception within which they are mutually complementary and supportive. The debunker does not investigate this possibility—perhaps because it assigns the theorist the humble role of witness to an objective rationality, with which role

---

[2] Alan Norrie, *Crime, Reason, and History* 2nd ed. (London: Butterworths, 2001); *Punishment, Responsibility, and Justice* (Oxford: Oxford University Press, 2000).

the debunker is dissatisfied. Yet until the possibility is decisively ruled out, the debunker has no right to pass final judgment.

None of the strategies sketched above will be followed in this book. Rather, I propose to explore the possibility just mentioned. That is, I propose a method that considers formal agency, real autonomy, and communal solidarity as each generating some of the liability conditions that distinguish punishment from unjust violence and that thus reconcile punishment with freedom. Then I depict each conception together with the liability rules it yields as an instance of a comprehensive conception of freedom that generates necessary and sufficient conditions of just punishment. Of course, adhering to this method will require justifying the comprehensive conception with arguments about the shortcomings of its rivals; but now the rivals will be preserved as constituent elements of the full conception rather than simply rejected or blended into the favoured one. As a result, the full conception will possess values each of its rivals lack, while none of its rivals will be able to make that claim with respect to the full conception. Call this the inclusive strategy.

The penal law as a complex whole

My choice of the inclusive strategy reflects a claim I make that the general part of the penal law, while forming a coherent unity, forms a complex rather than a simple unity. By that I mean that the unity is not based on a singular and exclusive fundamental idea such as welfare maximization, practical reasonableness, equal respect and concern, retributivism, or even the lexical priority of rights. The common intuition that no effort will succeed in fitting all the penal law or even all the defences into a single theoretical framework is confirmed in these pages. Nevertheless, I argue, the penal law forms a whole. Its unity is compatible with pluralism, however, because the penal law is a unity of *three distinct* legal paradigms or frameworks, each of which is organized around a particular conception of freedom, which nonetheless needs the others for its own coherence. This means that the penal law's unity has a quadripartite structure. There are not one but four ideas we must work with and whose interdependence we must show: namely, the three ideas—formal agency, real autonomy, and communal solidarity—that respectively order the three paradigms, and the idea that unites these three in a whole that preserves the distinctive ordering of each. So the unity of the penal law I propose is complex in that it is a unity of unities or a system of subsystems.

Conceiving the penal law's unity as complex enables one to understand the penal law as a whole without doing violence to it as it exists prior to theoretical reflection. In the way that it first appears, the penal law, far from presenting a picture of wholeness, seems shot through with fissures and paradoxes. In this section I'll simply indicate a few of these so as to make initially plausible the claim that any unity of the penal law must be complex in the sense just mentioned.

In the understanding of judges, lawyers, and textbook writers, the penal law is bifurcated into two broad spheres. In Anglo-American law, one is called the sphere of true crimes, the other the sphere of regulatory or public welfare offences.³ The category of true crimes includes offences against the person, property, the administration of justice, and the safety of the state, while that of public welfare offences includes violations of anti-pollution laws, highway and industrial safety laws, competition laws, and the like. I'll use the term "penal law" to cover both spheres together, reserving the term "criminal law" for the sphere of true crimes.

Judges have characterized the distinction between true crimes and public welfare offences in various ways (discussed in Chapter 5), but the characterization that perhaps best captures the difference focuses on the distinction between agency and welfare. In the sphere of true crimes, liability to punishment does not depend on setting back someone's welfare, that is, on inflicting harm to valued objects. Someone who obtains consent to intercourse by lying about his HIV status is guilty of a sexual assault even if the victim is never infected with the virus. The reason, of course, is that he has interfered with another person's agency by using his or her body without awaiting their independent choice to give it (their will was manipulated by deception). True, he has imposed a risk of grave harm, but this cannot be the gist of his crime, for a physician who injects a patient with a riskless and beneficial drug against his or her will (say the patient desires the benefit but misunderstands the risk) is also guilty of an assault, while one who administers high-risk medication and causes serious harm will be innocent of wrongdoing if the patient consented to the risk. So, whatever its prescriptive appeal, John Stuart Mill's (and Joel Feinberg's) harm principle of criminalization makes an awkward fit with the criminal law: harm to another, whether caused or risked, is neither necessary nor sufficient for criminal liability.⁴

By contrast, in the sphere of public welfare offences, what is penalized is precisely the imposition of a high risk of serious harm. Someone who drives in excess of the speed limit does not prevent others from pursuing ends of their own choosing; yet he is liable to a penalty just for risking harm to others. The same is true of someone who sells a narcotic to a willing buyer. So, whereas interference with agency or with the apparatus for protecting it seems to be the *gravamen* of true crimes (attempts, we'll see, is not the counterexample it appears to be), risking serious harm is the essence of public welfare offences.⁵ No doubt, one could try to characterize the interference with agency as itself a harm to an important value and in that way collapse the difference between crimes and welfare offences. However, doing so would commit the category mistake of treating the *a priori* possibility

---

³ European legal systems make a similar distinction; see George Fletcher, *The Grammar of Criminal Law* (Oxford: Oxford University Press, 2007), 71.
⁴ JS Mill, *On Liberty* (New York: Crofts, 1947), 9–14; Joel Feinberg, *The Moral Limits to the Criminal Law*, vol. 1, *Harm to Others* (New York: Oxford University Press, 1984).
⁵ Thus, Arthur Ripstein's "sovereignty principle" of legitimate prohibition is just as much an overgeneralization as the harm principle he criticizes; see 'Beyond the Harm Principle,' (2006) 34:3 *Philosophy and Public Affairs* 216.

of positing values—agency—as one value among others. This is somewhat like saying that the standard metre in Sèvres, France is a metre in length. Moreover, dissolving the difference between crimes and welfare offences would fly in the face of a practice that explicitly affirms these categories and allows the assignment of an offence to one or the other to carry significant doctrinal consequences, particularly with respect to fault.[6] Accordingly, I assume that a theory of the penal law that is faithful to its object must account for, rather than efface, this basic division.

The distinction between agency and welfare splits not only the penal law in its entirety, but also each sphere separately. In the realm of true crimes, as I said, liability to punishment is independent of causing or risking harm; what alone matters is the interference with liberty or free choice. Yet this sphere is far from being hermetically sealed against considerations of welfare, which figure in liability in a kind of adjunct or secondary way. Thus, while punishability is independent of causing harm, the *measure* of punishment for a crime depends crucially (though not exclusively) on the kind and extent of the harm caused or risked by a criminal interference. Assault causing bodily harm is punished more severely than assault, as is assault risking death. Assault causing death is punished more severely than assault causing bodily harm even though the underlying offence can be committed harmlessly. There are two mirror-image puzzles here that a satisfactory theory of the penal law must resolve. First, given that liability to punishment *simpliciter* is independent of causal luck, why should the measure of punishment depend on the chance causing of harm or of a particular kind of harm rather than simply on what the agent intended? Alternatively, why should harm be relevant to the measure of punishment and yet not to punishability as such? If the kind of harm caused or risked differentiates crimes from one another, why does not harm *simpliciter* differentiate crimes from nonpunishable acts, as Mill and Feinberg believed they should?

Furthermore, the kind of fault normally required for criminal wrongdoing (hence for liability to punishment of any severity) does not match the kind of fault required for criminal responsibility for the harm consequent on a criminal wrong (hence for liability to punishment of a certain measure). For example, the traditional (albeit controversial) doctrine is that liability to punishment for a true crime (for example, an assault) depends on a form of subjective fault: intention, conscious recklessness, or wilful blindness. But subjective fault is only one measure of criminal responsibility for harmful outcomes; one can also be punished for a harmful outcome one ought to have avoided, as in the crime of manslaughter. Why should this be so? If subjective fault is required for criminal wrongdoing,

---

[6] If a court decides that an offence is a true crime, it will normally interpret the offence as carrying a requirement of subjective fault—intention, conscious recklessness, or wilful blindness—unless a statute explicitly says otherwise; but if the offence is regulatory and the statute is silent regarding fault, then the presumption of subjective fault is dropped and the court will either impose liability without fault or read in a requirement of negligence; see *R v Sault Ste Marie* [1978] 2 SCR 1299; *Proudman v Dayman* [1941] 67 CLR 536.

why not for the consequences of wrongdoing? Or if objective fault is sufficient for consequences, why not for criminal wrongdoing as such?

The same fissure along the line dividing agency and welfare appears in the contrast between liability conditions, on the one hand, and justificatory and excusing conditions, on the other. While liability to punishment for a true crime is independent of causing or risking harm, the defences to liability that operate after the elements of liability have been proved make comparisons of harm decisive. Thus, one will be justified in stealing a loaf of bread if doing so is necessary to save a life, but at best excused for taking a life to save another life, and guilty for taking a life to save an item of property. Moreover, a plea of self-defence will succeed only if the kind of harm inflicted on the wrongdoer is proportionate to the kind avoided. It is surely an object of wonder that liability to punishment should be independent of harm while the defences to liability should be all about harm. This, at any rate, is something for which a faithful theory of the penal law must account; and a theory for which the penal law is a complex unity seems a more promising candidate in this respect than one for which the law is a simple unity.

If welfare is the shadow principle of true crimes, then freedom is the shadow principle of welfare offences. This is so because of an ambiguity in the notion of welfare. Welfare can mean the satisfaction of subjective ends, or it can mean the attainment of goods everyone needs to live a life reflecting self-authored ends. Some regulatory laws—competition laws, for example—aim to ensure the fair distribution of subjective satisfactions, but some—public health regulation, for example—aim to secure the conditions of living autonomously. A faithful theory of the penal law should attend to this difference and, to the extent that it is prescriptive, fashion liability and sentencing principles suitable to each sphere.

The difference between agency and welfare is not the only one that sunders the penal law. The difference between agency and virtue does so as well. Here the fault line lies between conditions that either negate wrongdoing or *exculpate* from wrongdoing (the admitted wrong is not criminal), on the one hand, and conditions that completely *excuse* culpable wrongdoing (the wrong is admittedly criminal but not punishable), on the other. Exculpatory conditions (such as mistake of fact and legal insanity) make no reference to virtuous motive or character and, indeed, can exist notwithstanding vice. Thus, blameworthy self-centredness, sexist prejudice, paranoid delusion, and even (in Australia) extreme drunkenness can exculpate if they cause cognitive mistakes negating the free choice to interfere with choice;[7] while, conversely, if the agent chose to interfere, it will not matter that its motives were pure: the agent who kills from compassionate love is just as culpable as the one who kills from hate or greed.[8] Nevertheless, virtue can excuse someone whose action was legally culpable—who (without justification) freely chose to interfere with choice or who freely chose to do what they ought to have

---

[7] *DPP v Morgan* [1975] 2 All ER 347; *R v O'Connor* (1980) 4 A Crim. R 348 (HC).
[8] *R v Latimer* [2001] 1 SCR 3.

known the law forbids. Thus, a mother forced to traffic in heroin under a threat of dire harm to her child will be set free because, though she chose to break the law, she showed no less fortitude against fear than one may expect of a fellow human being placed in her situation.[9] Yet in the absence of a complex theory these distinctions will seem bizarre. Why distinguish between exculpation and excuse so as to invite the paradox that someone may be at once legally culpable and morally blameless, morally blameworthy and legally innocent? If conformity to moral expectation renders punishment unjust, why (one might wonder) relegate it to the margin of excuse, while blameworthy mistake can win an unequivocal exculpation? Is this not to give bread to vice and a stone to virtue?[10]

In sum, the penal law that presents itself to theoretical reflection reveals bifurcation and paradox throughout. What is excluded in one place (welfare, virtue) is brought back in another, yet without disturbing the initial exclusion. A critical theorist fastens on this phenomenon and concludes that the penal law is hopelessly contradictory, hence unintelligible to any rationalizing theory.[11] But the fact of paradox means that the penal law must elude the grasp only of a certain kind of rationalizing theory—namely, one that seeks to understand the law in light of a single framework of justice. A theory that interprets the penal law as a unity of plural frameworks can realize the rationalist project while remaining faithful to the complexity of its object.

A complex theory unites external and internal viewpoints

Not only is the penal law a unity of legal paradigms ordered to diverse conceptions of freedom; its unifying theory synthesizes external and internal interpretive viewpoints. By an internal viewpoint I mean one from which jurists try to tell a coherent story about the law as they go about applying it in particular cases, describing it in legal treatises, or explaining it in scholarly articles. It is the viewpoint from which the law is self-consciously interpreted from within the practice of law itself by lawyers, judges, and legal scholars. By an external standpoint I mean one that reflects on the jurist's own narrative activity and sees in that

---

[9] *R v Ruzic* [2001] 1 SCR 687.
[10] So ascendant in the legal academy is the moral understanding of the criminal law that the idea of a possible coexistence of legal culpability and moral innocence will be resisted by many readers. Yet it is in the law. Thus there is firm authority for the view that (unless a penal provision stipulates a motive requirement that coercion can negate) duress is an affirmative defence presupposing the presence of both elements of legal culpability (*actus reus* and *mens rea*); see *R v Steane* [1947] 1 KB 997; *R v Lynch* [1975] AC 653; *R v Howe* [1987] 1 AC 417; *R v Hibbert* [1995] 2 SCR 973; ALI Model Penal Code, section 2.09. The Model Penal Code defines culpability solely in terms of the variants of *mens rea* (s. 2.02); duress presupposes culpability in this sense, and yet it is a complete defence. With this position the Canadian Supreme Court agrees. It has said that necessity and duress, though they render the defendant's action "morally involuntary" and any punishment unjust, nonetheless do not negate the "guilt" established solely by the presence of *actus reus* and *mens rea*; see *Ruzic*, ibid.
[11] Norrie, *Punishment, Responsibility, and Justice*, 10–13.

activity a thematic unity working itself out behind the jurist's back—a unity hidden from his or her professional range of vision. Though an external standpoint relies on an academic discipline outside that of legal studies—for example, philosophy, economics, or sociology—the difference between internal and external standpoints does not quite map onto that between "law" and "law and...". "Law and philosophy", for example, can provide an internal perspective if it sees itself as reproducing the intellectual work of legal actors at a higher level of abstraction and theoretical rigour. External standpoints, however, are by definition interdisciplinary; they interpret what legal actors say and do from a standpoint different from that of the legal actors themselves. I'll call the unifying theme seen from the external standpoint the latent theme of the penal law, and I'll call the unifying themes seen from the internal standpoint the overt or manifest themes.

The three conceptions of freedom sketched above—formal agency, real autonomy, and communal solidarity—are the manifest themes of the penal law. They are the law's internal organizing ideas, and the theoretical paradigms they structure are structures *of* the law; they are not heavenly constructs imposed on the law. That, at any rate, is a claim I make; and whether I persuade the reader of its truth should depend on how well the paradigms explain the basic features of the penal law described in the previous section, how faithfully they capture doctrines on which there is wide agreement, how well normative *lacunae* in the paradigms explain law-free zones in penal practice, how well logical tensions between conceptions of freedom explain perennial tugs-of-war in the jurisprudence, whether the logical transitions from one paradigm to another find parallels in historical shifts in the law, and so forth. In the positive law, the conceptions of freedom compete, engender doctrinal disputes and swings, in general give an appearance of intractable conflict. Nevertheless, they are, I argue, united within an inclusive whole that preserves the rule of each over a sphere reduced to one part of a unity of spheres. The theme that unifies the whole is the latent theme of each sub-whole, and the standpoint from which it is discernible is external to law.

There is, I believe, a prima facie appeal to a theory of the penal law uniting external and internal standpoints. For one thing, only such a theory can represent the penal law as a complex whole in which subsystems are preserved within an embracing unity. This is so because a complex whole requires both a distinction and an interdependence between latent and manifest themes. It requires a distinction, for only a theme distinct from the several immanent themes can unify rather than simply add to those themes. But a complex whole also requires that the latent and manifest themes be interdependent; for if the latent theme were alone the "true" one, there would be no ordering role for the manifest ones, which could thus be dismissed (as they are by economists) as "surface rhetoric"; and so the whole would not be complex. And if the manifest themes were the only eligible ones, then there would be a plurality of frameworks in the penal law but no unity.

Second, only a theory of the penal law uniting external and internal standpoints can reconcile ethical criticism of the law as a normative system with interpretive fidelity. Were we to understand the penal law solely with reference to conceptions of freedom internal to it, we would perhaps have achieved a faithful understanding; but we would not have justified the law as having normative force for anyone but those already committed to those conceptions. We could no doubt evaluate doctrines and procedures in light of the law's immanent norms, but this assessment would be incomplete without ethical scrutiny and criticism of the norms themselves. On the other hand, were we to interpret the penal law solely from an external normative standpoint, we would perhaps have shaped a law that is morally justified in our eyes, but we would not have understood the penal law as an autonomous normative system; nor would we have given jurists any convincing reason to prefer our evaluative standpoint to theirs. So, an interpretation of the penal law that is faithful to it without being uncritically deferential to its internal norms, and that is critical without ceasing to be faithful—such an interpretation must synthesize internal and external standpoints. It must show how, driven by their own logical inadequacies, conceptions of freedom internal to legal discourse move to an inclusive conception that has been latent in them all along and that preserves them as particular cases of itself, valid over a limited domain.[12]

Because the penal law must be understood from two points of view, I shall proceed in the following manner. Chapters 1–6 will give an account of the penal law's general part as a hybrid product of two conceptions of freedom internal to legal discourse and in apparent tension: formal agency and real autonomy. In Chapter 7, I introduce a third framework, one needed to explain excuse and resting on the idea of virtuous conformity to the moral expectations of a political community, also internal to legal discourse. In the final chapter, the three frameworks are integrated under an idea that is external to legal discourse and that I call dialogic community. I describe this idea as the mutual recognition of distinct agencies as having final worth. Finally, I show how this structure of mutual recognition is the latent theme of all three frameworks—formal agency, real autonomy, and communal solidarity—and how it maintains each within coherent boundaries.

Ideal law and positive law

What, it might be asked, is the relation between the penal law judged valid by penal law theory and the positive penal law of particular jurisdictions? Is the unity of the paradigms an ideal of penal justice having only prescriptive force? Or is it a model of the existing law claiming only descriptive accuracy?

The complex whole is a theoretical model exhibiting a unity and coherence not to be expected of the positive law itself. The positive law of any jurisdiction

---

[12] I might add that only a theory of law uniting external and internal standpoints is *inter*disciplinary. External standpoints that treat the internal discourse as "surface rhetoric" or as devoid of independent normative stature are pseudo-interdisciplinary.

is inevitably a mixture of stable and ephemeral doctrines; and, indeed, the ratio of ephemeral to stable is bound to be higher in the penal than in private law, where doctrinal controversies are less politically charged and where jurisprudence is better insulated against populist emotion and demagoguery. Because penal law issues arise in a social environment where anxieties about personal safety clash with the rights of a feared minority, they seldom receive the dispassionate reflection accorded to, say, mistaken assumptions in contract or liability for economic loss in tort. Thus we should not be surprised if the gap between the ideal and the actual is wider in penal law than in private law.

Nevertheless, the complex whole would not be a model *of* the law if it did not give the positive law the unity and coherence to which it aspires. Thus, there must be enough positive law accounted for by the model to enable us to say that the unity of the model is also the implicit unity of the positive law. Naturally, what is "enough" is, within limits, a matter of judgment concerning which reasonable disagreement is possible. However, in judging how well the model fits the positive law, we must keep in mind the borders of the positive law to which the model is accountable. Because the complex whole is a model penal law for societies committed to individual freedom, its factual touchstone is not any particular political jurisdiction, nor does it extend to all jurisdictions. The model need not account to penal law systems based on revelation, for example; while whatever mismatches it finds in one liberal jurisdiction may be discounted by matches elsewhere.

That the model claims to match the main outlines of the positive penal law of liberal legal orders does not mean, however, that the model is purely descriptive. The fundamental idea that organizes the whole is a normative conception of public reason purporting to distinguish official punishment from unjust violence; and so the model has just the normative force that its underlying conception has. Even if (as will turn out) the ideas of formal agency, real autonomy, and communal solidarity are not the fundamental norms they initially claim to be, they and the paradigms over which they preside will still retain the defeasible normativity of partial conceptions of freedom constituent of the one that is complete.

Penal law theory: legal, not moral

Most generally stated, this book's thesis is that a theory about how official penal force can be reconciled with the freedom and inviolability of the individual agent provides the most integrative and ethically satisfying view of the general part of a liberal penal law. If this thesis is correct, then the best theory of the penal law's general part is, as George Fletcher has maintained, part of a political and constitutional theory concerning when state coercion of the individual is legitimate.[13] It is not a theory about how the moral good of punishing evil is best served; nor is it a theory about when it is appropriate to express moral condemnation

---

[13] George Fletcher, *Rethinking Criminal Law* (Boston: Little, Brown, 1978), xix; *The Grammar of Criminal Law*, 152–55.

of blameworthy conduct or character through the penal power of the state; nor is it an account of what it takes for punishment to be a form of moral pedagogy addressed to a socially responsible agent rather than a tool for manipulating the behaviour of a rational hedonist. To put the point succinctly: the best theory of the penal law is a theory of penal right rather than one of penal morality.

The last statement, however, must be qualified in two respects. First, penal law theory is not coextensive with political theory. Rather, it is a narrowly legal theory, in that it specifies the conditions under which it is permissible to apply force to an individual agent who bears a right, founded on its worth, against coercion. Put otherwise, penal law theory is a narrow theory about just punishment (and penalization) rather than a broad theory of the legitimate state authority to coerce. Accordingly, it is not concerned with larger questions concerning the grounds and limits of political obligation; nor is it concerned with what justifies state coercion that is not penal, such as the issuing of commands backed by threats.

Second, while penal law theory is a distinctively legal theory, it is also a complex theory that makes room for a moral idea about when it is inappropriate to blame someone for intentionally engaging in proscribed conduct within the limited sphere of excuse, though not as a general theory of exculpation. That is, the legal theory of what reconciles penal force with freedom assigns moral theory whatever subordinate role it plays in a full account of judicial punishment. In that way, the legal theory makes sense of the idea of excuse, which is by definition a marginal legal phenomenon. Excuse (from *ex causa*) presupposes culpability for wrongdoing according to generally applicable legal criteria; it does not negate or even lessen culpability. Only the culpable require an excuse; and only the fully culpable need advance an explanation showing why punishment of a severity that is deserved according to the general rule should exceptionally be mitigated in their case. Thus, whereas exculpatory conditions (such as mistake of fact) issue from the core, nonmoral theory of liability, excusing conditions (such as duress and provocation) reflect a supplementary idea of moral blamelessness or diminished blameworthiness tailored to suit the authority of law (see Chapter 7). A legal theory of penal liability that accepts on its own terms a peripheral role for moral blamelessness will preserve the positive law's distinction between exculpation and excuse (a distinction reflected in that between conditions that negate an element of criminal wrongdoing and those raised in affirmative defence), whereas a generalized moral theory of blame will obliterate it.[14]

It should be apparent by now that, although I characterize the legal theory of criminal desert offered here as nonmoral, I do not mean by this that it is non-normative—that its subject matter is simply the facts that constitute criminal liability in some technical, value-neutral sense adapted to the managerial task

---

[14] Thus HLA Hart's "I could not help it" theory of excuse lumps duress in with insanity, reflex action, and mistake; see *Punishment and Responsibility* (Oxford: Clarendon Press, 1968), 152. See also Moore, *Placing Blame*, 483–5.

of crime control. Far from it. By a legal theory of criminal desert I mean one that investigates the conditions under which coercion of the agent is just rather than one that investigates the conditions under which censure of the character is appropriate. Accordingly, there would be nothing wrong with calling the legal theory a moral one of a certain sort, namely, a morality of the right rather than one of the good. However, I prefer to stay with the clear distinction between the legal and the moral.

Few besides Fletcher have advanced the thesis that penal law theory is about the justice of coercion, not about the morality of blaming.[15] Nowadays, the dominant tendency in criminal law theory is to derive the conditions of penal liability and of exculpation from a moral theory of inward blameworthiness for wrongdoing. Moral theories of the penal law come in two broad types: individualistic and Aristotelian/communitarian. Individualistic theories, such as those of Andrew Ashworth and Michael Moore view the subject of criminal responsibility as the agency or will of a human individual considered apart from his or her full moral character and social milieu; whereas Aristotelian or communitarian theories, such as those of Antony Duff, John Gardner, Jeremy Horder, and Victor Tadros see the subject of responsibility as a concrete moral character embedded in social and political relationships, with habits, attitudes, inclinations, and skills formed through the activities and roles comprising a life.

Both views will be engaged in the appropriate places. Here it is enough to say that this book defends a position contrary to the dominant view for a very simple reason. The forcible restraint of an individual's liberty by equal human beings requires a justification of an order altogether different from one suitable for expressions of condemnatory moral opinion, which the addressee is free to internalize or deflect. That judging the inward self is like shooting in the dark does not matter when the object of judgment can treat it as self-serving opinion and go on with his life. It does matter when the opinion carries a sword. Allowing a justification for moral blame and censure to count as a justification for physical restraint cannot sit with the equal worth of agents; for, each soul being inscrutable to another, human judgments of another's inward will or character are too subjective, too plagued by uncertainty and bias, to be enforceable against an equal.[16] Indeed, because such judgments are subjective and (at least partially) ignorant, the object of moral censure is always *entitled* to reject it, either in whole or in part.

---

[15] But see Hyman Gross, *A Theory of Criminal Justice* (New York: Oxford University Press, 1979), 13–33; Arthur Ripstein, *Equality, Responsibility and the Law* (Cambridge: Cambridge University Press, 1999), 135; Malcolm Thorburn, 'Justifications, Powers, and Authority,' (2008) 117 *Yale Law Journal* 1070. Fletcher has not adhered strictly to his original insight. In recent writing, he has sought to mix a political theory of criminalized conduct with a moral theory of culpability; see *The Grammar of Criminal Law*, 103–6, 154, 180–2, 217.

[16] Kant was surely right in saying that "the true morality of actions (merit or guilt), even that of our own conduct, remains...entirely hidden. Our imputations can refer to the empirical character only. How much of that may be the pure effect of freedom, how much should be ascribed to nature only, and to the faults of temperament, for which man is not responsible, or its happy constitution..., no one can discover, and no one can judge with perfect justice." *Critique of Pure Reason*, trans. F Max Mueller (Garden City, NY: Doubleday, 1966), 376.

He is entitled to relativize, contextualize, accept the grain of truth while dismissing the exaggeration, even debunk those who cast stones at him. But the legitimacy of penal force depends precisely on the convict's *not* being entitled to reject it.[17] And so the justification of penal liability must be a *sui generis* one geared to the requirement of non-rejectability.

To this objection from the inscrutability of the inward person Michael Moore offers two responses. First, he says, the objection is rarely put forward consistently. Everyone will agree that those innocent of wrongdoing do not deserve punishment and that those not deserving of punishment ought not to be punished. But, he argues, if we are confident in our judgments as to when someone does not deserve punishment, we cannot consistently be diffident about our assessments of when someone does.[18] Either we must impose criminal liability on the basis of conduct alone or admit that it is possible to determine a person's moral desert.

This argument fails, however, for it presupposes what Moore wants to demonstrate—that the morality of blaming and blameworthiness underlies legal judgments of innocence. The same worry about the limits of our knowledge as to when and in what measure someone inwardly deserves punishment applies equally to judgments about when someone inwardly does not. Of course, criminal trials do determine guilt and innocence. But a legal principle against punishing the innocent does not commit the law to judging the inward person, because the law's criteria of culpability and nonculpability are, I will argue, systematically nonmoral. They say nothing about the goodness or badness of individuals.

Moore's second response is to say that the virtue of an emotion is warrant for the epistemic reliability of the moral judgment it guides. "[I]f," he writes, "the possession of an emotion makes us more virtuous, then that emotion is a good heuristic for coming to moral judgments that are true."[19] Thus, if there is virtue in the emotion of moral revulsion one feels in beholding a horrific crime, then the moral judgment that the perpetrator deserves a severe punishment for the crime is very likely a true judgment. If one would feel "guilty unto death" for having committed that act, then this virtuous emotion is warrant for concluding that the perpetrator deserves the same suffering one virtuously believes would be due oneself.

There is, of course, a well-known problem of circularity in arguments that test the truth of moral judgments against intuitions that have already been winnowed for reliability in accordance with the judgments. Perhaps this problem of circularity is unavoidable or perhaps the circle is not vicious; I do not know. Yet, whatever one might think of the connection between virtuous emotions and sound

---

[17] In an interview given 11 years after his conviction for abducting, torturing, raping, and murdering two teen-aged girls, the reviled Paul Bernardo explained his behaviour as stemming from a "vice" rooted in insecurity around "sexual performance inadequacy." "I wake up every day," he said, "knowing I'm not psychopathic. I care about people. I cried during 9/11. I cried during Columbine." *Globe and Mail,* June 21, 2008. Bernardo is surely entitled to his opinion of himself; but he is not entitled to think his life sentence arbitrary.

[18] Moore, *Placing Blame,* 112–13. [19] Ibid., 134.

moral judgment in general, one surely exaggerates that connection in thinking that there is any reliable link between our emotions and our moral judgments *of other persons*.

To see this, imagine that the perpetrator of a terrible crime has the same feeling of revulsion toward his deed as we do—so much so that he is unable to derive any enjoyment from life for the rest of his days. His feelings of guilt are virtuous; they indicate a certain degree of self-dissociation from the character able to commit the crime, and so they bear on the extent of his moral blameworthiness as a character—on what or how much punishment he inwardly deserves. Yet these feelings are ultimately hidden from us. Even if they were manifested in words or behaviour, we could not know whether the outward display was genuine or fake. So, no matter how virtuous our anger in contemplating his monstrous act, our moral judgment of the perpetrator will be more or less blind. Moreover, our own hypothetical guilt feelings are not even a heuristic guide for estimating how much suffering the perpetrator deserves, for we lack necessary knowledge about what the perpetrator has already suffered inwardly; and what he has already suffered from his deed is a datum that a moral theory of desert must regard as relevant to a just measure of suffering now. Again, this is no mere contingent lack. Our judgment would lack that information even if the perpetrator manifested his guilt feelings, for we could not know how the emotion felt to him. The inscrutability of other souls derives from the separateness of souls.

There is a further problem here. Moral emotions such as anger are virtuous without qualification only in the ideally virtuous man, who feels them in the right way, toward the right objects, and in the right degree, as Aristotle says. In actual human beings, noble emotions are mixed up with base impostors. Thus moral anger may be righteous or a reaction formation against envy or self-hatred; guilt feelings may be appropriate or masochistic. Because there is no practical way of screening virtuous emotions for impurities, there is also no way of determining whether an emotion is suitable for expression through the public penal law. Accordingly, even if the moral emotions are heuristic guides to true moral judgments about what suffering other souls deserve, they are guides reliable enough for public enforcement only for the ideal character of practical wisdom, that is, for a rational idea, not for real human beings. Real people of imperfect virtue are capable only of subjective and fallible judgments of what suffering other persons inwardly deserve; and no one has the right to deprive an equal of his liberty pursuant to such judgments.

Moral and legal retributivism

The difference between legal and moral conceptions of desert is reflected in that between legal and moral conceptions of retributive punishment. Most contemporary moral theorists of the penal law subscribe to some version of a retributive idea of punishment, in that they view punishment as justified, not by its good effects, but by blameworthiness for wrongdoing or desert. Punishment is seen as the infliction of deserved suffering or, in Duff's account, as the "communication of deserved censure".[20] Some moralists, like Moore, regard the infliction of deserved suffering as intrinsically good, requiring no further justification;[21] others, like Duff, view punishment of the deserving as justified by a further good internal to retributivism, such as penance.[22] However, all moral retributivists believe that the state should punish for the sake of the good inherent in punishing the morally guilty.

The legal theory of the penal law presented in this book also defends a retributivist conception of punishment for crimes (though not for public welfare offences), but legal retributivism will look very different from moral retributivism. Whereas moral retributivism would order the penal law toward the moral good of giving evildoers what they deserve, legal retributivism would order it toward assuring a link between punishment and choice so as to respect the individual's inviolability—his right not to be forced to serve others' ends. With this right-based focus, legal retributivism dissociates itself from the moral thesis that has driven many a liberal thinker into the arms of consequentialism: that punishing those who deserve to be punished is good for its own sake, so that the sole and sufficient reason for punishing someone is that he deserves it. Because this thesis would use the public penal power to enforce a moral passion (hatred, outrage, indignation) no less self-interested than nonmoral passion and impossible to screen for contaminants, it has always made unfettered consequentialism seem enlightened by comparison and mixed theories seem unavoidable despite their incoherence. Yet legal retributivism is not that thesis. Nor is it a mixed theory that justifies punishment by crime reduction but allows that goal to be served in the particular case only if the recipient deserves to be punished. Legal retributivism is pure retributivism. Yet it is, I will argue, free of the problems besetting moral retributivism that, laid at the door of retributivism simply, have given consequentialist and mixed theories of punishment a borrowed life. So let us begin with an account of judicial punishment as seen by legal retributivism.

---

[20] Duff, *Punishment, Communication, and Community*, 30.
[21] Moore, *Placing Blame*, 87–91.
[22] Duff, *Punishment, Communication, and Community*, 106–30.

1

Punishment

1. The Concept of Public Reason

Let us begin with a few definitions. As I use the term, coercive action can mean either of two things. It can mean the communication of a command backed by a believable threat of unacceptable harm if the addressee fails to comply with the command; or it can mean the use of physical force upon a person to carry out a threat or to pre-empt, confine, or direct its bodily movements whether or not there was an antecedent threat. When the commander is a public official authorized by the constitution to issue commands, the command is a law or order, the threat a sanction, and the execution of the threat a case of penal force. When the commander is a private person with no authority over the addressee, the command is a naked command, the threat an assault, and the execution of the threat a battery, forcible confinement, or murder, all of which labels indicate that the actions they name are wrongful from the standpoint of a political sovereign claiming a monopoly on rightful coercion. Finally, penal force is either judicial punishment or the imposition of a penalty. It is judicial punishment if it is a reaction by the political sovereign to an antecedent culpable wrong; it is a penalty if, without being attached to a culpable wrong, it is directed toward the achievement of a public goal. By a culpable wrong I mean a wrong deserving of judicial punishment.

Now, the labelling of coercive actions by private actors as "assault," "battery," "murder," etc. from the standpoint of a sovereign's claim of monopoly on rightful coercion would be arbitrary if the sovereign's monopoly simply served its own private ends. For then there would be nothing to distinguish the coercion exercised by the sovereign from that of other private actors beyond the brute fact that the sovereign's claim of monopoly was widely accepted and its self-serving commands generally obeyed, while those who disputed the claim found their commands mostly ignored and their attempts to enforce them resisted. And that fact alone, even if it could distinguish sovereign from nonsovereign, could not distinguish right from wrong. So, it seems reasonable to think that, if coercive action by state officials is to be distinguished from the *wrongful* coercion of private actors, then it must be distinguished most basically by its serving a public interest. Here too definitions are in order. By a public interest I mean one that is shared by all subjects of a political authority bar none; by a private interest I mean one that is possessed by one or some of these subjects and not by others.

That the end of coercive action be a public interest is not, to be sure, sufficient to distinguish official from wrongful coercion. The person exercising force must be legally authorized to act for the public interest, and the force used must be no more than what is reasonably needed to protect the public interest. Yet the concept of a public interest is surely necessary to that distinction, for it is the only kind of interest to whose enforcement against recalcitrants everyone (including the recalcitrant) could rationally assent. Someone who coerces another to serve private ends coerces arbitrarily—that is, in a way that cannot be justified by reasons acceptable to the person coerced; and this holds true whether he coerces only this person now or a multitude into the future under a general command. In the hold-up situation writ large as a political tyranny, the gunman is still a gunman and his victim still a victim.

A public interest might be contingently shared or it might be necessarily shared. A contingently shared common interest is one that individuals possess coincidentally; a necessarily shared interest is one that individuals possess by virtue of their being the kind of beings they are. The problem, of course, with basing coercive authority on a contingently shared interest is that such an authority dissolves in the moment of its assertion, and so is no authority at all. Any wilful law-breaker denudes a coercive authority based on a contingently shared interest simply by his defection from that interest. His very challenge to authority transforms the public interest into a private one and therewith penal force into arbitrary force. So let us say that the public interest under which coercive authority is justified must be an interest that is necessarily rather than contingently shared—that is, shared by all subjects just by virtue of their possessing some common nature, whether of living things, animals, rational animals, or of rational agents. I'll call this kind of public interest "public reason", since it is an interest imputed by reason rather than inferred from behaviour or gleaned from self-reports and because it is the fundamental reason or purpose of collective action by people organized in a political society.[1]

The concept of public reason is very abstract, for it is as yet devoid of specific content. What public reason is has to be specified by particular conceptions of the fundamental purpose of political association, of which there are very many possible ones. Because our focus is on penal justice for a liberal society, we can short-circuit what would otherwise be a long discussion by zeroing in immediately on public reason as conceived by the denominations of liberalism. In that way, we bypass instances of public reason given independently of human agency, such as the perpetuation of biological life—its cycles, rhythms, and interdependencies—or

---

[1] As I use the term, "public reason" is both like and unlike Rawls's notion; see *Political Liberalism* (New York: Columbia University Press, 1993), 212–54. It is like Rawls's in that it refers to a shared normative framework by which individuals with diverse values can unite under a coercive political order. It is unlike Rawls's in that it is not identified with a particular conception of public reason set over against others—namely, the priority of the right. As the bare idea of a fundamental purpose of political association, public reason is hospitable to any plausible conception of a noncontingently shared human interest, including any plausible conception of a fundamental human good.

the ideal development of human nature, or the fullest possible development of human nature as preparation for a supernatural excellence. In contrast to these, liberal conceptions of public reason are conceptions of freedom—of what it means to be a free agent. The denominations of liberalism differ sharply in their understanding of what freedom is and of what the state must do to secure it, but they agree that freedom is the fundamental end of political society.

In the Introduction I distinguished three conceptions of freedom: formal agency, real autonomy, and freedom as citizenship. Ordered to each of these conceptions is a theoretical paradigm for justifying coercive action by officials claiming authority under the conception against those over whom they claim authority. Each paradigm generates a distinctive set of constraints on penal force by which the latter is reconciled with a particular view of the recipient's freedom and so distinguished from unjust coercion. Since, however, the conception of freedom to which a paradigm is ordered is a partial conception, no paradigm taken alone will yield liability conditions sufficient to distinguish official from arbitrary force. Each will leave a frontier—a kind of administrative badland—where penal policy may roam free of normative restraints. Together, however, the paradigms will generate all the law needed for freedom. The constraints on penal force yielded by the inclusive conception of freedom will comprise necessary and jointly sufficient conditions for distinguishing penal force from unjust violence. Hence these constraints are conditions of penal liability making up a model general part of a penal law for liberal states.

2. Public Reason as Formal Agency

If we think about why freedom is a plausible conception of public reason—a qualified candidate for the title of fundamental end of public authority—we will arrive at the particular conception of freedom that must form the starting point of any rational derivation of the general conditions of penal liability. Freedom, I suggest, is a plausible conception of public reason because of its emptiness of all interests that may be contingently held. Recall that the move to public reason from a contingently shared common interest was required by the idea of a stable coercive authority. To reach stable ground, therefore, we must abstract from every concrete interest or purpose that may or may not be held by individuals to the one end that is necessarily presupposed in the choice of any end whatever. As Kant taught, that end is the self, understood as a *possibility* or capacity for freely choosing ends and therefore a *potential* for achieving self-authored ends—ends reflecting a deliberative conception of the good. Here, however, it is the bare capacity for free choice that we fix upon, for any exercise of the capacity will once again engage the contingent and idiosyncratic ends from which we sought to abstract.

So isolated, however, the capacity for free choice can be grasped only negatively—as the capacity *not* to be causally determined to seek satisfactions according to behavioural laws. Because the self *can* reject a caused impulse (hunger, for example) as a motive for action, its following the impulse is something the self freely chooses even when it acts without deliberation or impulsively. Of course, this is not to deny that selves are alive in bodies that are embroiled in cause–effect relationships, nor even to deny that these connections operate with all the appearance of laws when deliberation is absent. What is denied is only that these connections are necessary ones. The possibility of not following an impulse makes following it the choice of a self to whom following the impulse is thus imputable and who is therefore "responsible" for following it. Moreover, as a chooser of its ends, the self is also the final end of action pursuant to its ends—that for the sake of which any action is performed. Because of its negativity and consequent emptiness of content, I'll call this final end formal agency, and I'll call the penal law paradigm it structures the paradigm of formal agency (or the formalist paradigm).

The paradigm of formal agency has as its fundamental end the protection of each agent's capacity to choose the ends of its action against pre-emption, interference, or destruction by the action of another. By pre-emption I mean prevention of the capacity's exercise by applying physical force to an agent so as to restrain or direct its movements according to physical laws. By interference I mean imposing by threat a binary choice upon the agent ("do this or suffer that"), one of which involves a normatively foreclosed acquiescence in wrongful pre-emption or destruction, so that the agent's capacity for choice is normatively pre-empted: it has no legally recognized choice but to obey. By destruction I mean the physical annihilation of the biological conditions (consciousness, life) of the capacity for free choice. All these actions are considered wrongful, not because they challenge the ruler's monopoly of coercion, but because they contradict the end-status of free agency. Were the ruler to pre-empt, interfere with, or destroy an agent's liberty outside its duty to protect the common liberty, it too would have committed a wrong.

Why not happiness?

It might be objected that formal agency is not the only end qualified by its abstractness for the title of public reason. Happiness too is such an end because, although each agent conceives happiness differently according to its subjective likes and dislikes, and although any agreement on what brings happiness would be fortuitous and short-lived, nevertheless happiness as such is necessarily desired by beings who are subjects of desire and are conscious of this. Such beings have not only first-order desires for this or that object but also a second-order desire that their first-order desires be satisfied insofar as satisfying them will yield an optimal level of satisfaction over the long run. The second-order desire is a desire for happiness simply, and it is necessarily shared by all beings who are conscious of themselves as desiring beings. So why begin from formal agency? Why could not punishment be distinguished from wrongful battery or forcible confinement by its being ordered to the greatest possible long-run satisfaction of desire across all those subject to a political authority? Why should we not say, with Bentham, that punishment is justified if the pain inflicted is necessary to prevent greater pain, and why should we not derive, as he did, liability and exculpatory conditions from this principle?

Despite its abstractness, happiness is not an eligible candidate for public reason. Its disqualifying feature is that, because it consists in the satisfaction of whatever prudent desires people may have, it cannot be pursued independently of seeking to satisfy those desires. As a result, it is prey to the same problem of fragmentation that afflicted a common interest contingently shared and that necessitated the move to public reason in the first place. As soon as the preferences of individuals are such that the satisfaction of some requires the frustration of others, the general happiness can be conceived only as the greatest net happiness, in which sum the sufferings experienced by some people will be justified by the greater gains obtainable by others. Since penal force against someone implies just such a fragmentation of interest, the public interest dissolves into a private one in the very act it was supposed to legitimate as being distinct from wrongful violence.

Formal agency is immune to this kind of disintegration. Because it is an *a priori* capacity to choose ends, formal agency may be respected and protected by a public authority independently of any secondary concern for facilitating the satisfaction of particular ends. Thus exercises of the capacity (for example, in offensive speech) inimical to the general happiness may be protected against interference provided they do not interfere with the capacity for free choice of others, while acts pre-emptive of formal agency (for example, confining people suspected of dangerous tendencies) may be proscribed even if they would yield a net gain of happiness. Unlike happiness, which, though an abstract idea, is still a compendium of satisfactions of subjective ends, formal agency transcends such ends, and this is what qualifies it to be a conception of public reason under which penal force may be distinguished from unjust violence.

The eudaemonist's objection

To this it might be further objected that the very feature of formal agency that recommends it as a conception of public reason disqualifies it as a worthwhile end of political association. Precisely because it transcends material ends, formal agency (it might be argued) is too vacuous an end upon which to base coercive authority. Why would any association take as its fundamental end—as the only end whose claim to satisfaction is indefeasible—something that, as a bare capacity to choose valued ends, is surely only one element of a life worth living? People might desire that their free agency be respected as an essential ingredient of their long-run happiness, but what would be the point of respecting agency in a particular case at the cost of everyone's long-run happiness? Better the happiness of a majority in which everyone may hope to participate than a universal formal agency which no one concerned for the general welfare would absolutize in isolation. Call this the eudaemonist's objection.

The eudaemonist's objection requires two responses. First, though certainly vacuous, formal agency has a special status among the ends forming a person's conception of a worthwhile life. That status derives from its being a condition of choice rather than something itself chosen. We can say that, as the end that is necessarily presupposed in the choice of all ends whose value depends on their being chosen, agency itself is an end whose value is unqualified. This means that, whereas the value of optional ends is relative to the agent whose ends they are, agency's value is absolute or valid for all agents. Moreover, whereas the agent may renounce or compromise the satisfaction of optional ends for the sake of its greatest possible happiness, agency itself is above such trade-offs. This is so because an end whose worth is absolute cannot suitably be treated as one among others, nor can an end that is prior to optional ends be disposed of by the agent as if it were itself optional. Agency, in short, is a locus of unconditioned and incomparable worth, which common parlance renders as "dignity".

So there is point to a public authority's treating agency as an end more fundamental than happiness even though it is formal and empty. The point is to treat agency with the respect due it as a locus of dignity. The way to treat it so is to treat it, in Kant's celebrated formulation "always as an end and never as a means only".[2] And this is why penal force against the agent cannot be justified by the happiness it secures to others, nor can liability and exculpatory conditions be derived from what is necessary for the maximum net happiness. Indeed, it is only because agents bear unqualified worth that their happiness is properly a concern, not only of each severally and of those bound to them by ties of love, but also of a public authority. While the general happiness cannot be the fundamental aim of a sustainable public authority (given its tendency to break up into the happiness of a part), a public authority may facilitate neutrally the pursuit of happiness by free agents whose dignity is what entitles them to such concern. It may do so, that is, subject to an indefeasible constraint of respect for agency. The public authority cannot self-consistently care for the happiness of its subjects at the expense of the very principle that makes the satisfaction of their subjective ends an appropriate object of public concern.

The residual force of the eudaemonist's objection

The foregoing argument, however, is not a complete response to the eudaemonist's objection. This is so because, however compelling the argument for treating agency as a locus of dignity or unconditioned worth, that argument does not establish agency as the *sole* locus of dignity nor, therefore, as the *fundamental* end of political association. The argument for its being fundamental presupposed the relativity of all goods to those who value them and hence the equation of welfare with "happiness",

---

[2] *Foundations of the Metaphysics of Morals,* trans. LW Beck (Indianapolis: Bobbs-Merrill, 1959), 47.

understood as the prudent satisfaction of subjective ends. If all material ends were subjective values, then formal agency would indeed be the sole unconditioned end and so would be exclusively entitled to the throne of public reason. But observe how all material ends came to be seen as subjective ones. In the negative movement to freedom of choice (as freedom *from* determination), the equation of material ends with biological ends was assumed, and then these ends had to be conceived as optional and subjective for agents rather than as necessary because of their capacity for free choice. Thus the subjectivity of all material ends followed from an initially assumed equation of material ends with biologically given ends; and so formal agency's claim to be the sole unconditioned end is self-contradictorily conditioned by that assumption. Moreover, the assumption seems far-fetched, for surely there are ends—life and good health, for example—that, though given immediately by biology, are valuable mediately through freedom and so valuable to *all* agents because necessary to acting from self-authored ends. If that is so, then the argument for the absolute priority of formal agency does not go through.

I take the latter objection to be unanswerable insofar as it contends against Kant's position that the dignity of formal agency is the fundamental end of coercive authority.[3] Yet the objection overshoots insofar as it views the argument against treating formal agency as *fundamental* as an argument for dismissing it also as an *autonomous* principle for justifying coercive action by public officials. From the fact that formal agency is not the fundamental end of coercive authority it does not follow that it can be immersed in some other fundamental end, such as self-determination or human flourishing; for it may be the case that the paradigm of penal justice ordered separately to formal agency is part of a complex system comprising several instantiations of a comprehensive public reason. Stated otherwise, it may be that the system of penal justice ordered to fundamental public reason is just the unity of the several systems autonomously ordered to constituent conceptions. Such a "federation" of justice paradigms is, after all, a conceptual possibility.

Furthermore, our doubts about whether formal agency is fundamental left its dignity unscathed, for formal agency may be a locus of absolute worth without being the sole such locus provided that plural loci are complementary rather than competitive; and that too is theoretically possible (after all, two agents are loci of mutually compatible claims to absolute worth). But if in rejecting formal agency's claim to be the fundamental end of coercive authority we also reject its claim to be an autonomous end, then we will have indeed denied formal agency's dignity along with its claim to being fundamental even though the latter denial does not entail the former. For, if the capacity to choose ends is valued simply as an ingredient of a common good (autonomy, for example), then the common good will

---

[3] That this is Kant's position is shown by *The Metaphysics of Morals*, trans. Mary Gregor (Cambridge: Cambridge University Press, 1991) 63: "Freedom (independence from being constrained by another's choice), insofar as it can coexist with the freedom of every other in accordance with a universal law, is the only original right belonging to every man by virtue of his humanity."

determine what respect is due agency, whose worth will thus be conditional on its furthering the good. There will thus be no independent worth to formal agency that an authority charged to promote the good must respect.

The foregoing considerations entitle us to proceed as follows. We begin with the paradigm of penal justice independently ordered to formal agency. We describe the structural features of this paradigm, elucidate its conceptions of right and wrong, and pinpoint the specific difference of criminal wrong. We then present the account of judicial punishment belonging uniquely to this paradigm and derive the liability and exculpatory conditions generated by that account. We also defend this account as one that *partially* reconciles liability to judicial punishment with the freedom and inviolable worth of the agent. Finally, we consider how treating formal agency as the fundamental end of coercive action leads to equivocations regarding the subjectivity of all material ends and permits a liability to noncriminal penalties that contradicts the dignity of agents. This will lead us to a new conception of public reason whose doctrinal offspring will fill out the system of constraints on penal force required by the agent's inviolable worth.

3. The Features of the Formalist Paradigm

The formalism of the formal agency paradigm consists in its isolating as the sole bearer of legal rights the capacity for freely choosing ends. While this capacity is also a potential for achieving self-authored ends, respect is here due the capacity whether or not the potential for achieving self-authored ends is realized or frustrated in the capacity's exercise. This means that there is a coercive duty to respect the capacity even if disrespecting it would better serve the agent's particular ends (happiness) or even long-run autonomy (welfare); that there is a coercive duty *only* to respect the capacity, not a duty to assist the realization of the further potential it carries; and that breach of the duty is a remediable wrong regardless of the beneficent motives of the one breaching. A few examples will bring into focus the difference between exercising the capacity to choose ends and realizing the potential for achieving self-authored ends.

If I act suddenly on an impulse to pocket a gold ring lying under glass in a jewellery store, I have exercised a capacity for free choice inasmuch as I could have rejected the impulse as a motive for action; no law of nature necessitated my behaving as I did. Nevertheless, there is a sense in which I have acted unfreely, because the end of my action was taken up as immediately given by an impulse rather than chosen upon reflection and deliberation. So, while the capacity for free choice was exercised, the potential it carries for acting from self-authored ends was badly realized—indeed hardly realized at all—in the exercise. Similarly, if I am faced with a choice between death by starvation or stealing, any choice I make will exercise my capacity for freely choosing ends, for it can always be said that I could have chosen otherwise than I did. But my choice will fail to realize my potential for acting from self-authored ends because the only available options are those that have been imposed on me by circumstances and that I would not choose were I empirically able to set ends for myself. Or again, I have a capacity to choose ends, but if my action begets unintended and adverse consequences for me that I could not have foreseen, then my product did not realize the specific ends I chose but was partly the result of extraneous causes owing to which my ends came to nought. Once again, my potential for achieving self-authored ends has been frustrated rather than realized in the exercise of my capacity for choice.

Now, we who are observing the formalist paradigm can see that the distinction between a bare capacity freely to choose ends ("I could have rejected the motive I acted on") and the greater potential it carries ("I can act from a self-authored end") is really one between two conceptions of freedom—a thin one and a more robust one—that we can call, respectively, liberty and real autonomy. But the formalist paradigm does not regard it so. Because it equates material ends with subjective ones having no standing in public reason (and which, apart from a reciprocal bargain, no absolute end could be forced to serve or accommodate), this paradigm must identify the public end with the capacity to choose ends and so make respect for this capacity its sole coercive norm. No distinction is drawn between subjective ends and goods all agents must value as conditions of a realized potential for autonomy; rather, all material ends are considered subjective, so that liberty appears as the only end that free agents could accept as coercively obliging them.

This is not to say, however, that formalism has no place for the idea of autonomy. On the contrary, autonomy is recognized (by Kant, for example) as the richer conception of freedom—the fulfilment of that for which free will is the potential. But autonomy cannot here have the status of a coercive public norm. Because material ends are treated as given biological goals that are subjectively ratified (or not), autonomy must be conceived as a condition one attains by setting aside material ends as motives and by acting purely for the sake of an intellectual end—the right.[4] This, however, makes autonomy a private and inward affair of disinterested motives rather than a coercive public end; after all, no one can be coerced to obey the law without regard to his material interest. So, the only coercive public end is liberty. This fundamental idea—call it the public priority of liberty—is reflected in the following defining features of the formalist paradigm: the equal dignity of agents, the independence of wronging from harming, the exclusion of civil and criminal liability for failing to benefit, and the independence of culpability from evil.

The equal dignity of agents

Because the formalist paradigm views all those with a capacity for choosing ends as bearers of unconditioned worth, it views all agents as equal right-bearers despite

---

[4] Kant, *Foundations of the Metaphysics of Morals*, 65.

yawning differences in ethical development and regardless of whether the potential for autonomy involved in the capacity is prevented from realization by infirmity or immaturity. Thus persons have rights, not just virtuous or autonomous persons. Career criminals, alcoholics, drug addicts, children, and the mentally ill have the same protection against other agents as everyone else; and whatever exculpatory conditions barring punishment the formalist paradigm prescribes (for example, involuntariness, mistake of fact) apply equally to them—even if their disability or immaturity is the cause of their meeting these conditions and will likely cause nonculpable transgressions again. The schizophrenic who kills a human being whom he perceives as an attacking animal may be nonpenally confined for prophylactic reasons because his disease disables him from realizing his metaphysical potential for achieving self-authored ends (see Chapter 8). But first he will be judged in court as a dignified agent capable of choice and declared not guilty because he chose no wrong.

Not only do all beings for whom free choice is possible have the same right to exercise their capacities for choice; they also have the same legal liabilities. Thus, conditions disabling them from realizing the potential in free choice for autonomous life-shaping do not by themselves disentitle human beings to the respect shown them when they are held legally responsible for their conduct. The mark of responsibility is not an empirical capability for acting autonomously, nor is it (as Duff and Gardner contend) an empirical capability for acting intelligibly from reasons and for being responsive to rational persuasion.[5] These capabilities are more advanced than those required for basic responsibility for conduct. The precondition for responsibility is nothing more than self-conscious agency—awareness of one's freedom of choice, which can exist even when the options one faces are delusional and the delusion fixed beyond argument. Thus infancy negates criminal capacity and so precludes a trial on the facts, but insanity does so only in the rare cases where it vitiates self-consciousness. Otherwise, the insane are tried like everyone else to determine whether, within the world as they saw it, the choices they made were culpable ones. Further, beings with a capacity for free choice cannot be subject to literally irresistible impulses while conscious, though addiction and mental disease might give inclinations a volcanic force to which even a person of reasonable self-control might yield. The formalist paradigm cannot recognize this condition of extreme heteronomy as negating responsibility, though it might admit it as partially excusing for reasons discussed in Chapter 7. In this way the mentally ill and addicted are accorded the dignity of agents who are responsible for their choices however powerful the inclinations they chose to follow.

The foregoing observations permit a glimpse of what would be lost if formalism's flawed equation of liberty with fundamental public reason were taken as a reason for ousting its autonomous legal ordering rather than simply its exclusive

---

[5] RA Duff, *Answering for Crime* (Oxford: Hart Publishing, 2007), 38–43; John Gardner, *Offences and Defences* (Oxford: Oxford University Press, 2007), 181–5.

ordering. The autonomy of the formalist paradigm alone guarantees the equal end-status of agents and hence the universality of legal rights. This is so because formalism alone sees unqualified worth, not in a moral excellence, but in the morally indiscriminate fact of self-consciousness. Accordingly, were this paradigm merged into one ordered to a richer conception of freedom, rights would be allotted by that conception, and so equality would be lost to an aristocracy of the autonomous. Those whose capacity for free choice cannot be exercised in autonomous or reasoned choices would command not even a defeasible respect for their choices; hence, they could not be wronged either by private actors or by public officials. Like infants, moreover, they would be ineligible for honourable punishment just because of their status—not even fit for judgment as guilty or not guilty—because a material capability for making autonomous choices rather than a capacity for free choice would be the basic precondition of responsibility for conduct.[6] Not only would the chronically heteronomous be vulnerable to coercion for therapeutic and prophylactic reasons (as I argue is justified in Chapter 8); such coercion would be unconstrained by a requirement that their freedom of choice be pre-empted only to the extent needed for public safety; for the capacity for free choice would not be a sufficient basis for rights. Thus they could be held at the sovereign's pleasure even without a determination that they pose a continuing danger. Indeed, since they could not be wronged, even more extreme conclusions could be drawn. Though far from fanciful (parts of this construct can be found in various imperfectly liberal jurisdictions), this picture obviously does not belong in a gallery of liberal legal practices.

The independence of wronging from harming

The formal agency model treats as a wrong any action that manifests disrespect for the capacity to choose ends even if the action inflicts no setback to the victim's ends and even if it actually furthers them. Wrong is simply the pre-emption of, or interference with, the capacity to choose ends.[7] Accordingly, someone who injects medication into an unwilling patient commits a battery even if the medication was essential to his living a productive life, even if the patient desired a productive life, and even if, contrary to what the patient believed, the medication carried no risk of serious side-effects. Conversely, someone who inflicts great harm will be innocent of wrongdoing if he did not interfere with the victim's capacity to choose ends, as in the cases of the business competitor and the tactless speaker, or if the injured person consented to the risk, as in the case of the prize-fighter who kills an opponent in the ring.

---

[6] See the judgment of McLachlin J in *R v Chaulk* [1990] 3 SCR 1303.
[7] The tort of negligence, I have argued elsewhere, lies at the border of the formalist paradigm, neither wholly in nor wholly out; see Alan Brudner, *The Unity of the Common Law: Studies in Hegelian Jurisprudence* (Berkeley: University of California Press, 1995), 200–1.

That the foregoing examples are commonplaces of the common law of tort and crime should tell us that the "harm principle" of liability, while a favourite of some philosophers, actually plays a very circumscribed role in the penal law. Harm (but not to subjective interests—hence the exclusion of civil liability for pure economic loss) is a condition of civil liability only in the tort of negligence; while in criminal law it plays an ancillary role as an aggravating factor relevant to quantum of punishment and as something whose avoidance might justify what remains a compensable transgression or excuse what remains a culpable transgression. Why harm should be irrelevant in the first instance to criminal liability and yet be secondarily relevant to measure of punishment and defence is a mystery that all single-end theories of the criminal law must find impenetrable. Yet we shall see that it is quite intelligible to the complex whole theory we are expounding.

That harm is irrelevant to wrongdoing in the first instance is explained by the reason for formalism's isolation of the capacity to choose ends as the sole coercive public end. That reason is its equation of goods with subjective values. Because this model identifies material ends with subjectively ratified biological goals, it equates welfare with the satisfaction of subjective ends, which (absent contract) no public authority may coerce absolute ends to serve or accommodate. There is thus no public conception of material interests harm to which could be legally cognizable as an objective harm. Specifically, the formalist model has no conception of welfare as the attainment of goods every reasonable agent must desire as essential to its living an autonomous life. Hence it has no public conception of harm as a setback to these goods. In a context where all material ends are subjective, the only public interest is the capacity to choose ends. And so the only coercive public norm for the formalist paradigm is an injunction to respect this capacity by refraining from pre-empting or interfering with its exercise.

The absence of positive duties

A related feature of the formalist paradigm is that it recognizes as coercible only negative duties not to interfere with the capacity to choose ends; it will not coerce the performance of any positive duties to which the agent has not freely consented in return for binding someone else. By a positive duty I mean a duty to confer a benefit on someone, to act for the sake of his or her welfare. The distinction between negative and positive duties is not, observe, a difference between liability for acts and liability for failing to act. If I fail to remove a car from someone's foot after driving onto it, I have breached a duty not to pre-empt free choice even though what occurred can be indifferently described as an act or an omission.[8] Conversely, if I walk away from someone dying in the street without offering assistance, I have failed to confer a benefit even though I have not been motionless. The difference between negative and positive duties is one between a duty

[8] *Fagan v Commissioner of Metropolitan Police* [1969] 1 QB 439 (CA).

to forbear from pre-empting another agent's capacity for choice and a duty to enhance another's welfare.

The formal agency model recognizes no positive duties, because it makes no distinction between interests relative to individual agents and interests that all human agents have in securing the conditions for living autonomous lives. It equates all interests with subjective interests and all welfare with happiness. And since no one has a right outside of contract to compel an absolute end to serve his or her subjective interests, the agency model will enforce no positive duty of concern.

Still, the absence of coercive positive duties as between private actors is not unique to the formalist paradigm. This feature of formalism will survive into the legal paradigm ordered to real autonomy. This is so because the positive entitlement to the conditions of an autonomous life will be correlative to a prior duty on the public authority to secure these conditions on pain of transformation into an instrument of the economically independent class. Thus a coercive duty on a private actor to promote a stranger's autonomy would amount to his or her unfairly shouldering the public burden, while a coercive duty unilaterally to promote another's happiness would still be inconsistent with his end-status. What is unique to formalism, however, is the absence of coercive positive duties of concern for autonomy even on the citizen. Where the sole public interest is the capacity to exercise choice, the only coercive duty on the citizen is to forbear from interfering with that capacity.

The independence of culpability from evil

Within the formalist paradigm, culpable wrongdoing consists in the choice to interfere with the capacity for choice. Just as the only legally cognizable wrong is interference with the capacity's exercise, so the capacity's exercise is the only legally cognizable criterion for liability to punishment. The wickedness or virtue of the character revealed by the choice is beside the point. This is so because, where all material ends are optional, there is no such thing as natural virtue in the Aristotelian sense of living as the best human would; for natural virtue presupposes that there are nonoptional ends (friendship, citizenship, wisdom) in human nature. But if there is no such thing as natural virtue, then distinctions between virtuous and vicious character themselves reflect subjective judgments having no standing in public reason and so incapable of coercively binding absolute ends. The only publicly acceptable basis of culpability for absolute ends whose ways of life are otherwise beyond public criticism is the choice to interfere with choice. No doubt formalism generates its own alternative to Aristotelian ethics in the ethics of Kantian autonomy. But we have seen why this must be an ethics of motive rather than one of character; and an ethics of disinterested motive cannot coherently be promoted by public coercion (whereas character can be formed by habits ingrained by obedience to good laws). Besides, whether an unlawful act is performed from self-interest or from a maxim of benevolence is a matter hidden from finite agents.

The upshot is that wickedness is neither a necessary nor a sufficient condition of culpability. Thus, it is irrelevant to culpability for wrong that the choice to interfere with choice was out of character for the defendant or that it was prompted by beneficent motives. As the court found, Robert Latimer's killing of his 12-year-old quadriplegic daughter was culpable even if he acted from a loving desire to end her incurable suffering from cerebral palsy.[9] Nor is it relevant to culpability that the choice to interfere with choice was morally blameless because in the circumstances (of duress, say) forbearance would have called for saintliness. As the positive law holds, this is a reason for excusing the culpable, not for exculpating.[10]

Neither is wickedness sufficient for culpability. Thus the wicked intention to harm another is not a culpable intention unless it manifests itself in an external choice to interfere with choice (though a completed interference is unnecessary to an external choice—see Chapter 3), even if there is abundant evidence of the intention and chance alone, not any change of heart, prevented its manifestation. Thus, the would-be arsonist who is interrupted by police while purchasing matches has not committed a culpable attempt even if he confesses his purpose.[11] Moreover, the wicked indifference to another's welfare shown in an unthinking imposition of an obvious risk of serious harm is not the choice to interfere with choice that formalism regards (for reasons that will soon become clear) as alone culpable.

If culpability is independent of wickedness, it follows that punishment cannot be justified as giving the wicked their just deserts. This may come as a surprise to those who associate formalism with Kant and Kant with moral retributivism. Actually, however, Kant is equivocal about what culpability consists in. Sometimes he equates it with wickedness. For example, in one passage in the *Doctrine of Right*, he argues that only the death penalty for murder and rebellion punishes all "in proportion to [their] *inner wickedness*" because the noble would prefer death to enslavement and the base would prefer the opposite.[12] Elsewhere, however, he implies that culpability consists simply in an action whose universalized principle rebounds against the actor. Thus he writes: "whatever undeserved evil you inflict upon another within the people, that you inflict upon yourself. If you insult him, you insult yourself; if you steal from him, you steal from yourself; if you strike him, you strike yourself; if you kill him, you kill yourself."[13]

Hegel is much clearer. In the *Philosophy of Right*, he explicitly distinguishes between the "moral attitude", which takes as essential "the subjective aspect of crime", and the juridical attitude, for which "crime is to be annulled, not because it is the producing of an evil, but because it is the infringement of the right as

---

[9] *R v Latimer* [2001] 1 SCR 3.   [10] See citations in Introduction, n. 10.
[11] Purchasing matches would likely be regarded as merely "preparatory"—too remote from the completed purpose to constitute an attempt.
[12] Kant, *Metaphysics of Morals*, 142–3. Emphasis in original.   [13] Ibid, 141.

right...".[14] Elsewhere he says that "[i]n formal right, there is no question of... the particular motive behind my volition"[15] and that in the theory of punishment "it is not merely the question of an evil or of this, that, or the other good; the precise point at issue is wrong and the righting of it".[16]

This gives rise to a puzzle. If punishment cannot be justified to absolute ends either as securing the greatest net happiness or as giving the wicked their just deserts, then it cannot be justified in either of the ways proposed by the two most prominent theories of punishment. How then can punishment be justified to absolute ends? Let us begin the story with the formalist account of right and wrong.

4. Formalist Right and Wrong

The formal agency model of penal justice is the system of liability and exculpatory rules organized around a familiar liberal idea: that the fundamental end of coercive authority is to protect the agent's liberty to pursue ends of its choosing insofar as its liberty is compatible with an equal liberty for others. The right to liberty is both a permission to act in all ways that do not interfere with another agent's capacity to act from ends it chooses and an enforceable claim to a remedy against interference by others. Let us first consider the permission and the limits thereof.

The limits reconciling the liberties of separate agents are drawn by property and tort law, whose principles concretize one basic idea: that publicly enforceable permissions to act are individual claims to the sufferance of others that can be recognized without self-abasement by agents equal in dignity to the claimant. That is, legal rights to act certify as suitable for public enforcement individual right-claims that have passed a validity test prior to enforcement; and that test is recognizability by another end. A claim of permission to an exercise of liberty must be confirmable by the agent (or agents) to whom the claim is addressed and who, to give an authentic confirmation, must be capable of remaining independent in recognizing the claim. If accepting the claim would be incompatible with the addressee's end-status, then the claim cannot be objectively validated by an independent other, and so the claim is unsuitable for public enforcement. Of course, there need not be an empirical acceptance by the addressee for a right-claim to be valid, for otherwise the addressee could dictate what the actor can do. It is enough that the addressee *could* accept the claim without compromising his equal worth.

Now, the only claims to another's sufferance that can be recognized by an equal end are those limited by a reciprocal and equal deference to the other's agency. An end can submit to another end without self-loss (and so without disqualifying itself as someone competent to give an effective recognition) if and only if the

---

[14] GWF Hegel, *Philosophy of Right*, trans. TM Knox (Oxford: Oxford University Press, 1967), para. 99.
[15] Ibid, para. 37.   [16] Ibid, para. 99.

other likewise submits to it. Accordingly, that a right-claim to liberty must be recognizable without self-abasement by the agent to whom the claim is addressed does not mean that I cannot hinder or harm another by my actions; after all, to act is potentially to foreclose the actions of others bent on identical objects and to initiate causal chains leading to harm. Rather, the recognizability condition means that hindrances and harms are permissible only under a rule allowing equal and reciprocal hindrances and risks. So, for example, I can disturb my neighbour through the use of my land only as long as I keep within the bounds of ordinary use; and I can accidentally injure another provided that the risk I imposed on him was within the bounds of the socially normal and reciprocal. These legal doctrines instantiate the idea that valid claims to act are those that can be validated by a free and equal other because they are limited by a reciprocal duty to respect his or her liberty. This, then, is the underlying idea of lawful liberty, and I'll call it by various names depending on what seems most natural in the context: the idea of *mutual recognition*, the idea of a *common will*, the intersubjective basis of valid claims of right, the legal norm, or sometimes simply Law.

The idea underlying lawful liberty in the formalist paradigm gives us the essential nature of wrong within that framework. Wrongdoing in general consists in an action whose permissibility cannot be recognized without self-loss by the agent who suffered the effects of the action because the action is incompatible with its equal liberty. If the idea of mutual recognition gives the limit of rightful liberty, then wrongdoing consists in the voluntary transgression of that limit through a choice unrecognizable by an equal. By "voluntary" I do not mean "intentional". A knowing or purposeful transgression is not essential to wrongdoing, because a mistaken belief in permission suffices to challenge the other's rightful boundary and so to require an answering "correction". On the other hand, crossing a boundary through involuntary motion (say, through a push) signifies no challenge to the boundary and thus requires no answering remedy. So, a voluntary crossing of another's rightful boundary without his or her consent is the necessary and sufficient condition of *transgressing* (wrongfully crossing) the boundary.[17]

Wrongdoing in general is particularized as transgressions of the several, more or less intersubjectively constituted, boundaries of the self. That is, while all valid right-claims to action issue from a relation of mutual recognition, not all boundaries of the self limiting others' action are themselves constituted within this relation; some are established nonrelationally or atomistically. The self's body, for example, is a boundary constituted outside of relation to another, so that the boundary is transgressed (the tort of trespass is committed) by any voluntary, nonconsensual contact, even if the defendant reasonably believed there was consent. Here no latitude exists for permissible but unwanted uses (see Chapter 2).[18]

---

[17] *Weaver v Ward* (1616) 80 ER 284; *Smith v Stone* (1647) Sty 65.
[18] *R v Ewanchuk* [1999] 1 SCR 33. True, action in crowded spaces carries an inevitable risk of jostling, and so there is a presumption of consent from a decision to enter such spaces. But if

Similarly, exclusive possession of things outside the body is constituted outside of relation (by unilateral first possession), and so the boundary is transgressed by a voluntary, unconsented-to encroachment or taking of what is in another's possession; that the trespasser reasonably mistook the thing for his own is irrelevant to his civil liability. By contrast, the landowner's boundary against disturbances of "quiet enjoyment" is itself constituted intersubjectively (because land use inevitably carries externalities), so that the boundary is transgressed, not by any unwanted disturbance, but only by those caused through extraordinary use. Similarly, the self's boundary against harm indirectly caused by another's action is itself a product of mutual recognition, and so the boundary is transgressed, not by any action causing harm, but only by those imposing a socially extraordinary risk. A voluntary, nonconsensual crossing of any of these boundaries is a *right infringement* or wrong, which may be nonculpable (a wrong remediable by compensation but undeserving of judicial punishment) or culpable (a wrong deserving judicial punishment) depending on conditions we shall now discuss.

5. Culpable Wrong and Formalist Punishment

Penal force (arrest, detention, fine, forced service, incarceration) is a right infringement. The official applying force voluntarily and without consent crosses the boundary of another agent's sphere of sovereign choice—the boundary delineated by its body or its property. Penal force is not a prima facie right infringement that an all-things-considered justification erases. It is a right infringement simply. This is so because penal force is not necessary to realize the right of the victim that the wrongdoer violated. If a transgression is threatened, pre-emptive self-defence or the defence of another by official actors realizes the right. If the transgression has already occurred, civil remedies realize the victim's right, for they restore wrongdoer and victim to the normative position of mutual recognition that the wrongdoer's action upset. In that the wrongdoer puts his victim back to where he was, he recants to the victim the claim of superiority his action implied, while the victim gains the wrongdoer's recognition for the right violated. In that sense a civil remedy corrects the injustice. Forcibly repelling the wrongdoer or forcing him to compensate his victim is not a right infringement, for he had no right to perform the action in the first place, and coercing him realizes the right his action challenged; it merely restores the parties to their rightful equilibrium.

However, if action against the wrongdoer's body or property that is *not* in pre-emptive self-defence and *not* compensatory exceeds what is necessary to prevent or correct the wrong to the victim, then that action is itself a right infringement. Since the civil remedy has already (or could) restore wrongdoer and victim to their

someone has clearly indicated nonconsent, there is technically a battery, and it is the doctrine *de minimis non curat lex* that shields the trespasser, not strict right.

rightful equality, any further action against the wrongdoer *sets him back* relative to that position and so is itself a wrong. Thus penal force is a right infringement that must be justified by reasons qualified to do so, not an apparent wrong to be explained away.

The formalist model's equation of the public end with the capacity for choosing ends determines the way it justifies the wrong that judicial punishment is. Since there is within this framework no good necessarily common to agents, penal force cannot be justified in prospective terms as a means to furthering socially desirable ends. Not even security against violence can qualify here as a public interest, since those forming strong alliances will have less to fear from a condition of insecurity than those more isolated; and so they will value additional security less in relation to liberty than those with more to gain from it. Thus, assuming a civil condition already exists guaranteeing rights through the public adjudication of disputes and the enforcement of civil remedies, the strong are likely to see an additional institution of punishment directed to deterrence and the incapacitation of threats as serving the particular interests of the vulnerable. Accordingly, where all good effects are preferences, penal force must be justified independently of its effects, which is to say that it must be justified in terms of formal right alone—as something required by the reality of rights. Given, however, that the victim's liberty right has already (or could) be realized by a civil remedy and that force not justified by pre-emptive defence or corrective justice is thus itself a right infringement, the requirement that penal force be justified in terms of right alone seems to entail a paradox. It places on the formalist justification of punishment the burden of showing how a right infringement is necessary to the realization of rights.

Criminal desert

The paradox could be resolved if we could identify necessary and sufficient conditions for distinguishing the right infringement that penal force involves from the right infringement of the initial wrongdoer. Where the institution of punishment is justified prospectively by the greatest net happiness, this distinction cannot be made, for on this view officials infringe the recipient's right for the sake of a particular interest (the happiness of the all-but-one they represent), and that is what all wrongdoers do. Moreover, whereas an institution of punishment justified by the general happiness could approve "punishing" someone unconnected to the wrong if doing so were necessary to avoid greater misery to others, one justified by the realization of rights could not. This is so because officials could not realize rights by an action that infringes a right unless there were a logical connection between the antecedent wrong done by the recipient of punishment and the wrong done to him by the punisher; for in that case (and in that case alone) the wrong of punishment would not be something officials do *to* the recipient but would rather be a kind of impersonal nemesis of the wrongdoer's deed that officials execute. Were we able to discern such a connection, therefore, we could say that the right infringement that punishment involves differs from the initial wrongdoer's in that it is reflexive rather than transitive. It is not something officials do to the recipient but is rather something the recipient brings on himself. Officials perform the act, but because the right infringement is (under conditions I'll discuss shortly) logically implied in the recipient's antecedent wrong, it is not their wrong, and so no remedial action lies against them in turn.

Let us call the connection between the recipient's antecedent wrong and the wrong he suffers "desert". Now, of course, there are many possible views as to what actions or psychological states deserve a punitive response of some kind. One may think, for example, that an adverse consequence is deserved by someone who acts immorally by being verbally abusive to a spouse, who harbours an immoral wish for a competitor, or who repeatedly causes harm to others through selfish inattention and insensitivity. All these evils deserve natural punishment (of which bad conscience is a form), but our sole interest is in judicial punishment, and the formalist paradigm dictates one particular understanding of what it means for punishment of this kind to be deserved.

Suppose Surgeon (S), while operating on Patient (P) to remove a cancerous prostate, also removes a healthy appendix, erroneously believing he has P's consent harmlessly to remove a potential source of trouble. S has wronged P, because he has pre-empted P's capacity to direct his body according to his own choice. He will thus have to pay P at least nominal damages for his trespass. Because, however, S's interference with P's freedom of choice was unwitting, it signified no denial of P's capacity for rights, hence no denial that agency is that capacity. Rather, it merely expressed a mistaken belief that P had, in exercising his capacity for choice, given S permission to remove his appendix. Therefore, S's transgression was limited to a transgression against P: it had no more general significance. It is therefore for P to decide whether he wants to assert his right against S; and once he has been fully compensated for the infringement, nothing remains to be done to vindicate the right, that is, to realize it in the face of an action inconsistent with its reality. Even if P decides not to pursue S, P's right is intact, for S is off the hook only by the grace of P—only by virtue of P's voluntary decision to forgo his right of action. Since, moreover, P's right can be fully realized by S's compensating him (and since P's right alone has been infringed), any coercive action taken against S not justified by a compensatory rationale is a gratuitous piece of violence by which S is unjustifiably wronged.[19]

Let's now vary the facts somewhat. Suppose that S removes P's appendix knowing that P has refused consent to any procedure not specifically authorized in advance. S has obviously still transgressed a boundary demarcating a sphere wherein P's choices rightfully rule, and so S will still have to compensate P. However, S's action now bears a significance transcending his infringement of P's right. Because S *knowingly* pre-empted P's capacity to choose for his body,

---

[19] I'll consider in a moment the possibility that penal force is justified by the need to deter those who would otherwise treat compensation as a worthwhile price for their wrongful activity. But the wrongdoer in our example has not done this, and so to punish him for that purpose would be to use him as a means only.

substituting his own choice for P's, his action signified a denial of P's end-status and so a denial that P is a right bearer. True, this is a specific insult to P's dignity requiring a compensatory award that reflects this additional dimension of S's private wrong. However, S's wrong is now not limited to a wrong against P. This is so because P, whose right-bearing status S denied, is an agent with a capacity for freely choosing ends. S may not have known this about P, but if P is functioning minimally as a specimen of *homo sapiens,* the thinking Agent in S's shoes will infer a capacity for choosing ends, and this inference can be imputed to S unless he delusionally mistook P for a nonhuman thing (which he did not). Since S can be taken to have assumed P was an agent, his intentional interference with P's body signified a denial that *agents* have rights to choose for their bodies just by virtue of their free will and that all agents are thus equal in dignity.[20] This, however, is tantamount to a denial of the possibility of rights, for (as we have seen) a claim of right to others' sufferance of one's action remains a subjective assertion unless it can obtain a validating recognition from the persons sought to be bound; and validation can come only from independent ends who can bind reciprocally. Rights can exist objectively only among free and equal agents. Accordingly, S's intentional pre-emption of P's capacity for choice signified a denial of the possibility of valid rights and therewith a claimed permission to an unlimited liberty.[21]

In the previous scenario, no such implication followed from S's action. There, on the contrary, S acknowledged the existence of a boundary to his liberty; he simply erred in thinking he had not crossed it. In this case, however, S either denies that boundaries to liberty exist (claims that each agent may do as it pleases) or he claims that, while existing for others, they do not bind him. In either case, he lays claim to an unlimited liberty. Whether such a claim actually crossed S's mind is irrelevant, for what counts is what the thinking Agent standing in S's shoes meant by S's choice to remove P's appendix without P's consent. The thinking Agent will draw the logical implication of an intentional interference with P's body, so that even if S merely excepted himself from the limits applying to others, the Agent will generalize the self-exemption to everyone who may similarly assert his or her special worth and conclude that rights do not exist. And that denial of rights can be imputed to S (the empirical agent) as a necessary implication of his choice to remove P's appendix against P's will.

But more than that can be imputed to S. If the thinking Agent in S's shoes denied the existence of rights to spheres of free choice in general, then it (the

---

[20] In crimes motivated by disdain for a group, this denial is conscious and explicit. Thus, someone may attack another believing that humanity is defined, not by agency, but by race, that only a few have rights, and that his victim is not among them.

[21] Thus Arthur Ripstein errs in thinking that the essence of crime is the denial of the *victim's* right rather than of rights simply; see *Equality, Responsibility, and the Law* (Cambridge: Cambridge University Press, 1999), 149. This error stems from Ripstein's tort-centred view of crime, according to which crime is a species of the genus tort differentiated by intention; 147–63. Jean Hampton fell into the same error; see 'An Expressive Theory of Retribution,' in W Cragg, ed., *Retributivism and its Critics* (Stuttgart: Steiner, 1992), 1–25. For a view of crime as *sui generis,* see Chapter 3 below.

Agent) by necessary implication also denied them for itself; and that denial too can be imputed to S just by virtue of his being an agent with a capacity to think. Moreover, given his implicit denial of his own right to liberty, S cannot justly complain if his freedom of choice is pre-empted in turn, for he has implicitly assented to this; he affirmed the right-denying principle ("I assert a permission to act unlimited by another's agency") by which his own liberty is pre-empted.[22] True, his denial of rights was mistaken, for agency is the bearer of an unqualified worth which no agent can claim without also recognizing it in others. This is why, despite S's implicit right denial, penal force against him is still an infringement of *his* right and why his implicit assent to being handcuffed, shackled, confined, etc., is assent to actions that *are* transgressions. It would thus be incorrect to say that S has forfeited his right to liberty. He has, however, forfeited his right to complain of a right infringement by virtue of his own (implicit) right denial. Accordingly, if S's right to liberty is indeed violated in turn, he may be said to have deserved this in the specific sense of desert understood by the formal agency framework. That is, he called it upon himself. He implicitly authorized it, so that there is no element of an external or transitive imposition in the penal transgression.

Observe that this conception of desert does not refer to a connection between an indeterminate evil (blameworthy deed, omission, or disposition) and an indeterminate detriment expressing blame, censure, condemnation, or whatever. Rather, it refers to a connection between a certain kind of right infringement (one in which a right denial is implicit) and judicial punishment, specifying when a *right infringement* is deserved. Thus, no matter how deserving of suffering an evil character may be, he does not deserve a right infringement unless he deserves it in the tight sense demanded by the formalist paradigm. That is, we must be able to say that actions amounting to an infringement of the wrongdoer's right are authorized by the right denial either explicit or implicit in his or her antecedent choice. So penal force is deserved if the recipient:

(a) interfered with agency with the aim of demonstrating the nonexistence of rights;
(b) interfered with agency in the belief that this human being had no rights or belonged to a group whose members were right-less;
(c) knowingly interfered with agency or knowingly took the risk of doing so (S's case); or
(d) performed actions short of actually interfering with agency but unambiguously manifesting an intention to interfere (see Chapter 3).

But if penal force is deserved under the condition that it be authorized by the practical right denial of the recipient, then deserved punishment is compatible with freedom and distinguishable from the initial wrongdoer's wrong.

---

[22] Why assertion without externalization is not enough is discussed in Chapter 3.

The point of punishing: a Kantian suggestion

So far, however, we have shown only how penal force can be reconciled with freedom *if* it is applied in response to an intentional interference. We have not yet shown why it generally ought to be applied. Failing a demonstration of purpose, however, we will have come up short in showing how punishment can be compatible with freedom and distinguished from the wrongdoer's violence. This is so because, if there is no end of punishment admissible by formalist public reason, then there is a logical gap between the crime and the punitive response such that the latter cannot be taken to have been strictly self-imposed. What is so far entailed by the criminal's intentional interference with agency is only his or her moral vulnerability to coercion, not the coercion itself. Crime gives the state a licence to apply force to the criminal but does not, as so far explained, demand use of the licence. But if the state has an absolute discretion to punish or not, then its arbitrary choice to punish cannot be conceived as self-willed by the recipient, and so it retains an element of external violence. Accordingly, we must show how the administration of punishment is itself self-willed by the recipient; and we do this by showing that there is a public reason to punish crimes as a general rule—one that the thinking Agent will endorse for the sake of its freedom and whose endorsement by the thinking Agent can be imputed to the empirical one.

Now it might seem that the formalist paradigm must falter here. Since it treats all material ends as subjective, formalism cannot regard the beneficial effects of punishment as a public reason to punish endorsable by the thinking Agent. Hence it cannot subscribe to a "mixed" theory of punishment according to which the latter is generally justified by socially desirable ends but can be imposed in the particular case only if the recipient deserves to be punished.[23] For formalism, desert cannot function simply as a constraint on punishing for ends unrelated to desert; rather, desert must somehow figure in the reason for punishing.

Does this mean that the only reason formalism can give for punishing is to give wrongdoers their just deserts? Indeed, most critics of the retributive theory of punishment take this as its reason for punishing and then have an easy time discrediting the theory because of the way it ties punishment to passion—to moral hatred, anger, vengefulness, and *hubris*.[24] However, the critics attack not retributivism, but *moral* retributivism. The retributivism generated by the formalist paradigm cannot regard meting out just deserts for its own sake as the point of punishment either; for we have just seen that crime entails only the coercibility of the criminal, not coercion itself, so that to give criminals what they deserve even after they have fully compensated their victims is an undetermined decision lacking a public purpose the agent could endorse. "Because they deserve it" cannot be

---

[23] HLA Hart, *Punishment and Responsibility* (Oxford: Clarendon Press, 1968), 1–13.
[24] Ibid, 169–73.

an adequate answer to "Why punish the guilty?" because desert does not necessitate punishment.

If formalism can regard neither the beneficial effects of punishment nor the meting out of just deserts for its own sake as its public reason for punishing, what purpose can it recognize? One suggestion is offered by Arthur Ripstein by way of an interpretation of Kant's view of punishment.[25] According to Ripstein's Kant, the point of legal punishment is to secure a "public rightful condition" (or what we would call the rule of Law) by deterring would-be strategic wrongdoers with the threat of having their wrongs visited back upon them. Were civil damages the sole remedy for a right infringement, those inclined to wrongdoing could treat damages as a worthwhile cost of pursuing their aims. They could thus "make the existence of a public rightful order the means through which they wrong others".[26] For Ripstein, this means that a legal order confined to civil remedies would "authorize" wrongdoing provided damages were paid. Payment of damages "could in principle *entitle* the criminal to wrong his victim, as a matter of right, simply by paying the requisite fee".[27] However, no self-respecting agent would acknowledge a duty to renounce self-help according to his private determination of right and wrong to an order that failed to actualize rights publicly. Accordingly, a threat of punishment for strategic wrongdoing is required to make such wrongdoing "normatively unavailable" so as to produce a public rightful condition. This is a public purpose consistent with the subjectivity of ends that the thinking Agent will endorse.

Alas, this argument fails. It cannot be true that wrongdoers' treating damages as a fee for wrongdoing *actually* makes damages a fee. From the fact that they can do so with impunity it does not follow that they cannot wrong their victims, provided there is a public system for adjudicating disputes and for civilly enforcing rights. If, as tort theory tells us, compensation for damages (including for the lost choice to alienate) corrects the defendant's injustice to the plaintiff, and if a system for enforcing court-ordered civil remedies exists, then rights exist in a civil order prior to punishment. Indeed, if rights did not precede the practice of punishment, all self-styled punishment would be an arrogation of punitive authority to enforce a private opinion of right. Accordingly, strategic wrongdoing is already normatively unavailable in a civil order, whether or not it is practically unavailable. The fact that wrongdoers can use the civil order for their purposes without hindrance means that freedom is insecure; it does not mean that rights are nonexistent. But if a civil order confined to enforceable civil remedies is one in which rights have crystallized, then it is one to which self-respecting agents can renounce their right of self-help.

Perhaps Ripstein means that, in a legal order without punishment, the strategic wrongdoer can wrong his victim but cannot do wrong by paying damages

---

[25] '*In Extremis*,' (2005) 2 *Ohio State Journal of Criminal Law*, 415.
[26] Ibid, at 417.   [27] Ibid, my emphasis.

as a price of wrongdoing. Hence *compensated* wrongdoing is permitted. Put this way, however, the argument does not take us to punishment for crime generally. The injunctive remedy backed by a threat of punishment for contempt of court is a forward line of defence making strategic wrongdoing normatively unavailable. If an injunction is unfeasible, strategic wrongdoing is rendered normatively unavailable by publicly invalidating the gains made from it. This is done by requiring the strategic wrongdoer to disgorge his profit (or its monetary equivalent if the profit is psychological); it is not necessary to punish him.[28] True, wiping out profits from strategic transgressions is often the point of what judges call "punitive damages", but they are punitive only in the sense that they exceed what is needed to compensate the victim; they retain the nature of the tort remedy in that they merely restore the wrongdoer to his position before the wrongful transaction (perhaps this is why the criminal standard of proof is thought to be unnecessary).[29] To punish in the strict sense, however, is to set the recipient back from the *status quo ante,* for at that position he was in enjoyment of his rights, whereas punishment violates them. Punitive damages, while they take away a gain from the defendant that does not belong to the plaintiff, do not violate the strategic wrongdoer's rights, for he had no right to a gain made from an invalid exercise of liberty.[30] Accordingly, since the forced disgorgement of ill-gotten gains publicly invalidates strategic transgressions, punishing the transgressor is not yet determined in the way that it must be if it is to be conceivable as self-imposed.

We could try to repair Ripstein's argument by saying that, because a legal order confined to civil remedies (including disgorgement) could not *deter* strategic wrongdoing, it could not adequately protect persons in their freedom; hence, self-respecting persons could not surrender their right of self-help to it. What is needed for a rightful condition is a threat of punishment for strategic wrongdoing sufficient to give everyone confidence in the public protection of their liberty. Though reminiscent of Hobbes, this argument appeals to dignity rather than felicity, for without a rightful condition, no one can wrong another by enforcing his own opinion of right.

Even as thus restated, however, the argument misconceives the basis of the duty to sustain a rightful condition as Kant himself understood it. The fact that, without an institution of punishment to supplement civil enforcement, there would be

---

[28] See *Edwards v Lee's Administrator* 265 Ky 418 (1936). It is immaterial that the wrongdoer may expect to consume his gains and be otherwise judgment-proof; for this goes to his idiosyncratic amenability to dissuasion, not to the systemic normative availability of strategic wrongdoing. After all, any particular strategic wrongdoer may also happen to enjoy the security of prison life.

[29] *Rookes v Barnard* [1964] AC 1129 (HL).

[30] It is because Ripstein fails to see the nonequivalence between punitive damages of this sort and punishment that he thinks the justification for the former can serve as an adequate justification of the latter; *Equality, Responsibility, and the Law,* 149–55. Of course, punitive damages might be assessed to deter rather than simply to remove ill-gotten gains, in which case they would be punitive in the true sense of the word. But the unanswered question is how the deterrent could be necessary to render strategic wrongdoing *normatively* unavailable so as to make a rightful condition possible. If a rightful condition did not precede punishment, what would punishment be for?

no assured disincentive to strategic wrongdoing cannot absolve from the duty to renounce self-help, for that duty is not conditional on the low probability of criminal events. Rather, it is conditional on the continuing existence of public institutions for adjudicating disputes and enforcing private rights.[31] Thus, if there exists a full range of civil remedies including injunctions, compensation for lost choice to alienate, and disgorgement of gains from strategic wrongdoing, and if a credible system for enforcing court-ordered civil remedies (through evictions, seizure of assets, penalties for contempt of court, etc.) exists, then a rightful condition exists and so too a perfect duty not to defect from it. The threat of punishment may then be necessary to deter intentional wrongdoing for reasons of public safety, psychological security, etc.; but it cannot be necessary to *make sense* of wrongdoing.

Moreover, the thinking Agent cannot accept an institution of punishment conceived in its nature as a threat aimed at securing people against criminal acts. Though empirical agents may or may not need the threat of punishment to deter them from strategic wrongdoing, the thinking Agent most certainly does not: having no subjective ends, it forbears from wrong (wills the right) for the sake of its dignity alone. Indeed, to the thinking Agent, punishment conceived as by nature an external threat is an affront to dignity, for, like any threat to freedom, it treats agents as manipulable objects rather than as ends. Though the thinking Agent will concede that its motive for forbearance from wrong cannot be relied upon by the civil order and that disincentives to wrongdoing are needed for some or even most, it will not allow that punishment be conceived *essentially* in this way; for if it is, then punishment is incompatible with its freedom. Rather, it will admit only that punishment is a threat relatively or contingently—that is, for those who happen to be inclined to wrongdoing whenever they can derive advantage from it. For itself, the thinking Agent will demand a justification for punishing that appeals to its interest in dignity without relying on the fear of disadvantage (for it has none).

The point of punishing: Hegel's solution

So what public purpose acceptable to the thinking Agent can the formal agency paradigm assign to punishment? In paragraph 97 of the *Philosophy of Right,* Hegel offers an answer:

> The infringement of right as right is something that has positive existence in the external world, though inherently it is nothing at all. The manifestation of its nullity is the appearance, also in the external world, of the annihilation of the infringement. This is the right actualized, the necessity of the right mediating itself with itself by annulling what has infringed it.

We can explain this terse passage by returning to the case of the Arrogant Surgeon. S removes P's appendix with knowledge of P's express choice that he not do so.

---

[31] Kant, *The Metaphysics of Morals,* 120–4.

We saw that this transgression signified S's denial of P's end-status *qua* agent and therewith a denial of the possibility of rights, which can exist objectively only among mutually recognizing ends. S's implicit denial of rights in general was also an implicit claim of permission to an unlimited liberty, for if there are no rights to respect for liberty, then S has an unlimited permission to act as he pleases, as does everyone else. However, a claim of permission to an unlimited liberty is self-contradictory, for its corollary when generalized is that no one, including S, may complain if someone pre-empts his liberty by physical force. Thus S's claim of permission to an unlimited liberty—a claim implicit in his intentional preemption of another agent's choice—is self-destroying. The public point of punishment is to manifest this aporetic result of S's claim by pre-empting S's liberty and, in doing so, to vindicate the truth (denied by S) that the only valid claims of permission to act are those that can be validated by equal ends. The thinking Agent will endorse an institution of punishment directed to this purpose, for it is one by which its right to lawful liberty is vindicated against a claim that, had it been allowed to stand, would have signified the right's nonexistence.

Observe that this is a reason for punishing that invokes neither material ends nor the bare fact of the wrongdoer's desert. The point of punishing is to realize everyone's right to act for any material end against an intentional interloper's denial of rights. Thus the criminal wrongdoer's desert—his practical denial of rights—while not a sufficient reason to punish, figures necessarily in the sufficient reason; for the vindication of mutual recognition (Law) as the sole ground of valid right-claims presupposes a challenge to its being this ground and consists precisely in manifesting the self-destructive result of the challenge. That the wrongdoer has authorized his own coercion by his claim of permission to an unlimited liberty shows that the only coherent claims to liberty are those limited by mutual recognition. Thus the right-vindicating purpose of punishment can be coherently furthered only against someone who deserves to be punished.

Neither compensation nor punitive damages suffices to invalidate the right-denying claim expressed by an intentional interference. Compensation adequately realizes P's right to choose his ends against S's mistaken claim that P is not a right bearer; but it fails to address the wider implication of S's intentional interference, namely, that (since P is an agent) there can be valid claims to act outside the bounds of mutual respect for agency. Moreover, to require only that S compensate P and that S disgorge his gain from the wrongful transaction merely restores S to the *status quo ante* where he enjoyed a right to mutually respectful liberty; whereas his claim is just that the *status quo ante* is invalid—that he has a permission to act unlimited by respect for other agents. The only remedial act qualified to answer that claim is one that listens to its challenge to the normativity of mutual respect, that then manifests the self-contradictoriness of the claim in the wrongdoer's own vulnerability to coercion, and that thereby vindicates mutual recognition as the sole ground of valid right claims.

It might be objected that all this can take place in a philosophy seminar. If the aim of an institutional response to crime is to vindicate mutual respect as the ground of rights by showing the self-contradictoriness of claims of right to nonrespectful liberty, why must the response take the form of punishment? Why not teach the truth about rights in school? If the wrongdoer's principle is a logical nullity, after all, then rights are invincible and require no conquest over a pitiful challenger to prove their strength. They can turn the other cheek. Moreover, if the application of punishment is not necessary to achieve this rarefied purpose, is it not a piece of gratuitous violence indistinguishable from the wrongdoer's?

Perhaps the lesson taught by punishment could be taught in school if the intentional interloper asserted his claim in the classroom. But he did not. He interfered with someone's agency, and his interference, because of its intentionality, expressed a right-denying principle. By *actualizing* a right-denying principle, however, the wrongdoer gave that principle an appearance of worldly authority, of existential force. He gave it, that is, the appearance of a law. That appearance would be allowed to stand if the nemesis of his principle were demonstrated by speech alone, for what is true in logic might not be true in the world; in the world, after all, there has been a violation expressing a claim to an absolute liberty—a claim that the civil remedy did not refute. So, by visiting the self-destructive consequence of the wrongdoer's principle upon him, punishment removes the appearance of its worldly validity and vindicates the worldly authority of Law.

One might further object that the authority of Law is inherently invincible and cannot be negated by logically absurd claims making pretences to existential validity. This is true. However, the invincibility of Law is a reason only for denying that the state *must* punish in all cases of intentional wrongdoing; it is not a reason for denying that the state ought to punish as a general rule. For if it did not, Law's authority would remain pervasively unrealized and hence no authority at all. Were private damages the sole remedy for an intentional interference, the authority of Law as mutual respect for liberty would remain deficient in two respects: first, the *existential* authority of mutual respect would depend on the plaintiff's contingent ability to sue; second (even if he did sue), the defendant's challenge to the *normative* authority of mutual respect as the sole ground of valid right claims would go unanswered because the civil suit takes that authority for granted. Corrective justice restores the parties to equality without addressing the intentional interloper's implicit denial that equality is Law.[32]

Of course, the foregoing argument need not deny that punishment may be used as a deterrent threat against strategic wrongdoing provided that its application is otherwise consistent with self-imposition. Nor need it deny that deterrence is the point of punishing from the everyday perspective of the empirical agent,

---

[32] In that corrective justice restores the parties to a *status quo ante* that it assumes is valid, whereas retributive justice sets the wrongdoer back from the *status quo ante* in order to demonstrate its validity, retributive justice is not simply a form of corrective justice. It must be regarded as *sui generis*, so that, *pace* Aristotle, there are three forms of justice, not two.

who must be assumed to act for the sake of self-interest, who therefore can be persuaded to forgo the advantage of crime only by the threat of greater disadvantage, and for whom it would be irrational to surrender its right of self-help to an authority no one would rationally fear. The point, however, is that deterrence cannot be the liberal *justification* of punishment, since the thinking Agent cannot consistently with its end-status endorse an institution conceived essentially as threat even if the threat were *empirically* required to secure a lawful condition; for that would make freedom dependent on unfreedom. The only reason it is permissible for the state to give criminals what they deserve so that others will be deterred is that punishment is independently justified to the thinking Agent as the practical annulment of a claim of absolute freedom that vindicates the normative authority of lawful freedom.

6. A Response to Critics of Retributivism

The theory of punishment I have presented so far may be called classical legal retributivism. It is classical in that it stems from the writings of the great philosophers who, present at the birth of the liberal *Rechtsstaat*, first articulated (though differently) its theoretical foundations. I mean, of course, Hegel's *Philosophy of Right* and Kant's *Doctrine of Right*. It is *legal* retributivism in that it justifies judicial punishment as vindicating the authority of Law rather than as giving evil its just deserts. How does this version of retributivism fare against the most common objections to retributivism?

The most common criticisms presuppose a certain portrait of the adversary. According to this description, retributivism is a deontological rather than a teleological theory of punishment in that it justifies punishment as a morally obligatory response to an antecedent evil rather than as a means for attaining socially desirable ends. More specifically, retributivism is (in the eyes of its critics) the thesis that punishment is justified by the moral duty to give those whose actions evince moral fault their just deserts and that the performance of this duty has intrinsic value quite apart from the consequential benefits punishment may yield in reducing crime. There are two parts to this thesis: first, people ought to be punished if and only if they deserve it; second, people ought to be punished with the severity and only with the severity they deserve.

The moral duty to punish evildoers

The portrait thus painted is of moral retributivism. Its critics commonly distinguish between a strong and a weak variant but typically regard the strong version as the only self-consistently deontological one.[33] Strong moral retributivism

---

[33] See Russ Shafer-Landau, 'The Failure of Retributivism,' in J Feinberg and J Coleman, eds., *Philosophy of Law*, 7th ed. (Belmont, Cal: Thomson, Wadsworth, 2004), 837–8.

argues that *all* those deserving of punishment ought to be punished with the severity they deserve because and only because they deserve it; weak moral retributivism holds that *only* the deserving *may* be punished with a severity *no greater* than they deserve. Critics regard the strong version as the only coherent retributivism, because if desert functions as a constraint on, rather than as a reason for, punishing, then forward-looking considerations tell us why to punish and, subject to the ceiling, how much. But if that is so, why should these considerations not also give us the reason for confining punishment to the deserving and so determine when that constraint may be exceptionally relaxed?

Yet strong moral retributivism is open to objections whose undoubted force has always made consequentialist theories of punishment look attractive by comparison. Take the first part of the "just deserts" thesis—that the wicked ought to be punished because and only because they deserve it. Here one might object that, unless the state is to enforce the whole of morality, a distinction must be drawn between criminal and noncriminal immorality. Yet strong moral retributivism by itself yields no criterion for this distinction. A "public harm" principle might draw the line but not without transforming strong retributivism into weak retributivism, for now judicial punishment in particular would be justified by harm prevention. But if no moral purpose can, compatibly with strong retributivism, separate criminal from noncriminal immorality, then moral anger as expressed in politics must do so; and so to make wickedness the object of punishment is to coerce the convict to satisfy the moral passion of others.[34] Retributivism, on this view, becomes the executive arm of legal moralism—the view that it is permissible to use the criminal law to enforce the socially dominant opinion as to which evils are most deserving of public retribution. But this view is illiberal because inconsistent with agent inviolability, which forbids coercing the agent to serve others' ends.

The logical gap between moral retributivism and state punishment causes a problem of a related sort. If we ask, "but why should the community give evildoers what they deserve?" the answer must be that its doing so is intrinsically valuable and hence self-justifying. There is no need for a justification to punish evil; that the agent is an evildoer is sufficient reason. But even if it is intrinsically valuable that the morally wicked receive the punishment they deserve, it does not follow that the state should do the punishing. Since other options are open (social censure, shunning, blacklisting, leaving to divine justice, for example), *judicial* punishment of the wicked requires a further justification referring to some end extrinsic to retribution—for example, the moral unity of the political community or the satisfaction of the community's moral indignation—to be achieved by the state's assuming the role of moral judge and enforcer. Yet once such ends are invoked, the whole of political prudence is also engaged; and so one must inquire whether these conjectural benefits of state punishment would justify the high cost of a police force, criminal courts, and prisons were crime reduction not

---

[34] James Stephen, *A History of the Criminal Law of England* (Macmillan: London, 1883), vol. II, 81; for a critique, see Hart, *Punishment and Responsibility*, 169–73.

also a consequence of legal punishment.[35] It would seem that, to obtain the state's sword, the moral retributivist must make a Faustian bargain.

Finally, critics point out that many actions involving no or trivial moral fault (such as unwittingly selling alcohol to a minor) are penalized for the sake of public goals, and no one suggests there is anything wrong with this. Thus, if evildoing is not a sufficient condition of *state* punishment, neither is it a necessary one.[36]

By now it should be clear that legal retributivism is untouched by criticisms such as these. First, legal retributivism nowhere argues that the reason for punishing is to give those whose actions evince moral fault their just deserts. From the broad class of evildoers, it singles out those whose actions manifest choices to which a denial of rights must be imputed, and it selects only these for retributive punishment. Thus, for legal retributivism, moral wickedness is not a sufficient condition for eligibility for judicial punishment, and so there is no need for politics or an extrinsic end to make the final selection; legal retributivism itself determines which wrongs are criminal. Nor is moral wickedness a necessary condition of criminal liability. The physician who, from a benevolent impulse (not amounting to the vice of excessive beneficence), injects a nonconsenting friend with life-saving and riskless medication is, for legal retributivism, a right denier deserving of punishment. Accordingly, judicial punishment is the executive arm, not of legal moralism, but of equal agency rights; and the convict is subject, not to moral opinion, but to the public reason of mutual recognition.

Second, legal retributivism nowhere claims that punishing those deserving of punishment is justified for its own sake. Not even Kant, whose famous plea for executing the last murderer in a society doomed the next day to extinction is usually invoked as the representative statement of this thesis, held this view. Rather, Kant vacillated between two views—one Hobbesian, the other Hegelian. The fact that he regarded a murder-or-die dilemma as robbing punishment of its justificatory point (because the threat of an imminent death defangs the threat of a future one) suggests he thought its justifying point was to deter crime so as to support the state's monopoly of coercion constitutive of a civil condition.[37] That is his Hobbesian side. However, his call for the execution of the last murderer in a moribund civil condition is inconsistent with that view and more consonant with his competing view that punishing the deserving is required by justice "as the Idea of judicial authority"—that is, as the realization of the authority of Law.[38] This is Hegel's univocal view. The point of punishing, Hegel writes, "is to annul the crime, which otherwise would have been held valid, and to restore the right".[39]

Such a justification eludes the deontological/teleological/mixed classification of punishment theories as well as the strong/weak classification of retributive theories, showing how simplistic these categories are. Because legal retributivism

---

[35] Shafer-Landau, 'The Failure of Retributivism,' 834.
[36] Ibid, 832.   [37] Kant, *The Metaphysics of Morals*, 60–61.
[38] Ibid, 143.   [39] *Philosophy of Right*, para. 99.

justifies punishment as vindicating the normative authority of mutual recognition, it can be called teleological; but because its end is right vindication rather than crime prevention or social welfare more generally, it may also be called deontological as opposed to eudaemonist or consequentialist. So, legal retributivism does not sell its deontological soul for the state's goal-directed sword. Yet it is not mixed either, because, viewing punishment as a denial of a denial, legal retributivism sees a necessary connection between the point of punishing and the restriction of punishment to the deserving. The authority of Law requires vindication only against one who denied that authority. Further, because legal retributivism regards desert as a constraint on, rather than a reason for, punishing, it appears to fall in the weak category. But because its reason for punishing is to deny a practical denial of rights that would appear valid were its self-contradictoriness not practically demonstrated, it holds that the state ought generally to punish those who have licensed their coercion whether or not doing so would prevent crime, and so it may also be called strong. We can say, then, that legal retributivism reconciles the view that desert is a constraint on, rather than a reason for, punishing with a nonconsequentialist view of the purpose of punishment. It thus shows how punishment can be justified by an end without losing its essential connection to desert.

Finally, the fact that the state commonly penalizes action inimical to the public welfare but evincing no moral fault does not tell against legal retributivism, for the latter's account of punishment presupposes crimes involving infringements of agency rights and so has application only to that sphere. Legal retributivism makes no claim to being a comprehensive theory of penal force; rather, it is a theory only of punishment for criminal right-infringements. How legal retributivism can be coherently integrated into a broader theory of penal force that covers public welfare offences is the subject of Chapter 5.

The moral duty to fit the punishment to the crime

Consider now the standard criticisms of retributivism understood as a theory prescribing a method for apportioning punishment to crimes. Here the usual objections run as follows. To punish according to desert is to make the punishment "fit" the crime—that is, to make it somehow equal to the crime. The only certain equation between crime and punishment, however, is an identity in kind between the physical injury the wrongdoer has inflicted and the physical injury done to the wrongdoer in return: an eye for an eye, a whipping for an assault, death for a homicide. But doing to wrongdoers what they have done to their victims ignores the possibility that the same injury may have different welfare impacts on different people. Suppose, for example, that the victim had only one eye and the wrongdoer has two, or that the wrongdoer was blind to begin with. This difficulty might lead us to think that, if equality with the crime is the measure of deserved punishment, what must be equalized is the suffering experienced by the victim and the wrongdoer. But interpersonal comparisons of suffering are impossible for an external judge, and, in any case, how could a schedule of equivalent sufferings be determined in advance by a general law applying to everyone? Punishments would have to be meted out case-by-case with no fixed limits, with the result that both legality and ordinal proportionality would be thrown to the winds. Sexual predators eager for the opportunities of prison life could be punished less severely than freedom-loving pickpockets.

Perhaps, then, the victim's suffering should be dropped from the equation and punishment simply fitted to the wickedness of the wrongful act. But this will not do either, for wickedness is a compound made up of the heinousness of the conduct and the cruelty of the inward disposition, and who can say whether a careless killing of many is more or less wicked than the malicious killing of one?[40] Further, inward dispositions are hidden from us, and crime types as well as the degrees of imputability called intention, recklessness, and negligence are at best crude *indicia* for them. The factors one must consider in judging evil are too numerous and variegated to be captured in a few legal categories, and everyone will weigh them differently.[41] Finally, even if there could be agreement on how wicked a wrongdoer is on a numerical scale, there is no principle for determining how much suffering any particular degree of wickedness deserves; and so convicts will be subject, not to a punishment they have imposed on themselves, but to the arbitrary opinions of the legislator and judge.

Accordingly, we are driven, it seems, to a rule of ordinal proportionality. Let more harmful crimes be punished more severely than less harmful ones; and let intentional inflictions of a particular type of harm be punished more severely than unintentional inflictions of the same type. But this will not work either, for we cannot proceed ordinally without some baseline noncomparative equality, and no such benchmark exists. Moreover, ordinal proportionality is obviously consistent with very cruel punishments: a scale that began with wrist chopping for minor theft and ended with drawing and quartering for murder would be ordinally correct. Thus, no sense can be made of the idea that the punishment must fit the crime.[42]

A defender of legal retributivism might respond as follows. The philosophic truth buried in the saying that "the punishment must fit the crime" is that punishment ought to be nothing other than the criminal wrongdoer's right-denying principle turned against him. Having practically denied an agent's right against interference with its freedom of choice, the criminal cannot complain when his or her own freedom of choice is interfered with in turn. However, this equality between crime and punishment is a purely conceptual one. It is an equality abstracted from any particular kind of crime or any particular measure of punishment. So the question becomes: how can this conceptual identity of crime and punishment be translated into a practical scheme of determinate punishments for determinate crimes?

---

[40] Hart, *Punishment and Responsibility*, 162.   [41] Ibid, 162–3.
[42] Landau, 'The Failure of Retributivism,' 836–7.

Now, when we seek to translate a conceptual identity into a physical world with qualitative and quantitative dimensions, we cannot expect a perfect replication. For what is identical in the concept may be incommensurable in the world. So we must be satisfied with the best approximation. One possibility is the biblical *lex talionis*, which has always possessed a seductive appeal for retributivists (Kant, for example), because it appears not to be an approximation at all but rather a perfect copy of the retributive idea in the sensuous medium of the world. The metaphysical identity of crime and punishment is rendered in the empirical world as an in-kind identity of physical injuries. But the sensuous replication is actually the crudest just because it is the most sensuous and therefore the least connected to the idea it is supposed to replicate. What is exacted in idea, after all, is liberty for liberty, not physical injury for physical injury. Moreover, because it seeks equality in sensuous terms, the *lex talionis* inevitably leads to absurdities when empirical circumstances bedevil the search for physical exactness (suppose the tooth-basher has no teeth) or when exactness would be shameful for the punisher (suppose the crime was rape).[43]

A modification of *lex talionis*, favoured by Kant, is an equality of suffering that takes into account the social and economic differences of the parties. Thus, argues Kant, a rich man who slanders another must be punished with a humiliation that compensates for his ability to tolerate a monetary penalty.[44] However, if the wrongdoer's pain threshold must be considered, why not the victim's? Must we not punish the thief more or less depending on the wealth of his victim, or the assailant more or less depending on his victim's emotional resilience? But this is to subject the criminal to a measure of punishment determined, not impersonally by public reason, but by the situation or sensibilities of the victim (an analogue to the expensive taste problem in securing equality of welfare).

The best approximation of real-world punishment to the idea of punishment as retribution would be attained if the thing to be equalized in the world corresponded with what is equal in the idea. In the idea, crime is an implicit denial of rights to liberty that entails the criminal's own vulnerability to coercion. Thus, whatever their qualitative and quantitative differences, all material crimes to which retributive punishment paradigmatically applies are interferences with liberty for which the fitting punishment is an interference with liberty.[45] Even a crime against property is ultimately an interference with liberty, since it transgresses the rightful boundary within which the agent's choices hold exclusive sway. Accordingly, deprivation of liberty (which may or may not involve incarceration) rather than corporal punishment or the infliction of suffering for

---

[43] In this case Kant, ever looking for physical analogues, recommends castration; see *Metaphysics of Morals*, 169.

[44] Ibid, 141–2.

[45] I say "paradigmatically" because interferences with the administration of justice are secondarily subject to retributive punishment as involving challenges to the legal authority making rights possible.

suffering is the mode of punishment best suited to the retributive idea. It is the most civilized of punishments just because it leaves behind the search for empirical equalities of outward injuries or of inward suffering and replicates the *idea* of punishment as retribution for a right denial.

Deprivations of liberty can be distinguished by the length of term during which the convict's liberty is restricted and by the scope allowed for liberty during the term. On their side, crimes can also be distinguished according to the importance to liberty of the interest harmed.[46] Thus, property crimes are less serious than crimes against the body, which are less serious than homicides. The question is whether there is any method for equating a particular (quantitative) term of detention with a particular (qualitative) impairment of liberty by the criminal. And the answer seems to be that, with a few exceptions, there is not. Murder is an exception because it is the only crime for which there is a known and determinate equal punishment. Nothing is equal only to nothing, and so the only punishment equal to a chosen extinguishment of liberty is an extinguishment of liberty.[47] Manslaughter is an exception because the part is less than the whole, and so (depending on the circumstances) an accidental taking of the rest of someone's natural life resulting from a chosen transgression can deserve a taking of liberty for the rest of the killer's life, but a partial impairment of liberty cannot. For the same reason, criminal conduct resulting in a significant permanent impairment of liberty can deserve a life term. All other crimes, however, involve more or less serious qualitative impairments of liberty, and we cannot know what quantitative term of detention (or even range of terms) equals what partial impairment.

Accordingly, the best approximation to the idea of retributive punishment attainable in the real world is an ordinal proportionality ensuring that crimes injuring or endangering interests more important to liberty than those injured or endangered by other crimes are punished with higher maximum restrictions on liberty than those lesser crimes.[48] Culpable homicides on the whole deserve stiffer sentences than culpable bodily injuries, which deserve stiffer sentences than culpable damage to property. Aggravated assault (endangering life) deserves more punishment than assault causing bodily harm. Moreover, intervals between harm types can be rendered ordinally proportionate to intervals between maximum sentences. So, the interval between the maximum punishment for assault and that for assault endangering life should be greater than the interval between the maxima for theft under $1,000 and theft over, and so on.

---

[46] Of course, the admission of harm at this point stands in tension with the formalist exclusion of welfare from public reason; I discuss this point in the next section.

[47] Yet the very absoluteness of the extinguishment in the case of the death penalty is a reason for doubting the state's right to execute because there is no corresponding absoluteness of knowledge as to whether the defendant is guilty.

[48] On ordinal and cardinal proportionality see Andrew von Hirsch and Andrew Ashworth, *Proportionate Sentencing* (Oxford: Oxford University Press, 2005), 137–43.

Granted, without a benchmark equation at the bottom of the scale, ordinally proportionate punishments could seem cardinally incommensurate with the crimes they punish. One day for theft and two for assault satisfies ordinal proportionality, as does twenty-five years for theft and thirty for assault. The response, however, is twofold. First, our ability to speak of cardinal incommensurability suggests that, even though no principle tells us what quantitative term of punishment a partial impairment of liberty deserves, a cultural sense of fittingness lets us know which punishments are beyond the pale or "unusual". This sense will thus determine the overall level of severity of the ordinal scale. Second, when the idea of retributive justice ceases to guide us, considerations extraneous to that idea can be introduced as a supplement provided their operation is consistent with the idea. Thus, within the bounds of ordinal proportionality, crime prevention concerns can militate against punishments that are too light, while moral concerns about cruelty can prevent punishments that are too harsh.

7. The Limits of Formalism

The formal agency paradigm of penal justice generates a conception of punishment that is compatible with freedom in two senses. First, liability to judicial coercion is implicitly self-willed by the recipient as the logical implication of his or her choice to interfere with a human being's capacity to choose its ends. Having implicitly denied the existence of rights against interference, criminals cannot justly complain if their own rights are violated. Second, the actual imposition of punishment is endorsed by the thinking Agent on behalf of the recipient as the vindication of the practical authority of agency rights against the criminal wrongdoer's challenge to that authority. Inasmuch as retributive punishment observes legal constraints (discussed in following chapters) guaranteeing its self-imposability, it respects the freedom and dignity of the recipient even as it turns the latter's right denial against him. In this way, punishment is distinguished from the violence of the wrongdoer.

Nevertheless, the formalist paradigm lacks the theoretical resources to produce a full account of just punishment. This is so for the following reasons. First, legal retributivism cannot operationalize the conceptual equality of crime and punishment in a practicable scheme of determinate punishments without tacitly acknowledging what its framework officially denies: the existence of material interests objectively important to freedom (hence to all agents) and so the existence of a public conception of welfare and of legally cognizable harms. If one were to adhere strictly to the formalist equation of the public interest with liberty, one would have to say that there is only one crime—an intentional interference with liberty implying a denial of rights to liberty—and that all crimes, however qualitatively and quantitatively differentiated according to the type and extent of the harm inflicted or attempted, must be punished identically. Of course, no one—not even the staunchest formalist—would seriously defend such a view. Even those who deny the relevance to penal desert of harmful outcomes because they are attributable to chance rather than to choice would vary punishments according to the harm intended or attempted.[49] But the inevitable grading of crimes according to the "seriousness" of the harm inflicted stands in tension with the formalist equation of material interests with subjective interests; hence it foreshadows a framework of penal justice ordered to a new conception of public reason, one that takes explicit account of the commonality to agents of some interests and harms.

Second, while the formalist paradigm generates a retributive idea of punishment requiring that punishability be implicitly self-willed through a chosen interference with choice and that the punishment mirror the crime, it generates no requirement that "the crime" be defined only by material outcomes that are themselves connected to the wrongdoer's agency. So, once liability to punishment *simpliciter* is self-willed by agents by virtue of a chosen interference, they become liable to state coercion directed at crime control for all resulting proscribed harms no matter how remote and unforeseeable. We see this, for example, in the thin-skull rule and in the definition of manslaughter as requiring the foreseeability only of nongrievous bodily harm.[50] In both cases, the crime description and measure of punishment are unconstrained by a requirement that the consequence for which the agent is punished be imputable to its agency in some degree, whether by intention, foresight, or foreseeability. Of course, these doctrines serve deterrence and the disabling of human threats; but the only reason these ends have full play here is that there is no requirement that punishable consequences be imputable to agency to limit their operation. Why should this be so? Why should it be necessary that punishment as such be connected to the wrongdoer's agency but not the outcomes for which he is punished?

The answer lies in the formalism of the formal agency paradigm. Given formalism's equation of the public interest with freedom of choice, it protects the agent against interferences with its liberty, but it does not protect the agent against vulnerability to blind chance—in this case to causal chains initiated by its culpable wrong that are beyond its power to foresee and control. Such protection is possible only under a richer conception of freedom than the one informing the formalist framework, one that understands by freedom not only undetermined choice but also self-determination, or the power to shape one's life in accordance with self-authored ends. Accordingly, once the agent has invited punishment through a chosen interference with choice, there is no public reason to stop its liability for all chance consequences of the wrong for the sake of deterrence, incapacitation, or whatever.

---

[49] See AJ Ashworth, 'Sharpening the Subjective Element in Criminal Liability,' in RA Duff and NE Simmonds, eds., *Philosophy and the Criminal Law* (Wiesbaden: Cambridge University Press, 1984), 79–89.
[50] *R v Holland* (1841) 2 Mood & R 351; *R v Larkin* (1942) 29 Cr App R 18, 23.

Third, the formalist paradigm generates no justification for a right infringement other than self-defence (defence of property, defence of others) and punishment for a crime. A right of self-defence is certainly intelligible within the formalist framework, since a right against interference with liberty is a right to defend oneself or others against transgressions if the public authority cannot intervene and provided one uses no more force than is necessary to repel the invader (see Chapter 6). However, justifications based on a comparison between the harm inflicted on an innocent and the harm avoided to a wrongdoer (for example, necessity) have no place in a theoretical framework for which all ends are subjective, all harms are relative to preferences, and for which liberty is the only public thing. If A values B's loaf of bread more than B does, then a bargain is in order, not a taking. The fact that A values B's bread so highly because he is starving and has a powerful aversion to death is here of no more consequence than if he desired the bread to satisfy a craving for carbohydrates. Since all ends are subjective, they are on a par. Accordingly, justifications other than self-defence presuppose a framework of penal justice ordered to a conception of freedom as self-determination—one for which objective harms are possible as harms to interests essential to acting from self-authored ends.

Finally, the formalist paradigm is powerless to regulate liability for offences (called public welfare offences) not involving either a right infringement or a violation of laws (for example, against bribery of officials) ministerial to rights protection. While formalism insists that a public policy of facilitating the agent's pursuit of satisfactions be subordinate to rights protection, it generates no constraints on liability for breaches of statutes having the general happiness as their aim. This is so because formalism's retributivist legitimation of penal force as implicitly licensed by the recipient has no application to the actions and omissions proscribed by these statutes. Since there is no right infringement in selling alcohol to a minor, for example, there is no invitation to a retaliatory right infringement in choosing to do so, nor can the point of penalizing be to vindicate the reality of rights. In this context, penal force is justified by prevention rather than by desert.

However, if public reason is identified with respect for liberty and if legal retributivism is thus considered an exhaustive account of penal justice, then the penalization of public welfare offences will occur in a normative vacuum. No liability-constraining rule will supplement the retributivist one for crimes, and so penalizing the faultless will be left free for rationalization in cost–benefit terms. Put otherwise, if there is no logical circuit between the intentional doing of the proscribed action and the coercibility of the doer, then no one can either deserve or not deserve punishment for these actions. Thus penal force cannot here be constrained by desert. But if penal justice is understood solely in terms of this circuit, then the penalization of activity not involving a right infringement will be constrained by nothing except cost–benefit rationality. And that rationality will likely favour no-fault liability, since the penalty and stigma for conviction are often light, while deterrence is perhaps much enhanced by the greater ease of conviction. Thus, the dichotomy in the penal law of many jurisdictions between a requirement of wilfulness for crimes and no-fault liability for public welfare offences is an offshoot of the formalist paradigm taking itself to be exhaustive of penal justice.

Still, these limitations of the formalist paradigm are not a reason for jettisoning it. They point only to the insufficiency of the framework as a full account of penal justice and hence to the need for integrating it within a more comprehensive account. That formalism is compelled to recognize tacitly the objectivity of some goods it officially denies is a reason for demoting it from an exhaustive theory of penal justice to a constituent one; it is not a reason for dispensing with it altogether. Moreover, to dispense with it would be to lose its contributions to a practice of punishment consistent with freedom, for we will see that the framework that supplies what formalism lacks cannot provide on its own what formalism contributes: an immovable desert-based constraint on punishment for crimes. It is thus a grave mistake to think that the valuable elements of the formalist paradigm can be salvaged within a new framework while the paradigm itself is sunk. How the formalist paradigm can be coherently preserved within a more inclusive framework remains to be seen.

2
Culpable Mind

In this chapter I develop from legal retributivism a liberal account of the culpable mind (*mens rea*) requirement of criminal liability. By a liberal account I mean one that interprets the meaning of *mens rea* in a way that reconciles liability to judicial coercion with the individual's inviolability as a free agent. To anticipate, I argue that the wrongdoer's free choice to interfere or to risk interfering with another agent's capacity to act on ends it freely chooses is the level of fault required to make punishment implicitly self-imposed by the recipient and thus distinguishable from the externally imposed violence of the wrongdoer. This is so because a free choice to interfere or to risk interfering with another's agency is a choice to which a *denial* of rights of agency may logically be imputed, a denial by which the wrongdoer implicitly authorizes his or her own coercibility. Accordingly, I argue that the fault threshold for criminal liability is the free choice to do that by virtue of which a denial of rights becomes logically imputable to the choice.

The latter thesis is a version of subjectivism because it holds that a punishable wrongdoer must have intentionally interfered with another agent's freedom of choice or knowingly risked such an interference; inadvertent interferences are insufficient. But it is a subjectivism that, I argue, is impregnable against the criticisms levelled against other versions by those who would punish for blameworthy inadvertence to risk. Specifically, the subjectivism I defend avoids the excessive empiricism of which critics complain, incorporating as it does the standpoint of an ideal thinking Agent whose inferences from the empirical agent's choices are imputed to those choices. Thus the subjective fault principle I defend incorporates a heavy dose of objectivism. Second, the thesis I defend draws a distinction between subjective fault for wrongdoing as the threshold condition for the deservedness of any punishment and subjective fault for consequential harm as only one of several degrees of criminal responsibility relevant to a just measure of punishment. Accordingly, the subjectivist thesis for which I argue applies to the threshold, but not to results. Third, the subjectivist position I defend is consistent, as we'll see, with the general rule that a mistake of law provides no defence to crime. Fourth, the subjectivism I put forward is one that, by its justifying theory, applies to criminal right infringements but not to public welfare offences. On the strength of all these features, the subjectivist thesis I defend may be described as moderate.

Along the way toward staking out defensible subjectivist ground, I criticize alternative accounts of *mens rea*—specifically, the character, choice, and opportunity theories proposed by Victor Tadros, Michael Moore, and HLA Hart. After justifying the particular version of subjectivism that I call the classical position on *mens rea*, I elaborate the interpretations of exculpatory conditions (involuntariness, mistake of fact, colour of right, insanity) flowing from this position. Finally, I address arguments put forward by Arthur Ripstein, RA Duff, and Jeremy Horder for eliminating the requirement of a conscious choice to do that which amounts to a denial of rights.

1. The Two Roles of *Mens Rea*

An account of the *mens rea* requirement of criminal liability must begin with a distinction that is often ignored in debates about the point and nature of that requirement. At common law, the various mental orientations toward wrongful deeds or risks (namely, intention, foresight, and wilful blindness) characterized by knowledge of the doing or awareness of the risk and that comprise what is called subjective fault have always played a dual role. First, subjective fault has traditionally (though not univocally) been viewed as the threshold level of fault for criminal wrongdoing and so for liability to judicial punishment of any severity.[1] That is, it has traditionally been viewed as the level of fault distinguishing crime from tort. But secondly, subjective fault has been treated as the highest degree of responsibility for the harmful result of a criminal wrong, calling for the most severe punishment meted out for that kind of result. Thus, someone who means to cause death and does so is responsible for the death to a higher degree (and liable to a more severe punishment) than if he had meant to cause bodily harm that he ought to have foreseen would result in death. I discuss the sense in which this agent is more responsible for the death in Chapter 4. But the distinction I want to highlight now is this: subjective fault has been both *the* fault threshold of criminal culpability for wrongdoing (hence for liability to any right-infringing punishment) and *one*—the highest—degree of responsibility for the harmful consequences of criminal wrongs (deserving a certain measure of punishment) once culpability for any consequence has been established. I'll call this the classical position on *mens rea*.

Corresponding to the different roles played by *mens rea* are two different ways in which a penal law might be criticized for failing to stipulate the appropriate level of fault for a crime. A statute might impose criminal liability in the absence of an intention to interfere with another's agency or without an awareness of the

---

[1] By "judicial punishment" I mean state coercion justified by criminal desert; sanctions justified by welfare goals I call "noncriminal penalties", which are typically imposed either without fault or subject to a due diligence defence.

risk of doing so, thus collapsing the difference between crime and tort. Or it might (as in constructive murder) punish and stigmatize equally two different grades of responsibility for harm consequent on criminal wrongdoing—intention and foreseeability of the harm to the reasonable person. The first failing is a mistake (I'll argue) about the threshold of criminal liability to punishment, the second a violation of proportionality in the measure of punishment.

In some crimes, the duality of roles played by *mens rea* is hidden. Take murder, for example. In murder, there is subjective fault with respect to the right infringement, which is the battery to the victim. This, according to the classical position, puts the wrongdoer into the criminal category, rendering him liable to punishment *simpliciter*. But there is also subjective fault with respect to the consequence of the battery—the death. This makes the criminal specifically a murderer liable to the most severe punishment meted out for a homicide. *Mens rea* is performing two normative tasks here—one authorizing punishment per se, the other authorizing a particular measure of punishment—but because the battery tends to be subsumed in the murder, it appears that the intention to kill is the only operative *mens rea*.

The tendency to elide the difference between the two roles of *mens rea* is responsible for much confusion in debates about the point and nature of the *mens rea* requirement. For example, although one can logically insist on a threshold requirement of subjective fault for criminal wrongdoing without committing oneself to a subjective fault requirement for responsibility for consequential harms once criminal liability for any outcome has been established, critics of the subjectivist position often ascribe both views to the subjectivist, who then becomes an easy target for criticism.[2] After all, who would seriously claim that we are answerable only for those harms we have consciously chosen? Who would deny Hart's claim that we are also answerable for those harms consequent on our actions that we could have avoided had we exercised our capacity for reasonable attentiveness and care?[3] Moreover, the straw man the critics have attacked has in some cases been made of real straw. Some subjectivists have themselves mistakenly thought that subjectivism regarding the threshold commits the law to subjectivism with respect to consequences, so that the maxim, *actus non facit reum nisi mens sit rea* must have the same subjectivist meaning for both.[4] But this view makes outliers of many result crimes and gives subjectivism a revisionist thrust too far-reaching for it to be credible as an internal elaboration of the criminal law.

---

[2] See, for example, RA Duff, *Intention, Agency, and Criminal Liability* (Oxford: Blackwell, 1990), 150–51; Arthur Ripstein, *Equality, Responsibility, and the Law* (Cambridge: Cambridge University Press, 1999), 174.

[3] HLA Hart, *Punishment and Responsibility* (Oxford: Clarendon Press, 1968), 145–57.

[4] For example, Glanville Williams saw manslaughter, where death need only be foreseeable, as "an exception to the requirement of full *mens rea* in crime". See *Criminal Law: The General Part*, 2nd ed. (London: Stevens, 1961), 106; see also JWC Turner, 'The Mental Element in Crimes at Common Law,' (1936) 6 CLJ 31.

Another example of the confusion concerns the case of *R v Caldwell*, a decision of the House of Lords.[5] This case has almost universally been taken to have introduced an objective standard of fault (an egregious failure to exercise reasonable care) for criminal liability and thus to have dealt subjectivism a severe blow in the United Kingdom. Yet in *Caldwell*, the penal statute that had to be interpreted made it an offence punishable by up to life imprisonment to destroy or damage any property "intending by the destruction or damage to endanger the life of another or being reckless as to whether the life of another would be thereby endangered". The accused had set fire to an inhabited hotel to redress a grievance he had against the proprietor but claimed that he had given no thought to whether he might be endangering life. The question for the court was whether "reckless" should be interpreted to mean having a conscious awareness of the prohibited risk or whether it should be enough that the risk would have been obvious to the reasonable person.

Now this question was not about the appropriate fault threshold for criminal liability, for that threshold had already incontestably been crossed by virtue of the defendant's having intentionally set fire to the victim's property. Rather, what was alone at issue in the application of the term "reckless" to the facts in *Caldwell* was whether a criminal arsonist who ought to have foreseen that he would endanger life but did not is to be held responsible for the endangerment. This is a question, not about whether the defendant is a criminal wrongdoer, but about the scope of a criminal wrongdoer's responsibility for consequential risks or harms. Accordingly, the court could have limited its view of recklessness as including egregious negligence to the responsibility issue, while indicating that this implied nothing for its view of what is required for culpability for *any* harm or risk. But the court drew no such distinction, and so, while nothing in the judgments really supports the view that objective fault marks the threshold of criminal liability, *Caldwell* is generally taken to have introduced this principle, and so that is what the case has come to stand for.

We see the same confusion in the leading academic literature on *mens rea*. For example, in his book, *Intention, Agency, and Criminal Liability*, RA Duff takes as the central target of his criticism and the foil for his own theory of liability the view that a conscious choice to bring about or risk a wrongful outcome is a requirement of punishability for the outcome, even though the classical subjectivist position holds no such view. He characterizes orthodox subjectivism as the view that "I should be guilty of an offence only if I acted intentionally or recklessly as to every element of its *actus reus;* and I act intentionally as to a result only if I aim to bring it about or am (almost) certain that I will bring it about, and recklessly only if I am aware that I may bring it about."[6] If this is orthodox subjectivism, then the offences known as manslaughter, assault causing bodily harm, causing bodily harm by an unlawful act, and aggravated assault are in conflict with it, and so this view would have to be called radically revisionist rather than orthodox. In fact, classical subjectivism subscribes to no such implausible position. It holds that a free choice to do that from which a denial of rights may logically be imputed to the

---

[5] [1981] 1 All ER 961 (HL).   [6] Duff, *Intention, Agency, and Criminal Liability*, 150.

agent's choice marks the threshold of criminal liability to punishment, but that once the threshold has been crossed, the criminal is punishable for the proscribed harms consequent on his crime that are connected *in some degree* to his agency; and here intention and foresight are only two of several degrees of connection. For classical subjectivism, restricting liability for results to intended or actually foreseen results would be inconsistent with the respect for free agency determining (in a way I'll explain) the subjectivist threshold; for it would treat human beings as unreflective, nose-to-the-ground seekers of satisfaction incapable of meeting expectations of foresight premised on a capacity for thought.

Because, moreover, Duff fails to distinguish between subjectivism with regard to culpability for wrong and subjectivism with regard to responsibility for consequential harm, he treats the cases of *Caldwell* and *DPP v Morgan* as raising the same issue of criminal liability.[7] In *Morgan*, the defendants sexually assaulted the wife of a friend who had invited them to have intercourse with her, falsely informing them that she had consented to intercourse simulating rape. The accuseds' defence was that, despite the victim's strong resistance, they honestly believed she had consented; and the question was whether, if believed, that story makes a good defence or whether, to exculpate, their mistake had to be reasonable. Now this is a case where the threshold requirement of criminal culpability is indeed in issue, since (if we believe their story) the defendants believed they had the victim's consent and that they were thus respecting her free will. So the issue is whether a grossly unreasonable mistake is the threshold of criminal liability or whether a conscious disdain for another's capacity for freedom is. But *Caldwell*, as we have seen, is a different kind of case. There the defendant unquestionably chose to interfere in the victim's exclusive sphere of choice, and so there is no doubt about his liability to punishment. In *Caldwell*, what is really at stake in the dispute about the compass of "recklessness" is whether a court ought to interpret a penal statute as conflating and punishing with the same severity grades of responsibility for consequential risks or outcomes as different as intention and objective foreseeability. I argue in Chapter 4 that this is to impose a measure of punishment disproportionate to responsibility.

Accordingly, it is important to keep the two roles of *mens rea* distinct. In this chapter I deal only with the level of fault necessary for crossing the threshold from tort to criminal liability—that is, for liability to punishment *simpliciter*. *Mens rea* as denoting the several grades of criminal responsibility for wrongful harms is the topic of Chapter 4.

2. Character, Choice, and Opportunity

Before elaborating an account of *mens rea* as the level of fault needed to connect wrongdoing with the coercibility of the wrongdoer so as to legitimate judicial punishment as implicitly self-imposed, I want to examine two other theories

---

[7] [1976] AC 182.

of *mens rea* that also see it as constituting criminal desert. Though very different, these theories share two common features. One, they are both theories of moral blameworthiness applied to the sphere of judicial punishment. Hence they both claim that, assuming punishment is otherwise justified by forward-looking ends, cases where it would be unjust to hold someone legally culpable for an unlawful action are parasitic on cases where it would be inappropriate to blame someone for the action. This means that, wherever it would be inappropriate to blame, it would also be unjust to hold legally culpable (that is, moral blamelessness entails legal innocence); and where there is no moral excuse, there need not be legal exculpation either (it would not be unjust to punish this person for whatever ends justify punishment generally). Two, they both derive an account of the culpable-mind requirement from a single theory of exculpatory conditions—that is, from a theory that seeks to explain with one idea defences as diverse as "I thought I had permission from the owner to use his cottage" and "Yes, I knew I was using the cottage without the owner's permission, but it was either break in or freeze to death."

The character theory

The character theory of *mens rea* holds that acting either purposely, knowingly, recklessly, or negligently with respect to proscribed conduct is necessary for criminal liability because these mental states allow us to infer a socially undesirable character trait from the wrongful conduct;[8] or they permit an interpretation of the wrongful conduct as expressive of,[9] or as reflective of,[10] or as constitutive of, a disposition of character deserving of blame.[11] Unlawful conduct by itself permits no such inference, because from a single unlawful action one can tell nothing about the settled features of an agent's character unless it performed the action purposely, knowingly, with reckless indifference, or with thoughtless preoccupation with its own interests. So the presence of *mens rea* is essential to our being able to presume a connection (whether of manifestation or causation) between an unlawful action and a blameworthy disposition or attitude. Obversely, exculpatory conditions such as involuntariness, mistake of fact, necessity, and duress either block the possibility of an inference of blameworthy character from the unlawful conduct or (in the case of necessity and duress) rebut the inference with evidence of extraordinary pressures that make moral blame and censure

---

[8] Michael Bayles, 'Character, Purpose, and Criminal Responsibility,' (1982) 1 *Law and Philosophy*, 5–20.

[9] George Fletcher, *Rethinking Criminal Law* (Boston: Little, Brown, 1978), 799–802; Nicola Lacey, *State Punishment* (London: Routledge, 1988), 68–78; Victor Tadros, *Criminal Responsibility* (Oxford: Oxford University Press, 2005), 47–53. Fletcher has now discarded the character theory; see *The Grammar of Criminal Law* (Oxford: Oxford University Press, 2007), 35–7.

[10] Tadros, *Criminal Responsibility*, 47–53.

[11] RA Duff, *Criminal Attempts* (Oxford: Oxford University Press, 1996), 188–9.

undeserved. Blameworthy character is not, of course, a sufficient condition of judicial punishment, since moral disapproval can be expressed in many ways. There must also be a harmful or dangerous action prohibited by law, because the end of judicial punishment, as distinct from that of informal types of social censure, is the prevention of crime. So the possibility of drawing an inference from action to character functions as a side-constraint on the state's pursuit of the goals of deterrence, incapacitation, and reform, ensuring that these aims will be furthered only on the backs of people who deserve public condemnation.[12]

Let us, because it is far too difficult a question to tackle, grant character theorists the assumption they need that we are responsible for our characters and can thus be appropriately blamed for vicious traits, dispositions, habits, and attitudes. And let us also assume that character theorists can demarcate with some precision the borders of the character for which we are responsible (does it exclude or include attributes formed through early childhood identification with parents; emotions, urges, etc. that *we* banish from our consciousness), so that judgments of actions as "in character" or "out of character" can be analytical and disciplined rather than subjective and result-driven. Even so, the character theory of *mens rea* is vulnerable to two lines of criticism: it fits too loosely the criminal law of which it is supposed to be an interpretation; and it provides an inadequate account of criminal desert.

Let's first consider the question of fit. Others have pointed out how precarious the act (or externalization) requirement of criminal liability becomes under a character theory of culpability, and so I will not belabour that point.[13] Suffice it to say that dangerous character traits that have manifested themselves in action do not go away just because the action is over and the character has been punished for it. They persist as a potential source of a stream of actions, and the character theory has no reason for waiting until anti-social characters strike again or even until they perform actions legally amounting to an attempt. If they are dangerous and blameable for their dangerousness, they are a fair target of preventive measures expressing public censure. In this way, the character theory of culpability has the potential to immerse punishment for actions in control of human threats.

Let us, however, leave aside the character theory's problems with the criminal *actus* and focus instead on its account of the *mens rea* requirement itself. Here I want to argue that the character theory of *mens rea* and of exculpatory conditions cannot plausibly claim to be the positive law's underlying theory.

Because it wants to link judicial punishment not to the culpable agency of an abstract person, but to the blameworthiness of a concrete and full moral character, the character theory requires distinctions among mental attitudes much finer than the criminal law typically recognizes. Criminal law generally attaches no practical

---

[12] But Lacey, because she is dubious about our responsibility for our characters, rejects attribution to character as a retributivist side-constraint, viewing it instead as integral to the forward-looking ends of punishment; see *State Punishment*, 72.

[13] See Duff, *Criminal Attempts*, 54–6; Michael Moore, 'Choice, Character, and Excuse,' (1990) 7 *Social Philosophy and Policy* 29, 54–6.

significance to the distinction between committing an unlawful action for the purpose of doing so, committing it knowingly but regretfully as a means to (or by-product of) achieving some other end, consciously imposing an unreasonable risk and being indifferent to whether the risk materializes, and consciously imposing an unreasonable risk but hoping it will not materialize. For purposes of punishability, these states of mind are treated as moral equivalents; when accompanying an unlawful action, any will suffice to move the wrongdoer across the threshold from civil to criminal liability. Yet they are far from equivalent from the standpoint of blameworthy character. Someone who, without justification or excuse, acts for the purpose of killing another human being has exhibited a more depraved character than someone who kills in anguish as a certain side-effect of achieving a different purpose; someone who is indifferent to whether an unreasonable risk will materialize deserves more blame than someone who hopes it will not. A character theory must distinguish between these nuances of fault as a matter of law binding on the judge; it cannot leave them to sentencing discretion, because, subtle as they are, the gradations are for it intrinsic to penal justice, not a matter of indifference to it. Accordingly, *mens rea* in law is far too blunt an indicator of blameworthy character to be plausibly considered as ordered to that function.

To the same point is the observation that the character theory cannot account for the law's general practice of treating *mens rea* as separate from motive and motive as irrelevant to culpability. The reason why someone commits an unlawful action is surely relevant to whether an inference can be drawn from the action to the actor's settled character as well as to what sort of inference can be drawn. Thus the individual who, from benevolent motives, force-feeds his hunger-striking friend has revealed a character far less deserving of blame than has someone who, to amuse himself, forces food down the throat of a stranger sitting beside him at a restaurant. The criminal law treats both of these cases as simple assaults and leaves to sentencing discretion the moral differences between them.[14] But the character theory is committed, if not to exculpating the benevolent force-feeder, at least to treating his crime as belonging to a different category (assault from benevolent motives, perhaps) than that of one who assaults from vicious motives.[15]

If *mens rea* in law is too undifferentiated to be a reliable indicator of character, it is also in some cases too narrowly focused on agency to permit the blaming of the blameworthy. I have in mind here the defences of mental disorder and intoxication. Where mental disorder is not genetic or biologically caused, it comprises a set of character vices (megalomania, paranoia, narcissism, lack of conscience, etc.) for which agents are as much or as little responsible as they are for any other formation of character. Thus, far from a condition blocking an inference from unlawful conduct to character, mental disorder is itself the connection. The same may be

---

[14] It is doubtful that even necessity will excuse from assault someone who tried to save a competent agent against his will.
[15] Tadros, *Criminal Responsibility*, 295: "…if the defendant has not shown herself in any way to have manifested bad character, it is difficult to see how criminal responsibility can ever be warranted."

said for voluntary drunkenness. Drinking to the point where one loses control of motor functions or even where one lacks the capacity to intend objects as means to further ends is, one may say, the sign of a character who disrespects his humanity, who is willing to "throw himself away", in Kant's phrase. From the standpoint of the character theory, therefore, the law's practice of permitting mental disorder to exculpate when it negates criminal intent and of allowing intoxication to exculpate from crimes of complex intent must seem exactly the opposite of the way these conditions ought to be regarded. Accordingly, the character theory would seem to be committed to eliminating or drastically reducing the scope of the defence of mental disorder and to admitting all evidence of intoxication as *inculpatory*.[16]

Not only does the character theory turn some legally exculpatory conditions into inculpatory ones; it also renders unintelligible the limitation of exculpatory conditions to a finite set of defences signifying that the defendant does not deserve punishment *for his action*. If the only significance of the legally recognized defences is that they preclude an inference from conduct to character, why not consider character evidence extrinsic to the action that might do so as well or that might at least reveal the action in a truer light? Indeed, since it is manifestly unfair to judge a person's settled character by an isolated action, the defendant ought, on the character theory, to be permitted to adduce character evidence, not simply to support a denial of commission or in discretionary mitigation of sentence, but as exculpatory in itself. Thus, if it could be shown that the criminal conduct was a momentary aberration from the defendant's enduring moral character, or if it could be shown that the action, while not disownable by the defendant, nonetheless belongs to a generally good character with all-too-human frailties rather than a bad one, he or she should be entitled to an acquittal or statutory (not discretionary) mitigation. Here the fit between the character theory of *mens rea* and the criminal law could not be much looser. Not only could the character theory convict before a blameworthy (and dangerous) disposition issued in an act; it could also acquit on the basis of a free-standing character defence someone who intentionally and without justification or excuse committed a crime.[17]

Victor Tadros seeks to rescue the character theory from implications such as these with two claims. One is that a character theory can coherently hold people responsible only for actions reflective of their character without making character

[16] Bayles, 'Character, Purpose, and Criminal Responsibility,' 17–19.
[17] Jeremy Horder seeks to avoid this result of the character theory by judging the defendant's criminal act against an idealized moral character for whom such an act would be impossible. But this takes the character theory out of the frying pan of act marginalization into the fire of no-fault criminal liability. Because the ideal moral character is a construct of reason, it is by definition unattainable by flesh-and-blood characters, who might uncharacteristically slip on occasion. To judge the real character as "bad" by an impossible standard of perfection, however, is to impose criminal liability without fault (and to turn every judge into a hypocrite). True, the defendant has broken the law with some form of *mens rea*; but the character theory (as modified by Horder) must see this as revealing a culpable character only because the real character has fallen short of the ideal one. And since he cannot help but fall short, this is to blame without fault. See Horder, 'Criminal Culpability: The Possibility of a General Theory,' (1993) 12 *Law and Philosophy* 193, 207–8.

the target of punishment and so without punishing dispositions independently of actions.[18] The other is that a character theory can avoid treating generally good character as a free-standing defence by limiting the circumstances under which one can properly say that an action was unreflective of character. An action, says Tadros, is not unreflective of character simply because it is an isolated or rare action for the agent; for even if exceptional, a bad action might reveal a blameworthy weakness in dealing with an unusual impulse.[19] Nor is an action unreflective of character just because the agent hates the desire that motivated it; for it could have been part of the agent's character to accept this disharmony between its desires and its values. Rather, argues Tadros, an action is unreflective of character only if committed by the agent during a "fundamental shift in character for which he is not responsible", one that might occur as a result of provocation or of involuntary intoxication that removes inhibitions.[20] Such a shift occurs when the agent acts from a desire from which it is "alienated"—that is, rejects as being discordant with other values it holds.[21] Since it is the agent rather than the action that is deemed worthy of punishment, the agent ought not to be punished for actions committed when he was not "himself".

Tadros believes that this reformulation of the character theory ties criminal responsibility closely to actions, but this may be doubted. To say that an individual deserves moral criticism, not for all his bad actions, but only for those reflective of his enduring character is to say that an individual deserves criticism not for his bad actions as such, but for the bad character he has manifested in bad actions. Thus, even if bad character is constituted rather than evidenced by bad actions, it is still manifested character that is the bearer of responsibility and the object of blame. But then there is no reason (absent a fundamental change of character) why one ought not to *continue indefinitely* to criticize people for the bad character they have manifested in past actions even if those actions have not been repeated; for it is the enduring character, not the single, over-and-done-with choice, that (for the character theory) deserves censure. So, if a danger exists that the bad action might be repeated, then the character theory must say that indefinite or pre-emptive punishment is deserved because of what the individual has revealed about himself through his past actions. Accordingly, the line Tadros wants to draw between holding people responsible only for actions reflective of their character and making character itself the target of condemnation is impossible to draw.

Second, defining out-of-character actions narrowly as those proceeding from fundamental shifts in character does not rule out a free-standing character defence even where D's criminal action at time *t* reflected D's character at time *t*. For if the individual is not responsible for actions committed while he was not himself, then he is also not responsible *now* for actions committed by a character he no longer is. If the unity of character can be disrupted during a period of "destabilization", it

---

[18] Tadros, *Criminal Responsibility*, 49, 295.
[19] Ibid, 296.   [20] Ibid, 297.   [21] Ibid, 31–5.

can also be discontinued owing to fundamental reorganizations of character such as might result from a religious conversion, or psychoanalysis, or just plain growing up. Tadros must therefore be willing to exculpate Paul for whatever criminal actions Saul committed before Saul became Paul if Paul is free of the desires that drove Saul to crime. But the criminal law will doubtless hold Paul responsible for what Saul did—for the following good reason.

Whatever fundamental changes characters undergo, the identity that persists throughout them is that of their formal agency; and, for the criminal law, this agency is the bearer of responsibility for deeds it chose whether it is now embodied in Paul or in Saul, or whether it is embodied in one's enduring character or temporarily destabilized one. Tadros acknowledges that the idea of responsibility requires an identity persisting over time on which to pin responsibility;[22] but he erroneously equates the identity required for *criminal* responsibility with that of character. The identity of character is an unsuitable bearer of criminal responsibility (though it is appropriate for moral responsibility) because coercion involving a right violation distinguishes judicial punishment from moral criticism. While moral criticism is doubtless directed at a character, judicial coercion coerces a free will or agent; and so it is the *agent* who must deserve (in the way explained in Chapter 1) judicial punishment. But because the agent is so abstract and characterless, it can persist throughout changes of character, so that judicial punishment is not undeserved just because the character clothing the agent has changed or because the agent chose an action unreflective of its character. And that is why octogenarians can be convicted of crimes committed when they were 20 with no questions asked about their present values.

Not only is the character theory at odds with well-settled and defensible features of the criminal law; it is also intrinsically deficient as a theory of criminal desert. On this theory, *mens rea* functions as a connector between a dangerous action and a character deserving of blame and moral censure. But if the blameworthy disposition revealed by an unlawful action committed with *mens rea* does not specifically deserve judicial punishment as distinct from blame generally, how can we say that a *mens rea* requirement acts as a desert constraint on the state's pursuit of crime prevention through punishment? Perhaps a character vice deserves blame in the abstract and judicial punishment is one way of expressing blame (i.e. of censuring) so that, by deserving blame, a character also deserves any of the specific manifestations it might take. But judicial punishment is not just a particular instance of censuring alongside professional discipline, verbal reprimands, and social snubbing. Nor is it even a particular instance of *public* censure alongside reports of public inquiries, parliamentary investigative committees, and press editorials. Because it comprises actions that are ordinarily themselves wrongful (indeed criminally wrongful), judicial punishment forms an altogether different category of responses to wrongdoing needing a distinctive justification—one

---

[22] Ibid, 47: "When we are punished, we are punished as agents who persist over time."

directed toward legitimating the violence it entails. Thus, something more than deserving blame and censure is required to deserve *it*.[23]

The same conclusion follows from attending to the difference between political and moral obligation. What is generally taken to distinguish them is precisely the authority of an official to whom a political obligation is owed to coerce obedience to norms that are otherwise binding only in conscience so that the official need not rely on angry remonstrations alone. The moral obligation to obey the norm is not yet a political obligation not to resist the might of the sovereign enforcer of the norm. Rather, the political obligation requires a distinctive justification by appeal to some common interest apart from the good of virtue, whether in self-preservation (Hobbes, Locke) or in civil independence (Rousseau, Kant). But if political obligation is categorically different from moral obligation, then the authority to punish that is correlative to political obligation is categorically different from the moral standing to blame, not simply a case of it. So to explain the *mens rea* requirement as needed to ensure a character's deserving blame, disapproval, or censure is still to leave judicial punishment undeserved. But then the pursuit of crime prevention through that means looks like arbitrary violence indistinguishable from the wrongdoer's.

The choice theory

The choice theory of the culpable mind is, like the character theory, an account of moral blameworthiness applied to legal punishment. The theory is quite simple and intuitively appealing. It says that, assuming punishment for a type of action is justified for forward-looking reasons, punishment of *this* person for an action of that type is justified only if blame is justified; and blame is justified for an unlawful action only if the agent had a choice between committing it and not committing

---

[23] Tadros argues that the specificity of the criminal justice system is that it communicates public "moral criticism" (ibid, 2–3) or "moral indignation" (82) toward individuals who have shown insufficient regard for the significant interests of others. But this cannot be right, for public inquiries and professional disciplinary bodies also perform this function. The rather obvious specific difference of criminal justice is that it deals violently with the people it criticizes. Horder argues that the possibility of an absolute discharge because of "wholly exceptional mitigating circumstances" shows that punishment is incidental to the criminal law, whose essential function is to institutionalize "ordinary practices of private moral condemnation" through the "public and official labelling of wrongdoing and wrongdoer"; see 'Gross Negligence and Criminal Culpability,' (1997) 47 *University of Toronto Law Journal* 495, 509 n.49. But the fact that a convict might be discharged because of exceptional mitigating circumstances does not show that punishment is incidental to the criminal law; it shows the opposite, for if punishment were incidental one would not need wholly exceptional circumstances to overcome the state's general duty to punish the guilty. Von Hirsch and Ashworth try to bridge the gap between censure and "hard treatment" with an argument about the need for deterrence to supplement moral inhibitions given fallible human nature; see Andrew von Hirsch and Andrew Ashworth, *Proportionate Sentencing* (Oxford: Oxford University Press, 2005), 21–34. But if the hard treatment is not specifically deserved (as they claim), then this argument approves coercing a moral subject so that others may have a motive for resisting temptation. This is to protect oneself against the Sirens by tying someone else to the mast—obviously a use of another no free moral subject could accept. Nor could the subject accept such a justification for the general institution of hard treatment, for it cannot endorse a justification that envisages moral subjects as animal organisms manipulable by external threats.

it—only if the agent could have chosen otherwise than it did. If the agent had no choice but to do what it did, it is not to blame for it. The culpable mind requirement of criminal liability embodies this truth of moral theory, for it confines punishment to those who could have done otherwise. In HLA Hart's words,

> What is crucial is that those whom we punish should have had, when they acted, the normal capacities, physical and mental, for abstaining from what [the law] forbids, and a fair opportunity to exercise these capacities. Where these capacities and opportunities are absent, as they are in different ways in the varied cases of accident, mistake, paralysis, reflex action, coercion, insanity, etc., the moral protest is that it is morally wrong to punish because 'he could not have helped it' or 'he could not have done otherwise' or 'he had no real choice'.[24]

Here Hart has run together two different pleas that might be meant by "he could not have helped it". That statement might mean that he lacked the *capacity* to choose otherwise, perhaps because he was a newborn infant. Or it might mean that he lacked a *fair opportunity* of exercising his capacity to choose otherwise, perhaps because he was unaware of the circumstances that made his conduct unlawful or because his will was overwhelmed by pressures much stronger than most people ordinarily face. Michael Moore, another proponent of the choice theory, distinguishes these senses by describing the first as a claim that one's choice was made impossible by factors beyond one's control and the second as a claim that one's choice was made very difficult by such factors.[25] Let's first consider the incapacity to choose otherwise as a condition negating *mens rea*.

There is, of course, an ambiguity here as well. To say that someone lacked the capacity to have done otherwise might mean that at the time he broke the law he lacked the capacity animals have for choosing the inclination they will yield to. This might be because he was asleep, or unconscious, or because a gust of wind blew him into another person. Alternatively, lacking the capacity to have chosen otherwise might mean lacking the capacity agents normally have for *freely* choosing whether or not to act on an inclination. This might be because the individual lacks awareness of its selfhood as the cause of its volitions, as in the case of an infant or a severely demented individual. There is even a third possibility. To have lacked the capacity to have chosen otherwise might mean that, while the defendant was a competent agent at the time of the breach, he lacked the strength of will to resist the powerful inclination to act as he did. Just as someone might say "I couldn't lift the 200-pound weights", someone might say "I couldn't resist the impulse to steal the watch."

Since the capacity for animal choice is included in the capacity for free choice, we need not consider it separately. Moreover, the third sense of "I could not do otherwise" cannot be exculpatory because, so understood, the statement adds

---

[24] Hart, *Punishment and Responsibility*, 152. Though a proponent of the choice theory, Hart did not see a could-have-done-otherwise requirement as connecting criminal liability to moral blameworthiness; rather he saw it as protecting individual autonomy: see *Punishment and Responsibility*, 181–2. Michael Moore, by contrast, espouses the choice theory as part of his moral retributivism; see 'Choice, Character, and Excuse,' 30–31.

[25] Moore, ibid, 35.

nothing to "I *did* not do otherwise." Since, counterfactually, I could have had the strength of will to resist the impulse (that is, resistance did not call for superhuman fortitude), the statement that I did not have the strength to resist is tautological for "I failed to resist." So it has no force to excuse the failure.

So let us focus on the second sense of incapacity mentioned above—the incapacity for free choice. And let us grant the choice theorist's assumption against determinists that incapacity in this sense intelligibly distinguishes the blameless from the possibly blameworthy. Assume, in other words, that a conscious, normally functioning human being has a capacity to accept or reject any impulse or motive that its body-psyche offers up as an end of action. By capacity is meant here not strength of will, but the bare possibility of asserting a will that distinguishes a conscious human being from other forms of life. A sunflower cannot reject the force of phototropism that causes it to turn toward the sun; a bloodhound cannot reject, except for the sake of a stronger impulse, the force of an instinct that causes it to pursue a scent. But a human being can reject the force of an emotion, drive, or inclination just for the sake of displaying self-mastery. It can do so because it is a self-consciousness—that is, an 'I' distanced from these emotions and drives and so capable of taking a stance toward them. This, no doubt, is a minimalist sense of capacity. Here capacity simply means that there is a rider on the horse, to use Plato's image, not that the rider possesses the strength or know-how to control the horse. So we can say that a capacity to have done otherwise in this sense belongs to any human being that is aware of itself as an 'I' or subject. And since this self-awareness is the possibility of choice undetermined by what is not-I, it is the condition of imputing choices to a subject and hence, as the choice theorist rightly maintains, the condition of blaming a subject for its unlawful deeds.

The difficulty for the choice theorist of the culpable mind, however, is that the presence of the capacity to have chosen otherwise says almost nothing about whether the defendant's mind was culpable. That D could have chosen otherwise when he shot V, while a minimum condition for culpability, fails by a wide margin to establish a culpable mind, for in a dark forest D may have reasonably believed V was a bear. Thus the culpable mind is determined, not solely by *whether* the defendant had a choice to do otherwise, but also (and indeed, primarily, as we'll see) by *what* he chose. This is why, in law, the mind's culpability is a function of its cognition rather than simply of its volitional capacity, of what the defendant knew or believed and thus thought he was doing. Thus, if he chose to shoot a bear but mistakenly shot a man he thought was a bear, he is not guilty of a homicide even though he could have chosen to flee. Even if, because of mental disorder, he delusionally mistook the man for a mouse, he is innocent of criminal wrongdoing even though he could have chosen not to kill the "mouse". Conversely, if, because of some condition negating self-consciousness (for example, unconsciousness), or determining physical motion irrespective of volition (for example, reflex action, forces of nature), the defendant could not have done otherwise, something more basic than a culpable mind is missing. In these situations, the law says that there is no *act*, because voluntariness is what differentiates acts from the genus of events. Accordingly, on its incapacity branch, the choice theory explains no more than the requirement that a culpable act be voluntary; it does not explain the requirement of a culpable mind—the requirement that the defendant have chosen something in particular. Hence it fails to explain the defences of mistake of fact and insanity, by virtue of which lawbreakers are acquitted despite having had the capacity that conscious subjects have to have chosen otherwise.

Perhaps the choice theory fares better when it argues that blameworthiness (and so punishability) depends on the agent's having had a fair opportunity to exercise its capacity for choice. This path seems more promising, because the agent who shot the man believing him to be a bear, though it had the capacity to choose otherwise, lacked the opportunity most people would have had for exercising this capacity, either because the mistake was reasonable (the forest was dark) or because the agent was suffering from a mental disorder that distorted its perception of the world. Moreover, the defences of necessity and duress can also be brought within the ambit of this theory, because they are put forward by people who, though they possessed the abstract capacity to have chosen otherwise, found their will overborne by pressures far above the ordinary. In these cases, the lack of strength to resist a drive or to overcome fear does have exculpatory force, potentially at least, because the plea does more than redescribe the failure to resist; it judges the failure as meeting the standard of moral strength that we are entitled to expect from our fellow human beings. The agent lacked a *fair* opportunity to exercise its capacity to have done otherwise.

Nevertheless, the fair opportunity branch of the choice theory also fails as a theory of the culpable mind. This is so because, if the capacity test established too little of what makes for a culpable mind, the fair opportunity test embraces too much, sweeping in states of mind that not even the most expansive view of *mens rea* found in the positive law views as culpable. Thus far, the outer limit to which courts have stretched the fault threshold of criminality is "gross negligence", understood as a failure to avoid a high risk of serious harm where the defendant had the capacity to do so but regardless of whether the defendant actually perceived the risk.[26] Any further expansion would breach the border between crime and noncriminal offences based on civil negligence and thus either (a) unfairly brand as criminals those whose fault was venial or (b) so inflate the criminal brand as to denude it of distinctive meaning. Yet the fair opportunity test of culpability would breach the border.

To see this, consider a classic civil law case of negligence, *Donoghue v Stevenson*.[27] As a matter of tort law, of course, it is immaterial whether the defendant had the

---

[26] *R v Adomako* [1994] 3 All ER 79 (HL); *R v Hundal* [1993] 1 SCR 867; Model Penal Code, s. 2.02.
[27] [1932] AC 562 (HL). The plaintiff drank from a bottle of ginger beer purchased from a café owner, in which bottle was found the decomposed remains of a snail. As a result, she suffered stomach pains diagnosed as gastro-enteritis. The plaintiff sued the bottler for damages, and the House of Lords acknowledged her cause of action, thus founding the modern tort of negligence as actionable outside the bounds of contract.

mental or physical capacity to conform to the standard of care that the reasonable person would have exercised in the situation; all that matters is whether or not he measured up to the standard. Thus civil negligence does not require that the defendant have been morally blameworthy for his having breached a duty of care. Suppose, however, that Stevenson did have the basic capacities needed to meet the required standard of consideration for those likely to drink his ginger beer—to contemplate the risk that some of his bottles might become adulterated and to inspect them prior to sealing them. In that case we would say that he breached a duty of care owed the plaintiff and injured her despite having had a fair opportunity to have done otherwise—to have taken the precaution that would have avoided injury to the plaintiff. This, according to Hart's fair opportunity test, makes Stevenson blameworthy for his negligence, and so it does. Does it also make him culpable and criminally liable to punishment (assuming there are good goal-oriented reasons to punish)? Not according to the most expansive view of *mens rea* found in the positive law, because his having had the capacity to foresee the risk and avoid it has not changed the magnitude of the risk, which (we may assume) was not sufficiently excessive to warrant a finding of egregious negligence. Nor does his capacity indicate anything more than venial thoughtlessness. He is not indifferent to the risk, for had it been brought to his attention, he would no doubt have taken the appropriate action to remove it. Nor was the risk of adulteration so obvious that only someone indifferent to the risk could have failed to notice it. If this is nonculpable negligence when he lacks capacity, it is still nonculpable negligence when he has it. So here we have a case where, though the defendant is morally to blame for his negligence, it would still be unjust to punish him (though not unjust to impose noncriminal penalties that need not be deserved either by culpability or moral blameworthiness). But this only tells us what we already knew: that the blameworthiness that gives the wronged party the standing to blame is not yet the culpability that gives the state the right to punish.

If the presence of a fair opportunity to exercise one's capacity for choice against wrongdoing does not map onto legal culpability for wrongdoing, we should suspect that the lack of a fair opportunity to avoid wrongdoing is not the legally relevant common theme of the conditions that exculpate. Of course, it is natural to think that, even if those morally blameworthy for their unlawful actions are not necessarily criminally culpable for them, at least the morally blameless are necessarily nonculpable. But this is not as obvious as it seems.

Both the American Model Penal Code and the Supreme Court of Canada distinguish between *exculpating* conditions that negate an essential element of culpable wrong (culpable action or culpable mind) or that justify what in ordinary circumstances would be a culpable wrong, and *excusing* conditions that presuppose a culpable wrong.[28] This is just the distinction, well ensconced in Anglo-American

---

[28] Model Penal Code, ss. 2.02, 2.09; *R v Ruzic* [2001] 1 SCR 687. The MPC includes absence of excuse among the elements of the offence but distinguishes between culpability and absence of excuse (s. 1.13[9]). This leaves logical room for someone culpable for proscribed conduct to be excused.

criminal law, between pleas (such as mistake) that deny a criminal offence and those that affirm a defence, the crime being admitted. Duress is an affirmative defence. Now let us grant that T's believable threat to kill D if D does not kill V excuses D for murdering V, because D lacked a fair opportunity to exercise his capacity for choice and is therefore morally blameless (his doing otherwise would have been morally heroic, supererogatory). According to the Model Penal Code and Canadian law, D's blamelessness does not exculpate him from the wrong; rather, it (at most) gives a reason for excusing D from a culpable wrong, for holding him safe from punishment despite his legal culpability. The fair opportunity theory, in conflating moral blamelessness and legal innocence, fails to capture this nuance of the law. Moreover, if the morally blameless are not necessarily nonculpable legally, then the lack of a fair opportunity to do otherwise cannot explain why mistake of fact and insanity *exculpate*. But this is what we suspected all along. For, even prior to any theoretical reflection, it seems intuitively plain that the reason why someone who kills a man thinking he is a bear is not culpable for his wrong (liable to judicial punishment) is not that he lacked a fair opportunity to exercise differently his capacity for choice, but that his actual choice (to shoot a bear) is nonculpable.

But (it will be protested) have we not, with this separation between exculpation and excuse, driven a wedge between the answers to a criminal accusation, thereby precluding a coherent theory of defence? Whatever their failings with respect to fit with the positive law, after all, both the choice theory and the character theory have the advantage of providing a unified theory of defences. And is it not the chief virtue of a theory that it unifies into a coherent explanation the phenomena of which it purports to be an account?

Wedge yes, incoherence no. There is no reason to consider it an advantage of a theory that it explains with one idea defences as disparate as "I thought he was a bear" and "I knew he was a man, but it was either him or me." We should rather think that such a theory oversimplifies. But neither is there any reason to think that preserving the distinction between exculpation and excuse is incompatible with a coherent theory of defences; for an account of defences can be unified without being unitary. That is, it may be possible to unify the defences, not through a single idea that effaces the difference between exculpation and excuse, but through a parent idea that manifests itself differently in each, that shows their kinship and compatibility, and that thus shows how they fit together, different as they are, within a coherent account of the defences. This is the subject of Chapter 7.

3. A Legal Account of *Mens Rea*

The character and choice theories of the culpable mind derived legal culpability from moral blameworthiness and legal excuse from moral excuse. They carried implications at odds with well-settled features of the legal tradition and failed to connect blameworthiness to judicial punishment. By contrast, the theory of *mens rea* I shall defend is a distinctively legal account that explains the fault threshold of criminal liability as the one specifically required to legitimate a judicial infringement of rights.

The account of *mens rea* I propose flows from the retributivist justification of punishment belonging to the formalist paradigm of penal justice. That paradigm, as we saw, rests on a certain conception of the public reason that justifies official coercion; specifically, it rests on the dignity inherent in the self's capacity to act from ends it freely chooses. The protection of that dignity is, for the formalist framework, the fundamental end of criminal law and of state coercion under it.

The account of *mens rea* derived from formalism is meant to have both explanatory and prescriptive force. That is, it claims to fit the common law of criminal fault well enough to have earned the credentials to issue prescriptions for the law to jurists—to label outliers as missteps and to call approved changes organic developments. But the formalist account of *mens rea* is also meant to be prescriptive in a stronger sense—in the sense needed to persuade someone with liberal convictions of the normative cogency of the account. The liberal conviction the argument assumes in the interlocutor is, I believe, uncontroversially generic to the various schools of liberalism: that the individual agent possesses an inviolable worth that makes it wrong for others physically to restrain and confine the agent for their particular ends. On the empirical plane, judicial punishment does just this, and so the question becomes: how must penal coercion be constrained so as to reconcile it with the individual's inviolability? The following account of the culpable mind forms part of an answer.

The fault threshold

Let us recall the legal retributivist account of punishment presented in Chapter 1. If D knowingly interferes with V's capacity to act from freely chosen ends (whether by threatening one of the essential conditions of V's freedom, by physical force, or by interfering in the proprietary domain over which V's choices rule), his act signifies something more general than an infringement of V's right so to act. Since V is a human agent with a capacity for self-actuation, D's choice to interfere with this capacity signifies for the thinking Agent standing in D's shoes a claim of permission to act that is unlimited by respect for the agency of another human being. However, claims of permission binding others can be objectively validated as rights only by free others whose liberty to act is reciprocally respected. Therefore, D's choice to interfere with another agent's freedom is impliedly a choice to act against the framework of mutual respect that makes rights (as distinct from subjective claims) to act possible. Accordingly, D's choice to interfere with V's agency signifies (to the thinking Agent) a challenge to the very idea of a valid permission to act or to a permission to act that others must respect.

However, if (according to the challenge) no one has a valid permission to act, then no one can validly protest (i.e. make a protest that others must heed) if another agent impedes his or her movements through physical restraint or confinement. No one, including D. Thus, the necessary implication of D's choice to interfere with V's agency is the denial of an inviolable sphere of liberty for D. Having implicitly denied the existence of rights (claims recognizable by a free self) to act, D cannot now turn around and assert a right against interference with his own agency. This constitutes the *aporia* or self-contradictory result of the criminal's implicit claim of permission to an unlimited liberty. Because this claim was mistaken, it would be impermissible for V or anyone acting from self-interest to take advantage of the licence the criminal has granted to coerce him. However, a state agent could do so for the public purpose of demonstrating the *aporia* so as to vindicate mutual respect as the sole ground of solid rights. Judicial punishment is justified to free agents by this purpose, which therefore provides a normative frame within which alone punishment may also be directed to material ends, such as crime control and reform. By availing itself of the criminal's licence to coerce him, the state shows the downfall of his claim of right to an unlimited liberty; and it thereby publicly vindicates mutually recognized liberty as the framework for real rights. Since doing so also vindicates the criminal's right, the thinking Agent in his shoes would accept retribution as the actualization of valid human worth. Accordingly, the necessary implication of D's wilful interference with V is his own moral vulnerability to coercion for the purpose of right vindication, and this connection between wilful wrongdoing and liability to punishment is what we call criminal desert.

We can see that what launches this story is an intentional interference with another human being's capacity for free agency. Choosing to do that from which a denial of rights of agency can be imputed to the choice triggers the circuit from wrongdoing to coercibility. *Why* one chose so as to imply a right denial—one's motive, whether wicked or benevolent—is irrelevant to whether the circuit goes through, as it is to culpability in the positive law. Moreover, *only* a choice implying a right denial initiates the circuit. An unwitting interference does not set the logic in motion, for if D mistakenly thinks he has permission from V, then his choice is just to pursue his object (surgery, sex, acquisition, etc.) within the bounds of respect for V's agency; and from this act description no denial of rights can be imputed to his choice, hence no authorization of his own coercion either. Coercion is then external violence incompatible with the inviolability of the person.

Observe, however, that nothing in this argument determines that an intentional interference is required for a right infringement (i.e. a wrong or tort). Where D interferes with V's agency under a mistaken belief that he has permission from V, a boundary has nonetheless been crossed, and D will not be able to raise his mistake to defend against a civil action for battery, entry, or conversion.[29]

---

[29] Thus the oft-heard argument that subjectivism ignores victims tells a half-truth. It forgets that subjectivism does not stand alone but comes on top of a theory of tort that sees tort law as vindicating the rights of victims and so as the proper sphere for objective standards of fault and even (in some cases) strict liability. Subjectivism assumes that the parties to a criminal action are the state and the accused; the accused is criminally culpable, not because he infringed this particular victim's right but because, in wilfully infringing this particular person's right, he denied the

This is so because D's subjective perceptions and beliefs cannot, consistently with mutual respect for agency, be allowed to dictate the boundary between D's and V's zones of permissible activity. That boundary must be determined impartially—in accordance with a principle securing the greatest extent of equal liberty. Hence D's beliefs about whether he has transgressed V's boundary are irrelevant to whether he has in fact transgressed it.

However, in the criminal action, the question is whether D can be physically restrained and confined for his transgression, and now his subjective perceptions become relevant as determining whether he has made a choice from which an assent to coercion may be implied. If, given his perceptions and beliefs about the circumstances or likely consequences of his action, it would be incorrect to describe his choice as one to interfere with V's free agency, then nothing connects his choice to his own coercibility. Thus, even to interfere unwittingly where a reasonable person would have known of the interference (i.e. to make a negligent mistake about permission) is not yet to interfere culpably either in theory or in law.[30] Nor is an unwitting interference culpable where the interference would have been glaringly obvious to the reasonable person, though the obviousness of the transgression would be strong evidence against a plea of inadvertence. Though the reasonable person would have known of the interference, D did not, and so he made no choice from which a denial of rights can logically be inferred.

Whereas, however, a choice to do that from which a denial of rights can be imputed to the choice is essential to culpability, *knowledge* of the *interference* is not the only way to make such a choice. A denial of rights to respect for agency can also be inferred from a choice to impose an extraordinary risk of interference—that is, a risk over and above the magnitude that agents reciprocally accept as an inevitable cost of freedom of action in a certain social context. I choose to impose an extraordinary risk, however, only when I am aware of such a risk or only when I suspect that one exists and so actually foresee the likelihood of an interference. If I am unaware of the risk, then no matter how apparent it would be to a reasonable person, I have not chosen to impose it, and so I have chosen nothing implying a denial of rights (though my bare assertion of ignorance need not, of course, be taken at face value). Thus recklessness understood as proceeding despite advertence to one's imposing an unreasonable risk of interference with others' capacity for freedom or a wilful blindness regarding such a risk are culpable states of mind both in theory and in law; but gross negligence is an outlier for

---

very idea of a right and gave this denial practical force. Accordingly, to exculpate someone on the ground that, through an unreasonable mistake, he did not deny rights is perfectly compatible with a finding that he infringed this victim's right and is therefore liable in tort. Fletcher thus errs when he attributes to legal retributivism the view that only those who signal disrespect for others' rights are wrongdoers; see *The Grammar of Criminal Law*, 57.

[30] Though this can be deterred by a noncriminal penalty for a public welfare offence, for which the penalty need not be deserved and to which other constraints protective of individual autonomy apply; see Chapter 5.

the theory and (we may say) a mistake in law. Moreover, a denial of rights can be imputed to the choice to impose an unreasonable risk whether one would regret the risk's materializing, or be indifferent to it, or rejoice in it. Thus mental orientations toward actions and outcomes one would want to distinguish in assessing and calibrating moral blame are juridically equivalent as denials of rights authorizing one's own coercion, and they are so treated by the positive law.

Observe that, while this account of the culpable mind provides an argument for subjective *mens rea* as the fault threshold of criminal liability, it is not crudely subjectivist in the sense decried by many advocates of an objective standard of criminal fault.[31] That is, it is not concerned solely with what is empirically going on in the mind of a monadic agent, and so it does not judge him exclusively by his own knowledge, beliefs, and self-interpretations, ignoring the interpersonal meaning of his action. True, the foregoing account of *mens rea* focuses on what situational facts the agent knew or believed existed or on what risks he foresaw in order to determine what he chose to do. But it does not judge the agent solely by what he subjectively thought his choice *meant;* rather it judges him by what is logically imputable to his choice and thus by what the thinking Agent in his shoes meant by his choice.[32] If D knowingly operates on V against V's will thinking that this shows love and concern for V rather than disrespect, the foregoing account will still treat him as having implicitly denied rights of agency and authorized the interference with his own. So too if D reports that he thought he was ignoring only V's will, not denying rights of agency as such, or that he knew V was a human being but didn't know he was an agent or even what an agent is. Accordingly, the foregoing account of criminal desert generates a subjectivism that, by virtue of incorporating the public standpoint of a thinking Agent, is immune from the charges of excessive atomism or empiricism brought against other versions.[33]

Yet, one might ask (with George Fletcher), if right denials may be imputed to those who do not empirically deny rights, why impute them only to those who intentionally interfere (or risk interfering) with agency? Why not impute them

---

[31] Duff, *Intention, Agency, and Criminal Liability*, 159–62; Ripstein, *Equality, Responsibility, and the Law*, 178; Fletcher, *The Grammar of Criminal Law*, 313–4.

[32] It follows that there is no "mismatch" between the factual psychological states relied upon by subjectivism and the normative work of inculpation they are supposed to do; see Alan Norrie, *Punishment, Responsibility, and Justice* (Oxford: Oxford University Press, 2000), 170. Right denials cannot be imputed arbitrarily to any empirical choice. To an empirical choice to accept (what one mistakenly believes to be) an invitation to enter another's home one cannot impute a denial of rights of property.

[33] But now the empiricist will protest: why is it legitimate to fix the empirical agent with the knowledge, choice, and assent of the thinking Agent? Why should the thinking Agent's consent to punishment count as that of the empirical agent, who, after all, must be assumed not to consent? One response is that a public standpoint is required to make law, crime, and punishment conceivable, and a public standpoint is possible only if we conceive the empirical human being as a particularized agency—a self individuated in various ways. But if the empirical individual is a particularized agency, then he or she may be fixed with the universal capacities (logical thought, free will) belonging to agency without external imposition; these capacities are not alien to the empirical agent, however well or ill the agent may realize them.

also to those whose negligent interferences manifest a noncaring attitude toward rights?[34] The response is that imputations cannot be arbitrary; they must be anchored in something that logically permits the inference. From an attitude one can infer only another attitude; one cannot infer a choice. Attitudes are imputable to attitudes and choices to choices. Thus, an attitude of disrespect for rights is imputable to an attitude of thoughtlessness manifested in a failure to make sure of one's invitation before crossing a boundary. But a choice to deny rights is imputable only to a choice to coerce; and only an implicit choice to deny rights is an implicit assent to judicial coercion, for assent must proceed from the will. Accordingly, an implicit assent to punishment requires anchoring in an empirical choice to coerce; it cannot be inferred from an attitude of indifference as to whether one is transgressing a boundary or not.

Observe, further, that the foregoing account of the culpable mind determines that a form of subjective fault is the threshold of criminal liability to judicial coercion in the abstract. It says that a choice from which a *right denial* may be implied is essential to deserving a *right infringement*. This means that, once the agent has made a choice implicitly authorizing a right infringement in the abstract, the account's subjectivist requirement is spent. There is no further need that the criminal have intended or foreseen the harmful result of his transgression in order that the severity of punishment properly reflect that result. Of course, the self-imposition requirement at the threshold rules out punishing the criminal for all consequences of his wrong, no matter how unforeseeable; for it would be self-contradictory to say that punishment per se must be implicitly self-imposed but that the measure of punishment can be abandoned entirely to chance (see Chapter 4). However, the self-imposition requirement does not entail that the criminal can be punished only for those results he intended or actually foresaw; for in choosing to coerce someone in a world of cause–effect chains it knows might extend beyond its purpose, the thinking Agent in the criminal's shoes accepts responsibility (in the appropriate degree) for those outcomes of its right-denying action that are imputable in some degree to its agency; and intention is but the highest of several degrees of imputability (foresight and foreseeability are the others). Hence the relaxed fault requirement applying to results is quite consistent with the self-imposition constraint determining the stringency of the threshold. Indeed, one can go further. A requirement of intention or foresight for results would be *inconsistent* with the respect for free agency determining the subjectivist threshold, for it would imply that human beings have no capacity they may be expected to exercise to think beyond the immediate effect of their actions. It follows that nothing in the foregoing account of subjective fault as the threshold of criminal *culpability* determines that subjective fault is also required for criminal *responsibility* for harmful results once the threshold for liability to any punishment has been crossed.

Finally, the legal retributivist account of *mens rea* reveals subjective fault as belonging to the sphere of crimes involving interferences with agency, for it is the

---

[34] Fletcher, *The Grammar of Criminal Law*, 313–14.

denial of rights implied in intentional interferences that connects wrongdoing with the coercibility of the wrongdoer. Because the account has no application to breaches of statutes aiming at the public welfare, it leaves the fault requirement of these offences to be determined by a generic autonomy constraint on the state's pursuit of welfare, which constraint is satisfied by a due diligence defence coupled with a rule against imprisonment for negligence (see Chapter 5).[35] On the other hand, the retributivist justification of physical restraint applies by extension to *intentional* breaches of laws (against perjury, bribing officials, etc.) supporting the enforcement of rights and even to intentional breaches of public welfare laws. This is so because the reality of rights may be said to depend on the rule of law. A knowing breach of a statute involves a choice to which a denial of law's authority may be imputed and hence also a rejection of the condition for the possibility of effective rights. Accordingly, for every public welfare offence involving a risk of harm to others (a qualification required by proportionality, for otherwise an intentional breach of a no-jaywalking ordinance could incur a prison sentence), it would be permissible for a liberal state to enact a separate offence for committing the breach knowingly (to which ignorance of law would thus be a defence) punishable by imprisonment.

Exculpatory conditions

The legal retributivist account of the culpable mind is also an account of the conditions that exculpate because, and to the extent that, their presence means that the defendant did not make a culpable choice: mistake of fact, colour of right, and legal insanity. These conditions exculpate, I'll argue, to the extent that they preclude the inference of a right denial from the defendant's choice.

Of course, if, because his bodily movements were externally forced or automatic, the defendant made no choice at all, then he could not have made a choice to which a right denial is imputable. Indeed, he could not have made a choice that engages the right at all. Similarly, if, because he (as an infant) lacks self-consciousness, he lacks the capability for free choice, then he could not have made a free choice to which a right denial is imputable. Thus, involuntariness and infancy exculpate, not because the doer could not have done otherwise (a condition that fails to distinguish legal innocence from moral blamelessness), but because they negate the basic precondition—freedom of choice—for a right-denying free choice. Hence they negate the wrongdoing without which there cannot be criminal wrongdoing. This explanation accords better with the positive law's own understanding of involuntariness than does the choice theory's account; for instead of developing involuntariness into a general theory of exculpation, it captures the law's sense that involuntariness negates only a basic precondition of culpability. Accordingly, the

---

[35] In confining a subjective fault requirement to the sphere of right violations, the subjectivist position I defend departs from that of Jerome Hall, who would have banished negligence from the penal law generally; see 'Negligent Behavior Should Be Excluded from Penal Liability,' (1963) 63 *Columbia Law Review*, 632.

capacity for free choice may be called the condition of basic responsibility. As the necessary and sufficient condition for ascribing behaviour to a self, that capacity is a precondition for ascribing an interference with free choice to the free choice of a self, hence a precondition for imputing a right denial to that choice.

Mistake of fact exculpates, not because the defendant lacked a fair opportunity to exercise his capacity for choice, nor because it blocks an inference from action to character, but because—and only to the extent that—on the facts as perceived by the defendant, he made no choice which for the thinking Agent in his shoes would have been a choice to deny rights of free agency. Thus, if D chose to shoot a bear and instead shot a man thinking it was a bear, he chose nonculpably unless he chose to risk shooting a man. But if he chose to shoot Peter and instead shot Paul thinking he was Peter, he in any case chose to kill a human being, which for the thinking Agent in his shoes is a denial of rights, and so his mistake is not exculpatory even without the fiction of a "transferred intent". If D shoots V under a mistaken belief that V is about to shoot him, then, however unreasonable the mistake, D does not make a choice from which a right denial may be inferred; for, on the contrary, the thinking Agent with D's perceptions and beliefs is asserting his right against a transgressor, and so D's choice, while not actually justified, is nevertheless nonculpable (though D may be subject to noncriminal penalties for a negligent homicide).[36] But if D shoots V who is not threatening him or anyone else but who D mistakenly believes has forfeited her right because her evil ways have brought dishonour to the family, he has made a choice from which a right denial may be inferred; for he has acted on a belief that an agent's right depends on his pleasure. Here D's mistake is inculpatory.

In the latter case, no doubt, D has made a mistake of law rather than of fact. However, the reason his mistake fails to exculpate is not that it belongs to one category of mistake rather than another but that, even in the personal world that D inhabits, he chose what for the thinking Agent is a choice to deny rights. Indeed, as it applies to right infringements, the rule that mistake or ignorance of law does not exculpate simply reflects the idea that the thinking Agent knows the self-contradictoriness of right claims to act unlimited by respect for others' agency and that the knowledge of the thinking Agent is imputable to the defendant. That is why Bailey was culpable for shooting Truscott on the high seas even if he could not be aware of a new statute extending the King's writ to British ships in mid-ocean;[37] and it is why some mistakes of law (such as D's in the above example), far from being exculpatory, denote culpability itself. But this means that if, in the particular situation, the thinking Agent would not necessarily know the illegality of D's deed, then D's mistake of law can exculpate if it means that he chose to act within the bounds of his permission and so respectfully of V.

Consider these examples. If D takes V's property under a mistake of positive law that the thing is his own, he has chosen to act within his permission (under

[36] *R v Williams (Gladstone)* [1987] 3 All ER 411, 415 (CA).
[37] *R v Bailey* (1800) 168 ER 651.

"colour of right"), and so his mistake of law exculpates both in theory and in law. But then similarly, if D makes sexual contact with V mistakenly taking an equivocal communication for consent, he chooses nonculpably (assuming no recklessness or wilful blindness) even if, for reasons of social policy, consent (unknown to D) is defined by statute as an unequivocal communication of "yes" rather than as an inward mental orientation toward the contact.[38] So, too, if 15-year-old D has sexual contact with a 13-year-old willing partner believing the statutory age of consent is 13 when it is in fact 14. What matters is whether, given his beliefs, D made a choice from which a right denial may be implied, not whether his mistake was one of fact or law; hence it should make no difference whether D mistakenly thought his partner was 14 or mistakenly thought the legal age of consent was 13, for in either case he chose lawful sex. While D may be subjected to noncriminal penalties for a negligent mistake, he is not liable to punishment as a criminal, for he has made no choice from which a right denial may be inferred.

The defence of insanity as circumscribed by the rules in *M'Naghten's case* perfectly reflects the legal retributivist view of what constitutes culpability and exculpation.[39] First, insanity is not treated as necessarily depriving human beings of the capacity for free choice (hence for basic responsibility), because this capacity—for nondetermination by causal laws—is too thin to be affected by cognitive and emotional disorders short of advanced dementia and automatism. So the mentally disordered are not generally regarded as infants to whom judgments of guilt or innocence do not apply; they are not, for example, exempted from the criminal process upon a psychiatric diagnosis of clinical insanity, as infants are exempted just because of their age. Nor are they (except in some American jurisdictions) exculpated for reasons that would not be exculpatory for other conscious agents with a capacity for free choice, for example because of "irresistible impulse" or incapacity to conform one's behaviour to the law. The capacity for free choice is just the capacity to conform.[40] Rather, they are treated as agents who can be culpable for their choices and who are exculpated only if their disorder engenders cognitive mistakes that would be exculpatory absent their disorder.[41] So if D kills

---

[38] I deal below with the objection that the thinking Agent would define consent only as publicly given.
[39] [1843–60] All ER 229.
[40] *R v Borg* [1969] CCC (4th) 262; contrast Model Penal Code, s. 4.01. However, the fact that capacity is present leaves open the question whether an extraordinary difficulty to control impulses because of mental disease might afford a partial defence of diminished responsibility mitigating crimes carrying a mandatory sentence.
[41] Hence it is a mistake, both as a matter of normative theory and legal description, to equate criminal capacity (or basic responsibility) with a higher-order capacity to deliberate with respect to reasons for action and to be responsive to reasons; see RA Duff, *Answering for Crime* (Oxford: Hart Publishing, 2007), 38–43; John Gardner, *Offences and Defences* (Oxford: Oxford University Press, 2007), 181–5. This view, by treating insanity as negating basic responsibility, would transform the insanity defence from a plea that one made no culpable choice into an admission that one is subhuman. It is enough for basic responsibility that the defendant is aware of the causality of his choices. In Chapter 8 I'll argue that their inability to respond to reasons is justification for detaining the innocent insane for prophylactic reasons, not for denying their basic responsibility.

V delusionally thinking V is a snake, he has made no choice from which a right denial can be implied, and so the mistake is exculpatory. So too if D kills V thinking that he (D) is a public executioner carrying out the verdict of a court. But if D kills V under the delusion that he is guaranteed protection against penal consequences by a cosmic shield or that he is a god to whom the law does not apply, his choice is culpable regardless of his delusion, for a right denial is imputable to it.[42]

Just as mistakes of law may exculpate when, exceptionally, the thinking Agent would not necessarily know the law (for example, pertaining to property) determining when a boundary has been crossed, so may they when the thinking Agent with the defendant's beliefs would consider that a right infringement is tragically justified, as in the case of a public necessity. So if the defendant delusionally believes in the existence of exigent circumstances that the thinking Agent would consider justify a wrong, he has not chosen culpably even though he has mistaken a wrong action for a right one—that is, has made a mistake of law. And this is so both in theory and in law; for the *M'Naghten* rules exculpate not only those unable because of mental disease to understand the nature and effect of their actions, but also those incapable of knowing that what they are doing is something they ought not to do.

Some regard the latter reason for not punishing the insane as relevant to something more basic than the existence of a culpable choice, since no other adults are exculpated because they could not know right from wrong; knowledge of right and wrong is rather imputed to them. An incapacity to know right from wrong seems to make a culpable choice impossible rather than simply absent, as it does for the infant. That is, it negates a precondition of imputing culpable choices to the defendant, for an individual cannot impliedly *deny* the validity of rights if he or she does not impliedly know the *purported* basis of rights in human agency. The insanity defence, on this view, belongs not with mistake, but with infancy. Someone who pleads it denies his *capacity* to make a culpable choice.

Now, it may be that some mental disorders (dementia, for example) infantilize the sufferer to the point that he is no longer aware of his agency. Such an individual indeed lacks criminal capacity, for he lacks the self-consciousness that allows us (a) to ascribe his behaviour and its results to a free choice and (b) to impute to his understanding the thinking Agent's knowledge of right and wrong. Such an individual will also be unable to understand the nature and point of the trial process, and so will be unable to give a hypothetical legitimating assent to any judgment rendered against him. For this reason he will be exempted from trial.

However, it cannot be said *a priori* of all mentally disordered individuals that their disease is incapacitating to the extreme of robbing them of their basic humanity. Moreover, if this were the type of defendant envisaged by the insanity defence, would it make sense for a judge or jury to decide the question of capacity to know right from wrong after a trial instead of a team of psychiatrists after a series of examinations? The fact that the clinically insane defendant is tried under

---

[42] *R v Abbey* [1982] 2 SCR 24.

specific criteria for *legal* insanity reflects the fact that, unlike the infant, his capacity for guilt or innocence is assumed, and the inquiry is into whether his choice was actually culpable or not, given his beliefs. Sometimes his choice will be nonculpable because he laboured under a delusion that he was performing an act quite different from the one he was actually performing. But sometimes it will be nonculpable because, looking at the world from the defendant's deluded perspective, the thinking Agent would conclude that in this case a wrong is justified by public necessity and so would choose a justified act. Thus, no denial of right can be imputed to the defendant's choice. To be sure, the defendant, in erroneously believing his act was justified in the real world, has made a mistake of law; but we have seen (in the "colour of right" doctrine) that if a mistake of law blocks the inference from the defendant's choice to a denial of rights, it is no less exculpatory than a mistake of fact. Accordingly, that an insane defendant may be exculpated for an incapacity to know that his act was prohibited is no reason to think that the defence of insanity belongs with infancy rather than with mistake.

The difficult case, however, is one where the deluded defendant thinks himself justified in a wrong by a standard transcendent of the legal order. Of this kind is the case of Hadfield who shot at the King in order to fulfill a divine commandment to sacrifice himself to avert the world's destruction.[43] This type of case presents difficulties because, though the defendant was hallucinating when he committed a crime, the thinking Agent with his perceptions chose to subordinate the public authority of law to a private belief in a higher law, which is to deny the reality of rights. Indeed, since crime on the legal retributivist theory is just the claim to a permission to act unlimited by respect for others' agency—that is, a claim of right to do wrong—the religiously inspired accused's plea in defence looks more like an admission of culpability.

Nevertheless, there may be a way of distinguishing the psychotic who knowingly commits a wrong in obedience to a divine voice he "hears" from the fanatic who subordinates public rights of agency to a private religious inspiration. If the defendant's disorder is of a kind (a matter of expert evidence) that deprives him of the ability to distinguish between a private inspiration or dictate of conscience and a public command from the sovereign of sovereigns, then he is in the same position as the man who kills in the insane belief that he is the King's public executioner. His choice is then nonculpable, for no claim of permission to a liberty unfettered by law is imputable to it.

4. A Response to Objections

In this section I discuss whether the version of subjectivism outlined in the preceding pages is vulnerable to the strongest objections that have been directed

---

[43] *Hadfield's Trial* (1800) 27 St Tr 1281.

against a subjective fault threshold for criminal liability. I will not deal with the objection (associated with HLA Hart) that one can be morally responsible for an outcome one has not chosen, for the response to this objection is the same as the one given to the character theory of *mens rea*: to be morally responsible for an unlawful outcome is not yet to deserve the infringement of one's right to agency that judicial punishment distinctively entails.

Subjectivism and mistake of law

One persistent objection against subjectivism has been raised by Oliver Wendell Holmes and George Fletcher and has lately been reformulated by Arthur Ripstein.[44] It is that a consistent subjectivism is committed to abolishing the well-settled distinction between mistakes of fact and mistakes of law and to treating even negligent mistakes of law as exculpatory. This is so, argue the critics, because the subjectivist requires for criminal liability a conscious choice to do wrong or to break the law, so that a defendant unaware, even through moral blindness or negligence, of the legal prohibition must be acquitted. But this position obviously undermines the authority of the legal standard and runs contrary to the positive law of all Western legal systems. Hence subjectivism must be discarded as offensive to "basic sensibilities of justice".[45]

The classical subjectivist position I have delineated is immune to this criticism. For while it softens the dichotomy between mistakes of fact and mistakes of law, it does so only to the extent that the positive law itself acknowledges, in the doctrine of colour of right, an exception to the rule that a mistake of law does not exculpate. Moreover, far from abolishing the rule, classical subjectivism provides theoretical support for it insofar as the rule applies to the sphere of crimes and leaves it standing in the sphere of public welfare offences. In the sphere of crimes, classical subjectivism does not require for criminal liability that the empirical agent consciously choose to do wrong; on the contrary, it treats the thinking Agent's knowledge of the rightful limit of action in the free will and ownership of others as imputable to the empirical agent. What is required, rather, is that the empirical agent choose to interfere with a person's freedom of choice; reason then imputes to this choice a denial that rights to free choice exist. This is enough to break the objectivist's lances, for on the classical subjectivist position, the defendant's ignorance of his wrong will not exculpate him if the thinking Agent in his shoes would be choosing a wrong; and it will positively *inculpate* him if his ignorance is shown in an explicit challenge to the normativity of rights such as might be expressed in the claim, "I am above the law" or "right is the interest of the stronger".

---

[44] Oliver Wendell Holmes, *The Common Law*, ed. M Howe (Cambridge, Mass: Belknap Press, 1963), 41–43; George Fletcher, 'The Theory of Criminal Negligence: A Comparative Analysis,' (1971) 119 *University of Pennsylvania Law Review* 401; Ripstein, *Equality, Responsibility, and the Law*, 179–214.

[45] Fletcher, 'The Theory of Criminal Negligence,' 422.

It is true, however, that where knowledge of the law cannot be imputed to the empirical agent as a matter of reason, a mistake of law can exculpate if it precludes an inference of a right denial from the agent's choice. So, if the defendant took or damaged another's property believing it was his own, he is exculpated from theft or mischief; or if he defended with reasonable force what he mistakenly thought was his property against someone legally entitled to possess it, he is exculpated. But these exceptions to the rule that mistakes of law do not exculpate are those recognized by the positive law itself.[46]

Further, the subjectivist position I have described leaves the rule regarding mistakes of law untouched in the welfare context. This is so because the retributivist argument for subjectivism applies only to right infringements or to what are called "true crimes"; it does not apply to welfare offences punishable by noncriminal penalties, for the logical circuit between an intentional doing of what the law forbids and coercibility is not initiated where the law furthers a public goal rather than protecting a right of agency (though it would be by an intentional breach of the law). In Chapter 5, I argue that negligence is the appropriate fault threshold for noncriminal penalties, so that negligent mistakes, whether of fact or law, will not excuse (a defence of mistake of law would be available only against a separate offence of knowingly breaching the statute).

Arthur Ripstein has mounted a critique specifically directed against the classical version of subjectivism I have sought to revive. He observes that classical subjectivism maintains a distinction between mistakes of law as not exculpatory and mistakes of fact as exculpatory by imputing to empirical agents the thinking Agent's knowledge of the wrongfulness of acts interfering with other agents' capacity to act from freely chosen ends. That knowledge comes from grasping the self-contradictoriness of a claim of right based on agency to a liberty disrespectful of agency. This idea, Ripstein argues, raises three problems. First,

> ... [A]ny concept of respect for the agency of others thin enough to be presupposed by all action will be incompatible with every action. On the face of it, the criminal who decides on reflection that his commitment to his gang is more important than any commitment not to take the lives of strangers has done something awful, but has not contradicted himself. If we presume (as the argument requires) that the criminal's commitment to respecting agency as such flows from the fact that he acts for reasons he recognizes, then whatever he decides to do, he will end up honouring it. (Or if he does not, his act will show that it is after all possible to act without that commitment.) In order to show that some implicit commitment has been violated, the commitment must both be implicit in every act, and yet violated in criminal acts. The question for the subjectivist is not whether or not the agent could be made aware of the law, but whether he was aware of it at the time of the offense.[47]

This objection confuses throughout the thinking with the empirical agent. The agent whose commitment can alone be self-contradictory is the thinking

---

[46] Criminal Code, RSC 1985 c. C–46, ss. 39(1), 322(1), 429(2).
[47] Ripstein, *Equality, Responsibility, and the Law,* 186.

Agent shorn of all commitments but the one to liberty. That agent's commitment to liberty is self-contradictory when it lays claim to a liberty disrespectful of the liberty of other agents. The criminal who prefers his gang loyalty to respect for others' freedom is an empirical agent, and it is obviously true that no single empirical commitment of his can be self-contradictory. But in giving effect to his preference in a wrongful action, the criminal implicitly (i.e. for the thinking Agent in his shoes) acts from an *a priori* commitment (to a right claim based on agency to a liberty nonrespectful of agency) that is self-contradictorily destructive of rights; and this right denial can be imputed to the criminal insofar as he is an agent. Further, the fatal presumption that Ripstein attributes to the subjectivist is one that the subjectivist will certainly disclaim. The subjectivist's argument need not presume that "the criminal's commitment to respecting agency as such flows from the fact that he acts from reasons he recognizes", nor does it in fact presume any such thing. Rather, the subjectivist's argument presumes that the thinking Agent's commitment to respecting agency as such flows from its laying claim to a liberty to act, period. From this it hardly follows that the empirical agent will always end up honouring its commitment to respect agency whatever it does; for, first, it may have no such commitment, and second, it may act for empirical ends in a way that contradicts its *a priori* right claim to action. Thus the subjectivist meets the condition of success Ripstein identifies: "in order to show that some implicit commitment has been violated, the commitment must be both implicit in every act and yet violated in criminal acts." The meaning of the last sentence in the long passage reproduced above is obscure. The question for the subjectivist is not whether the agent was aware of the law at the time of the offence, because the thinking Agent's knowledge of the law proscribing wrongs is imputable to it.

The second problem allegedly faced by the classical subjectivist, according to Ripstein,

is that even if we grant that all agents are implicitly aware of the conditions of their agency, and that that implicit awareness implicitly commits them to a recognition of the wrongfulness of certain acts, that awareness needs to be made explicit. Given the subjectivist's readiness to excuse mere inadvertence about matters of fact, why not also excuse inadvertence about one's implicit commitments?[48]

This argument too rests on a misunderstanding. The subjectivist's readiness to "excuse" inadvertence about matters of fact does not flow from a belief that only advertent wrongdoing is culpable. It flows from the proposition that a right denial cannot be imputed to an empirical agent's choice if, on the facts as perceived by the agent, it did not choose to interfere with another agent's capacity for self-actuation. This reason for allowing mistakes of fact to exculpate has no general application to mistakes of law, nor any application at all to "inadvertence about one's implicit commitments". If the agent did choose to interfere with another's agency, then a

[48] Ibid, 186.

right denial can be imputed to its choice (because it is an agent) whether or not it was empirically aware that such an interference is wrong. Indeed, since it is an agent who (unlike the infant) *can* discern right from wrong, its mistaking an intentional interference for a permitted act is just the right denial that constitutes culpability. So why would the subjectivist treat such a mistake as grounds for exculpation?

The third difficulty for classical subjectivism, Ripstein says, "goes deepest".[49]

In order to make unreasonable mistakes of fact exculpate, but unreasonable mistakes of law inculpate, the subjectivist must provide a conception of agency that does two seemingly incompatible things. It must both incorporate some account of reciprocity into the very concept of agency, yet at the same time remain monadic. It must incorporate reciprocity because if it does not, the conditions of agency will fail to implicate the protected interests of others. If it fails to incorporate the interests of others, it will lack the grounds to distinguish mistakes of fact from mistakes of law, because the very possibility of acting will not implicitly include knowing the rights of others. At the same time, the account of agency must not be too reciprocal, for otherwise it will incorporate reasonableness tests, that is, tests that seek to be fair to both parties in situations of risk. For the argument from agency to lead to subjectivist conclusions, agents must know the rights of others and those rights must not include the right to have others only violate their apparent interests on reasonable grounds. No amount of analysis of the concept of intention could establish such a thing.[50]

What Ripstein is saying here is that the idea of mutual recognition (or reciprocity, in his language) that delimits valid permissions to act must also draw the boundary of the self in reference to which a boundary crossing is determined. This means that the self's boundaries must fall out of a determination of what is a reasonable impingement or imposition of risk as between two parties in interaction, so that a boundary is crossed, not by any imposition, but only by an unreasonable one. Classical subjectivists, Ripstein argues, are ambivalent about the role of reciprocity in drawing boundaries to permissible action. On the one hand, they must be committed to the view that, conceptually, valid claims to individual liberty fall out of mutual respect for liberty, for otherwise the thinking Agent could not know the wrongfulness of acts disrespectful of another's liberty; but on the other hand, they are committed to atomism in drawing the self's boundary outside of interaction with others and thus independently of a standard of reasonable impositions. This is why the classical subjectivist can speak of an unreasonable belief in consent (i.e. a belief held despite outward behaviour that a reasonable person would interpret as nonconsent) as a mistake of fact about what is going on in the private mind of the victim; for the subjectivist, the victim's monadic will determines when her consent to bodily contact has been given, and what she inwardly wills is a fact about which one can be mistaken against all outward evidence. The monadic perspective also explains why the classical subjectivist can treat unreasonable mistakes about consent as exculpatory: if the complainant's monadic will determines when her consent to bodily contact has been given, it must be open

---

[49] Ibid, 187. [50] Ibid, 187–8.

to the defendant to say (subject, of course, to an evidentiary burden) that he was honestly mistaken about her inner will, even if his belief was held in the face of clear manifestations of resistance or without any effort to ascertain her will; and if in fact the defendant did not choose to touch (or to risk touching) the complainant against her will, then no right denial is imputable to him.

Ripstein's own view, however, is that whether a person consents to bodily contact is determined in the same way that consent to a contract is determined—interpersonally. So, if a reasonable person would interpret the complainant's words or actions as consent, then she has consented in law, no matter what lay in her inner will—a reasonable belief in consent cannot be mistaken. Conversely, if a reasonable person would interpret her manifestations as nonconsent, then she has not consented, and there is no room for an inquiry into her private thoughts. Therefore, someone who claims a mistaken belief in consent despite clear manifestations of nonconsent or despite a failure to make reasonable inquiries (i.e. someone who has made an unreasonable mistake about consent) has made a mistake about what consent is; he thinks consent is a matter of one's inner will rather than one's public manifestations. This, however, is a mistake of law. And since he is making a mistake about what consent in law is, to exculpate him for this mistake is to subvert the authority of law and to allow the defendant to dictate when the complainant consents. The subjectivist, concludes Ripstein, in allowing an unreasonable mistake about consent to exculpate, gives exculpatory force to a mistake of law.[51]

Now it is partly true that the classical subjectivist is monadic when it comes to drawing the boundaries of the self. I say partly, because the subjectivist is monadic in drawing some boundaries but not others, though this discrimination reflects (I'll argue) attention to nuance rather than ambivalence. The self's body, the subjectivist believes, is a boundary that is set prior to and outside of interaction. As a consequence, there is no latitude for legally permissible but unwanted incursions on the body based on reasonable apprehensions of consent. The subjectivist, however, is not monadic when it comes to drawing boundaries against unwanted disturbances to the enjoyment of one's property or against injuries resulting from the risks attendant on action in the world. Here boundaries are determined by standards of reasonableness.

Why the difference? One could say that personal autonomy requires that the agent determine alone when its consent to bodily contact is given rather than handing this decision over to a meeting between agents. But there is a more conceptual reason. To use one's property and to act in the world is necessarily to create noises, smells, and risks, so that for my right to liberty to coexist with yours, there must be space for reasonable mutual impingements. But my self-possession can coexist with your self-possession without allowing scope for unwanted bodily incursions based on reasonable apprehensions of consent, because self-possession requires no external action. My body is openly mine without my having to take

---

[51] Ibid, 209–14.

action to occupy it publicly. But because a person's body is hers absolutely, consent to bodily contact is determined from the subjective perspective of the person whose body it is. If in her mind she was not consenting, then she was not consenting, regardless of how the reasonable person would interpret her behaviour. But the corollary to this is that the defendant must be permitted to say that he was mistaken about what was going on in her mind whatever her outward behaviour (though the unreasonableness of the belief will be strong evidence against its sincerity) and despite his failure to make inquiries. And if this was an honest mistake without advertence or wilful blindness to the risk of nonconsent, then his choice was not to touch her or to risk touching her without her consent, and so no right denial is imputable to his choice. Of course, he may be subjected to a noncriminal penalty aimed at educating him and others to sexual communication undistorted by stereotypes; but he may not be punished for a criminal assault.

So the dispute between Ripstein and the classical subjectivist comes down to this: who is right about the boundary of the self's body? Is that boundary drawn relationally or nonrelationally? Is there scope for legally permissible unwanted incursions on the body as there is scope for legally permissible impositions of risk in acting? Is there room for a defence of mistake of fact as to whether someone has consented to bodily contact or are all mistaken beliefs in consent mistakes of law?

To say, as Ripstein does, that consent to bodily contact is determined relationally is to say that my control over my body is not absolute *vis-à-vis* other persons but is limited by their qualified liberty to use my body against my subjective will. This implication is surely at odds with the liberal premise of individual inviolability. Further, the common law denies that consent is relational even with regard to possession (not enjoyment) of an ordinary item of property. If I take your Lexus from your driveway under the reasonable but mistaken belief that you gifted it to me (you said, handing me the keys, "take the car in my driveway—it's yours", thinking it was the Lada), I do not get to keep the car. If I enter your land uninvited, you can eject me even if I reasonably believe I had just bought it (because of a clerical error on the deed). In other words, civil liability for an interference with proprietary sovereignty (not for harm) is strict.[52] Perhaps Ripstein thinks this settled law is mistaken. But if not, then his relational view of consent to bodily contact requires us to believe that tort law affords greater protection to land and chattels than it does to the body.

Further, I'll pose two cases where I believe the intuition against the relational view of consent to bodily contact and in favour of the monadic view is overpowering. Suppose D is about to force himself on V, who has recently broken off a relationship with D. V thinks to herself that, if D knows he is raping her, he might very well kill her to remove the only witness to his crime. So she resolves out of fear for her life to feign reconciliation and consent, and she thinks that her self-preservation

---

[52] Restatement (Second) of Torts, s. 217: "It is not necessary that the actor should know or have reason to know that [his] intermeddling is a violation of the possessory rights of another."

depends on her being as convincing as possible. Suppose her pretence would be convincing to any former lover and that she succeeds in masking her fear. I do not believe that anyone would comfortably say that V has consented to intercourse in this case, but that is what Ripstein's relational view of consent requires us to say.

Second, suppose (counterfactually) that in *Morgan* the husband's story to his friends was true, that his wife had indeed invited intercourse with his friends simulating rape and that she was a willing participant in the game throughout. The relational view of consent requires us to say that no consent is given here and that the defendants' "mistaken" belief in consent is a nonexculpatory mistake of law. By contrast, the monadic view yields the sensible result in both cases (no consent in the first, consent in the second). But if consent to bodily contact is indeed determined outside of relation with another, then an unreasonable but honest belief in consent is an exculpatory mistake of fact, not a mistake of law.[53]

Subjectivism and practical indifference

RA Duff has fashioned an intricate argument countering the position that criminal liability ought to require a conscious choice to do that which is proscribed as wrong, or a conscious choice to risk what is so proscribed.[54] The argument is meant to establish that inadvertent recklessness—a failure to notice and avoid an obvious and unreasonable risk one had the capacity to notice—can sometimes supply the blameworthiness needed to justify punishment. Duff's strategy is to determine, first, what makes an agent blameworthy in what he calls the paradigm cases of responsible agency and then to see whether penumbral cases of responsible agency, namely advertent recklessness (acting in the face of a foreseen risk of a wrongful outcome) and inadvertent recklessness, can be brought within the same reasoning. The paradigm cases are "intended agency", where the agent aims to bring about a wrongful outcome, and "intentional agency", where the agent pursues an object by means that will certainly bring about a wrongful outcome but where that outcome is not itself the aim of the action. Duff's argument proceeds as follows.

If the agent's choice of a proscribed outcome underlies criminal responsibility for outcomes in the two paradigm cases, then advertent recklessness is the only kind of recklessness we can punish, since only the advertently reckless person chooses to risk a wrongful outcome. But choice, while it underlies the paradigm of intended agency, does not necessarily define intentional agency, where the agent produces an outcome it knew would certainly come about as a result of doing what

---

[53] Does the monadic view of consent to bodily contact collapse the distinction between choice and wish? No, because there is room for the distinction even within the agent's private perspective. Thus, in the case of the rape victim fearful that her assailant will murder her if he knows he is raping her, we can intelligibly say she is choosing to feign acceptance while wishing she could manifest her rejection. To map the distinction between choice and wish onto that between the external and inward dimensions of the self is to settle a normative question by definitional fiat.

[54] Duff, *Intention, Agency, and Criminal Liability*, 139–42.

it intends. The reason for blameworthy responsibility in the case of intentional agency, Duff argues, is the attitude of indifference toward the victim's important interests that it shows. The agent is willing to sacrifice the victim's important human interests for its own particular ends. But if that is why we punish agents for unlawful outcomes produced through intentional agency, then we can also punish agents for unlawful outcomes they produce through inadvertent recklessness, because (and to the extent that) they also manifest a callous indifference to the victim's important human interests. And since we are punishing agents who manifest this attitude of indifference, we are still subjectivists about *mens rea*, argues Duff, albeit not subjectivists in the classical sense of requiring a conscious choice to run a prohibited risk. Choosing to run an unreasonable risk of a wrongful outcome is only one way of manifesting indifference toward whether it materializes; one may also display this attitude through inadvertent recklessness. Thus, criminal liability based on inadvertent recklessness can be defended on subjectivist grounds, provided that we broaden the notion of the subjective to include an attitude of practical indifference to the important human interests of others.[55]

Duff emphasizes that the attitude of practical indifference is not an empirical psychological state, for which the outward act is evidence. Rather, it is a practical attitude constituted by conduct that fails to consider a human being's important interests when the danger to those interests is obvious. We should say that the attitude is reflected or manifested in the conduct rather than evidenced by it. However, not all failures to notice or avoid obvious risks constitute practical indifference. Some are not culpable at all, because the agent lacked the capacity to appreciate the risk; and some are blameworthy but not criminally culpable because the agent failed to notice the risk for reasons other than indifference—for example, from an undervaluation of the victim's interests in comparison with its own. This Duff calls gross negligence.

Duff comes to practical indifference as the unifying theme of culpable agency by a curious logic. Choice, he says, characterizes intended agency, but there is an ambiguity about what constitutes culpability in intentional agency: it could be that the agent chooses to bring about the outcome it is certain will occur, or it could be that the agent is willing to ignore another's important human interests for the sake of its ends. Duff opts for the second of these possibilities for no other reason than that an attitude of practical indifference toward others seems highly blameworthy and condemnable. He then reinterprets all the other cases of responsible agency, including intended agency, as instances of practical indifference and then brings inadvertent recklessness into the tent.

There is, however, no connection between the blameworthiness of practical indifference and judicial punishment involving an infringement of rights. Nothing tells us that practical indifference deserves judicial punishment as distinct from other kinds of social response to blameworthy conduct. So Duff's

---

[55] Ibid, 157, 163.

reason for opting for practical indifference rather than choice as the key to culpable agency in the case of intentional agency is not a good one. There is, however, a good reason for opting for choice. Choice of a proscribed outcome is culpable in the case of intended agency because it is the only orientation toward the outcome to which a denial of rights is imputable, and this imputation is what makes the coercion of the agent self-willed. Intentional agency is also a culpable agency, because, though the agent does not aim at the proscribed outcome, it knows the outcome will certainly occur, and so it chooses the outcome, thus implicitly denying the validity of rights, including its own. Advertent recklessness and wilful blindness are also culpable as implicit right denials authorizing punishment, because the agent chooses a wrongful risk. And that is where the logic stops. The inadvertently reckless agent does not choose the unreasonable risk, and so no right denial is implicit in its choice, however obnoxiously narcissistic its character may be in being oblivious to the important interests of others.

Because Duff makes the moral blameworthiness of practical indifference the key to criminal liability, he has no way of stopping his logic from extending past practical indifference to gross negligence and even to ordinary negligence, assuming the agent has a capacity to appreciate the risk. He distinguishes practical indifference from gross negligence on the basis that the practically indifferent agent does not care about others' important human interests, whereas the grossly negligent agent, in its preoccupation with its own ends, simply undervalues those interests while overvaluing its own.[56] Yet these attitudes are surely gradations along a continuum of moral blameworthiness rather than qualitatively different kinds. They differ, as Duff admits, only in degree, whereas one needs a categorical distinction between culpable and nonculpable instances of moral blameworthiness to be able to attach criminal liability to one but *not* to the others. Ordinary negligence, where the agent has the capacity to appreciate and avoid the risk, is likewise on the continuum, and so the distinction between crime and tort or between crime and regulatory offence disappears.[57] Indeed, it would seem that any plausible rationale for punishing practical indifference (whether moral blameworthiness, deterrence, or reform) will also justify punishing with

[56] Ibid, 164–5.
[57] Larry Alexander's idea of "insufficient concern" as the unifying idea of culpability is also vulnerable to this slide into negligence. Alexander wants to unify culpability under advertent recklessness, but since the "basic moral vice" underlying culpability is the insufficient concern for others' interests shown by imposing unjustified risks, it is unclear why this lack of regard is not also shown by unreasonable mistakes (caused, say, by partiality to oneself) concerning when one's interests sufficiently outweigh those of others to justify imposing risks on them. Alexander believes that negligence is morally nonculpable even if the agent had the mental capacity to notice and appreciate the unjustified risk, because one has no control over one's absent-mindedness unless one foresaw it. But why should this be true absolutely given that someone might fail to appreciate an unjustifiable risk, not from absent-mindedness, but from a narcissistic tendency to overvalue his interests and undervalue others'? Even if forgetting or failing to notice is never blameworthy (a doubtful proposition in itself, since they might be caused by self-absorption), negligence needn't always take these forms. It may consist in misvaluing the interests at stake because of insufficient concern. See Larry Alexander, 'Insufficient Concern: A Unified Conception of Criminal Culpability,' (2000) 88 *California Law Review*, 931.

lesser sentences gross negligence and negligence as criminal forms of fault. What is needed, therefore, is a justification for punishing criminal negligence that will not extend to ordinary negligence. But the only such justification of which I am aware is that in criminal negligence, the actor chooses to impose (what it knows or suspects is) an unreasonable risk of interference with another's agency, hence implicitly denies rights of agency, including its own.

Aware of the icy slope on which he has trodden, Duff tries to rescue practical indifference by distinguishing it from other forms of inadvertent imposition of wrongful risk. The practically indifferent agent, he says, is unaware of a specific risk, for example, of death, whereas the negligent agent is merely unaware of a general risk to safety or health.[58] This distinction, however, is difficult to fathom. Specific and general risk can distinguish different forms of advertence (I foresaw the danger to her welfare but I didn't foresee death, whereas you foresaw death), but how can they distinguish different forms of inadvertence? To be inadvertent with respect to a specific risk is either to be inadvertent with respect to risk generally or to be advertent to risk generally but not to the specific risk. The latter possibility is ruled out, because the practically indifferent agent who is inadvertently reckless is not advertent to general risk either, for otherwise he would be indistinguishable from the advertently reckless agent; and the former possibility does not distinguish the practically indifferent agent from the negligent one. So, for Duff's distinction (between practical indifference and ordinary negligence) to make sense, it would have to be possible for the practically indifferent agent to be at once inadvertent to risk generally and specifically inadvertent to a particular risk. But this is not possible (try not to think about artichokes).

Jeremy Horder has sought to repair this flaw in Duff's reasoning by showing how practical indifference of a certain kind can be brought within the classical subjectivist criterion of criminal culpability.[59] Horder distinguishes between weak and strong practical indifference. Weakly indifferent agents do not deny that another agent's agency interests should be taken into account in one's practical reasoning as to what course of action to take. They simply tend in their haste to overvalue their personal interests and to be thoughtless regarding the other's agency interests. If the risk to the other's agency interests were brought to their attention, their practical reasoning would change and so too their conduct. By contrast, strongly indifferent agents deny the weight of the other's agency interests altogether; even if the risk to those interests were brought to their attention, they would still prefer their own particular ends. Accordingly, Horder argues, in denying weight to the other's agency interests, strongly indifferent agents implicitly deny the validity of rights, and so invite punishment in the sense demanded by classical subjectivism even though their recklessness is inadvertent.[60]

---

[58] Duff, *Intention, Agency, and Criminal Liability*, 165.
[59] Jeremy Horder, 'Gross Negligence and Criminal Culpability,' (1997) 47 *University of Toronto Law Journal*, 495.
[60] Ibid, 502–9.

Horder's effort is valiant, but unfortunately it falls short. This is so because strong indifference is now ascertained by means of a counterfactual situation. The agent's action itself tells us nothing about whether the agent is strongly or weakly indifferent to the victim's agency interests. Of course, if the agent was advertently reckless, we could say that it did in fact choose an unreasonable risk of a wrongful outcome and was thus strongly indifferent toward another's agency interests. But if the agent did not advert to the risk, we can determine strong indifference only by imagining a hypothetical scenario; if it had known of the high risk to the victim's important human interests, would the agent have chosen the risk? But this is now a question about the agent's underlying character, not about its culpability for this action in particular. In this action, it did not choose the risk. And if punishment is to be directed against a character who is strongly indifferent toward others' important interests, why require a wrongful action at all? Suppose that, in acting, the agent did not bother to consider the likely impact of its action on the agency interests of others, but that its action was not unreasonably risky. Yet someone was hurt. Why not ask: if the action had been unreasonably risky and if the agent had adverted to the risk, would it have chosen the risk? If so, the agent is strongly indifferent and criminally culpable, on Horder's theory, for an injury that was not even wrongful. The *actus reus* requirement of culpability drops out, because the agent's action cannot be interpreted as a sign of strong as opposed to weak indifference, and so it becomes a contingent piece of evidence that can be buttressed or countered by evidence of what the agent would have done in the counterfactual situation. Duff avoided this problem by emphasizing that inadvertently reckless action is not evidence of a practically indifferent attitude lying behind the action but practical indifference itself. But this is precisely what one cannot say about strong indifference in particular. The only *action* that manifests strong indifference is an advertently reckless one.

5. Conclusion

Judicial punishment is not simply an instance of expressing moral blame. Alone among other forms of censure, judicial punishment violates rights of agency; and there is no connection between moral blameworthiness and liability to a right violation in virtue of which one could say that the former deserves the latter. What is required for criminal desert is a specifically legal sense of culpability that connects wrongdoing with the coercibility of the wrongdoer. Culpability of that sort is given only by a free choice to which a denial of rights of agency is logically imputable. But the only choices to which a denial of rights of agency is imputable are choices to interfere or to risk interfering with another agent's capacity to act from freely chosen ends and choices to break the law. Accordingly, the defendant's free choice to interfere or to risk interfering with another person's agency or to break the law is the level of fault without which coercion of the person is external violence indistinguishable from the criminal's rather than just punishment self-willed by the criminal and so consonant with his inviolability.

From this perspective, the oft-heard argument that negligence might reflect egocentric attitudes worthy in some cases of public condemnation is true but beside the point. No doubt the egregious negligence of a competent actor is blameworthy in a moral sense relevant to the assessment of its character and so deservedly attracts the censure of the community. Doubtless, too, an actor who failed to advert to a high risk of interference where it had the capacity to do so is morally responsible for any harm it causes, civilly liable for damages, and (as we'll see) publicly liable to noncriminal penalties that are in their nature disincentives rather than punishments. However, no blameworthy state of mind short of an intention to interfere with another's agency or advertent recklessness with respect to the risk of interfering has juridical in addition to moral significance as a denial of right; hence no other blameworthy disposition is culpable in the sense of exhibiting a tight connection with judicial coercion that renders that particular consequence specifically deserved, leaving no room for the instrumentalist manipulation of the person.

Once the culpable mind is understood in this way, exculpatory conditions (not excusing ones) such as mistake of fact, colour of right, and legal insanity can be explained as conditions that block an inference from the defendant's choice to a denial of rights. Involuntariness and infancy, because they negate choice and free choice, respectively, *a fortiori* preclude a right-denying free choice. Accordingly, exculpatory defences ought to be structured so as to allow any honest misperception that blocks the requisite inference to exculpate regardless of its unreasonableness. Negligent mistakes can be penalized as lesser included public welfare offences with monetary disincentives.

The subjectivist position on criminal fault delineated in this chapter can deflect the criticisms perennially levelled against subjectivism by those who equate it with weaker versions. Classical subjectivism does not judge the defendant solely by his own understanding of his deed's import; it does not apply to public welfare offences; it does not entail a subjective fault requirement for criminal responsibility for the results of wrongdoing; nor does it require more inroads into the rule that mistake of law does not exculpate than the positive law already implicitly recognizes in the colour of right defence to property crimes.

3

Culpable Action

In this chapter I propose an account of the culpable action (*actus reus*) requirement of criminal liability and elaborate its implications for certain perennial trouble spots in the theory and practice of criminal law: whether and to what extent criminal liability should extend to omissions, to inchoate criminal endeavours (attempts, counselling, conspiracy), and to statuses (being in the possession of, being a member of, etc.). I should emphasize, however, that what follows is an account, not of the so-called act requirement of the penal law, but of the *culpable action* requirement of the *criminal* law. We shall see that, if by "act" is meant a voluntary bodily movement, there is no such thing as an act requirement of the penal law, either as a matter of normative theory or positive law. Both voluntary at-rest states and involuntary motion will turn out to be culpable (deserving of punishment) in some cases, and both voluntary at-rest states and statuses will be fair game, given appropriate constraints, for penal disincentives under public welfare statutes.[1] However, I do not deal with nonculpable offences here. This chapter's focus is on the culpable action requirement of liability to judicial punishment.

Because, however, actions such as shooting or hitting are built on acts such as moving a finger or swinging an arm, the term "culpable action requirement" might suggest that only voluntary bodily movements can be culpable. To avoid this suggestion, I shall have to employ some unusual terminology. There being no convenient English word naming the genus of which, in the context of a law of punishment, acts, omissions, and involuntary motion are species, I'll henceforth use the term "*actus*" to denote any externalization of a culpable choice, whether by an act, voluntary motionlessness, or involuntary motion, and the term "*actus reus*" to denote the kind of externalization necessary and sufficient for criminal liability. Thus, an account of the *actus* requirement in criminal law (or of the "criminal *actus*") is a theory about why an externalization of the agent's culpable choice is essential to criminal liability or why an evidenced culpable intention is not enough. An account of

---

[1] By voluntary at-rest states I mean something in between at-rest states generally (of which death and unconsciousness are instances) and intentional forbearances from X (which exclude negligent omissions). I mean the motionlessness of an agent who had a choice whether or not to move. I believe that only such motionlessness can sensibly be characterized as an "omission" to X, but I need not enter the essentially semantic debate on this point between Michael Moore and George Fletcher; see Moore, *Placing Blame* (Oxford: Clarendon Press, 1997), 262–6; Fletcher, 'On the Moral Irrelevance of Bodily Movements,' (1994) *University of Pennsylvania Law Review*, 142, 143–53.

the *actus reus* is a theory about what sort of externalization is normatively required for liability. Of course, these two accounts are connected, for an answer to "why" will also yield an answer to "what". To anticipate, I argue that the sort of externalization normatively (and, generally speaking, positively too) required for liability to judicial punishment is a public manifestation of a choice to which a right denial is imputable. By a *public* manifestation I mean one that another mind could not reasonably interpret otherwise than as externalizing a right-denying choice.

The account of the *actus reus* I defend is derived from the legal retributivist justification of punishment belonging to the formalist paradigm of penal justice. This means that it is part (in conjunction with the account of *mens rea*) of a legal theory of what justifies penal force infringing an agent's right to act from ends it chooses. As was the case with *mens rea*, I develop this account in opposition to the moral theory of the *actus* that is dominant nowadays and that sees an unlawful action as constituting the morally blameworthy choice that makes punishment deserved.

Because the theory of the *actus reus* I offer is derived from the formalist paradigm of penal justice, that theory is only as strong as the formalist paradigm is normatively cogent. To this point, we have seen that formalism, while generating an account of punishment that is normatively compelling (to a liberal) as being consistent with the freedom and inviolability of the person, is nonetheless precariously dependent on an assumed equation of human goods with subjective values and of harms with subjective hurts. Indeed, it is just this rejection of a common human good (equivocated, as we saw, in the grading of crimes according to seriousness) that guaranteed the tying of punishment to the criminal's antecedent choice rather than to a public goal, which connection is just what made punishment compatible with personal inviolability. Accordingly, whether the legal retributivist justification of punishment (and the accounts of *mens rea* and *actus reus* that derive from it) can itself be justified ultimately depends on whether the formalist paradigm can be preserved despite its congenital blindness to human goods within a more comprehensive conception of penal justice.

1. The Austinian View of the *Actus*

Treatises on criminal law often speak of an act requirement of criminal liability.[2] This element of liability is supposedly made up of a simple act that factually causes an outcome proscribed by law. A simple act is so called because it is, as Hart put it, "the simplest thing we can do".[3] It is a voluntary movement of the body, like swinging an arm or crooking a finger, which may be further simplified into

---

[2] Alan Mewett and Morris Manning, *Mewett and Manning on Criminal Law*, 3rd ed. (Toronto: Butterworths, 1994), 125, 129; Don Stuart, *Canadian Criminal Law*, 5th ed. (Toronto: Carswell, 2007), 79. But contrast, JC Smith, *Smith and Hogan Criminal Law*, 10th ed. (London: Butterworth, 2002), 30.
[3] HLA Hart, *Punishment and Responsibility* (Oxford: Clarendon Press, 1968), 98.

a voluntary muscular contraction. A voluntary bodily movement causing an outcome is a complex *action*—for example, of taking, hitting, or killing. If a complex action exemplifies a complex action-type proscribed by law, then it constitutes a criminal offence. The essential elements (voluntary motion, causation of outcome) of the proscribed action-type make up what is called the *actus reus* of the offence.

On this view, accordingly, there is both an act requirement and an *actus reus* requirement of criminal liability. The act requirement is the requirement that the defendant have caused a proscribed outcome by a voluntary bodily movement. The *actus reus* requirement is the requirement that the defendant have performed a complex action that matches the definition of an action-type prohibited by law. Very different considerations apply to the justification of these two requirements. To justify the act requirement, one would try to explain why criminal liability is properly restricted to voluntary bodily movements (why not involuntary motion, voluntary at-rest states, statuses, thoughts?). To justify the *actus reus* requirement, one would try to explain why criminal liability is properly restricted to complex actions of the type proscribed by fairly precise and contemporaneous legal norms (why not norms of morality generally or retroactive laws?).[4]

This way of understanding the criminal *actus* has an old and venerable lineage. It is adumbrated by Bentham,[5] made explicit by Austin,[6] repeated by Holmes,[7] and largely accepted by the drafters of the Model Penal Code.[8] Michael Moore adopts it hook, line, and sinker.[9] Indeed, so well ensconced is this view in the textbooks that Moore can call it, not without some justification, the "orthodox view of the act requirement".[10] Because, however, *ortho* means correct and because the correctness of this opinion is what is at issue, I shall refer to it as the Austinian view or sometimes as the conventional view.

There is, as some have observed, something peculiar about the Austinian view of the *actus*.[11] I mean there is something about reducing criminal actions to willed bodily movements causing a proscribed outcome that must strike the criminal law theorist as peculiar, for I cannot presume to speak for the metaphysician of action. The peculiarity is this. Even though it is for what they do or fail to do that people are liable to judicial punishment, neither the empirical action that incurs criminal liability nor the elements of the proscribed action-type that the empirical action must match makes any reference to culpability. This may be because

---

[4] Michael Moore, *Act and Crime* (Oxford: Clarendon Press, 1993), 47, 239–44.
[5] Jeremy Bentham, *An Introduction to the Principles of Morals and Legislation* (Darien, Conn: Hafner, 1970), 70–81.
[6] John Austin, *Lectures on Jurisprudence*, 4th ed. (London: John Murray, 1879), vol. 1, 376–77, 423–9.
[7] Oliver Wendell Holmes, Jr., *The Common Law* (Boston: Little, Brown, 1923), 54, 91.
[8] Ss. 1.13(2), 2.01.   [9] Moore, *Act and Crime*.   [10] Ibid, 44.
[11] For critiques see Hart, *Punishment and Responsibility*, ch. 4; Hyman Gross, *A Theory of Criminal Justice* (New York: Oxford University Press, 1979), 49–57; Douglas Husak, *Philosophy of Criminal Law* (Totowa, NJ: Rowman & Littlefield, 1987), 122–8; George Fletcher, *The Grammar of Criminal Law* (Oxford: Oxford University Press, 2007), 269–73.

the holders of the Austinian view are mind–body dualists for whom culpability is a quality of the mind rather than an attribute of external actions, which they view as intelligible only in causal and value-neutral terms. Or perhaps they are legal positivists (of course, Bentham, Austin, and Holmes were) who wish to keep the notion of illegality separate from that of culpability as part of the general positivist project to divorce valid law from morality. Whatever the reason for it, however, the exclusion of culpability from the conventional definition of the criminal *actus* seems to contradict the most famous maxim of the criminal law: *actus non facit reum nisi mens sit rea*. Moreover, if willed bodily movements attended by consequences are the only actions there are, then talk of an act requirement of the criminal law flies in the face of the many crimes (for example, criminally negligent homicide) that can be committed by doing nothing at all.

A not-so-far-fetched analogy

An analogy that may initially seem far-fetched actually helps us see what is wrong with the Austinian view of the criminal *actus*. That view has features in common with the way 17th-century mercantilists understood wealth. The mercantilists saw wealth as an autonomous object in the external world detached from human intention. Thus, instead of understanding wealth generically and purposively as the power to summon resources for satisfying human ends, they identified it with one particular physical object conventionally taken as the medium for exchange—bullion. So too the Austinian theory of the criminal *actus* rests on an understanding of human action as having an autonomous existence separate from the purposiveness borne by rational agency. What individuates actions on this theory—what makes them the specific actions they are—is not the purpose of the action but the consequence of the bodily movement; and so, out of all the ways in which purposes can be externalized in choices, the bodily movement is singled out as the one definitive of an *actus*.

No doubt, the Austinian view insists on the connection between action and volition, for without volition, there are events or behaviours but not actions. And it does seem true that a simple act can be understood apart from intention, because the simple act of, say, moving an arm is sufficiently distinguished from the bodily event of an arm's moving by the event's being willed for whatever reason. Hence one has no need for the concept of intention to distinguish simple acts from the genus of events to which they belong. However, because the Austinian view reduces all complex actions to simple acts, it indiscriminately views complex actions themselves without reference to intention—as willed bodily movements causing X. Thus, signalling the end of a Grand Prix race and conducting the London Philharmonic are basically the same willed arm movements with different consequences.

Hans Welzel stood to the Austinian (or "causal," as he called it) view of action as Adam Smith stood to the mercantilist conception of wealth. Opposing ideas in 19th-century German criminal law akin to Austin's, Welzel elaborated a purposive theory of action (*finale Handlungslehre*) according to which human actions must be understood not as willed bodily movements causing effects, but as teleological unities individuated (as signalling, conducting, etc.) by the ends to which action is directed.[12] Because all human action is for a purpose, Welzel argued, actions are the particular actions they are by virtue of the ends consciously animating them, not by virtue of the outcomes caused by micro-volitions of which no one is aware. For Welzel, the volition-causing-outcome theory fundamentally misconceived the nature of human action as mechanistic and blind rather than goal-directed; and so the thing to do was to discard it and reorganize criminal law around the purposive theory.

Welzel's theory of action attracted George Fletcher, who, however, amended it so as to eliminate its polemical one-sidedness.[13] For Fletcher, the volition-causing-outcome picture of action was not so much wrong as incomplete. Fletcher saw that, while complex actions denoted by factual gerunds such as killing and injuring are individuated by their consequences, those signified by the value-charged verbal nouns used in the criminal law are further individuated by intentions as intersubjectively interpreted within a meaning-giving context.[14] Thus, a killing is a willed bodily movement causing death, but whether the killing is an "execution" or a "murder" depends on what the agent must, in the circumstances, be taken to have intended by moving its arm. Causing the sexual penetration of a female person is an act of love or of rape depending on whether the female is a consenting partner and on whether the male knew she was consenting or knew she was not. Of course, the same linguistic refinements appear outside the criminal law. Hitting can be done accidentally, but slapping, spanking, and boxing are kinds of hitting that, it would seem, can only be done intentionally within an interpretive context.

Accordingly, there seems to be a kind of complex action whose distinguishing feature is that its members are externalizations of intentions into a public world rather than mere consequences of simple acts. More specifically, they are externalizations of intentions to produce the outcome embraced by the less complex description. And yet the equation of complex actions with simple acts attended by consequences obstructs vision of this distinctive kind. It precludes seeing purposiveness as constituting a unique kind of complex action—call it externalization—that is irreducible (except physiologically) to a simple act, whose nature is definable apart from any purpose. Translated into the criminal law context, this means that the Austinian view of action cannot see what the agent must be taken to have intended by its physical motion as itself a constitutive part of the "*reus*-ness" of any *actus*. Rather, intentions belong in a separate compartment—the *mens rea*—and what makes an *actus* "*reus*" is just its matching an offence definition. Accordingly,

---

[12] Hans Welzel, *Abhandlungen zum Strafrecht und zur Rechtsphilosophie* (Berlin: de Gruyter, 1975), 7–22, 120–32, 93–119.
[13] George Fletcher, *Rethinking Criminal Law* (Boston: Little, Brown, 1978), 433–9; *The Grammar of Criminal Law*, 289–90.
[14] *The Grammar of Criminal Law*, 281–85.

for liability to flow, the severed action must *coincide* with the presence of a culpable mind, a requirement expressed in the idiom of "concurrence".[15]

Severing the criminal *actus* from the culpable mind produces a pattern of thought one might call object fetishism or the reification (making into an autonomous object) of that whose nature is constituted only within a relation to a human purpose. The features of the pattern are the following.

First, the *actus*, abstracted from the culpable (right-denying) intention that might draw in diverse instances (as the power to summon resources to satisfy human ends draws in ownership of many things besides bullion), becomes identified with its most common instance (like wealth with bullion), leaving other instances as troubling exceptions leading to conundrums in actual cases. So, for example, the Austinian view treats a voluntary bodily movement as the basic unit of any *actus reus*, thereby excluding the voluntary at-rest state from eligibility as another way of *externalizing* a culpable intention. Second, the Austinian view privileges the proscribed action-type that includes causing a certain outcome (e.g. homicide) as the central case of an *actus reus*, leaving attempts, incitement, and conspiracies to commit unlawful actions looking like anomalies where what is punished is really only an intention or disposition.[16] Third, the Austinian view privileges a naturalistic conception of causation according to which only motion can cause outcomes because nonmotion is "nothing at all".[17] This leaves voluntary at-rest states out of the causation picture even if an agent's failure to act is the means she chooses to effect her purpose, as in the case of a mother who, intending the death of her infant, achieves her object by not moving a muscle to feed it. Finally, the Austinian view treats the proscribed complex action as the primary element of criminal liability (most criminal law text- and casebooks begin with the *actus reus* requirement), for it is that which the law seeks to prevent. Mental states are relevant only as determining whether the penal sanction could have threatened the actor in the circumstances or whether the actor is to blame and thus answerable for the unlawful action. On this view, a complex action matching a proscribed action-type is temporally joined to a deterrable or responsible mind to produce a punishable offence.

Stresses in the Austinian structure

It does not take long for the weaknesses in this structure to manifest themselves in stress points. If a criminal *actus* rests on a simple act, what are we to make of a case like *Fagan v Commissioner of Metropolitan Police*, where the defendant accidentally drove his car onto a policeman's foot, but then intentionally let it rest there?[18] On the conventional understanding of a criminal *actus*, one would have to say that when there was a simple act, there was no guilty intention, and when there was

---

[15] *Smith and Hogan Criminal Law*, 92–4.
[16] *R v Ancio* [1984] 1 SCR 225; *R v Whybrow* [1951] 35 Cr App R141, 147.
[17] Moore, *Act and Crime*, 28.   [18] [1969] 1 QB 439 (CA).

a guilty intention, there was no simple act. It looks like Fagan should have gone free for want of concurrence, but of course he did not. To resolve its difficulty, the court invented the device of "a continuing act" beginning when Fagan drove onto the officer's foot and extending over the time during which the car (and Fagan) lay at rest, and upon which the guilty mind eventually supervened.[19] This is perhaps not too fanciful a construction in a case like *Fagan,* but what if, as in *R v Miller,* the defendant accidentally drops a lit cigarette onto a mattress, and then, upon wakening to the sight of flames, intentionally omits to take measures to prevent the ensuing fire?[20] How can we ascribe a continuing act to someone who was asleep?

Fictitiously extending simple acts forward is one device used to convict those who seem intuitively culpable despite their passivity *vis-à-vis* the proscribed outcome and despite the lack of concurrence between unlawful act and culpable mind. Looking backward from a nonact to a culpable mind is another. Thus, suppose, as in *R v Marison,* that the defendant lost consciousness at the wheel of his car as a result of a hypoglycaemic episode and killed someone as a result.[21] At the time of the proscribed event, Marison was certainly not "acting", and so he appealed the trial judge's ruling that the defence of automatism was unavailable on a charge of dangerous driving causing death in his case. Yet no one will think that a plea of involuntariness should exculpate Marison if, as was the case, he knew he was prone to hypoglycaemic black-outs and drove anyway. The Appeal Court did not, and so it dismissed the appeal. For the same reason, those who choose the risk of ingesting alcohol to the point of automatism and hit someone while in that unconscious state cannot plead unconsciousness in total exculpation; for they are at least guilty of criminal negligence causing the proscribed outcome. Evidently, neither the involuntariness of a proscribed transaction nor the absence of simultaneity of *actus reus* and culpable mind is necessarily a bar to conviction.

It may be objected, however, that there was a voluntary act before the unconscious episode—bringing a glass to one's lips, setting a car in motion—that brings these cases within the conventional act paradigm. However, this will be true even of cases where involuntariness would be a good defence (as where a driver is not informed of the soporific effect of medication), so that what makes *Marison* and the intoxication-causing-automatism cases stand out is that one judges the involuntary transaction to be *itself culpable* to the extent that the agent foresaw it and chose to risk it. In these cases, then, what turns an involuntary transaction into an *actus reus* is its connection to a culpable mental orientation—recklessness toward the risk that the involuntary state will occur. Not only is an involuntary transaction admitted here to be potentially an *actus reus*; also acknowledged is an inward connection between the criminal *actus* and the culpable mind such that the *actus* becomes *reus* only in connection with a *mens rea* and the *mens* becomes *rea* only when actualized in an external choice. Thus, the conventional view of the two

---

[19] The Model Penal Code makes an exception for omissions "accompanied by" acts; see s. 2.01.
[20] [1982] 2 WLR 937.   [21] [1996] Crim LR 909.

elements of culpability—that they are separate essences that coincide temporally in crime—is silently breached. The same inward connection between *actus reus* and *mens rea* is acknowledged when, as in *R v Black,* passive spectators at the scene of a crime are convicted of complicity in the crime if their omission was "for the purpose of aiding" it.[22]

Cases like those mentioned above show that there is no reason to take a proscribed complex action initiated by a simple act as the standard case of an *actus reus*. Both voluntary motionlessness and involuntary motion can also be culpable if they manifest choices to risk interfering with another agent's exclusive sphere of choice or to let materialize the risks one has accidentally imposed. All are instances of something more general, and so there is no act requirement of criminal liability, either descriptively or normatively. There is, however, an *actus reus* requirement. And yet this too must be understood differently from the way legal positivists like Bentham and Austin saw it and from the way Moore has recently characterized it.[23] For if a failure to act can be constituted as an *actus reus* by a culpable intention, then the *actus reus* requirement cannot be understood separately from the culpable mind as simply a requirement that a punishable action match an action-type proscribed by law. Rather (and more straightforwardly), the *actus reus* requirement must be a requirement that the defendant's action, or inaction, or status (or whatever) be *reus*—that is, culpable in its own right. The action-type proscribed by law can then be seen as itself an instance of a more general type—*actus reus*. But in what does the distinctive culpability that belongs to the criminal *actus* consist?

The interdependence of *actus reus* and *mens rea*

Perhaps an *actus reus* is a certain kind of tort. That is, perhaps it is a specific kind of transgression or infringement of an agent's right to be free from interference with its capacity to act from ends it chooses. Such transgressions may occur as a result of simple acts (trespass) or as a result of voluntary motionlessness amounting to a failure to take reasonable precautions (negligence); they may occur without fault (for example, through reasonable mistakes about ownership), through negligence, or intentionally. The tort is the transgression itself, prescinded from any inquiry into the tortfeasor's intentions. If, however, the interference with agency is chosen or intentional, then the tort has become the specific kind of tort known as crime, and the transgression has become an *actus reus* as well as a tort. So an *actus reus*, on this view, is that species of transgression or right infringement distinguished by an intention to interfere with the free choice of another. Transgressions are thus the primary thing. Crimes are standardly intentional torts.[24]

---

[22] [1970] 4 CCC 251.   [23] Moore, *Act and Crime,* 169.
[24] For an elaboration of this point of view, see Markus Dubber, *Victims in the War on Crime* (New York: New York University Press, 2002). See also Arthur Ripstein, *Equality, Responsibility, and the Law* (Cambridge: Cambridge University Press, 1999), 147–9.

This view is an advance on the conventional one for two reasons. One, it does not make a fetish of simple acts; voluntary at-rest states can be transgressions if there is a duty to act to avoid a risk one has created, and they can be crimes if one chose to let the risk materialize. Two, it does not see the *actus reus* as constituted independently of the culpable mind, as if there could be a *criminal* wrong without a criminal mind. Rather, the *actus reus* is constituted *with* a culpable mind and vice versa. A tort is a culpable *actus* only with a *mens rea* directed toward the interference; an immoral wish is a legally culpable choice only as externalized in a wrongful *actus*. Each (*actus reus* and *mens rea*) is what it is only in relation with the other. Just as a man is a husband only with a wife and a woman a wife only with a husband, so an *actus* is *reus* only with a *mens rea* and a mind *rea* only with an *actus reus*. The requirement of temporal concurrence is merely a metaphor for the inward connection, and so it may be relaxed when, as in *Fagan*, *Miller*, and *Marison*, the connection exists without concurrence.[25]

Nevertheless, a great difficulty remains. Its symptom is the exclusion of inchoate crimes—which do not involve transgressions and are thus not a species of tort—from the paradigm of crime. As a consequence of this exclusion, inchoate crimes, though they might have an act requirement, are not seen as having a *culpable* act requirement; rather, their criminality is said to lie in intention or disposition alone, and whatever statutory act requirement they possess is said to be merely evidentiary for a firm intention or disposition.[26] This gives inchoate crimes the look of something that belongs not to a legal regime of punishment of free persons (*Strafrecht*), but to a technocratic regime for managing socially hazardous objects (*Verwaltungsrecht*).[27] And as long as they are so regarded, no judicial effort will be made to reclaim them for the *Strafrecht* by insisting on a public manifestation of a culpable choice that fulfils the normative requirement of an *actus reus*.

What is the conceptual difficulty with equating an *actus reus* with a tort committed intentionally, of which the exclusion of inchoate crimes from the paradigm of crime is a symptom? The problem lies in a failure to push the insight into the interdependence of *actus reus* and culpable mind to its logical conclusion. We saw that the tort-centered view of the *actus reus* sees the latter as constituted only in conjunction with a culpable intention. But if a transgression can become an *actus reus* through a culpable intention, why should it be the case that *only* a transgression can do so? After all, the interference with agency became an *actus reus* only because it was the outward manifestation for others of a culpable choice (this will be argued in section 3 of this chapter). But then why restrict such manifestations to

---

[25] See also *Thabo Meli v R* [1954] 1 All ER 373. This way of viewing the relation between *actus reus* and *mens rea* may be called holistic, but it is not holistic in contrast to "structured", as Fletcher would have it, since the two elements of criminal culpability are distinct and mutually essential, not merged or conflated. It is holistic in contrast to fragmented. See Fletcher, *The Grammar of Criminal Law*, 56–7.

[26] *Whybrow*, 147; JWC Turner, ed., *Russell on Crime*, 12th ed. (London: Stevens, 1964), 175.

[27] They appear so to Dubber; see *Victims in the War on Crime*, 20–3; 137–8.

interferences? If a manifestation of a culpable choice can transform a nonculpable tort into an *actus reus*, then it should also be able to transform a nontortious action into an *actus reus*. Crime, understood as the public manifestation of a choice to which a right denial is imputable, will then have become a *sui generis* category distinct from tort; and inchoate crimes, properly monitored by judges for the adequacy of their *actus* requirement, could then be domesticated to the *Strafrecht*.

The claim so far put forward (and which requires a theoretical derivation) is that an *actus reus* is the public manifestation of a culpable choice and that the *actus reus* requirement of criminal liability is the requirement that there be such a manifestation. A public manifestation of a culpable choice can occur through simple acts, voluntary motionlessness, or involuntary motion, through right infringements or inchoate criminal endeavours, perhaps even through public commitments to associations organized for criminal purposes. We shall presently see how this conception of the *actus reus* fits into the legal retributivist account of what makes punishment deserved outlined in Chapter 1. We shall also see what constraints the conception imposes on the act "beyond preparation" requirement for inchoate crimes laid down by positive law. But to prepare for these discussions, we must first see how a competing view of criminal desert fares with respect to the requirement of criminal liability that there be an externalization (*actus*) of a culpable choice.

2. The Moral Account of the *Actus*

If there is any one proposition that commands general agreement among theorists and practitioners of the penal law, it is that judicial punishment ought not to be inflicted for private thoughts, wishes, inclinations, or states of character where these have not manifested themselves in conduct. Theorists from otherwise opposing philosophic schools converge on this principle. Utilitarians support it, because there is no public mischief in inner thoughts to justify the evil of punishment. Right theorists adhere to it, because liberty within the sphere of the inner life needs no limitation to render it compatible with the equal liberty of others. Perfectionists honour it, because the threat of punishment for inner vice appeals to motives inconsistent with virtue. Thus, quite apart from practical problems of detection and proof, there are reasons of principle for everyone militating against punishing what goes on in the mind.

One suspects, though, that behind the different reasons against punishing inward states derivable from opposing schools lies a deeper and shared reason, one so powerful that the inability of a philosophic perspective to criticize such a practice for its own reason (and *a fortiori* its approval of the practice) would be felt as cause for profound embarrassment. I suggest that this shared reason is just that punishing someone for his or her private thoughts, feelings, and motives is violence done to one individual to calm the anxiety of others for their physical security or psychic integrity, or simply to achieve dominance for their moral opinions, and that is to treat the agent as a means to others' ends. Moreover, it can make no relevant moral difference whether the oppressor hides behind a mask or robes.

Assuming the injunction against punishing inward states is common ground, let us consider a desert-based account of the *actus* requirement of criminal liability alternative to the one I'll present in the next section. I leave aside accounts of that requirement drawn from purely consequentialist theories of punishment, for the problems with these are well known. While there is no public mischief in imagining or wishing, there is danger in dispositions toward law breaking likely to manifest themselves in conduct as well as in nonvolitional, harm-causing transactions likely to recur whether or not the agent induced or foresaw the unconscious episode. For the pure consequentialist, these perils become fair game for coercive measures aimed at incapacitating the dangerous, and so the *actus* requirement drops out. What pretends to be punishment is really just the administrative quarantine of human threats without the public emergency needed to justify it.

The desert-based account of the *actus* I want to consider is the moral account offered in different ways by Michael Moore and Douglas Husak. In *Act and Crime*, Moore writes: "It is the choice to do evil on a particular occasion that makes a person morally responsible for any wrong that flows from such choice, irrespective of whether such choice expresses bad character or not."[28] With this sentence, Moore means to distance his account of moral responsibility from a character-based one for which acts are meritorious or blameworthy depending on whether they express good or bad character. For a character theory, bad acts are blameless if they are out of character, while bad character is blameworthy whether or not it has yet manifested itself in conduct (perhaps it has revealed itself in speech or in a repeated failure to show appropriate emotions). By contrast, Moore's understanding of moral responsibility seems to make blameworthiness hinge on acts. We are morally responsible for our choice to *do* evil, where by evil Moore means the violation of a norm of moral obligation. To do evil, according to Moore, is to will bodily movements that end up as complex actions breaching moral obligations. Further, for Moore, moral responsibility for choosing to do evil is sufficient for criminal responsibility. Thus, he says, to will bodily movements that violate moral norms of obligation "is to do moral wrong and thus deserve punishment".[29]

All this, however, is only to affirm the sufficiency of a choice to do evil for punishment. It is not yet to explain why an evil act is also necessary for punishment. There are two separate issues here. One, does the moral account of the *actus* explain why a willed bodily movement is necessary? Two, does this account explain why an externalization of a culpable intention is necessary? Since I have already argued that to confine the possibility of culpable agency to willed bodily movements is to restrict that possibility too narrowly, I will not blame Moore if his act requirement proves unstable. Instead I'll hold him to account only if the redundancy of an act on his theory is part of a more general redundancy of an externalization.

[28] *Act and Crime*, p. 51.   [29] Ibid.

If, as Moore holds, responsibility for violating norms of moral obligation makes a person deserving of judicial punishment, why should we not deserve punishment for failures to conform to our moral obligations ascribable to vices we can choose either to indulge or control but that typically manifest themselves in omissions? For example, meanness is a character flaw that manifests itself in an omission to act generously when one ought to do so. Why, on Moore's account of criminal responsibility, should we not deserve punishment for a failure to act generously toward another person when a norm of moral obligation requires us to do so if the reason for the failure was not a lack of resources but meanness of character? Observe that to punish in this case would not be to punish *for* the omission, since the omission itself could be explained by nonblameworthy factors such as a lack of adequate resources or the pull of a competing duty; the omission by itself is morally neutral. Rather, to punish on the occasion of the omission would be to punish the agent for choosing to indulge a vice of character of which the omission is found to be an expression.

Moore deals with the problem that blameworthy omissions pose to his act requirement by construing our positive moral obligations toward others narrowly. Essentially, he denies that we have positive moral obligations toward strangers we have not imperiled, even if they are dying and we could prevent their death with negligible cost to ourselves. Macaulay's surgeon, according to Moore, has not even a moral obligation to travel from Calcutta to Meerut to save the person needing an operation "even though the journey is not risky, just inconvenient to his other interests".[30] For Moore, easy rescues of strangers are supererogatory—cases of saintliness or heroism. The only exception he acknowledges is the duty owed to others' children, to which case I'll return. Moore concludes: "once we concede that... there was no obligation to prevent harm, there can be no wrong done in omitting to prevent harm".[31] Hence no retributive justice would be achieved by punishing.

Moore's construal of the scope of our positive moral obligations is idiosyncratic. Why should we concede, in the absence of argument, that shouting "Look out!" to a blind man to warn him of a precipice is an act of heroism? And why should we concede that a failure to warn because one has chosen to indulge an inclination toward *Schadenfreude* is not to breach a moral obligation? Certainly, the common law's refusal to punish omissions to perform easy rescues for strangers has never assumed that there is no moral obligation in these cases. Rather, this refusal has been based on the idea that, while there is a *moral* duty, there is no *coercive* duty correlative to a right.[32] And I believe that the generally accepted idea of a supererogatory rescue is that it is one involving nontrivial risk or cost to oneself.

Moore concedes that we have a positive moral obligation to rescue another's child if we can do so at no cost to ourselves. He does not say why children and not adults should trigger this obligation, but let us leave this omission aside. Having acknowledged a positive moral obligation to act in this case, Moore, to save his act requirement, has to explain why a failure to rescue should not be punished. His

[30] Ibid, 55.   [31] Ibid, 56.   [32] *People v Beardsley*, 113 NW 1128 (1907).

explanation is that, because the moral force of our negative obligations is stronger than that of our positive obligations, we "do much more wrong when we kill than when we fail to save [from death]".[33] Hence, in the case of positive duties, he says, the value of the liberty to make the wrong choice outweighs the value of retributive justice in punishing the wrong. Our negative obligations are stronger than our positive ones, according to Moore, because breaching a negative duty makes the world a worse place, whereas breaching a positive duty simply fails to improve it.[34]

However, Moore's distinction between negative and positive duties proves unsustainable. If the wrong of breaching a negative duty consists in making the world a worse place, why should we not be able to consider the character of the victim and the motive of the wrongdoer in estimating the overall seriousness of the wrong? Indignantly killing a solitary, psychopathic, serial murderer makes the world a worse place because of the killing, but not as bad a place as the sadistic killing of a decent husband and father. But if some breaches of negative obligations are morally worse than others because of the character of the victim and the motive of the wrongdoer, why could not breaching a positive obligation make the world a worse place than breaching a negative one in some cases? Why, for example, does not the failure to save a saint because of a choice to indulge one's envy of him make the world a worse place than altruistically ridding the world of a monster? More to the point, how do we know whether it does or not? And if we cannot know—if the weighing is subjective and discretionary—how can we know that omissions from blameworthy motives are never punishable? Presumably they will be punished when the judge to whom the legislature has delegated moral discretion under a general Good Samaritan statute feels they make the world a worse place than some crimes of commission.

In *Placing Blame,* Moore revises his earlier view that the difference in stringency between negative and positive moral duties rests on the difference between making the world a worse place and not improving it. He now bases the stringency differential on the difference between duties to specific persons, which are indefeasible by consequentialist reasoning, and agent-neutral duties, which are products of such reasoning.[35] Negative duties are owed to specific persons, whereas positive duties to the children of strangers are agent-neutral, so that one can omit saving this particular drowning child if doing so is necessary to save more or to perform an agent-specific duty (say, to save one's own child). Thus, according to Moore, negative duties are stringent because indefeasible by ordinary consequentialist reasoning, whereas positive duties are less so because there is a moral discretion to do good optimally.

Yet the flaw in this argument is readily apparent. Choosing against saving one child in order to save more, or to save one's own, does not count as a breach of any positive moral obligation precisely because the obligation is agent-neutral. Someone breaches a positive moral obligation to perform an easy rescue only when he or she

---

[33] *Act and Crime,* 58.   [34] Ibid, 25, 54, 58.   [35] *Placing Blame,* 280–81.

chooses not to rescue from an immoral motive, such as cowardice or meanness. But the moral prohibition against failing to rescue from an evil motive is just as stringent as the negative duty not to do evil from whatever motive; for what morality sets its face against is evil.[36] Hence Moore's moral account of criminal desert provides no reason not to punish failures to rescue the children of strangers from evil motives. That is to say, it provides no reason not to punish inward vice.

Furthermore, even granted Moore's premise that the breach of a positive moral duty can never be as serious a wrong as a breach of a negative one, it is nevertheless on Moore's view still a wrong. Why then is there a value in the offending liberty that has to be weighed against the value of justice? After all, we do not say in the case of murder that the value of justice outweighs the value of the liberty to commit this crime, as if we were trading something important. We say that, because murder is wrong, there is no right to the liberty to kill and so nothing of moral significance to weigh in the scales. Nor do we say that, because petty theft is a less serious wrong than murder, the value of the liberty to steal small sums weighs more relative to the value of justice than the value of the liberty to kill. We say that, however minor the wrong, there is no moral value in the liberty to commit the wrong just because it is a wrong; hence there is no moral loss in giving it up. Why then should we not also say this when the wrong is a breach of a positive duty?

Perhaps the answer lies in Moore's observation that positive commands take away more of our liberty than negative ones, because a positive command to X forecloses every action but X, whereas a prohibition of X forecloses nothing but X.[37] We can say that positive commands foreclose action in an all-but way, whereas negative commands do so in a nothing-but way. Accordingly, the moral account of the act requirement could explain the rule against punishing breaches of positive obligations by pointing to the greater value of the liberty that would be forgone relative to the case of negative obligations.

However, this move does not help Moore for two reasons. One, even granting his premise that the liberty to breach a positive moral obligation is valuable, positive commands will not even generally deprive us of much more liberty than negative ones if they can be breached only by indulging vices. For then they do not require us to forgo the liberty to allocate our limited resources according to our moral judgment; they simply require us to forgo the liberty to act immorally. And that is just what, on Moore's account, negative obligations do. If, in other words, the positive moral command enjoins us to do good optimally, then it forecloses *nothing but* evil, as does the negative command. Two, the argument still assumes that the duty to exact retributive justice prevails when negative obligations are breached only because the value of the forgone liberty is lower in relation

---

[36] This does not mean that cruelly letting die when one can easily save is *as* evil as wrongfully killing; from the moral point of view the former may deserve less punishment than the latter. The point is that the moral prohibitions of both are equally resistant to consequentialist reasoning, so that, if judicial punishment serves morality, there is no reason to punish one but not the other.
[37] *Placing Blame*, 278.

to the duty's force than it is when positive obligations are violated. But what is the value in the forgone liberty to murder, rape, steal, etc.?

In *Placing Blame,* Moore attempts to defend his ascribing value to the liberty exercised in wrongdoing (and *a fortiori* to the liberty exercised in omitting the performance of a positive obligation).[38] He argues against egalitarian liberals that there is value, not only in the basic liberties to express our identities (freedom of speech, etc.), but also in the natural liberty to do as we please; for there is value in the free choice to do right or wrong. This is why, he says, any legal limitation of natural liberty must be justified by good reasons. But what exactly is the moral loss inflicted by the law, say, against murder that has to be justified by the moral gain in punishing the evil of murder? It is, says Moore, the same loss that would be inflicted by laws coercing the performance of positive obligations: the lost room for autonomously and virtuously choosing against evil that legal coercion implies.

We have seen, however, that, for the moral retributivist, this loss shadows negative and positive obligations symmetrically.[39] Punishing breaches of negative obligations to avoid evildoing, and punishing omissions from evil motives to do good, achieve retributive gain at the same cost of space for virtue: both foreclose action in nothing-but form. The negative command forecloses no action but the proscribed action; the positive one forecloses no action but that springing from vice. Thus Moore cannot accept the trade-off of liberty for justice in the case of negative obligations without also accepting it in the case of positive ones. And that is to accept judicial punishment of inward vice.

Moore's house collapses entirely, however, when he concedes that a breach of a positive obligation to save one's own child is punishable both morally and in positive law. His explanation is that the obligation to protect one's own child is stronger than the obligation to protect another's, and so the value of retributive justice here outweighs the value of the liberty to do wrong. Yet Moore acknowledges the impossibility of knowing whether the difference in the force of these two obligations is great enough to justify punishing in the one case and not in the other, and so he finally admits uncertainty as to whether a rightly conceived penal code might punish both sorts of blameworthy omission.[40]

However, once Moore concedes the possibility of punishing a blameworthy omission to fulfill a moral obligation, a more serious problem for the moral account of the *actus* emerges. We saw (on page 110) that an omission to perform an agent-neutral charitable duty is by itself morally neutral because it might be explained by exculpatory reasons such as the pull of a competing duty. I do not breach a duty of easy rescue in leaving Athos to his fate if this is what I must do to save Porthos and Aramis. Omitting performance of an agent-neutral positive

---

[38] Ibid, 282–3.
[39] Not for the legal retributivist, because legal coercion enforces rights rather than promoting the good, and so it leaves the inward self free.
[40] *Act and Crime,* 57.

duty becomes blameworthy only by virtue of a choice to indulge rather than resist a vicious passion (envy, hatred) or disposition of character (meanness). But if that is so, why not punish indulgences of vice that breach a moral obligation owed only to oneself? Why not punish gluttony, envy, or sloth?

Moore's answer is that "those who lack virtue, but who do not exhibit it through bad actions, have done no wrong. They have wronged themselves, by being less worthy persons than they should be; but they have not wronged anyone else."[41] Here the claim in one sentence that those who lack virtue have "done no wrong" is retracted in the next. They have done wrong, Moore admits, but they have not wronged "anyone else". This is true, but the answer simply assumes what must be explained, namely, why, on the moral theory of criminal responsibility, punishment for moral wrongs should be confined to wrongs against others. That the envious and slothful have not *done* wrong cannot be the reason for the moral theory's forbearing to punish, because the moral theory could not rule out punishment for blameworthy omissions to perform duties toward others' children.

Moore might respond that threatening inward vice with punishment would not produce virtue, for external threats appeal to motives for virtue whose driving force renders abstinences and actions nonmoral. However, exactly the same can be said for punishing breaches of one's moral obligations, including even negative obligations, toward others. The moral duty not to kill is the duty to forbear from killing for the reason that it is morally wrong to kill. Forbearing from fear of disadvantage would not count as fulfilling the moral duty, since the same motive that inclines in this case to forbearance will, under different circumstances, incline toward wrongdoing. So Moore cannot rely on the self-contradiction in coercing virtue to rule out punishment of inward states without also forswearing punishment for evil choices generally. Nor can he rely on this argument without abandoning moral retributivism. For Moore (and for moral retributivism generally), the state ought to punish evil, not in order to produce virtue, but because evil deserves to be punished.

Like Moore, Douglas Husak believes that criminal liability ought to (and generally does) track moral responsibility for wrong.[42] That is, he thinks that moral responsibility for wrong ought to be (and generally is) a necessary and sufficient condition of criminal liability to punishment. Unlike Moore, however, Husak sees clearly where this position logically takes us with respect to whether criminal liability ought to require an *actus* and stoutly accepts the implication. Therefore, I shall simply expound his argument.

The argument is elegantly simple. Husak begins by asking what it is about acts that makes us responsible for them and deserving of punishment for proscribed actions. His answer is: we choose our acts. He then asks what the relevance of choice is for responsibility and criminal desert. His answer is: we control our

---

[41] Ibid, 53.
[42] Douglas Husak, 'Does Criminal Liability Require an Act?' in RA Duff, ed., *Philosophy and the Criminal Law* (Cambridge: Cambridge University Press, 1998), 60–64.

choices. But, he argues, we are able to control far more than our choices to act. We can also control our choices to abstain from acting. We can also control whether we create risks for others even when we do not consciously choose them, and so we can control whether or not these risks materialize in harm. We can also control whether we are in possession of something, whether we are a member of some association, or whether we are found in a certain place or in a drunken state, and so on. Indeed, Husak says without flinching, we are even able to control what thoughts we allow to linger before our minds through "mental acts" like imagining, planning, deliberating, and deciding. Thus, the reason for holding people criminally responsible for their unlawful actions does not support an act *requirement*—a rule that we punish only those whose unlawful actions stemmed from willed bodily movements. Instead, Husak says, that reason supports a control requirement. Criminal liability for a state of affairs ought to (and generally does) depend on whether it is reasonable to expect the defendant to have prevented that state of affairs from coming about.[43]

Accordingly, if criminal liability ought to track moral responsibility for wrong, there can be no principled objection, Husak argues, against crimes of omission, negligence, possession, status, or even of wicked mental acts provided that a defence of lack of reasonable control is available. To make the pill of thought crimes easier to swallow, Husak argues that we already punish for mental acts when we punish for attempts.[44] This is so, he says, because although attempt crimes have an act requirement, the requisite acts are not what the actor is punished for, since these acts are by definition innocent. Rather, the actor is punished solely for a criminal intention, and the function of the act requirement is just to give evidence of resolve. But suppose there is evidence of resolve without an act corroborative of intention—for example, from a confession. In such cases, Husak argues, the same preventative rationale that justifies punishing people for attempts and conspiracies could justify punishing them for mental acts under their control.[45] Accordingly, concludes Husak, there is no bodily act requirement of criminal liability either as a matter of prescriptive theory or positive law. *Nor is there even an externalization requirement.* There is only a requirement that the defendant have been able to avoid running afoul of a legal prohibition of immorality.

3. A Legal Account of the *Actus*

The moral account of the *actus* failed to preserve it as a necessary element of criminal liability. Such an account can have no principled objection to punishing evil motives for failing to rescue, wrongs to oneself, nor to punishing the solitary planning of, or deliberating on, a crime. Moore recoils from this destination of his theory, and for good reason. To punish mental acts or inward vice is to coerce the

[43] Ibid, 73–7.   [44] Ibid, 89–90.   [45] Ibid, 90.

agent for the sake of the particular interests—whether peace of mind or the satisfaction in seeing one's moral judgments of others enforced—of other individuals. Such coercion seems indistinguishable from wrongful violence. Moreover, the moral account of the *actus* also fails as a theory of the positive law. For the only phenomenon it can point to as corroborating its approval of thought crimes is the law of attempts as interpreted from its own point of view. If, however, there is an interpretation of inchoate crimes that gives their act requirements a co-ordinate role in criminal liability rather than the instrumental one of evidencing a culpable mind, then the only thread tying the moral account's approval of thought crimes to the positive law will have been cut. No doubt, the moral account of the *actus* can compass omission, possession, and status offences, whereas the traditionally narrow view of the "act" requirement cannot. But we shall see that the complete legal account (which includes an account of public welfare offences) can also compass these things without, however, embracing thought crimes.

Why an *actus*?

Why, then, does criminal liability require an *actus*? Why does the law require the punishable agent to have externalized a culpable state of mind? For what I believe is the answer, we have to revisit the legal retributivist conception of judicial punishment derived from the formal agency paradigm of penal justice.

Punishment, according to that conception, differs from criminal coercion in that it is the recoiling against the wrongdoer of the right denial implicit in his choice to interfere with another agent's capacity to act from ends it chooses. What deserves judicial punishment is not the choice to violate any norm of moral obligation; rather, it is the choice to violate the specific obligation to respect rights of agency constituted within a mutual recognition between ends and giving reality to the worth the violator claims in isolation. Such a choice implies a denial of rights; and so it implies acceptance of the permissibility of state interference with one's own agency for the purpose of vindicating mutual recognition as the sole ground of stable worth-claims. Accordingly, penal interferences with agency are legitimate only if they can be conceived as implicitly self-imposed. We saw that this account of judicial punishment selected the various forms of subjective *mens rea* (intention, advertent recklessness, wilful blindness) as the fault threshold normatively required for criminal liability, because only if the agent chooses to interfere or to risk interfering with another's agency can a right denial be imputed to its choice and the circuit between crime and punishment triggered. However, what role, if any, does this account of punishment assign to the *actus*? If a right denial is what bestirs the Eumenides, why is not a silent commitment to the proposition "everything is permitted" enough to invite retribution?

An *actus* is required because without it, one cannot impute to the mental act a claim of objective or public reality for the right denial. By public reality I mean reality for another agent as well as for oneself—that is to say, for all agents who exist or may exist. To deny rights of agency in thought is to say to oneself, "I believe there are no rights." To interfere with someone's agency in imagination is to think, "I wish there were no rights." To proclaim before an audience that everything is permitted is to say, "in my opinion, there are no rights." None of these mental or speech acts entails one's moral vulnerability to coercion, because none gets beyond subjective belief, fancy, or assertion into public reality. None gives objective reality or an appearance thereof to the right-denying claim because none alters the world everyone inhabits in light of the claim. Or we can say that none gives the right-denying claim the force of a practical principle or law purportedly valid for everyone. But if there is no giving the right denial the force of law, then there is no logical impetus to turn the denial back onto the denier, and so punishment will not be conceivable as implicitly assented to. It will be external violence. By contrast, to externalize a right denial in an action or omission publicly interpretable as embodying a right denial is to change the world everyone inhabits in light of that right-denying principle. It is thus to give the right denial the force of a law applicable to everyone including the denier. Thus the right denier cannot complain if he is brought under the law he himself set up.

Observe that this account of the necessity of the *actus* also tells us what kind of *actus* is *reus*—that is, what kind of externalization is culpable in the sense that it triggers the circuit between wrongdoing and punishment. That *actus* is alone *reus* that embodies or realizes in the public world a choice to which a right denial is imputable. To embody such a choice in the public world is to create a state of affairs that other agents could not reasonably interpret otherwise than as manifesting a right-denying choice. I'll call such a state of affairs a public manifestation of a right denial. Accordingly, the *actus reus* requirement of the criminal law is a requirement that the defendant have committed an action or omission (or anything else) that amounts to a public manifestation of a denial of rights. Obviously, a civil wrong committed intentionally or with advertence to the risk of interference satisfies this test of an *actus reus*. But what else does?

Failing to benefit

If by an omission is meant the absence of a willed bodily movement, then the claim that there is no criminal liability for omissions is clearly false as a descriptive statement about the law. Motionless acquiescence in a crime is complicity in the crime if the defendant's passivity is for the purpose of aiding it; and criminal negligence causing harm can be committed through a reckless omission to perform a legal duty to render assistance whether the omission consists in motionlessness or in doing something else. Nor are these cases of liability for motionlessness exceptions to a general rule. The theoretical account of the *actus reus* requirement just given provides no reason for treating a wilful failure to move one's body as lying outside the paradigm of a criminal *actus*. As the *Fagan* case shows, voluntary motionlessness too can be a public manifestation of a culpable choice.

However, if by an omission is meant a failure to confer a benefit on someone (i.e. a stranger) who has no right to demand it specifically from the defendant, then it is true that there is no criminal liability for an omission of that sort, no matter what the motive for the failure. A public welfare (Good Samaritan) statute may create liability for failing to perform an easy rescue of a stranger, but in doing so, it places on someone with a clear opportunity to rescue a civic obligation to discharge the state's duty to secure the basic welfare of its citizens. In effect, individuals are conscripted into public service unless the state compensates them for their efforts, in which case they are fairly taxed. The moral account of the *actus* could not explain why there is no criminal liability for failing to rescue a stranger for an immoral reason, inasmuch as (*pace* Moore) there would seem to be a moral obligation either to perform an easy rescue or to abstain from a proper motive.

The legal account, however, can explain this. The wicked soul who watches his rival for a woman's affection sink in quicksand when he could easily throw him a rope has not publicly manifested a choice to which a right denial is imputable, because the person in need had no right to the rope holder's beneficence or virtue nor, absent a statute, a right to his shouldering the public burden. The rope holder's duty is a noncoercive one to act virtuously. That duty is both self-regarding (a duty of self-perfection owed oneself) and subject to a moral discretion as to how best to discharge it; hence it is a duty owed to no other person in particular. Since the rope holder's choice infringed no right, no right denial can be imputed to it, hence no authorization of his own liability to coercion. No doubt the rope holder has publicly manifested a wicked character and for that has earned our contempt. But between wickedness and loss of liberty there is no connection.

Of course, in positive law there is a coercive duty to provide assistance to those with whom we have a special relationship of protector (whether by status or contract) or to those whose lives or safety we have inadvertently endangered; and we can be criminally liable for a reckless failure to perform the duty if the person to whom the duty is owed suffers harm as a result. But these cases accord well with the foregoing account of the *actus reus* requirement, because they are cases, not of failing to benefit, but of a public manifestation of a right denial.

Take first the case of unknowingly imperilling someone, because it is the easiest. If I inadvertently endanger a person or his property, but then, with knowledge that I have imposed this danger, decide not to remove it, I have chosen to allow an unreasonable risk that I have imposed to materialize. But that is no different from choosing to impose an unreasonable risk in the first place; for it cannot matter at what point during the life of the risk from inception to materialization the risk is chosen as long as it is a risk I have created. Thus, had Miller smoked in bed realizing the danger of his falling asleep and igniting what he knew to be a highly flammable polyurethane foam mattress, he would have publicly manifested a choice to which a right denial is imputable had the worst occurred. But then he does so as well if he wilfully allows the fire he inadvertently set to take its course.

Neither are the special relationship cases exceptions to the rule against criminal liability for failing to benefit. They too are cases of criminal right-infringements. If I induce someone to rely on me in emergencies, I make him more vulnerable to the risk of death than he would otherwise have been, for he is now dependent for his preservation on my choice to help him or not. However, the formalist paradigm cannot countenance a relationship in which an end is dependent for its existence on another's choice; and so it places me under a coercive duty to help him in emergencies if I can reasonably do so. By binding my choice, this duty reconciles his dependence on me for necessities with his end-status and hence with his capacity for rights. Breach of the duty is thus a right infringement rather than a failure to benefit, for I have induced someone to depend on me for necessities without observing the condition under which alone the other's dependence is compatible with his status as a right bearer. And if I breach the duty with knowledge of the attendant risks and harm results, then I have crossed the line dividing unpunishable immorality and punishable crime; for the world has now changed in a way that reflects the right-denying principle implicit in my choice to treat an end as servile.

Possession and status offences

Much sterile debate has swirled around whether possession and status offences are counterexamples to a supposed act requirement of criminal law or ways of punishing previous acts of coming into possession or of acquiring a status.[46] The debate is sterile because, as we have seen, there is no act requirement of criminal liability either positively or normatively. The only interesting questions regarding possession and status offences are whether the *actus* of possessing a proscribed article (for example, a narcotic, a firearm, a concealed weapon) or of having a proscribed status (for example, being drunk in a public place, being a member of a criminal syndicate) meets the *actus reus* requirement of self-willed punishment, and if it does not, whether the appropriate kind of penalty for a public welfare offence has been legislated and whether appropriate defences to a public welfare offence are available to the defendant.

Discussion of these issues must await an account (in Chapter 5) of how public welfare offences fit into a complete liberal theory of the penal law. This is so because most possession and status offences do not punish right violations or even inchoate right violations but rather penalize some conditions to avert harm to the public welfare. This is the case with laws proscribing possession of a narcotic as well as with laws against being drunk in a public place or being found in a house of prostitution. Because they do not punish crimes in the true sense (i.e. public manifestations of a right-denying choice), most possession and status

[46] Moore, *Act and Crime*, 19–22.

offences will not meet the *actus reus* requirement of criminal punishment; though there may be exceptions, neither possessing something nor being something will unambiguously manifest in the public world a right-denying choice.

But that is not the end of the matter. For even though an *actus* may not be *reus*, it may nonetheless be potentially harmful and so properly curtailed by noncriminal penalties for negligent breaches of a statute prohibiting it. Further, once a public welfare law is in place, a *knowing* violation of that law is a choice to which a denial of law's authority may be imputed and therewith too a denial of effective rights (since the rule of law is a necessary condition of effective rights) making hard treatment legitimate as implicitly self-willed. So, *provided that ignorance of law is permitted to exculpate,* there is nothing wrong with punishing as quasi-crimes intentional breaches of public welfare statutes making illegal the voluntary possession of harmful articles or prohibiting voluntary statuses inimical to the public welfare.

There may, however, be exceptional cases where the possession of something or the being of something might not reasonably be capable of interpretation otherwise than as manifesting a right-denying choice. In that case, the possession or status would qualify as an *actus reus* deserving punishment if the defendant knew he was in possession of the proscribed article or intentionally entered the status, whether or not he knew of the positive law proscribing the *actus*. I do not believe the unlicensed possession of a weapon is such a case, since weapons may be used for legal purposes. Nor is possession of a narcotic such a case, for an intended interference with choice is not signified by such possession, not even if an intention to distribute is. It might be argued that the possession without authorization of a cache of high-powered weapons, or of explosives, or of burglary tools would meet the public-manifestation requirement of criminal desert, for innocent explanations of such possession do not come easily to mind. Still, it is difficult to view any concealed or even private possession as altering the world everyone inhabits in light of a criminal principle. For this reason, possession offences are best penalized as regulatory offences with noncriminal penalties unless the defendant knew he was breaking the law. On the other hand, voluntary membership in an association notoriously organized for criminal purposes might be considered an incursion into public reality of a criminal principle. But this is a borderline case about which reasonable disagreement is possible.

4. Inchoate Crime

In this section I discuss how the foregoing account of the *actus reus* requirement of criminal desert can be applied to time-worn problems raised by the so-called inchoate crimes. What is the meaning of "beyond preparation"? What is the relevance of impossibility to culpability for attempts? What is the *actus reus* of criminal counselling? Can punishment for conspiracy be justified on desert grounds or is it explicable only as an instrument for incapacitating threats?

Because I am arguing that intentional torts form only one species of crime understood as the public manifestation of a culpable choice, the term "inchoate crime" becomes a misnomer insofar as it reflects an anachronistically tort-centred view of crime. The assumption is that only actions consummating a criminal purpose are complete crimes, whereas those falling short are crimes, not in the strict sense, but in one that is derivative or borrowed from the paradigm case; they are not-yet-crimes that are nevertheless "punished" for prophylactic reasons or else to give the wicked what they, whether contingently successful in their evil designs or not, deserve. Because the foregoing account of the criminal *actus* challenges that assumption, I am tempted to use the term "victimless crime" instead of inchoate crime for crimes of unfulfilled purpose. However, if by an inchoate crime we understand one in which the defendant's criminal aim is unrealized rather than one in which the defendant has not committed a complete crime, then we can continue to use the traditional term.[47]

It is most likely an historical fact that the crimes of attempt and conspiracy originated in the infamous organ of Tudor and Stuart despotism known as the Court of Star Chamber, where they were used as instruments of crime prevention, political repression, and the incapacitation of human threats.[48] Given this provenance, the dominant tendency among judges and commentators has been to identify the criminality of inchoate crimes with blameworthy intention alone and to see in their *actus* element only a requirement that there be clear evidence of dangerous resolve.[49] And while this approach has engendered the fairly strict "substantial step" test for attempts of the Model Penal Code, there is no necessity that it do so.[50] On the contrary, since the act's only function is to provide evidence corroborative of dangerous intent, the *actus* requirement of inchoate crimes tends to atrophy as other evidence of the defendant's dangerousness presents itself.[51] In this way, inchoate crimes, true to their origins in the secret Court of Star Chamber, shade into thought crimes.

Nowhere has this tendency been more evident than in the case of criminal attempts. At the time of writing, the impossibility of a train of acts' culminating in a crime has no bearing whatever on an agent's culpability for an attempt to commit the crime.[52] This means, for example, that someone who purchases an item from a discount store under perfectly innocent circumstances but who mistakenly believes the item was stolen is guilty of an attempt to handle stolen goods even though all that is culpable here is an intention. And if a protest is raised to the effect that this is to punish for immoral thoughts or dangerous tendencies alone, the inevitable retort is: "But since the actions are always innocent, that

---

[47] If crimes of unfulfilled purpose can be complete crimes, it would appear that the legal account of culpability has the same difficulty the moral account has in explaining why successful attempts are punished more severely than unsuccessful ones. I discuss this question in Chapter 4.
[48] See *The Case of Duels* (1615) 2 St Tr 1033.
[49] *Russell on Crime*, 12th ed., 175; *Whybrow*, 147, *per* Lord Goddard; Model Penal Code, Commentary to s. 5.01, 323, 331. The Model Penal Code test is acts "strongly corroborative of the actor's criminal purpose": s. 5.01(2).
[50] S. 5.01(1)(c).
[51] *R v Sorrell and Bondett* (1978) 41 CCC (2d) 9 (Ont CA).
[52] *R v Shivpuri* [1986] 2 All ER 334; *United States of America v Dynar* [1997] 2 SCR 462.

is just what the law of attempts is meant to do!" The retort is inadequate, however, because whatever the historical rationale for inchoate crimes, we can still ask whether these crimes can be redeemed by a liberal theory of penal justice and, if so, how such a theory would structure them. Let us begin with attempts.

Attempts

Most Anglo-American jurisdictions punish actions furthering a criminal design but falling short of achieving it if the actions have gone beyond the stage of "preparation". The fact that not all actions furthering a criminal intention are regarded as culpable suggests that the line between furthering and attempting in law is not simply a quantitative one of empirical proximity to the goal. For if furthering a culpable intention does not by itself constitute a culpable action, then it can make no difference how far down the road the furthering extended if nothing happened to transform the furthering into something qualitatively different. The "beyond preparation" formula is the law's way of marking the qualitative transformation from furthering to attempting in law. But what does the formula mean?

In *R v Barker,* a New Zealand case of 1924, Sir John Salmond of the Supreme Court proposed a test for determining whether the actions of a defendant were more than preparatory.[53] "That a man's unfulfilled criminal purposes should be punishable," he wrote, "they must be manifested not by his words merely, or by acts which are in themselves of innocent or ambiguous significance, but by overt acts which are sufficient in themselves to declare and proclaim the guilty purpose with which they are done."[54] Later in the same judgment, Justice Salmond made clear that words could count as acts unambiguously manifesting a criminal intent if, as in solicitation for unlawful sex, they were the means used to achieve the defendant's purpose. Further, it was an essential part of his test that, in deciding whether the defendant's actions unambiguously manifested a criminal intent, the judge was to ignore all evidence of intent from sources extrinsic to the action in its circumstantial context. Confessions, confidences to others, and so on were admissible as evidence of intent but not as establishing whether the defendant had gone beyond preparation.[55]

The exclusion of intent evidence extrinsic to the action holds the key to the meaning of Justice Salmond's test. The point of the test is not to look to the defendant's actions for evidence of a firm intent, but rather to judge whether the defendant has outwardly embodied or publicly manifested his intent in actions that, in their context, would thus signify to the reasonable observer a culpable choice. Obviously, a judge could not decide this question if he allowed evidence of intent from external sources to assist his understanding of the action's meaning. On Justice Salmond's test, accordingly, the defendant's actions play a role in determining criminal liability distinct from that of the culpable mind. The defendant is punished,

---

[53] [1924] NZLR 865.   [54] Ibid, 875.   [55] Ibid, 876.

not for his thoughts alone, but for externalizing a culpable purpose into public reality, where the principle imputable to his choice claims general validity. To decide whether the defendant's actions have gone "beyond preparation" into public reality, one asks whether, viewed in context, the actions can be reasonably interpreted otherwise than as serving a culpable purpose.

Justice Salmond's test has come to be known in the common-law world as the unequivocality test for attempts. Though it has garnered support from a few legal scholars, it has been almost universally rejected by common-law courts and treatise writers.[56] It was even overruled by statute in New Zealand, the country of its birth. Today, it is mentioned in textbooks only as a straw to be cut down along with all the other tests that seek to concretize the "beyond preparation" formula. But what is so wrong with the unequivocality test?

In his treatise on *Criminal Law: The General Part*, Glanville Williams levelled two criticisms against the unequivocality test—criticisms one finds continually repeated in textbooks and judgments without much critical scrutiny. One is that, since actions falling short of achieving a criminal purpose are by definition innocent, none will unequivocally manifest a criminal intent unless one presupposes the very criminal purpose that the action is supposed to manifest independently. If that is so, we must either let all attempters go free or else abandon the artificial exercise of ignoring what we know about intent from other sources.[57] Williams gave the example of a man bent on setting fire to a neighbour's haystack, who places a pipe in his mouth before lighting the match. The example is meant to show that the unequivocality test will acquit the guilty unless we allow evidence of intent to assist our interpretation of ambiguous actions.

Williams's second criticism is a variation of the first. He argued that no actions falling short of an accomplished criminal purpose will unequivocally manifest a *specific* criminal intent, and of course it is always a specific attempt with which the defendant is charged. The example he gives is that of a masked prowler discovered in someone's backyard at night.[58] Unless we take into account what we know of the prowler's intent from other sources (suppose he tells the police he meant to burgle the house), we shall never be able to conclude whether he intended burglary, or arson, or whatever, and so he will go free. Indeed, it was a case of this kind that led to the statutory overruling of the unequivocality test in New Zealand. In *Campbell and Bradley v Ward,* the defendants, who had been caught breaking into a car, were convicted of attempting to steal a car battery, one accomplice having confessed this purpose to the police.[59] Applying the unequivocality test to which he felt himself bound by precedent, the appeal judge decided that the

---

[56] In favour are George Fletcher, 'Constructing a Theory of Impossible Attempts,' in P Fitzgerald, ed., *Crime, Justice, and Codification* (Toronto: Carswell, 1986), 87–113, and Ripstein, *Equality, Responsibility, and the Law*, 235–40. Against are RA Duff, *Criminal Attempts* (Oxford: Clarendon Press, 1996), 48–53; Williams, *Criminal Law*, 629–31; *Shivpuri*; *Deutsch v The Queen* [1986] 2 SCR 2.

[57] Williams, *Criminal Law*, 630.   [58] Ibid.   [59] [1955] NZLR 471 (SC).

defendants' acts of attempted entry were consistent with an attempt to steal any number of things, and so, unable to use the confession to resolve the ambiguity, he quashed the convictions. He concluded his reasons by inviting the legislature to change the law if it, like he, found it unsatisfactory.

Both these criticisms, however, attack a caricature of the unequivocality test; they do not touch the unequivocality test itself.[60] It may be true that no nontortious action taken in isolation will reasonably exclude all innocent interpretations; but there is no reason to consider the defendant's action in isolation from its circumstantial context. Justice Salmond himself was clear that evidence of surrounding context is admissible, as it must be if the focus is on whether the defendant has publicly manifested a culpable choice.[61] Nor is there any reason to require that the actions in context *conclusively* manifest a culpable choice. As long as they are actions from which, absent other evidence, a reasonable observer would infer a criminal purpose, the defendant will either have manifested a culpable purpose or be acquitted because he has brought forward exculpatory intent evidence. "Presumptive criminality" might thus better describe the test than "unequivocality", and I shall henceforward call it by that name.

The presumptive criminality test easily handles the case of the pipe-smoking arsonist. If he lights his match in broad daylight, his actions are ambiguous with respect to a criminal purpose, as he may be engaged in nothing more than a country stroll.[62] But if he is surprised in his neighbour's field at night, his actions presumptively betoken a criminal purpose, pipe or no pipe, which purpose may be confirmed or thrown into reasonable doubt by extrinsic evidence of intent. The fact that the defendant goes free in the first case means that someone with a blameworthy intention who has gone a considerable distance toward executing it will go free. But this is just what it means to punish someone only for publicly

---

[60] The caricature probably stems from JWC Turner, 'Attempts to Commit Crimes,' (1935) CLJ 5, 230–47.

[61] *Barker*, 876.

[62] Duff has him kneeling beside a corn-stack and says that his act of lighting the match with a pipe in his mouth is nonetheless equivocal, showing that the test can acquit the guilty: *Criminal Attempts*, 51. The simple response is that we need more facts: Is it day or night? Is it windy or calm? The presumptive criminality test will doubtless often acquit those who have gone a long way toward completing their criminal purpose, but to say that it would acquit the *guilty* is to assert what needs to be argued: that ambiguous acts can be guilty though they have fallen short of consummating a criminal design. To show that the test can also sometimes convict the innocent, Duff adduces the example of someone who buys a gun from a criminal intending to use it in an armed robbery (51). Duff thinks this action unequivocally manifests a criminal purpose. But does it? Since guns can be used for legal purposes, buying one from a criminal (though it might itself be an offence) does not presumptively manifest a criminal use for the gun. Though critical of the "unequivocality test" Duff himself presents a test that engages the same rationale as that test but without translating the rationale into reasonably determinate language. Preparatory acts, Duff says, have "only a shadowy existence in the public world". (387). Attempts are acts that have acquired "a sufficiently concrete form as an active engagement in the public world" (390). Duff's own formula of "embarking on the commission" (393) is either a last-step test (which he rejects), a mere restatement of the "beyond preparation" formula, or a less perspicuous way of saying "not reasonably capable of an innocent interpretation".

manifesting a culpable choice rather than for immoral thoughts, and for threat management to be constrained by criminal desert.

It may be objected, however, that the nocturnal actions of the pipe-smoking trespasser are not even presumptively the actions of an *arsonist*. He may be on his way to burgling the farmhouse or murdering its inhabitants. This is Williams's second criticism, and it is equally beside the mark. The presumptive criminality test requires only that the defendant's actions in context manifest *a* criminal purpose; they need not presumptively manifest the specific one of which the defendant is accused. This is so because at issue at the first stage of the inquiry is whether the defendant has by his conduct exposed himself to punishment *simpliciter*, leaving aside the question of the appropriate measure of punishment. This depends on whether he has committed a crime. He has committed a crime if and only if he has publicly manifested a choice to which a right denial is imputable. Accordingly, if his actions in context can reasonably bear an innocent interpretation, he must be acquitted, for there is nothing here but a morally blameworthy intention and a threat short of one justifying defensive force. However, once it is determined without recourse to intent evidence that the defendant's conduct presumptively manifested a criminal purpose, there can be no objection to admitting extrinsic evidence of intent to determine the specific offence he was trying to commit and hence the appropriate range of sentences.[63] If the specific offence intended is not among those reasonably inferable from the conduct at the first stage (if the nocturnal pipe-smoker was actually on his way to robbing a candy store), then the defendant is innocent of an attempt to commit the specific offence he intended, though guilty of attempted crime in the abstract, if such an offence has been legislated. Properly construed, therefore, the presumptive criminality test convicts the defendants in *Campbell v Ward;* the appeal judge applied the test incorrectly.

Impossible attempts

Once the presumptive criminality test (properly construed) is accepted, cases in which the attempted crime cannot possibly be completed cease to present the conundrums they otherwise do. Completion of an attempt, as the courts tell us, may be either factually or legally impossible.[64] Completion is factually impossible if circumstances prevent the fulfilment of a project which, if successfully executed, would constitute a crime (the pocket the pickpocket tries to pick is empty). Completion is legally impossible if the agent, even were it to accomplish everything it set out to do, could not commit a crime (the wallet the pickpocket takes turns out to be his own).

Take first the case where completion is impossible because of some circumstance preventing the achievement of the actor's aim. Here the general rule that

---

[63] *Jones v Brooks* [1968] 52 Cr App R 614, 616–17.
[64] *R v Smith* [1973] 2 WLR 942 (CA).

factual impossibility is irrelevant to culpability for an attempt runs up against hypothetical cases such as that of the believer in voodoo who sticks a pin into the effigy of an enemy, intending to kill him. Everyone who discusses this example agrees that the voodoo enthusiast's action falls short of an attempt because of its remoteness from its object. And yet, without a presumptive criminality test of remoteness, one struggles to articulate the sense in which the voodooist's action is more remote from its intended object than that of a terrorist who tries to detonate a bomb with a remote control device whose battery is dead. With the presumptive criminality test, these cases fall out as they should: the voodooist's action, considered apart from our knowledge of his intention, can be interpreted as a cathartic expression of anger, whereas we know (because we know there is a bomb and that the device is rigged to detonate it) what the man pushing the button is up to. Without that test, however, the cases are indistinguishable: someone with a criminal intention uses all the means he believes are necessary to accomplish it, but the means are, as it turns out, ineffective. From a moral point of view, the voodooist and the frustrated terrorist are equally blameworthy.

Take another example. Without a presumptive criminality test for remoteness, how does one distinguish between a man in an unlit public street who stabs a tree he mistakenly believes is a person and an intruder who, in the dark, fires a gun into an empty bed? The intruder is by general agreement an attempted murderer, but without the presumptive criminality test to decide this, so also will be the tree stabber; for he too has done everything within his power to achieve his criminal intent only to be foiled by happenstance. From both a moral and a threat-management standpoint, the cases are indistinguishable.

Consider next the case where completion is impossible because no crime can be committed by the agent even were it to accomplish everything it set out to do. This situation may arise either because the crime the agent imagines it is committing does not exist or because the real crime the agent believes it is committing cannot, for lack of a circumstantial element of the proscribed action-type, be instantiated in this case (for example, the goods the agent is handling are, contrary to its belief, not stolen). Here the difficulty is that, if the proximity of the agent's actions to the completed offence is determined by how close the agent came to instantiating the proscribed action-type, then legal impossibility will always negate an attempt, for no action will bring the agent closer to a crime it cannot commit; yet this is counterintuitive in the case of an intruder who, intending to kill, shoots in the dark into a dead body lying in bed. On the other hand, if proximity is determined by how close the agent came to instantiating a proscribed action-type assuming the facts had been as it perceived them, then legal impossibility will never negate an attempt, for on the facts as it perceived them, the agent has committed the offence it was attempting; yet this is counterintuitive in the case of someone who, believing he is stealing an umbrella from a cloakroom, actually takes his own.

Properly applied, the presumptive criminality test resolves the conundrum posed by legally impossible attempts. Consider first the example of an imaginary crime. Suppose D commits adultery mistakenly believing that adultery is a crime. Though controversy around legal impossibility is rife, on one point there is general agreement: there can be no liability for an attempt if the crime the agent believes he is committing is nonexistent. Reasons vary, but two predominate. One is that the agent who intends an imaginary crime poses no threat to society that requires pre-emption or incapacitation;[65] another is that, had the agent discovered his mistake, he would have proceeded anyway, showing that the correct description of his action is a successful attempt to commit adultery, not an unsuccessful attempt to commit a crime.[66] The first reason is weak, however, because someone who was willing to commit what he thought was a crime to achieve his ends may next time be willing to commit a comparable real offence (say, infidelity to stockholders) if the law stands in the way of his objective; he has shown a disposition toward subordinating the law to his strongly felt desires. The second reason invokes a consideration—dominant motive—to exculpate for an impossible attempt that would not exculpate for a possible one. Someone who tries to take jewellery belonging to another is not acquitted of attempted theft if he would still take the gems were property abolished. How ordinary language would describe an action (trying to take those jewels) is not conclusive for the legal description (attempting theft).

The only cogent reason for not punishing for an attempt someone who thinks he is committing a crime that is in fact nonexistent is that to punish him would be to punish for thoughts alone. But then how is the law to deal with a man who has consensual intercourse with an adult woman erroneously believing she is under the age of consent? Here the crime he thinks he is committing is real, but the reason for not punishing in the case of an imaginary crime applies with equal force to this case. This individual too must be acquitted of attempted rape, for, as the woman is actually a consenting adult, to punish him would be to punish for thoughts alone. But does this reason apply in the case of someone who, intending to kill, breaks into a home and fires a bullet into a body in bed that, unknown to him, is already dead? No, because this individual has externalized his criminal intention in an action that cannot reasonably be interpreted otherwise than as serving a criminal purpose. This cannot be said of the adulterer or the self-imagined rapist, and so the presumptive criminality test again sorts out the cases properly. But without the presumptive criminality test, what is there to distinguish the case of the gun-firing intruder from those two? The answer is 'nothing.' In all three cases, we have a criminal intention and executing actions that, had the facts been as the agent believed them to be, would have constituted a crime. And so if the moralist and threat manager are inclined to punish the gun-firing intruder because he has done everything in his power to accomplish his criminal intent only to be saved by luck, then nothing but a salutary incoherence will keep them from punishing the self-imagined rapist as well as the attempter of an imaginary crime.

[65] *USA v Dynar*, 492.
[66] Bruce Chapman, 'Agency and Contingency: The Case of Criminal Attempts,' (1988) 38 *University of Toronto Law Journal* 355, 372–4.

It may be objected that the reasonable observer knows at once too much and too little to resolve the legal impossibility cases in a satisfactory way. The observer cannot be invested with knowledge of the agent's intention, for extrinsic evidence of intent must be excluded on the presumptive criminality test for the sufficiency of the conduct. But if the reasonable observer knows the legal truth (the woman is a consenting adult, the umbrella is the taker's own, etc.) without knowing the agent's intention, will it not always conclude that the conduct is innocent? On the other hand, if the observer is assumed not to know the legal truth, is this not arbitrarily to exclude from its awareness a crucial piece of the surrounding context?

The reasonable observer must indeed be invested with knowledge of the legal truth. However, this does not mean that the observer will interpret the agent's actions as innocent in all cases. This is so because sometimes the circumstances will give the observer reason to infer that the agent does not know the legal truth; while in other cases, the circumstances will lead the reasonable observer to infer *wrongly* that the agent does know the legal truth. For example, the observer will infer (without help from extrinsic sources) that the intruder who shoots into the bed in a dark room does not know the body is dead, and so it will interpret his actions as attempted murder. But (except under rare circumstances) the observer will wrongly assume that the umbrella taker means to take his own umbrella from the cloakroom, and so it will interpret the taker's actions as innocent.

Accordingly, while impossibility of completion should not necessarily preclude culpability for attempt, liability should be excluded where, applying the presumptive criminality test for remoteness, a reasonable observer could interpret the defendant's action as innocent. In most circumstances, this principle will exclude liability in the cases where jurists agree that liability should be excluded: taking one's own umbrella from a cloakroom thinking it belongs to someone else, selling a genuine Picasso believing it is fake, purchasing a DVD player in an open market erroneously believing it was stolen.[67] However, if, as has occurred in the common-law world, the presumptive criminality test is abandoned for reasons that apply only to a caricature of the test, then nothing but prosecutorial discretion will stop liability for thought crimes such as these.

Counselling and conspiracy

In *Barker*, Justice Salmond argued that words could constitute an attempt if they were the means used to further the defendant's criminal purpose and if, understood in their discursive and circumstantial context, no reasonable observer could interpret them as having an innocent import.[68] *Barker* was a case of solicitation for unlawful sex, but the presumptive criminality test is generally applicable to culpable speech, known to the law as counselling, procuring, or inciting. At present, the *actus reus* of counselling in positive law is usually expressed in the form of action

[67] Anderton v Ryan [1985] 2 All ER 355.   [68] Barker, 876.

verbs—encouraging, urging, importuning, etc.—that fail to focus the mind on what makes words culpable in their own right as public manifestations of a right-denying choice. As a result, judges may, on the one hand, sweep into criminality hortatory words that a reasonable observer could interpret as not seriously meant or as meant in a humorous vein, and on the other, exclude from liability words publicly manifesting a culpable purpose but thinly disguised in instructional and nonhortatory language (as in manuals for home-made bombs).[69] Conceiving counselling as a kind of attempt and applying the presumptive criminality test to determine the culpability of the words would redeem for liberal penal justice a crime historically intended for threat management, while perhaps even achieving greater protection against threats to public order.

In the crime of conspiracy, the *actus* on which criminal liability hinges is nothing more than an agreement between two or more persons to commit an offence. No actions toward achieving the common design are necessary. The redundancy of an action together with the historical roots of conspiracy in the Court of Star Chamber have led commentators to view conspiracy as a crime even more inchoate than attempt, reflecting the subordination of criminal desert to the exigencies of crime prevention and the incapacitation of human threats.

However, this appearance may be deceiving. If by inchoate crime is meant unfulfilled criminal purpose, then conspiracy certainly pushes the line at which liability takes hold further back toward conception. But if by inchoate crime is meant not yet a full crime, conspiracy is no more an inchoate crime than attempt is; each is itself a crime by virtue of the public manifestation of a culpable choice. In conspiracy, the agreement between minds does the work in triggering criminal desert that unambiguous actions do in attempts, and that is why actions form no part of the *actus reus*. The mutual commitment to commit an offence is itself the externalization into public reality of the criminal choice of each conspirator.

This will be so, however, only if there has been a firm agreement as distinct from negotiations, deliberations, or imagining in common, which do not go beyond the expression of thoughts. And, while actions furthering the plot are theoretically unnecessary for culpability, it is difficult to see how a firm agreement could be evidenced without them. Accordingly, some executing actions, even if too ambiguous for attempt liability, could be evidence sufficiently probative of an agreement—indeed, would normally be essential to proof beyond reasonable doubt. However, the agreement itself is essential, not as evidence of dangerous resolve (which may be obtainable elsewhere) but as signifying the stepping of private purpose into public reality, whereby each conspirator gives interpersonal force to the right-denying principle implicit in his intention. Moreover, conspiracy can be a crime deserving of punishment only if it is an agreement to break the law, for only then does the agreement embody a right denial applicable to

---

[69] For an error of the former type, see *R v Mcleod* (1970) 1 CCC (2d) 5 (BC CA).

the denier. The branch of common-law conspiracy that punished combinations likely to effect a public mischief but that contemplated no action for which a lone individual could be punished was a true child of Star Chamber.[70]

5. Epilogue

The foregoing is a legal account of the culpable action requirement of criminal desert that, unlike the moral account, preserves the *actus* as a co-ordinate and essential element of liability to punishment rather than as merely evidence of a blameworthy mind. Moreover, it is an account that, in fully separating crime from tort, provides a way of disciplining status and inchoate crimes to a law of punishment so that they need not be abandoned to an administrative regime ordered to crime prevention and the management of human threats. The basic idea is that criminal desert requires an externalization of a culpable intention because the right denial implicit in a criminal purpose must claim public validity if there is to be a logical impetus toward turning the denial against its author. This means that an action or omission (or anything else) is an *actus reus* deserving of judicial punishment just in case it is a public manifestation of a choice to which a right denial is imputable. Such a manifestation may take the form of an actual right violation, but it need not do so. Attempts and counselling crime are also public manifestations of a culpable choice if (and only if) the defendant's actions or words, understood in context but apart from other evidence of intent, cannot reasonably be interpreted otherwise than as serving a culpable purpose. A conspiracy is likewise such a manifestation if there have been executing actions evidencing a firm agreement among the conspirators to break the law. Thus the formal agency account of penal desert at once incorporates, legitimates, and subjects to substantive constraints offences normally regarded as justified by crime control rather than by desert.

[70] *Shaw v DPP* [1962] AC 220 (HL).

4

Responsibility for Harm

1. Public Reason as Real Autonomy

Hitherto we have dealt with the threshold elements of criminal culpability—those that distinguish crime from tort and that reconcile punishment in general for crime in general with the agent's inviolability. We now deal with the agent's responsibility for the harmful results of its culpable conduct assuming that the threshold of criminality has been crossed. The agent deserves to be punished, but for what specifically and how much?

At issue here is not basic responsibility (whether the doer had the capacity for free choice) but *outcome responsibility* (for what results of its culpable choice is the free agent punishable?). Here the questions for discussion are: should results matter to the deserved measure of punishment and, if so, why? If they do matter, are there limits on liability to punishment for results and, if so, where is the line to be drawn? At results caused intentionally? At results caused with foresight of their likelihood? At results caused negligently? When does a cause intervening between the defendant's culpable conduct and the proscribed result shield the defendant from criminal liability for that result? We will see that answers to these questions cannot be derived from the formal agency paradigm of penal justice and so require transition to a new framework, which I'll call the paradigm of real autonomy. How the two frameworks are united within a coherent account of penal justice is the subject of Chapter 9.

Formalism, strict liability for results, and fault-undifferentiated crimes

At the end of Chapter 1, I pointed out certain limitations of the formalist paradigm considered as a complete account of penal justice. One of these concerned the idea of a punishable harm. Because formalism equates goods with preferences and the public interest with the capacity for free choice, it cannot without equivocation recognize harms to common goods as distinguishing crimes by level of gravity; nor can it even recognize the differential impacts on liberty of interferences with bodily and proprietary sovereignty. Hence it cannot generate a scale of punishments relating severity to the kind of agency interest interfered with or the kind of harm caused.[1] For a theoretically self-contained formalism, there is only one crime—an intentional or reckless interference with liberty—and only one punishment—restraint. Moreover, to this problem we can now add another that was revealed in our discussion of the criminal *actus*. Because formalist crime is completed in a publicly manifested right denial that can occur just as well with an unsuccessful as with a successful attempt, formalism cannot account for the relevance of outcomes to criminal desert in the positive law: for it, unsuccessful and successful attempts are the same crime. While this view has some currency among academics, it is totally unsupported in legal practice.[2]

Because formalism cannot coherently acknowledge harm as a factor aggravating criminal wrongdoing, it yields no principle for determining when resulting harm should figure in the description of the crime the wrongdoer committed and the wrongdoer be punished for it. Therefore, as long as formalism is considered a complete theory of penal justice, this question will be left free for decision on nondesert or instrumentalist grounds. Exigencies of crime control will determine liability for harm. Since, moreover, general deterrence from the graver crime is served by punishing the wrongdoer for consequential harm *whenever* the harm materializes, liability for harm within the formalist paradigm depends on unbridled chance. Resulting harm is punishable when it results. We see this, for example, in the crimes of manslaughter and constructive (or felony) murder as well as in the "thin-skull" rule, all of which make criminal liability for the harmful results of criminal wrongs strict—that is, independent of any degree of the result's imputability to the wrongdoer's agency. Since the idea of imputability will figure prominently in the discussion that follows, a clarification is in order.

A result is imputable to an agent, I will assume, if the agent either chose it, chose the risk of it, or could have avoided the result had the agent chosen to exercise its capacity for ordinary foresight and care. An agent chooses a result if it either aims to produce the result with means it believes are adequate to the task, acts knowing that the result will certainly (barring a miracle) ensue from its deed, or chooses to perform an action (such as spying for the enemy) that logically entails the result (assisting the enemy). An agent chooses the risk of a result if, and only if, the agent is aware of the risk and knowingly takes it. An agent could have

---

[1] Here the formalist might object that the immediate preferences abstracted from in the first instance are not the freedom interests that have now come into view, and so formalism can accept these interests without revision of its foundations; see Ernest Weinrib, 'Right and Advantage in Private Law,' (1989) 10 *Cardozo Law Review* 1283, 1286. If only matters were that simple. Remember that the *identification* of goods with preferences underlay the whole nonteleological system of legal thought called the priority of the right, of which legal retributivism is a part.

[2] For support see Andrew Ashworth, 'Sharpening the Subjective Element in Criminal Liability,' in RA Duff and NE Simmonds, eds., *Philosophy and the Criminal Law* (Wiesbaden: Cambridge University Press, 1984), 79–89. HLA Hart, *Punishment and Responsibility* (Oxford: Clarendon Press, 1968), 129; S Kadish, 'Foreword: The Criminal Law and the Luck of the Draw,' (1994) 84 *Journal of Criminal Law and Criminology* 679; Joel Feinberg, *Doing and Deserving* (Princeton, NJ: Princeton University Press, 1970), 33; Hyman Gross, *A Theory of Criminal Justice* (New York: Oxford University Press, 1979), 423–36.

avoided a result if, and only if, it had the cognitive capacity to foresee the result as well as a choice whether or not to attend to and avoid the risk.

Under the formalist paradigm, penal liability for results is unconstrained by a requirement that the result be imputable to the agent in one of these senses; it is enough that the agent caused the result as a matter of fact. Factual causation is necessary, because the authorization the criminal gave for punishment *simpliciter* was not a totally blank cheque. Since the authorization was implied in his deed, it did not extend to "punishment" for events having no connection with his deed (any more than it extended to punishment for crimes committed by unrelated others). Nevertheless, factual causation is sufficient for formalism. Thus, in many common-law jurisdictions, one can be punished for manslaughter, and even for murder during a felony, though death was unforeseeable; and in general, one can be punished for the harmful consequence of a criminal wrong even if the consequence would not have occurred but for an unknowable and unusual susceptibility of the victim.[3]

To be sure, the retributivist legitimation of punishment belonging to formalism demands that penal force in the abstract be implicitly self-willed by the wrongdoer through a chosen transgression in the abstract. However, it generates no requirement that the results determining the severity of his punishment be confined to those connected in some degree to his choice, whether by intention, awareness of risk, or unexercised capacity to foresee and avoid. This is so because, while the formalist equation of public reason with the capacity for free choice yields a right against unauthorized pre-emptions of the capacity by other agents, it gives no insurance against the vulnerability to brute chance of one's power to exercise the capacity. Thus, once the wrongdoer has crossed the threshold into criminality by virtue of a chosen transgression, he may be punished for all the proscribed harms that ensue from his wrong regardless of whether he could be expected to have foreseen them. I'll call this phenomenon strict penal liability for results.[4]

Not only does the formalist paradigm permit punishment for results that are unconnected (beyond factual causation) to the criminal's agency; it also permits punishment that is untailored to the degree to which the result is imputable to his agency. By degrees of imputability I mean differences in the relative contribution to a result of choice and chance. So, if the criminal wrongdoer produced

---

[3] *R v Holland* (1841) 2 Mood & R 351; *R v Larkin* (1942) 29 Cr App R 18, 23; *R v Creighton* [1993] 3 SCR 3; *State v Frazer* 98 SW (2d) 707 (1936).

[4] Andrew Ashworth discusses two variants of this position: the "unlawful act theory", which bases strict liability for results on any unlawful act requiring intention and "moderate constructivism", which requires the punishable result to be a harm belonging to the same "family of interests" as that to which the interest attacked at the threshold belonged; see 'A Change of Normative Position: Determining the Contours of Culpability in Criminal Law,' (2008) 11 *New Criminal Law Review* 232, 233–42. The former view underlies the English and Canadian law of manslaughter; the latter view is favoured by some academics. If the "family of interest" restriction is not a proxy for foreseeability of the punishable harm, it is not clear what normative work it is doing; and if it is such a proxy, why not require foreseeability directly?

the result purposely (aimed to produce it either as end or means) or having known that (given the laws of physics or logic) it would certainly ensue from, or be implied by, pursuing another purpose, imputability is tightest, for he has chosen the result. Even though he may by chance have failed in his efforts, the successful outcome is his without remainder because he chose it. If he chose only the risk of the outcome and the risk materialized, then imputability is weaker, for chance has played a role in the happening of the result just in the degree to which the result is underdetermined by his choice. If he chose neither the result nor the risk thereof but the result was avoidable had he chosen to exercise the foresight of which human agents generally and he in particular are capable, imputability is weakest; for here choice has played a role in the event's occurrence only in a counterfactual sense: the result could have been avoided had the criminal who factually caused it chosen otherwise, as he could have done. Call these three degrees of imputability intention, recklessness, and negligence, respectively.

Now the formalist paradigm generates no requirement of penal justice that the severity of punishment for a proscribed result (for example, death) be proportioned to the degree to which the result is imputable to the criminal's choice as distinct from ascribable to chance. Instead, it permits extrinsic considerations of crime control to conflate under the same criminal label (for example, murder), and to punish equally, different degrees of imputability. Any adjustment of the sentence to the defendant's responsibility for the result is left to the trial judge's discretion (assuming no mandatory sentence)—a sign of formalism's indifference to whether punishments are actually calibrated to imputability or to whether those who are alike in respect of outcome responsibility are treated alike. Proportionality is not a lexically prior and system-wide justice constraint on the pursuit of other sentencing goals; it is simply one of several ends for the trial judge to consider and weigh.

I'll call the product of conflating different degrees of imputability a fault-undifferentiated crime. Constructive murder is an example, for besides allowing punishment for an unforeseeable death, it labels (hence stigmatizes) and punishes the same those who intentionally kill and those who kill where death was only foreseeable. So too murder, which in Canada blurs the distinction between those who kill intentionally and those who kill through an intentional interference with the body having foreseen the high risk of death.[5] Accomplice liability is another example, for a party to a crime is typically held responsible for any further crime he ought to have foreseen would ensue, to the same degree as the principal who intentionally committed it.[6] Yet a further illustration is the common-law rule regarding the exculpatory force of intoxication evidence. Such evidence is inadmissible to negate a simple intention to do the proscribed deed (though it is admissible to negate the intention to do it as a means to some further end) because, it is said, the unlawful deed and resultant harm are sufficiently

---

[5] Canadian Criminal Code, RSC 1985, C–46, s. 229 (a)(i) and (a)(ii). Model Penal Code, s. 210.2
[6] Canadian Criminal Code, s. 21(2); Model Penal Code, s. 2.06(4).

connected to the defendant's agency by virtue of his having intentionally or recklessly become extremely intoxicated.[7] But since the recklessness relates here to the getting drunk rather than to the unlawful deed, the latter is connected to the defendant's agency at most through negligence. Thus, negligently causing an unlawful outcome is branded identically to, and punished with the same maximum as, intentionally causing it.[8]

The formalist paradigm of penal justice does not *produce* strict liability for results, nor does it *entail* fault-undifferentiated crimes. Rather, it is simply silent in the face of the state's use of these tools for purposes of deterrence and the incapacitation of the dangerous. Formalism, we can say, leaves punishment for results to a legal void. Because it takes the bare capacity for choice as the sole public end, formalism has no theoretical resources for limiting penal liability for chance consequences once the fault threshold authorizing any punishment has been traversed; for the right against forcible pre-emptions of the capacity for free choice is not yet a right that the vulnerability to chance of one's actualized capacity be limited by, and proportioned to, imputability.

The transition to the real autonomy paradigm

Nevertheless, the transition to a framework of penal justice that generates such a right is already implied in the formalist conception of public reason. Formalism identified public reason with freedom and freedom with an agent's capacity to act from ends it could have rejected. This capacity for undetermined choice is also a potential for self-determined choice—for shaping one's life according to self-authored ends. Nonetheless, formalism did not treat the realization of this potential for self-determination as itself part of the freedom protected by law; rather, juristic freedom was understood only negatively—as freedom *from* causal determinism.

However, if freedom is equated with negative freedom, then much of what is generally regarded as crime could not be said to violate an agent's right to freedom. Actions that pre-empt exercise of the capacity for free choice through the physical application of force would do so; but actions that allow room for the capacity's exercise and only direct the victim's choice to ends not his or her own would not. Thus, killing a human being pre-empts his capacity for free choice, as does pushing him, holding him, hitting him, abducting him, confining him, or wresting something from him. However, taking property not in the owner's physical grasp does not pre-empt the owner's capacity for undetermined choice; rather it interferes in the sphere reserved for the agent's use of means to achieve self-authored ends. Similarly, influencing another to serve one's ends by threatening him with reputation loss if

---

[7] *DPP v Majewski* (1976) 62 Cr App R 262 (HL).
[8] The Model Penal Code countenances fault-undifferentiated crimes, for it denies exculpatory force to negligent mistakes of fact if the same crime can be committed negligently or intentionally; see ss. 3.02(2), 3.09(3).

he refuses does not pre-empt his capacity for free choice; rather, the victim exercises his capacity but in a way that fails to execute a self-authored end. Nor does obtaining property or consent to physical contact by fraud pre-empt capacity; again, the victim exercises his capacity for free choice, but, because of the deception, his action misfires as a realization of his purpose. Indeed, if freedom is simply freedom from causal determinism, then one is free whatever one does as long as one moves consciously and is not moved or prevented from moving by external physical forces. Accordingly, in which direction must liberal penal theory go: toward reducing crime to pre-emptions of the capacity for free choice, or to criminalizing actions that interfere with the capacity's exercise in action from self-authored ends?

The answer, of course, is that liberal penal justice must encompass as crimes actions that interfere with the capacity's exercise in autonomously motivated action—in action from ends reflecting the agent's own purposiveness, its potential for authoring ends. This is so because the idea behind formalism's right against the pre-emption of capacity is agency's right to respect for its end-status or dignity. That right is violated, however, not only by pre-emptions of capacity through physical force, but also by interferences with its autonomous exercise by threats and fraud; for unless agents act from self-authored ends, they are not the ends of their actions but are rather instruments for another. Thus no one will deny that enslavement, which is an interference with autonomously motivated action rather than a pre-emption of action as such, is inconsistent with an agent's end-status. So if, as the formalist paradigm claims, the agent is a final end, then it has a right, not only to act, but also to act from ends it autonomously projects.

However, once liberal legal thought acknowledges a right to action from self-authored ends, it cannot stop at a right against interference with autonomy by other agents; for such interference is only one way in which the freedom to act from self-authored ends may be subverted. That freedom may also be short-circuited by poverty, disease, and disabling accident, as a result of which the agent is reduced to acting from ends—survival, avoidance of pain—given by biology rather than conceived autonomously. Accordingly, liberal thought must go on to recognize a robust right to the protection of autonomous action against fortuities beyond one's human capacity to foresee and control—against blind fate, as I shall call it. For if the freedom to act from self-authored ends were vulnerable to uncontrollable contingencies, then freedom would not be an end in relation to the sphere of causes and effects; it would instead be the plaything of the aimless forces operative within that sphere. But the end-status of freedom is the fundamental public reason of liberal justice in its formalist interpretation. Thus, liberal legal thought is driven by the logic of formalist principle to a framework of justice ordered to a conception of public reason richer than the formalist one—to a conception of public reason I'll call real autonomy.

Under this conception, agents not only have a right against interference with autonomous action on particular occasions by other agents; they also have a right to the general protection of autonomous action against contingencies of all sorts—including poverty, illness, accident, crime, and, yes, even the unforeseeable consequences of their criminal actions. This general entitlement is not, however, held against all agents as private individuals; for, as an entitlement unfolded from the idea of a liberal public reason, it is correlative to a prior duty on the person claiming coercive authority under public reason as its human representative. That person (as well as those who legislate, administer, and adjudicate in his or her name) is alone duty-bound to satisfy the entitlement as a condition of its valid authority to coerce.

There is yet another logical route from formalism to the right against unlimited penal liability for the results of criminal wrongs. Formalism conceived the capacity for free choice as the sole public end, hence as the only end qualified to justify coercion by the state. Yet, in the retributive conception of punishment belonging to formalism, there is already implicit a public end richer than the bare capacity for free choice. In that conception, recall, punishment is distinguished from the wrongdoer's coercion to the extent that it is possible to impute self-imposition on the part of the recipient as an implication of his right-denying choice to interfere with another's agency. This means that retributive punishment discloses a potential in human agency not taken into account by formalism—namely, a potential for the agent's authoring the fate it suffers in being judicially coerced. But this potential is one for real autonomy rather than simply for nondetermination by external causes, for it is a potential for reconciling vulnerability to fate with autonomous life-shaping.

Moreover, as a potential inherent in agency, authorship of one's fate is a public end that those claiming authority under liberal public reason are duty bound to actualize. Fulfilling this duty, however, requires more than confining the *incidence* of penal force to cases where it is implicitly self-willed; it requires too that the *measure* of his punishment be self-authored by the criminal wrongdoer. But the criminal may be said to author the measure of his punishment only if the results of his wrongdoing that are reflected in the severity of his punishment are imputable in some degree to his choice and only if severity is proportioned to the degree of imputability.

2. The Features of the Real Autonomy Paradigm

The public reason under which rulers exercise legitimate coercive authority is now conceived as the real autonomy of their subjects. By real autonomy I mean realized potential for acting from self-authored ends (for autonomous life-shaping or self-motivated action). The right to real autonomy is specified in the following ways. It is

(a) a right against pre-emption by other agents of the capacity for free choice through physical force,
(b) a right against interference by other agents with the self-motivated exercise of the capacity through threats of serious harm or fraud,

(c) an entitlement *vis-à-vis* those claiming coercive authority under liberal public reason to an administration of penal justice that, through its procedures (for example, a fair and open trial by jury, a right to counsel) and substantive legal doctrines (for example, subjective *mens rea* for crime), enlists the agent's rational assent to the judgment and fate pronounced against him, and

(d) an entitlement *vis-à-vis* the same authorities to the protection of autonomous life-shaping—of investments in a life plan—against fortuities beyond a human agent's power to foresee and control.

I'll call the sum of the conditions for the realized potential for living according to self-authored ends the public welfare; and I'll call the framework of penal justice ordered to the public welfare the paradigm of real autonomy. That framework exhibits the following essential features.

Agency goods and objective harms

First, the paradigm of real autonomy introduces the idea of goods that are necessarily common to agents because they are essential to realizing the agent's potential for acting from self-authored ends. Life is obviously necessary for living autonomously, and so it is good regardless of whether this or that particular agent values it. Physical health and bodily integrity are preconditions for acting from self-authored ends, for the chronically ill or seriously disabled are, tragically, too preoccupied with the functions necessary to preserve life to be able to live out a conception of what makes life valuable. Owning property is good because it is essential to one's independence of others' ends and because it is a sphere for the exclusive operation of one's self-authored goals. An impartial administration of justice is good because necessary to the protection of rights of self-determination as well as of life, health, and limb against wrongdoers. Finally, laws and public services ordered to health, safety, and insurance against misfortune are good because necessary to the protection of autonomous life-shaping against accidents not necessarily caused by wrongdoing. I'll call the things necessary to real autonomy agency goods.

Second, because agency goods are noncontingently common goods, harm to these goods can be legally recognized as figuring into the objective gravity of criminal wrongs and hence also into the deserved measure of judicial punishment for these wrongs. Thus, crimes can be objectively distinguished and graded as more or less serious depending on whether harm to an agency good has ensued from the crime. Results can matter to the public description of what the criminal has done because harms to agency goods distinguish criminal wrongs according to seriousness publicly understood. Thus a simple assault is less serious than assault causing bodily harm, aggravated assault less serious than manslaughter, and attempts in general are less serious than completed crimes. Moreover, because an item of property is less important to the realized potential for self-motivated action than bodily health or integrity, and because the latter is less important than life, the kinds of harm resulting from criminal wrongs can themselves be graded as more or less serious depending on the importance to real autonomy of the agency good harmed or interfered with.[9] Thus, a scale of punishments relating severity ordinally to the seriousness of the type of harm caused becomes theoretically coherent under the real autonomy paradigm, whereas formalism could adopt it only at the price of equivocation.

To be sure, the existence of agency goods is insufficient by itself to explain why results do and should matter for criminal liability, if indeed they should. We still need to know whether, and if so why, criminal wrongdoers are properly held responsible for harmful results whose materialization is a matter of chance and, conversely, why they should (if indeed they should) benefit from the chance non-materialization of the harms they fully intended. We also need to know whether, and if so why, assuming criminal wrongdoers are properly accountable for results, they are properly punished for harmful results they did not intend. None of these questions is adequately answered simply by pointing to the existence of agency goods. Nevertheless, the universality of agency goods is a necessary condition of punishability according to result, for (absent a contract of mutual benefit) free agents cannot assent to having their freedom curtailed according to the harms they cause to others' subjective interests.

Public welfare offences and noncriminal penalties

Not only does the real autonomy paradigm provide a theoretical framework capable of explaining the differentiation of crimes and scale of punishments that formalism could not; it also provides a framework for comprehending and disciplining to legal norms noncriminal offences against the public welfare. Because those claiming authority under public reason now have a duty to safeguard the conditions of real autonomy against all fortuities, they cannot wait until harms to agency goods are caused or threatened by criminal conduct before intervening with penal force. They must also prevent harms that might occur accidentally, and prevention requires intervention before the dangerous activity causes harm or even impinges on another's liberty. Thus they legislate so-called public welfare offences, proscribing excessively risky activity irrespective of whether the risk has materialized or whether the agent was aware of the risk.

In this context, the retributivist legitimation of penal force as impliedly self-willed has no application, for there is no logical circuit between the intentional doing of what a regulation proscribes and a penal consequence. Apart from a statute, someone who drives faster than 100 kilometres per hour on an otherwise deserted highway does nothing to which a right denial is imputable; and so the rationale for penalizing him cannot be to vindicate the reality of rights, nor can it

---

[9] This largely agrees with the criterion of seriousness proposed by Jareborg, von Hirsch, and Ashworth: harms are more or less publicly serious depending on whether they affect "means or capabilities" more or less important for achieving a valued life; see Andrew von Hirsch and Andrew Ashworth, *Proportionate Sentencing* (Oxford: Oxford University Press, 2005), 144–6, 186–219.

be said that he has authorized his punishment. But if a statute sets the speed limit at 100 kilometres per hour, he may be penalized even if he exceeded the limit inadvertently. Here the penalty for an infraction is legitimated not by desert but by the prevention of harm to agency goods. This means that the doctrinal constraints on liability to punishment discussed in the previous two chapters—those ensuring that it is deserved in the sense of being impliedly self-willed—do not apply to non-criminal penalties; and we saw that this nonapplicability of legal retributivism left a normative void as long as the formalist paradigm was considered exhaustive of penal justice. The question as to what alternative constraints on noncriminal penalization are generated by the real autonomy paradigm is discussed in Chapter 5.

Authoring fate

The real autonomy paradigm generates an entitlement *vis-à-vis* those claiming coercive authority under public reason to the conditions for realizing the agent's potential for shaping a life according to self-authored ends. We saw that one of these conditions is that the vulnerability to blind fate of one's investment in a life plan be brought under rational control. But what exactly is blind fate, and what does it mean to bring it under rational control?

Dramatic literature offers us depictions of different conceptions of fate. As we can distinguish between the kinds of tragedy respectively portrayed in *Romeo and Juliet* and *Oedipus the King*, so we can distinguish between the two kinds of fate by which the heroes of these tragedies are brought low. One may be called natural fate because it is what befalls someone as a result of causes (microbes, earthquake, human misadventure) in the physical world—death, illness, disability, financial loss, and so on. This is fate in the sense of fortune or luck, which is capricious, aimless, unpredictable, indeed often unforeseeable. Natural fate itself appears in different shapes. It can take the form of happenings or situations that occur independently of human action, such as disease, natural disaster, birth advantages, and the like; or it can take the form of happenings—called accidents—that are the effects of causes supervening on action and deflecting it from its object. The fate depicted in Shakespeare's tragedy is of the latter sort. Thus, it was through sheer blind luck that Friar John was prevented from delivering the letter to Romeo that would have informed him of the plan to fake Juliet's death.

The other kind of fate may be called moral fate because it is what befalls someone as the result of the execution of a judgment. This is fate in the sense of nemesis, which is inexorable and implacable—the kind of fate that stalked Oedipus from infancy. Unlike natural fate, moral fate is purposeful; but in its tragic form, the purpose is wholly independent of the agent's purposes, and it is dark, hidden, knowable only to oracles and sightless prophets. Here fate executes a predetermined judgment impossible to avoid, and its independence of human agency is shown in the way that it works through unforeseeable accident, turning natural fate to its own end. Thus it was through no doing of

Oedipus that he is ignorant of his true parentage or that he is attacked on a country road by his father, Laius, whom he kills in self-defence: these things simply befall him. Whereas, moreover, the blindness pertaining to natural fate is a blindness *of* the fate—its aimlessness—that pertaining to moral fate is a blindness *to* the fate. Oedipus's destiny fulfils itself behind his back. He unwittingly brings it to pass by the very means he uses in trying to escape it. His actions are mere instruments of an external and unknown purpose; his own purposes are beside the point.

Now, the right to real autonomy entails, first, an entitlement to protection against an uncontrolled vulnerability to natural fate. Thus it entails an entitlement to the panoply of regulatory laws and public insurance measures by which the agent's exposure to accident, illness, and economic fluctuation is limited. But second, the right to real autonomy entails a right that Oedipus's tragedy be a thing of the past: that one be subject to no moral fate that one has not implicitly self-authored through one's conscious choices and whose deservedness is not clear to rational insight. This is a right that one's moral fate not be unqualifiedly enmeshed, as it was for Oedipus, with natural fate—that it not be unavoidable—and that it be intelligibly connected in some degree to what one chose to do.

It is the latter entitlement that will occupy us in the rest of this chapter. Specifying its meaning will fill out our account of the relevance of results to criminal culpability; for unless penal liability for results is consistent with authorship of one's moral fate, it will not matter that the harmful outcome of a criminal wrong figures objectively into the seriousness of what has befallen the victim. As we have seen, the fact that harms to agency goods distinguish criminal wrongs according to a public measure of seriousness is a necessary but not sufficient condition for branding and punishing the criminal for, and in proportion to, the harmful result of his wrong. It must also be the case that the criminal is rightly answerable for the result.

3. What Does the Right to Author One's Moral Fate Entail?

Why results matter to penal liability

It is not crazy to think that the right to be subject to no moral fate one has not self-authored requires a rule that the criminal not be punished for *any* result of his wrong. No less a figure than Kant argued for such a rule with respect to moral blaming; and it is not obvious why, if the autonomy he reserved for private ethics becomes a political end, the rule should not also apply to punishment.[10] Some have called this idea a subjectivist thesis about criminal liability, but it should not be confused with the subjectivist thesis I defended in Chapter 2. There I argued

---

[10] *Foundations of the Metaphysics of Morals*, trans. LW Beck (Indianapolis: Bobbs-Merrill, 1959), 10.

that a choice to do that from which a right denial is imputable to the choice must be a condition of criminal liability if punishment is to be reconciled with the agent's inviolability; and so punishing for inadvertent interferences with choice is impermissible. That, of course, is far from a claim that no results of criminal wrongs are properly imputable to the wrongdoer.

Nevertheless, it may plausibly be argued that the subjectivist thesis I defended regarding culpability for wrong commits its proponent to the further claim that the criminal ought to be punished only for wrong and not for harm. This is so because the subjectivism I endorsed turns on the idea that punishment, to be distinguishable from external violence, must be implicitly self-chosen. One must be able to conceive oneself as the author of one's moral fate. But of course results are not at the beck and call of choice. All that belongs exclusively to choice, one might argue, are one's intentions and one's efforts to carry them out. What turns out in the world belongs to chance rather than to choice, for one's efforts might fail through the intervention of any number of contingencies; and if they might fail through bad luck, then it is partly through good luck that they succeed. Thus the outcome of a choice seems to be extraneous to the choice itself. But, the argument runs, since the right to author one's moral fate entails a right to be punished only for one's choices, it also entails a right to be insulated from criminal responsibility for everything but one's wrongful attempts.[11] Call this the extreme subjectivist thesis.

Though not crazy, the extreme subjectivist thesis is nonetheless wrong. To see why it is wrong and not entailed by the subjectivism I endorse, we need only consider how chance is necessarily bound up with *any* exercise of the capacity for choice. The proponent of extreme subjectivism assumes that, while the outcomes of acts belong partly to chance, acts themselves belong exclusively to choice. But do they? After all, it is only by chance that I am able to move my body to execute an intention to X; things might have turned out differently. Indeed, it is only by chance that I formed an intention to X; had circumstances been different, nothing of the sort might have occurred to me. So if we wish to subtract from agency everything that does not strictly belong to it, we are left with nothing but pure agency itself—the metaphysical capacity for free choice.[12] That is to say, we are left with nothing but nothing.

What this *reductio* shows, however, is not that empirical agents are inevitably heteronomous—that there is no human potential for autonomy. Still less does it imply (as Thomas Nagel feared) that agency must, in diving into action, drown itself in the broader class of events. What the *reductio* shows, rather, is that any exercise of the capacity for free choice in a particular choice *necessarily* engages chance, so that an agent who chooses to perform some action in particular implicitly (for the thinking Agent in his shoes) *chooses* to submit to the power of chance over its action. This does not mean that the agent assents to an unlimited subjection to

---

[11] Ashworth, 'Sharpening the Subjective Element in Criminal Liability,' 79–89.
[12] See Thomas Nagel's and Bernard Williams's famous reflections on this point in *Mortal Questions* (Cambridge: Cambridge University Press, 1979), 24–38 and *Moral Luck* (Cambridge: Cambridge University Press, 1981), 20–1, respectively.

chance, as I'll argue in a moment. But it does mean that the agent cannot disown the result of its act simply because chance has had a hand in it. Having chosen to act under the material conditions for acting, the agent also implicitly authorized natural fate to interfere with its act. Thus, when Faust blames Mephistopheles for the chain of events subsequent to his seduction of Gretchen and ending in her destruction, the devil responds appropriately: "Will you fly and be safe from dizziness? ... Who was it that plunged her into ruin? I or you?"

We may conclude, then, that results matter to the description and punishment of criminal wrongs because (on the objective side) harms to agency goods figure objectively into the seriousness of a wrong and (on the subjective side) because at least some results belong to acts by virtue of the actor's having implicitly authorized natural fate to meddle with them (given the necessary connection between action and contingency). Of course, luck may play with acts, not only by taking them in unintended directions, but also by foiling them or by favouring them; hence these interventions too are authorized by acting. This is why people whose criminal attempts succeed author more punishment than those whose criminal attempts fail, and it is why people who culpably cause a particular kind of harm author more punishment than people who culpably choose to risk that harm without causing it.

Why penal liability for results does not depend on intending or foreseeing the result

The same line of reasoning tells us that criminal responsibility for results is not limited to aimed-at results or to results one knew would certainly occur as a by-product of one's action. Choosing by acting to submit to the power of chance precisely means accepting the possibility that one's deeds will produce consequences one did not mean to produce or know for certain would result. So, when Mrs Hyam set fire to her rival's home aiming only to scare her away from Mr Jones, she implicitly accepted ownership of any deaths of the inhabitants that might ensue.[13] She cannot disown that result simply because she did not choose it, for, given the necessary connection between action and contingency, she implicitly chose to expose her intended object to natural fate. Thus, punishing her for an unchosen result is not inconsistent with her authorship of her moral fate (though whether she was rightly punished for murder is a further question I'll consider later).

Nor is punishing the criminal for a result he did not subjectively foresee as likely inconsistent with his authorship of his moral fate. Assuming a risk of harm above the socially expected as well as normal human intelligence in the actor, whether an actor does or does not notice the risk he creates depends on himself—on whether or not he chooses to engage his human capacity to think beyond the immediate object of his action. But authorizing by acting natural fate's power over one's act precisely means submitting to a power independent of

[13] *Hyam v DPP* [1975] AC 55 (HL).

one's choices. That is what natural fate is. It would be inconsistent with authorizing a power independent of one's agency to limit liability for results to those one empirically foresaw, for this makes liability depend solely on one's own choice. But because authorizing a power independent of one's agency is what one does by choosing to act, punishing the criminal for a result he did not subjectively foresee does not by itself violate his right to author his moral fate.

All this explains more fully what we could only partly explain in Chapter 2: why a subjectivist position on the fault threshold for punishability for wrongdoing does not entail a subjectivist position with regard to punishability for the harmful results of wrongs once the culpability threshold has been crossed.[14] Punishability for a wrong is consistent with the agent's inviolability only if a right denial can be inferred from the wrong, one that licenses the infringement of the denier's right; and a right denial can be inferred from the wrong only if the wrongdoer intended, foresaw, or was wilfully blind toward his interference with another human being's agency. But once a punitive right infringement *simpliciter* has been authorized, the question of measure is (partly) decided by the harmful results of the criminal transgression; and one authorizes punishment for results beyond what one intends or foresees by virtue of the necessary connection between acting and engaging chance. Because in choosing to act for a particular end, one implicitly authorizes the meddling of chance with one's choice, penal liability for the unintended and unforeseen results of chosen transgressions is consistent with the right to author one's moral fate.

Accordingly, offences such as manslaughter and assault causing bodily harm are not exceptions to a rule requiring subjective *mens rea* for criminal liability. This is so, not because they require subjective *mens rea* for the result, but because there is no such blanket rule. There is neither a positive nor a normative requirement that subjective fault extend to the result elements of a crime, though there is (as I argued in Chapter 2) a normative requirement of subjective fault for the underlying transgression.

Why penal liability for results cannot be strict

But now we come to an issue of controversy. Does choosing by acting to expose one's act to contingency entail authorship of *all*, including the unforeseeable, consequences of one's criminal wrong, as Oedipus (whose accusing conscience

---

[14] John Gardner explains this by rule of law considerations. Subjectivism at the threshold ensures that the agent will have had notice that his contemplated deed will incur penal liability; but once the threshold has been crossed, publication of the law suffices to give him notice that he will be punishable for unforeseen consequences; see 'On the General Part of the Criminal Law,' in A Duff, ed., *Philosophy and the Criminal Law* (Cambridge: Cambridge University Press, 1998), 243–4. As Andrew Ashworth argues, however, publication cannot by itself make fair a rule of liability that might be substantively unfair. It must be explained why liability for unforeseen results is substantively fair because consistent with authorship of one's moral fate; see Ashworth, 'A Change of Normative Position,' 247.

exacts self-punishment) believes? Or does the right to real autonomy set limits on penal liability for results? More concretely, is an assailant rightly punished for manslaughter if his battery factually caused the victim's death no matter how death came about? Or is he punishable for an unforeseen death only if an agent with normal capacities would have appreciated the high risk of death from the harm inflicted and he possesses those capacities? Is he, for example, punishable for a death if he inflicted a finger wound on the victim, who then contracted lockjaw from the wound and died because he refused an amputation that would have saved him?[15] Or is he punishable in this case only for an assault causing bodily harm? We saw that the formal agency paradigm was powerless to constrain penal liability for results and that the positive law of manslaughter by and large reflects this failing. Does the real autonomy paradigm fare any better?

The real autonomy paradigm generates an entitlement (subject to human mortality) *vis-à-vis* public authority that one's ability to act from self-authored ends be protected against natural contingencies beyond one's human power to control. This is so, as we saw, because otherwise purposive agency would be hostage to aimless cause–effect relations instead of being the end liberal justice takes it to be. The human entitlement to protection against unforeseeable natural fate sets limits on the consequences of his action the criminal actor may be deemed to have authored for purposes of determining the extent of his penal liability. Specifically, the criminal has a right to repudiate authorship of consequences that were beyond his power to foresee and avoid unless his deficiency of power was itself due to choices he made. This means that the criminal is punishable only for those unforeseen results of his crime he could have foreseen and avoided by exercising normal human intelligence unless he possesses subnormal intelligence or extraordinary experience and skill. These qualifications require some elaboration.

Inability to appreciate a risk for want of common knowledge, or ordinary education, or because of thoughtless self-absorption does not exculpate for a result, for these deficits could themselves have been avoided.[16] Because one is properly protected only against uncontrollable consequences of criminal wrongs, one cannot invoke in exculpation for a result deficits or frailties for which one is responsible. Thus, only immutable incapacity to avoid a normally foreseeable result (owing to mental or physical disability) can exculpate.[17] Extraordinary skill would not expose one to a personal standard of care in tort law (it would do so only to a professional one), for the location of the boundary between persons must be drawn impersonally, hence without attention to individual idiosyncrasies. But here the question is not whether a boundary has been crossed but whether the criminal transgressor can be punished for a result of his transgression. And the answer depends on whether he personally could have avoided the result. So an experienced drug dealer who

---

[15] *R v Holland*, note 3 above.
[16] But this principle might require qualification in the case of unjust societies; see Conclusion.
[17] *R v Creighton*, note 3 above.

accidentally kills someone by injecting her with a standard dose of cocaine whose unusual potency he failed to determine is responsible for the death even though someone with common knowledge would not have appreciated the risk.

The agent's right to repudiate authorship of unforeseeable consequences makes the thin-skull rule of criminal law unjust. The maxim "you take your victim as you find him" would be sound if it meant simply that the exact medical aetiology of an unlawful harm is not part of its legally relevant description and so can be ignored in determining whether the death that occurred ought to have been foreseen by the defendant. It would be sound, too, if it merely stated that, by acting in the world, agents implicitly accept an action's exposure to luck and so cannot disown a foreseeable result simply because they did not foresee it or because things might have turned out differently had the victim been healthy (after all, if you must take your victim *where* you find him—perhaps remote from medical facilities—why not *as* you find him?). Or it would be sound if it meant (as it does in tort law) that, by acting in the world, the wrongdoer took the risk of whatever *extent* of harm befell his victim within a foreseeable *type* of harm, so that if he foreseeably causes bodily harm (a head injury), he is responsible for grievous bodily harm (paralysis) that would not have occurred but for the victim's peculiar susceptibility. Confined within any of these limits, the thin-skull rule is perfectly consistent with the right (under the real autonomy paradigm) against strict penal liability for results.

However, the thin-skull rule in the positive criminal law means none of these things. Rather, it means that, once having wronged someone, the criminal becomes responsible for a resulting death even though death was not reasonably foreseeable—even though it would not have occurred but for the victim's hidden and peculiar susceptibility. Foreseeability of the harm type is not a requirement of punishability for harm of that type. Thus, in *R v Smithers*, the defendant kicked his victim in the stomach causing him to vomit.[18] Because of a malfunctioning epiglottis, the victim inhaled his vomit and suffocated. The defendant's conviction for manslaughter was upheld on the principle that any blow beyond the *de minimis* range and resulting in death will incur guilt for manslaughter even though death would not have occurred but for an existing abnormality.[19]

The "beyond *de minimis*" qualification is puzzling. It is not a proxy for foreseeability of death, for it is only necessary that bodily harm (not necessarily serious) be foreseeable. Nevertheless, the qualification seems to embody the principle that factual causation is insufficient for criminal responsibility, that there is a limit to the risks the wrongdoer may be deemed to have accepted in acting wrongfully. And so there is, according to the real autonomy paradigm. But if the limit is not drawn at *some* degree of the punishable harm's imputability to the wrongdoer's choice, why have a limit at all and where is it to be drawn? Foreseeability of death

---

[18] [1978] 1 SCR 506.
[19] The "beyond *de minimis*" qualification to the but-for test was also applied in *R v Cato* (1976) 62 Cr App R 41.

is the lowest degree of the death's imputability to the agent, for an unforeseeable death is an unavoidable death, hence one wholly ascribable to natural fate.

No doubt the wrongdoer could have avoided the death by forbearing from wrong in the first place. But he will be justly punished for that wrong, and the question now is whether he can be punished *additionally* for the resultant death. Thus the point from which to assess avoidability of the death is during or after the assault. The question is: could the agent have avoided the death having chosen to wrong? If not, then any additional punishment for the death is not in any degree self-chosen; and if it is not self-chosen, then it is a moral fate that befalls the agent, not one it authors. Accordingly, the "beyond *de minimis*" qualification to the thin-skull rule is an incoherent half-way house between punishment for results based on factual causation alone and punishment for results based on imputability.

So far I have argued that the right to real autonomy entails a right in the criminal wrongdoer to be punished *only* for results controllable by him. But the point may also be stated positively: the criminal has a right to be punished for controllable results rather than simply for results he intended or foresaw as likely. This is so because agents realize their potential for autonomous life-shaping more or less depending on the degree to which they can limit the influence on their lives of accidents. This they can do by pulling back from myopic attention to their immediate objects and by surveying the whole of the projected action with its probable consequences. Because the capacity for free choice is also a capacity for such thoughtful foresight, and because the capacity for free choice is what accords agents their dignity, respect for an agent's dignity demands respect for its capacity for foresight; hence it demands the imputation to its agency of consequences it could have foreseen whether or not it actually foresaw them. To limit responsibility for results to what the agent empirically foresaw is, as Hegel remarked, to treat the agent "as devoid of the dignity of being a thinker and a will".[20]

We may conclude that the right against those claiming authority under public reason to author one's moral fate, when qualified by the entitlement against an unlimited vulnerability to natural fate, limits penal liability for results to those the agent could have avoided had it exercised capacities it either possessed or could reasonably be expected to acquire. Both the common law of manslaughter and statutory constructive murder provisions violate this right, for they punish for unforeseeable deaths. What else does the right to author one's moral fate entail?

Proportionality

All avoidable results of criminal wrongs are imputable to the wrongdoer, but (as we saw) not to the same degree. Aimed-at results as well as results the agent knew would certainly ensue from, or necessarily go with, its action belong to the agent without residue because it chose the result. Chance is involved only

---

[20] *Philosophy of Right*, trans. TM Knox (Oxford: Oxford University Press, 1967), para. 120.

negatively—all the things that could have happened to frustrate the end's achievement did not happen, leaving the agent's choice as the sole cause of the result. Results the agent foresaw as likely belong less tightly to agency, for here the agent chose the risk of the outcome but not the outcome itself, which was thus partly the effect of causes external to its will; hence the outcome belongs partly to agency and partly to chance. Results the agent did not foresee but could have avoided belong to the agent most tenuously, for they are its only in the sense that they would not have occurred but for the agent's failure to exercise its capacity for thoughtful foresight and care; for the rest, they are ascribable to chance.

Here we should pause to observe that the various mental orientations toward the results of criminal wrongs known to the positive law as intention, recklessness, and negligence, though grades of responsibility (or fault) for the result, are not grades of evil or wickedness. They are rather disposition-neutral grades of imputability reflecting different relative contributions to a result of choice and chance. They refer, accordingly, not to degrees of inward affirmation of the result but to degrees of *external* connection between choice and result that are knowable and amenable to objective comparison by finite beings. They cannot be grades of wickedness, because there is no strict correlation between greater responsibility for a result in law and greater wickedness. Someone who purposely kills in anguish to end suffering is less wicked than someone who kills by drunk driving, having foreseen the risk and demonstrated callous indifference to it. Yet the first is a murderer and the second a manslayer. Someone who purposely kills to save another life and someone who kills as a certain side-effect of action aimed at saving a life are equally responsible for the death in law (though they may be excused) but unequally blameworthy in the court of conscience (indeed the Catholic double-effect doctrine turns on this distinction).[21]

Nor do the grades of responsibility in law function as rough proxies for wickedness. Why consider them so when they can be explained more elegantly as exact measures of differences in imputability? An intended result always belongs to choice more tightly than a result foreseen as likely, which always belongs to choice more tightly than a result caused negligently. Moreover, that responsibility in law should be independent of blameworthiness in morals and religion is required by the right to author one's moral fate. Judgments of wickedness are inherently variable and subjective, for they depend on how the individual judge weighs conduct, result, context, motive, and character. To be subject to such judgments is thus to be ruled by the opinions of others, whereas to be subject to judgments of imputability is to be ruled by an objective and public criterion of responsibility all can accept.

Now, the right to author one's moral fate requires that the severity of punishment for crimes be ordinally tailored, not only to the seriousness of the harm caused, but also to the degree to which the harm is imputable to the agent's choice as distinct from chance. Thus, given a certain type of harm consequent

[21] *Re A* [2000] 4 All ER 961 (separating joined twins).

on a criminal wrong (property loss, bodily harm, grievous bodily harm, death), those who cause that harm intentionally deserve more punishment than those who do so recklessly, and those who cause that harm recklessly deserve more punishment than those who do so negligently. Punishment proportional to imputability is entailed by the right to author one's moral fate, for it ties the measure of one's punishment to the degree to which one's choice caused the wrongful harm rather than to a policy of crime control or to visceral judgments of degrees of villainy. The less responsible one's agency is for harm of a certain type, the less punishment one has willed in causing it. Crime control is a secondary end—rightly pursued only within the constraint imposed by proportionality.

Because the legal measure of responsibility for an outcome is the degree of external connection between outcome and choice rather than the level of inward affirmation of the outcome, the relevant description of the outcome for purposes of calibrating responsibility is a concrete rather than an abstract description. That is to say, it is a description that includes the causal path to the outcome, as in death by lightning or death by shooting; for that is the event that occurred and whose degree of connection with the agent's choice must be determined. Were the wickedness of a killer the thing to be determined, it would not matter that the specific death he intended—for example, death by shooting—was not the death the victim actually died; as long as the shooting led to death, he achieved his evil purpose. Even if the gunshot wound had healed and the victim died from the effects of an intubation performed during surgery, the killer would still be a murderer because he intended and caused death.[22] Similarly, if the killer, in assaulting his victim, foresaw the likelihood of death but (because of intervening causes) the death that occurred was outside the ambit of the risk he contemplated, he would still be a reckless killer; for he showed a wicked indifference to life and caused death.

Not so from a juristic standpoint. At that vantage point we are concerned not with judging the inner self, but with reconciling public coercion with freedom and so with ensuring that the criminal authors his moral fate. He may be said to author his moral fate, however, only if he is punished for a result in a measure proportional to his agency's trace in the result. But if that is so, then what matters is the degree of connection between the outcome *that occurred* (the death the victim died) and the criminal's choice. So if he intended death by shooting but caused death only through a doctor's botched intubation, he committed manslaughter (and attempted murder) rather than murder, for the death that occurred was connected to his agency in the degree known as negligence.[23] And if the victim died from an unforeseeable cause that resulted from the gunshot wound—if while in hospital he slipped on a wet floor and fractured his skull—the defendant is guilty only of attempted murder, for the specific death that occurred was not an event he ought to have foreseen. Finally, if the agent chose the risk of death, but the

---

[22] *R v Cheshire* [1991] 3 All ER 670.   [23] Model Penal Code, s. 2.03(2)(3).

death that occurred was outside the range of those he risked, he is responsible at most for a negligent homicide.

Contrary to received wisdom, therefore, there is nothing arbitrary about the choice whether to describe an outcome abstractly or concretely for purposes of determining the agent's legal responsibility for it.[24] A description that includes the causal path to the outcome is determined by the requirement of penal justice (in its real autonomy interpretation) that the agent not be subject to a moral fate that is unqualifiedly enmeshed in natural (causal) fate—that he be punished for a consequence only in the degree to which it is connected to his choice. Given that constraint, the relevant consequence is the specific event that occurred, not a generic one.

Further, because punishment proportional to imputability is a requirement of liberal penal justice under the real autonomy paradigm thereof, it cannot be left to sentencing discretion. To discretion is properly left aims of punishment to which penal justice is indifferent and which may be pursued only once the demands of penal justice have been satisfied—aims such as deterrence, incapacitation, and reform. Punishment proportional to imputability is not such an end. Thus, it is for legislatures to differentiate crimes by level of fault as a prior, system-wide constraint on sentencing or for judges to interpret statutory fault requirements for results in line with proportionality (or to strike them down under constitutional laws against unjust deprivations of liberty if they cannot be so construed).

4. Fault-Undifferentiated Crimes

Let us now see what implications the foregoing arguments have for some current controversies in the law of criminal responsibility for homicide.

Punishing someone for an unforeseeable result is one way of violating his right to author the measure of his punishment; it is not, however, the only way. We also violate this right when we fail to discriminate in our public brandings and maximum sentences between degrees of imputability—between intending, foreseeing the likelihood of, and having the capacity to avoid, a proscribed harm. We fail in this way when we create fault-undifferentiated result crimes—crimes whose result element can be produced either intentionally, recklessly, or negligently. Conflating degrees of imputability in a single offence violates the right to author one's punishment, for when we brand with the same name and subject to the same maximum sentences those who choose a proscribed harm, those who choose only the risk of it, and those who merely could have avoided the harm had they perceived the risk, we inflict a punishment that, because disproportionate to

---

[24] For a representative statement of scepticism concerning the notion of foreseeability, see Michael Moore, *Placing Blame* (Oxford: Clarendon Press, 1997), 363–99. Contrast HLA Hart and Tony Honoré, *Causation in the Law*, 2nd ed. (Oxford: Clarendon Press, 1985), 256–8.

imputability, is still partly imposed rather than self-authored.[25] We can illustrate this problem with the example of murder.

The legal situation

The American Law Institute's Model Penal Code (MPC) defines murder in section 210.2 as criminal homicide that is committed (a) purposely or knowingly or (b) recklessly under circumstances manifesting extreme indifference to the value of human life. Further, recklessness and indifference are presumed by the Code if the actor is engaged (as principal or accomplice) in the commission of, or in flight after committing, various felonies. With this provision, the MPC has conflated under the rubric of murder three well-marked degrees of responsibility for a criminal homicide: choosing the victim's death (purposely, knowingly), choosing the high risk of death (recklessness), and failure to avoid a foreseeable death during the commission of a felony (constructive recklessness). Thus the accomplice to a felony whose partner kills with a weapon the accomplice did not know he possessed is branded and punished equally with the principal who purposely killed or knew that death would certainly occur.

Murder based on foreseeability of death has been abolished in Canada[26] and the United Kingdom;[27] but sections 229(a)(i) and (ii) of the Canadian Criminal Code define murder as a culpable homicide where (a) the agent means to cause death or (b) means to cause bodily harm that it knows is likely to cause death. Thus choosing the high risk of a person's death is equated with, and punished the same as, choosing a person's death. There is no room for sentencing discretion to separate what the legislature has joined, even were that a sufficient cure; the punishment for murder is a mandatory sentence of life imprisonment.

In the United Kingdom, the *mens rea* or fault element for murder has generated a prolonged controversy in the Supreme Court. In *Hyam v DPP*,[28] the Court held that the intention requirement for murder is satisfied if the defendant either aimed at, knew the virtual certainty of, or foresaw the probability of, death or "really serious" bodily harm.[29] So Mrs Hyam, who meant to scare but not to kill her rival, was convicted for murder because she foresaw the risk of death to the inhabitants of the house she set ablaze. However, in more recent cases, the Court has abandoned its position in *Hyam*, holding that foresight lies outside the concept of intention; only purpose and knowledge of virtual certainty suffice. Thus, in *R v Woolin,* the Court substituted a conviction of manslaughter for murder for

---

[25] Of course, punishing for an unforeseeable result also violates proportionality by treating the same those who negligently cause the result and those who do so non-negligently. For a proportionality argument against strict liability for results, see Douglas Husak, 'Strict Liability, Justice, Proportionality,' in AP Simester, ed., *Appraising Strict Liability* (Oxford: Oxford University Press, 2005), 93–99.
[26] *R v Martineau* [1990] 2 SCR 633.   [27] Criminal Justice Act 1967, s. 8.
[28] Note 13 above.   [29] Ibid, 69, *per* Lord Hailsham.

a defendant who, in a fit of temper, had thrown his 3-year-old son against a wall, killing him.[30] This, on our view, is the correct position (or would be if it did not now conflate foresight and foreseeability of death under one offence); for it distinguishes culpable homicides as murder or manslaughter according to the degree to which the death is imputable to the killer's choice as distinct from chance.

However, in the Supreme Court and in academic commentary on these cases, the debate over whether recklessness is properly a form of *mens rea* for murder has focused mainly on the correct meaning of "intention", as if the concept of intention possessed an identical content across different spheres (legal, moral, religious) of normative discourse, and as if analysis of the concept could by itself resolve what is at bottom a normative issue.[31] This focus is misguided, as I'll try to show, for two reasons: first, because the scope of the legal concept of intention is determined by the unique work the concept does within legal discourse; second, because even if recklessness and intention are morally equivalent for some normative practices (and even for one purpose within criminal law), they are non-equivalent for purposes of assigning criminal responsibility for results.

Are knowledge and recklessness forms of intention?

In *R v Steane,* the Nazis had forced the defendant, an English journalist, to broadcast war propaganda on pain of losing his family to a concentration camp if he refused.[32] After the war, he was charged in England with doing acts assisting the enemy with intent to assist the enemy. In defence, he argued that he broadcast the messages with the intent, not of assisting the enemy, but of saving his family, and this argument succeeded in the House of Lords. Assuming his story was true, did Steane intend to assist the enemy?

I have argued that, for purposes of assigning legal responsibility for a result, aiming at a result and knowing that (barring a miracle) it will certainly occur as a necessary side-effect of one's action are properly lumped together as "intention", because in both cases, one chooses the result. No doubt, in some cases (that of *Steane,* for example) aiming at a result and knowing it will certainly occur as a side-effect can reflect vastly different levels of self-identification with, or inward endorsement of, the result. But this is a consideration bearing on the state of one's soul, which only an omniscient observer can judge objectively and so punish justly. For purposes of determining *legal* responsibility for a result, purpose and knowledge of certainty are the same, for they both forge the tightest possible connection between the result and choice, leaving no role for chance. I may have been lucky to achieve my aim, but only in the sense that fate did *not* interfere with my efforts. Equally, where I act knowing a side-effect to be determined by

---

[30] [1998] 3 WLR 382; see also *R v Moloney* [1985] 1 All ER 1025.
[31] See W Wilson, 'Doctrinal Rationality after Woolin,' (1999) 62 MLR 448.
[32] [1947] KB 997.

physical laws (for example, knowing a patient will die from the morphine dose necessary to alleviate his pain) or by logical entailment (knowing that broadcasting propaganda for the enemy will assist the enemy), luck is involved in the effect only in the sense that *no* miracle intervened. Since in both cases, nothing intervened between the outcome I chose and the outcome that materialized, my will (and my will alone) caused the outcome.

By contrast, to distinguish between intention and knowledge of certainty is necessarily to blur the line between intention and motive, which is just the line separating impersonal judgments of imputability and personal judgments of wickedness. To say that Steane did not intend to assist the enemy in broadcasting war propaganda for the Nazis is to say that he would have intended to assist the enemy only had he broadcast the messages *in order to* assist the enemy rather than to save his family. But then assisting the enemy would have been his motive for broadcasting the messages, and so intention becomes identical with motive. For some normative practices—those concerned with judging the inner self—this usage makes sense, for one would want to distinguish between levels of self-identification with the outcome and hence between purposely and knowingly producing it. Juridically speaking, however, Steane *did* intend to assist the enemy even if, in moral or religious discourse, he did not. He intended it because he chose it. This, however, is not to say that Steane was improperly acquitted, only that the proper ground of acquittal was excusing duress rather than lack of intent.[33]

Foreseeing the probability of a result, however, is not the same as aiming at, or knowing the certainty of, a result (that is, not the same as "intention" in the extended legal sense). This is so because here the connection between the result and choice is looser: one chooses the risk but not the result, and so chance (causes independent of one's will) plays an independent role in bringing about the result. Lord Diplock argued, in judging Mrs Hyam, that foresight of probability was a kind of criminal intention, because whether one aimed at the result or foresaw its likelihood, one demonstrated a willingness to produce it, and this is culpability for murder.[34] But "willingness" is an inward disposition rather than an external connection between will and result; and if we are to punish willingness to kill, why not impose strict liability for murder if there is evidence that the agent would have been willing to cause death had he adverted to its remote possibility? Hart too thought that purposely killing and killing with foresight of death could be treated by law as equivalents, because in both cases the killer "has control over and may be considered to have chosen the outcome".[35] But having "control over" the outcome is hardly the same thing as choosing the outcome; for one also has

---

[33] It may be objected that if the law excuses Steane, it smuggles in the moral judgment it excluded from the analysis of responsibility. I deal with this issue in Chapter 7. Suffice it to say here that this is a "smuggling" only if moral excuse stands in logical tension with nonmoral responsibility. But I argue in Chapter 9 that there is no such tension. See also the conclusion of this chapter for a short discussion of this issue.
[34] *Hyam*, 86.   [35] *Punishment and Responsibility*, 293.

control over the outcome if one has a capacity to foresee and avoid it but does neither. No doubt the killer who perceived the risk *knew* he had control over the outcome and yet chose not to avoid it. But this is still different from having chosen the outcome, because there was room for believing and even hoping the outcome would not materialize as well as for being indifferent to whether it would. So, whereas both recklessness and purpose/knowledge involve a choice not to avoid the outcome, only purpose and knowledge involve choice *of* the outcome.

Is recklessness as culpable as intention?

Even if analysis of the legal concept of intention in terms of choosing the result tells us that recklessness (choosing the risk) lies outside it, this would not decide the normative issue at the heart of *Hyam* and *Woolin*. That issue is whether an assailant who is reckless regarding death deserves the same punishment and the same criminal label as the intentional killer. If normative theory concludes that he does, then there would be nothing wrong with calling recklessness "constructive intention" or with simply allowing both recklessness and intention to count as fault elements for murder.

Antony Duff has argued that, although recklessness lies outside the core meaning of intention (which in his terminology includes intended and intentional agency, meaning purpose and knowledge or expectation, respectively), some forms of it may nonetheless suffice as blameworthiness for murder.[36] A distinction can be drawn, he argues, between someone who aims to create a risk of death (aims to frighten with death but not to kill) and someone who knowingly imposes a risk of death as a side-effect of pursuing another purpose (for example, speeding to make an appointment). The first, Duff says, is guilty of murder if the victim dies, whereas the second is guilty only of manslaughter. This is so because the first "relate[s] [himself] so closely" to the homicide as to display a "wicked recklessness" of another's life sufficient for culpability for murder, whereas the second has kept himself more distant from the result.[37] This attitude of wicked recklessness of life, argues Duff, makes Mrs Hyam as guilty of murdering Mrs Booth's children as if she had aimed at their death. Similarly, he says, someone who means to cause very serious injury that he knows is certain to risk death also aims at the risk and so, by the previous argument, is a murderer if the risk materializes.[38] Finally, the agent who aims to cause very serious injury but does not realize that a probability of death would be an inseparable consequence of the injury, though he does not aim at the risk, nevertheless shares with the one who aims at the risk a common culpable attitude sufficient for murder if the victim dies. That attitude is wicked recklessness of another's life. His "very failure to notice" the risk, says Duff, "displays just the same kind of recklessness of his victim's life as is displayed

---

[36] *Intention, Agency, and Criminal Liability* (Oxford: Blackwell, 1990), 173–9.
[37] Ibid, 177.   [38] Ibid.

by one who knowingly endangers his victim's life".[39] Indeed, Duff goes so far as to say that this person, who never adverted to the risk of death, "wilfully endangered", even "chose to endanger", the victim's life.[40] With this hyperbole, Duff marches resolutely backward to "implied malice" or "constructive murder".

I have already criticized Duff's notion of practical indifference considered as a kind of fault sufficient to constitute the threshold of criminal culpability for any harm.[41] The argument against "wicked recklessness" or "extreme indifference" (as he elsewhere calls it) considered as a level of criminal responsibility for a particular harm (here death) equivalent to intending the harm is different. The gist of the former criticism was that blameworthy indifference to another's important human interests cannot be shown to deserve judicial punishment in particular (a right infringement) as distinct from censure generally. The criticism of "wicked recklessness of life" as constituting criminal responsibility for death equivalent to aiming at death is that it relies on a notion of responsibility that is not legal.

The key phrase in Duff's argument is "relates himself closely". The reason why the agent who deliberately creates a risk of death is more responsible for the ensuing death than one who knowingly creates the risk as a side-effect is that the first "relates [himself] more closely" to the death. Indeed, so intimately does he relate himself to the death that his responsibility is indistinguishable from that of one who actually aims at death (not just the risk); for what makes purposeful killing the central case of responsibility for a homicide is just the agent's inward affirmation of the result. Duff's claim is that reckless killers are just as responsible for the deaths they cause as purposeful killers to the extent that their agency is as enmeshed in their deeds as the agency of purposeful killers is enmeshed in theirs (so only some reckless killers are murderers).

This is, of course, the language of the Catholic doctrine of double effect. Indeed, Duff explicitly says that he means to draw from this doctrine an "alternative view" of legal responsibility.[42] The difficulty, however, is that this conception of responsibility, while suitable for some normative practices, is unsuitable to criminal law—that is, to a practice whose specific difference from other normative practices is that coercion follows human judgment. Such a practice requires an objective, public, and impersonal measuring rod of responsibility such that the convict (or the thinking Agent in his shoes) could accept a judgment of responsibility as well as the measure of punishment flowing from it as his own. The relative contribution to a result of choice and chance is that measuring rod, while intention, recklessness, and negligence are its calibrations.

For Duff, however, the yardstick by which a human judge should measure another human being's responsibility for a wrongful result is not the impersonal one of the result's imputability (and degree thereof) to agency as distinct from chance. It is rather the degree of the agent's inward *affirmation* of the deed—the

---

[39] Ibid.   [40] Ibid, 178.   [41] See Chapter 2.
[42] *Intention, Agency, and Criminal Liability*, 111.

sort of affirmation that moral discourse would call evil and that religious discourse would call sin. This is why Duff wants to maintain—contrary to now settled legal doctrine—a nonequivalence between aiming at a result and producing it as a virtually certain side-effect.[43] The agent who tries to kill is enmeshed more thoroughly in the wrongful death than someone who merely expects death to occur as a result of trying something else. Such a conception of responsibility is incompatible with a practice of punishment ordered to freedom, because it requires judgments of more or less wickedness that are subjective, personal, and ill-informed, hence externally imposed rather than self-authored.[44]

Just how personal such judgments can become is discernible from Duff's own moral judgments. He would say that the killer who meant to cause serious bodily harm but failed to notice the obvious risk of death this entails has displayed just as much wickedness as the one who apprehended the risk. But one may wonder how he knows and what he could say to someone who disagreed. Suppose the failure to notice the risk stemmed from low intelligence, or from momentary anger resulting from cumulative stresses, rather than from depravity. Or suppose the assailant, had he apprehended the risk, would have preferred that it not materialize, whereas the one who did apprehend it was indifferent to whether it did so.

These ruminations show that judgments of comparative wickedness, besides being subjective, are inherently context-sensitive; hence they are inappropriate at the legislative stage, where general rules of responsibility must be laid down in advance of conduct. Generalizations about what makes actions more or less evil are bound to be heuristic and tentative—hence defeasible by more information about the case and about the defendant before the court. In particular, concepts such as intention, foresight, and failure to foresee the obvious (as Hart pointed out) are poor proxies for relative wickedness; at best they raise weak presumptions. And the more considerations bearing on the final judgment, the more room there is for discretion in weighing them.

This is not to say that judgments of wickedness have no place in criminal trials. But where they belong is in the space for sentencing discretion left *after* the principles of penal justice have done all the work they can do. Penal justice for free agents cannot be defined as giving the wicked what a legislator guesses they deserve or what a judge, in his or her discretion, feels they actually deserve; for this imports subjectivity into the definition of the just itself. But within the legislatively mandated bounds of punishing result crimes in proportion to the degree of connection between choice and result, judges may tailor sentence ranges geared to imputability to the reform needs of the convict and to the heinousness of the particular crime.

---

[43] Ibid., 113.

[44] Thus one can say that "[m]oral issues concerning motive press to be included within the analysis of what it means to intend to commit a crime, if law is to judge conduct criminal" only on the dubious assumption that to judge conduct criminal is to judge its agent wicked; Alan Norrie, *Punishment, Responsibility, and Justice* (Oxford: Oxford University Press, 2000), 172. Expelling the old language of "malice" from the legal concept of murder signifies the positive law's rejection of that assumption.

Is meaning to cause bodily harm that one knows is likely to cause death ever as culpable a form of homicide as meaning to cause death? On Duff's criterion of the intimacy of one's agency with the deed, perhaps it is (who knows?), but on the imputability yardstick, it definitely is not. Whereas intention and advertent recklessness are indeed juridically equivalent levels of fault at the *threshold* of culpability for wrong (see Chapter 2), they represent different levels of responsibility for consequential harms. They are equivalent at the threshold because choosing to interfere with someone's agency and choosing a risk of interference known to be excessive both imply a denial of the agent's right to act on ends of its own choosing; and this is what makes judicial punishment as such deserved in the sense of self-willed. However, the assailant who kills having foreseen the likelihood of death does not deserve the same *measure* of punishment *for the death* as the assailant who kills intentionally. This is so, not because there is a necessary connection between that severity of punishment and an intentional homicide, but because two different grades of imputability of death (and hence two different grades of legal fault for results) are involved here. The reckless killer chooses the risk of death, leaving death to chance; the intentional killer chooses the death, leaving nothing to chance.

Observe that this judgment of comparative imputability will *always* be true irrespective of context, so that the yardstick of imputability is inherently suited to judgments of responsibility under a general law everyone can understand and accept. There is nothing rough or tentative about the correlation between imputability and legal responsibility, as there is about the connection between imputability and wickedness; hence there is no need for personal discretion to complete the judgment of responsibility at the sentencing stage. All that is left for discretion are matters that are indifferent from the standpoint of penal justice and whose relativity to the individual case makes disparate treatment fair treatment: social protection, rehabilitation, censure, etc. Notice also that the yardstick of imputability makes no reference to the inner person and so cannot be mistaken about what it cannot know. On both counts the differential punishments flowing from judgments of comparative imputability can be conceived as self-authored.

The moralist might object that the difference between choosing to kill and choosing to inflict bodily harm one knows is life-threatening is legally technical and morally insignificant if the reckless killer did not care whether death occurred. For whether he does not care about causing death on the way to achieving his end or aims to kill as a means of achieving his end might depend on nothing more than the contingent content of his current aims. Indeed, the difference between intention and recklessness seems vanishingly trivial from a moral standpoint if the killer hoped but doubted that death would result from his paltry efforts at homicide (say he succeeds in killing a giant with a slingshot). Even the difference between choosing someone's death and foreseeably causing it is morally insignificant if the killer intended death by shooting but through lack of skill inflicted only a minor wound and the victim then died as the result of improper hospital treatment. From a moral standpoint, one might as well call all these killers murderers.

However, from the fact that these differences are morally insignificant it does not follow that they are technical, legal distinctions devoid of normative significance; for the penal law lies under its own normative firmament. The differences between choosing an outcome, choosing the risk of the outcome, and foreseeably causing the outcome are always juridically significant, because judicial punishment differs from the wrongdoer's violence in being self-authored rather than externally imposed; and punishment is self-authored only if the actual harmful results for which one is punished are connected in some degree to one's choice, and if the degrees of connection are reflected in degrees of culpable harm-causing having distinct names and punishments. So, labelling and punishing identically reckless and intentional homicide (or foreseeable and reckless homicide) violates the agent's right to author its moral fate, for it imposes on the reckless (or negligent) killer a stigma and measure of punishment disproportionate to the degree to which his agency caused death.

5. The *Novus Actus Interveniens*

How does the foregoing analysis of legal responsibility for outcomes handle the problems arising from intervening causes? Consider the following situations:

(1) D assaults V not intending to kill him but inflicting a wound carrying more than a theoretical risk of death. In hospital, V is inadvertently given the wrong treatment, from which he dies. Is D responsible for V's death?

(2) D assaults V not intending to kill him and knocks V unconscious. He leaves V lying in the street of a neighbourhood where a serial killer is widely known to be preying on helpless people. The serial killer dispatches V. Is D responsible for V's death?

(3) D shoots V intending to kill him. As V lies slowly dying from his abdominal wound, he deliberately cuts his own throat and dies soon after.[45] Is D responsible for V's death?

(4) D stabs V intending to kill him. In hospital, V's stab-wound has almost healed, but V dies after a doctor negligently gives him an antibiotic to which V is allergic.[46] Is D responsible for V's death? If so, is D guilty of murder or manslaughter?

These situations raise the problem as to when a cause intervening between the defendant's action and the proscribed result his action factually caused negates the defendant's criminal responsibility for the result. An intervening cause having this legal effect is called a *novus actus interveniens* (*novus actus*).

Sometimes an intervening cause will be a *novus actus* because it renders the causal path toward the proscribed result one the defendant could not have been expected

---

[45] *People v Lewis* (1899) 57 P 470 (Cal SC). [46] *R v Jordan* (1956) 40 Cr App R 152.

to foresee. The standard example has D knocking V unconscious on the seashore, where V is later killed by a bolt of lightning. The reasonably circumspect person would foresee death by drowning as likely but not death by lightning, and so D is not responsible for a death that instantiates death by lightning. But sometimes an intervening cause will be a *novus actus* even though the causal path toward the proscribed result ought to have been foreseen by the defendant as a likely consequence of his action. For example, it was perhaps reasonably foreseeable that a prostitute knocked out and left lying in a Whitechapel street in September, 1888 would have been murdered by Jack the Ripper. Yet, however likely this prospect, it is doubtful that the first assailant would have been guilty of manslaughter had it materialized. The questions for discussion in this section are: what legal principle determines this result? Under what circumstances must the principle be qualified?

The common-law response

The common-law response to the *novus actus* problem is couched in language notorious for its imprecision. In *R v Smith*,[47] Lord Parker declared that an intervening cause shields the defendant from responsibility for a result he factually caused only if the defendant's action is "merely the setting in which another cause operates" or only if the intervening cause "is so overwhelming as to make the original wound merely part of the history" leading to the unlawful outcome.[48] Though not incorrect, these formulations are unhelpful because they state as a criterion of a *novus actus* what is simply an effect of such an action, namely, that the original action recedes into causal insignificance. We still do not know what transforms an intervening cause into a *novus actus* having this effect. We are told, to be sure, that the intervening act must be "overwhelming" in its causal significance; but this merely restates the point that the *novus actus* makes the first actor's responsibility pale into nothing by comparison. We want to know precisely what it takes to do this.

In *R v Cheshire,* the English Court of Appeal suggested a two-pronged test for the *novus actus*.[49] There, Lord Beldam said that an intervening cause is a *novus actus* only if it was "so independent of [the defendant's] acts, and in itself so potent in causing death, that [the jury] regard[s] the contribution made by his acts as insignificant".[50] Unfortunately, Lord Beldam did not make clear what he meant by "independent" and "potent", and none of the meanings he might have intended makes these criteria satisfactory. If the requirement of independence means that a *novus actus* must be causally unconnected to the defendant's action, then an ambiguity arises. An intervening cause can be causally independent of the defendant's action either in the sense that it did not result from the action or in the sense that it was an unforeseeable result of the defendant's action. If "independent" means "not a result of the defendant's action", then there will never be a *novus actus*, for either the defendant's action provided the opportunity but for

[47] (1959) 43 Cr App R 121.   [48] Ibid, 131.   [49] Note 22 above.   [50] Ibid, 677.

which the intervening act or event would not have caused death then and there, or it was not a but-for cause whose causality was "interrupted".[51] If, however, "independent" means unforeseeable, then Lord Beldam's test (if he meant this as a necessary condition of a *novus actus*) will counterintuitively ensnare the D in situation 2, who merely provided the opportunity for Jack the Ripper to murder again. It seems that there is a class of cases in which an intervening cause blocks the first actor's responsibility for a result notwithstanding that the result was within the risk he ought to have perceived.

Nor is the criterion of "potency" more helpful. On one reading, it seems to suggest a comparison of the causal force of the first and intervening agents. Of the two causes, the intervening one contributes so much more to the result that the other's contribution becomes insignificant by comparison. So interpreted, however, the criterion of potency proves inadequate, for it fails to explain why the *novus actus* cancels the responsibility of the first actor instead of simply incurring more responsibility than that actor. Suppose D inflicts a life-threatening wound on V intending to kill him and in hospital V is negligently given the wrong treatment and dies. Presumably, Lord Beldam would say that the first cause is far more potent than the second. Yet in this case the more potent cause will not cancel the responsibility of the physician, who will be liable civilly. If, however, the sequence were reversed so that the intentional killing succeeded a negligent exposure to danger, the more potent action would very likely be held to negate the responsibility of the lesser one. Since the same difference in causal potency exists in both situations and yet only one exhibits a legal cause exclusive of others, the idea of potency sheds no light on what makes an intervening cause a *novus actus*.

Perhaps, however, "in itself so potent" means "sufficient by itself" to cause death. Yet this formula leads to a counterintuitive result in *People v Lewis* (situation 3), where the intervening suicide was both "independent" (why should Lewis have foreseen that his victim would commit suicide?) and sufficient to cause death, and yet the defendant who intentionally inflicted the mortal wound was also held responsible for the death (rightly, I shall argue).[52] Further, in *Cheshire* itself, the gunshot wound inflicted by the defendant had mostly healed, and the victim died from an obstruction of his windpipe caused by a badly performed tracheotomy. Here was an intervening action sufficient in itself to cause death, and yet the defendant was held to be punishable for a homicide.

---

[51] D's knocking out V on the seashore did not cause the lightning bolt, but the lightning bolt would not have struck V then and there had D not prepared the conditions. Thus D's action is part of a causal chain that can be broken. But if V had died on the seashore because his biological clock had run out, his natural death could not be described as a *novus actus interveniens* (though it empirically prevented death by drowning), because D's action, not being a factual cause of death, is not even a candidate for legal cause.

[52] Note 45 above.

The Hart-Honoré approach

A more promising approach to the *novus actus* question is provided by HLA Hart and Tony Honoré in their book, *Causation in the Law*.[53] The originality of their thesis lay in the suggestion that the criterion of a *novus actus* might have something to do with the mental state of the intervening actor. According to Hart and Honoré, "[t]he free, deliberate, and informed act or omission of a human being, intended to exploit the situation created by the defendant, negatives causal connection".[54] Although this principle is presented as a descriptive generalization about the law, it is also one that Hart and Honoré endorse. For them, an intervening action should insulate the first actor from legal responsibility if the intervention is "voluntary" in the sense of "free, deliberate, and informed". If the action meets these requirements, it does not matter that it miscarried and produced results unintended by the intervening actor. It is enough that the intervenor freely acted upon an informed decision in order to exploit an opportunity created by the first actor.

While setting the law regarding the *novus actus* onto a promising new path, Hart and Honoré did not themselves fulfil the promise their insight bore. To begin with, the requirement of an intention to exploit a situation created by the first actor seems redundant. If D intentionally kills someone left vulnerable in the street by a hit-and-run driver, D is solely responsible for the death whether he knew he was exploiting an opportunity created by the driver or thought his victim had suffered a heart attack. It would be odd if the driver's liability for the death depended on what D knew about the provenance of his (D's) opportunity.

Second, the criterion of free, deliberate, and informed activity embraces cases that common sense would exclude from the category of a *novus actus*; and so, to achieve the exclusions that common sense demands, Hart and Honoré must stretch the notion of *in*voluntary conduct well beyond its ordinary meaning. A few illustrations will show the linguistic contortions into which Hart and Honoré are forced by their voluntariness test.

Suppose a policeman involved in a gunfight with a robber accidentally kills an innocent bystander in a crowded street. He thus freely and deliberately acts in accordance with an informed decision but produces an unintended (though not unlikely) result. In *Commonwealth v Almeida,* the Supreme Court of Pennsylvania held the robber criminally responsible for the bystander's death based on its foreseeability to him, and Hart and Honoré agree.[55] Their explanation is that the policeman's action was involuntary (hence not a *novus actus*) because done to carry out a legal duty.

Yet this explanation is unconvincing, for it is difficult to see how an act intentionally performed to discharge a legal duty can be regarded as involuntary. Since

---

[53] Note 24 above.
[54] Hart and Honoré, *Causation in the Law,* 136. This formulation was adopted by Lord Steyn in *R v Latif* [1996] 2 Cr App R 92, 104 (HL). See also *Pagett v The Queen* [1983] 76 Cr App R 279 (CA).
[55] (1949) 68 A2d 595.

the agent has a choice between obedience and disobedience, and since he chooses to obey because the law commands him, his act is not only voluntary but free in the most demanding of Kantian senses. The fact that the agent is liable to a penalty for failing to perform his duty does not render his conforming act involuntary; for even if he is moved by these considerations, he must still weigh the costs and benefits of shirking and make a choice.

Further, let us juxtapose the following two situations. In one, V, on being held up at gunpoint by D, tries to flee down a flight of stairs, falls, and dies. In the other, V tries to flee by leaping from a tenth-floor window and dies. To account for the intuition that D is responsible for V's death in the first case, Hart and Honoré must say that V's act of escape was involuntary because done for self-preservation (even though V could also have preserved himself by doing what the gunman commanded). But if acts of self-preservation are involuntary, then neither does V's reckless jump from the window qualify as a *novus actus*, and so D is guilty of manslaughter in the second case as well. To avoid this result, Hart and Honoré draw a distinction: an act reasonably done for self-preservation is involuntary, but an act unreasonably done for self-preservation is voluntary.[56] With this move, however, the idea of voluntariness has obviously ceased to perform any independent work in identifying a *novus actus*. Rather, an intervening act is called voluntary or involuntary depending on whether it seems right or wrong on some other unarticulated ground to hold the first agent responsible for the proscribed result.

Next, consider example 3 above. D inflicts a mortal wound on V intending to kill him. To cut short his suffering, V commits suicide. Since V's act is here voluntary in the Hart-Honoré sense, it should on their test shield D from responsibility for V's death. In *Lewis*, the court held that it did not, and Hart and Honoré agree. To account for this type of case,[57] they introduce another qualification to the voluntariness test: if the first wound is sufficient to cause death, the first agent may be responsible for the death notwithstanding the free, informed, and deliberate act of the second.[58] Yet this qualification raises a further problem. Suppose D's gun discharges accidentally, inflicting on V a life-threatening wound, after which V commits suicide to end his pain. In that situation, the case for calling V's intervening suicide a *novus actus* seems more compelling even though the initial wound was mortal. This suggests that it is not the causal sufficiency of the initial action that resists the power of the intervening cause but rather the first actor's mental orientation toward the outcome. I'll return to this point.

Comparative imputability

Let us now examine the *novus actus* problem in light of the comparative imputability of a proscribed result (here death) to an actor's choice as distinct from

---

[56] *Causation in the Law*, 331.
[57] See also *R v Dear* [1996] Crim LR 595 (CA).
[58] *Causation in the Law*, 329.

chance. An approach that focuses on the degree of a result's imputability to the intervenor's choice will corroborate the Hart-Honoré thesis that the intervenor's mental state is crucial for determining whether his action was a *novus actus*; but it will suggest the following modifications to that thesis. First, what is relevant is not the intervenor's mental state taken in isolation but rather his mental orientation *toward* the unlawful outcome of his action. That is to say, what is important is not whether the intervenor acted free of duty or pressure and after informed deliberation but whether he produced the unlawful outcome intentionally, recklessly, or negligently. Second, we must not only attend to the intervenor's mental orientation toward the outcome; we must also compare the mental orientations of the first and second actors.

Consider situation 1 above. Since neither D nor the intervening actor aimed at V's death nor foresaw it as certainly following from their actions, neither chose it. Hence V's death is an accident, which is to say that it is the effect of innumerable blind causes—of causes not aiming to produce it. As an accident, V's death remains, despite the doctor's negligent intervention, amenable to explanation in terms of all the blind causes but for which V would not have died then and there, of which D's act is one. If death from medical negligence is a kind of death whose risk from inflicting a serious wound is sufficiently high that one ought to have perceived it, then the first actor is criminally responsible for the death based on its being an instance of the type foreseeable to him. He cannot rely on the negligence of the intervening agent to relieve him of responsibility, for this is just the sort of bad luck he authorized by acting.

Now consider situation 2. Given the serial killer's intentional killing of V, he chose the very result that occurred. Hence that result belongs to the serial killer's agency in the tightest possible sense. It is his without remainder—that is, since he chose *it* rather than simply the risk of it, one can no longer explain the outcome as an accident resulting from blind causes independent of his will. "Accident" and "blind cause" are correlates. So, since there is nothing accidental in the outcome that can be considered the effect of a blind cause, there is nothing that can also be imputed to the person who acted without intent to kill. This is so even if the path toward death was foreseeable to the initial actor, for if the death is not an accident, it cannot have been co-ordinately caused by a blind cause. D's action has become a subordinate precondition of the serial killer's intentional killing rather than a co-ordinate cause—has become "merely the setting in which another cause operates"—for there is no residue of accidental fact that blind causes could cause.

Contrast situation 4, where the stabbing with intent to kill precedes the negligent homicide by the doctor. Here the death that actually occurred is not the one contemplated by the first agent and so not the one chosen by him. D chose V's death by means he employed for the purpose, but the means he employed did not medically cause death; rather, the wound he inflicted had healed, and death resulted from a causal path outside D's actual contemplation. True, D intended death under a generic description and might have *wished* the victim's death from whatever cause; but he cannot be said to have *chosen* a resultant death his means did not bring about. Hence the outcome is not exclusively his; it is also the effect of blind causes, and this is why the first actor's responsibility does not preclude that of the succeeding negligent one even though the first actor acted with homicidal intent. Since, moreover, a death caused by an intervening negligent agent is not chosen by the intervenor, it is an accident amenable to co-ordinate causal accounts, as in situation 1. Hence it does not necessarily preclude the responsibility of the first actor. However, since the death that occurred is not the one the first actor chose, he is not guilty of murder; rather his responsibility for the death is based on the foreseeability of death by medical negligence from a life-threatening wound. Hence he is guilty of manslaughter (and attempted murder).[59] Had the causal path toward death lain outside the risk he ought to have perceived (had the victim died from a car accident while leaving the hospital), he would have been guilty only of attempted murder.

Now consider situation 3 (the situation in *Lewis*). Here we have an intentional suicide supervening on an earlier shooting with intent to kill. If (as we assume) the initial wound is still physically contributing to the death through the victim's loss of blood, then the path toward death is still within the contemplation of the first actor despite the intervening suicide. The initial actor chose death by means he employed and that is what partly happened. Accordingly, the outcome belongs to both actors in the tightest sense (they both chose it), and so there is no reason why the intervening suicide should cancel (or even reduce) the first actor's responsibility, even if the suicide is voluntary, deliberate, and informed.[60] True, the intentional killing by the intervening actor leaves no remainder of accidental fact to be ascribed to blind causality. But the first actor did not produce death through the operation of blind causality; rather, he too intended it. Hence the two agents are co-owners, as it were, of the outcome (as the court held).[61]

More difficult is the case where advertently reckless conduct intervenes between the defendant's negligent action and the unlawful outcome. In such situations, the risk to the victim imposed by the reckless intervenor may be so high as to approach the certainty of intention, in which case we will be strongly inclined toward viewing the intervention as a *novus actus* cancelling responsibility based on foreseeability. The hold-up victim's jump from the tenth-floor window is a case in point. It is foreseeable that someone will run extraordinary risks in such a situation, but there comes a point where the intervenor must be taken to have chosen death and so where his death belongs exclusively to his choice, leaving nothing to be explained by blind causes. However, let us assume that the intervenor's

[59] Model Penal Code s. 2.03(2) agrees. Jordan and Cheshire should have been convicted of manslaughter rather than murder.
[60] This is *a fortiori* true if the intervenor is an unwitting instrument of the first actor. Thus, if D, intending to kill V, tells X to administer a poison D misrepresents as medicine and X does, X's action is not a *novus actus* because D chose to kill V by means he employed and succeeded.
[61] Lewis, though, was convicted of manslaughter.

recklessness consists in his conscious indifference to a degree of abnormal risk that falls well below certainty. Suppose, for example, that a policeman fires at a fugitive holding someone as a shield and kills the hostage. Is the fugitive guilty of manslaughter, or is the policeman's action a *novus actus*?

Here the death does not belong to the policeman without remainder, for it was neither intended nor foreseen as certain. Hence he chose not the death, but only the risk of death, leaving that outcome open to explanation in terms of coordinate blind causes.[62] And since the human shield's death from the policeman's fire was a causal path the hostage taker ought to have foreseen, he remains responsible as a manslayer for the death. In *Pagett v The Queen,* the English Court of Criminal Appeal concluded likewise, though on the dubious ground that the policeman's act was involuntary because done for self-defence (it was not necessary for self-defence) and in the line of legal duty.[63]

We can summarize the foregoing discussion as follows. An intervening actor will be capable of excluding a prior actor's responsibility for an outcome based on foreseeability only if he purposely produces the outcome or foresees it as a virtually certain result of his act; for the outcome is then wholly determined by the intervenor's choice. It is not necessary that the intervening agent have acted with full information or deliberatively or free of duty; nor is it sufficient that he acted voluntarily. Rather, the outcome he brought about must be the one he chose to produce. Even this is not a sufficient condition of a *novus actus*, however, for we must still inquire whether the prior actor also chose the outcome. If so, (and if the proscribed outcome *that occurred* was within his contemplation when he acted), the first actor's responsibility is unaffected by that of the intervening actor. Finally, if, owing to intervening causes, the proscribed outcome that actually occurs is not the specific one contemplated by the first actor, then, though he intended the outcome under a generic description, the first actor is not legally responsible for it in the degree known as intention. Rather, his responsibility is reduced or negated depending on whether the path toward the outcome was within the risk he ought to have perceived.

6. Conclusion

This brings to a close our discussion of the conditions of the criminal culpability of free agents—of their liability to punishment both for wrongs and for resultant harms. The rest of the book deals with the conditions of their liability to non-criminal penalties and with their defences. Having completed our picture of the

---

[62] This reasoning also explains the result in *R v Roberts* (1971) 56 Cr App R 95, where a woman suffered injury after jumping from a moving car to escape an assailant. The defendant's conviction for assault occasioning actual bodily harm was upheld. Likewise *R v Williams and Davis* (1992) 95 Cr App R 1.

[63] Note 54 above.

kind of criminal liability free agents could accept, we can now stand back and observe what is perhaps its most conspicuous feature.

The criteria of criminal culpability for free persons are rigorously abstract, impersonal, and nonmoral. They are as far removed from the standards by which we categorize and judge concrete moral characters as legal codes are removed from novels. The key to a culpable wrong is the practical denial of agency rights imputable to a choice to interfere or to risk interfering with another's liberty. Because culpability depends exclusively on what external choice a person has made, everything pertaining to his inward self is irrelevant to a judgment of culpability. Thus, the motive for his choice is set aside, as is the individual's inward attitude toward his choice—the degree to which he identifies himself with, or distances himself from, the choice he has made. Anguish, regret, wish, hope, indifference, affirmation—all the psychological attitudes that are relevant to an assessment of what the individual's deed reveals about his character—are ruthlessly expunged.

Likewise irrelevant are the emotions the wrongdoer chose to act upon as well as the qualities of character reflected in the action. Hence love, compassion, and moral anger are on a par with hostility, lust, greed, vengefulness, and jealousy. Indifference in the face of risk to others is treated the same as quixotic rashness, rashness the same as deliberateness in choosing a risk to avoid a greater evil. Obversely, exculpatory factors are simply those negating a choice to interfere or risk interfering with another's agency; and so they exculpate even if they reflect moral vice, censurable stupidity, or vulgar prejudice. The upshot is that, while social disgrace usually follows a criminal conviction, there is really no necessary connection between deserving punishment and deserving disgrace, or between exculpation and social vindication (consider the defendant who is acquitted of murder because he was too drunk to form the intent to kill).

The criteria of responsibility for culpable harm are likewise impersonal. Culpable harms are harms, not to values individuals hold, but to objective goods essential to freedom. And degrees of responsibility are marked, not by shades of evil, but by the degree to which a harmful result is ascribable to choice rather than to chance. Thus the man who kills intentionally from compassion is punished more severely than the man who kills accidentally from a reckless indifference to another's life.

It may come as a surprise to some that a conception of culpability so seemingly unnatural, so purged of considerations pertaining to the inward self, should be the product of a retributivist conception of punishment. Retributivism, after all, is usually identified with the view that the wicked should receive their just deserts; and it is no doubt this identification that led utilitarians to think that an impartial and objective science of punishment had to abandon the notion of desert in favour of rational principles of crime prevention. But legal retributivism is not this view. It is rather the view that judicial punishment is distinguishable from criminal violence and so consistent with the individual agent's inviolability only to the extent that it can be conceived as self-imposed both as to its incidence and its measure; and this desideratum requires criteria of culpability and responsibility so austerely geared to external choice that all free agents could accept them as conditions and yardsticks of desert whatever their personal opinions about what makes conduct more or less wicked, or whatever their opinions about other people's estimations of their moral character. Thus the nonmoral nature of the legal criteria of culpability and responsibility flows from the requirement that judgments of criminal desert be self-imposable, that human beings not judge other human beings pursuant to their moral opinions in a sphere where a person's liberty hangs on the judgment.[64]

But that is not the end of the story. For while impersonal and nonmoral criteria of culpability and responsibility are essential to a punishment consistent with freedom, they run into trouble at the margin when treated as exhaustive of penal justice—just because they isolate a few features from a full ethical picture of what the defendant has done. In these cases, sentencing discretion will be inadequate to the task of setting things right, because the defendant has something stronger than a plea for a judge's compassion or understanding or consideration of the whole person. He has a claim *resembling* an exculpatory defence. Given the abstractness of the legal criteria of culpability, it will sometimes be the case that the defendant has (what I'll call) a *quasi*-right to an acquittal despite meeting the legal criteria of culpability or responsibility for the graver crime. This will be so because an intransigent application of these criteria will sometimes inculpate someone who, though he set his abstract *will* against the juristic common will, has not deviated from the public standard of self-control by which passionate human beings are judged morally strong or weak by their fellow citizens of a political community.

Of course, these cases are dealt with through the excuses, which are themselves part of the criminal law. In Chapters 7 and 9, I'll propose a theory of the moral excuses that endeavours to integrate them with a legal theory of culpability geared to the self-imposability of punishment and that, in doing so, accounts

---

[64] Alan Norrie aptly refers to the agency-based principles of legal culpability and responsibility as a "morality of form". Yet his criticism of the "poverty" of this morality misses its point; for it ignores the specific role the morality of form plays in reconciling judicial punishment with freedom within the narrow precinct of penal justice. Norrie represents the virtue of the morality of form—its setting aside judgments of inner wickedness—as a vice, while denigrating legal degrees of imputability as "psychologistic" and "technical", as if there were no moral stature in a body of principles securing the distinction between punishment and unjust violence. True, the thinness of legal desert creates the possibility of tension between legal culpability and moral blameworthiness. Blameworthy people might be exculpated and blameless people might be inculpated. But the criminal law leaves the former problem to social censure (where, in a free society, it belongs) and deals with the latter problem through the concept of excuse (see Chapter 7). Accordingly, there is nothing "false" or "artificial" about the separation between legal and moral desert (is it artificial for a secular state to forbear from punishing as a murderer someone who would have been willing to cause death had he adverted to its remote possibility?); nor is there need for hand-wringing about the "necessity" of the "impossible". See Norrie, *Punishment, Responsibility, and Justice*, 7–9, 170–93.

for their being excuses given culpability (that is, pleas in the affirmative) rather than exculpatory conditions. Some criminal law theorists, mesmerized by the moral idea behind the excuses, try to develop that idea into a general ethical theory of criminal culpability.[65] Culpability then tracks moral evil and whatever blocks an inference from outward action to "who we are" exculpates. For reasons already discussed, this approach is mistaken. Apart from obliterating the difference between exculpation and affirmative excuse, it leads to a regime of secular punishment expressive of fallible human judgments about the moral worth of other human beings. Coercion of that sort cannot sit with the freedom and equality of persons.

---

[65] John Gardner, *Offences and Defences* (Oxford: Oxford University Press, 2007); Jeremy Horder, 'Criminal Culpability: The Possibility of a General Theory,' (1993) 12 *Law and Philosophy* 193.

5
Liability for Public Welfare Offences

Those claiming authority to coerce under public reason conceived as real autonomy have a duty to provide (to those owing a duty to obey them) the conditions for living according to self-authored ends. Therefore, they must protect the individual's autonomy not only against criminal transgressions but against all excessive risks of harm to the goods essential to autonomy. The performance of this duty gives rise to the myriad regulatory laws of the administrative state. Though enforced in common-law jurisdictions through the criminal courts, these laws are regarded by judges as creating a type of offence distinct from crime, one they call the "public welfare offence" or sometimes the "regulatory offence"; and they are correspondingly viewed as expressions of the state's "police power" (so called because of its direction toward "policy") rather than of its power to punish criminals. The most important consequence of the distinction between crimes and public welfare offences in the positive law is that people can be convicted of a public welfare offence without a finding of fault.

The question for discussion in this chapter is: under what substantive constraints can autonomous agents be penalized for a public welfare offence?[1] To anticipate, I'll offer a justification for dispensing with a subjective fault requirement for public welfare offences. Then I'll derive from the real autonomy paradigm an injunction against liability for breach of a regulatory statute in the absence of any fault (against strict liability), an injunction against imprisoning for negligent breaches of public welfare statutes, and a prescription for a general defence of non-negligent ignorance of regulatory law.

1. What is a Public Welfare Offence?

To begin with, we must ask: what are public welfare offences and how are they distinguished from crimes? From a eudaemonist perspective, or even from one that treats the real autonomy paradigm as exhaustive of penal justice, the distinction

---

[1] Because this chapter discusses liability conditions suitable for autonomous agents, its arguments apply only to natural agents. I do not discuss corporate liability for public welfare offences, which liability may be subject to different constraints.

between public welfare offences and crimes will appear illusory.[2] For if coercive authority is just only as directed toward the general happiness (of which liberty is an ingredient), or only as ordered to the public welfare conceived as the totality of conditions for autonomous action (of which legal protection from criminal coercion is part), then punishing interferences with liberty and penalizing excessively risky activity are simply two species of the same genus. Criminal law, no less than regulatory law, protects the public welfare. The only difference, it would seem, is that the criminal law typically waits for a wrongful harm to occur before punishing, whereas regulatory law is pre-emptive. And of course even this distinction disappears when one considers the plethora of inchoate, possession, and reckless endangerment (for instance, impaired driving) crimes found in most criminal codes. Nevertheless, despite widespread scepticism among academic writers, Anglo-American positive law clearly recognizes a border between public welfare (regulatory) offences and "true crimes"; and it attaches markedly different liability conditions to each.[3] I believe the common law is right about this, and what follows in this section is a defence of the border.

To be sure, the judges' and treatise writers' own explanations for the difference are not very convincing. Some have said that criminal law differs from regulatory law in that the former protects individual interests whereas the latter protects the public interest as a whole;[4] or in that criminal law prohibits certain kinds of harmful activity outright whereas public welfare statutes regulate otherwise lawful activity in the interest of public health and safety;[5] or in that criminal law consists of "fundamental rules" essential to society whereas welfare statutes consist of "non-fundamental rules" merely useful to society;[6] or in that the criminal law typically imposes harsh penalties in order to prevent harmful activity carrying negligible social benefit, whereas regulatory law "prices" activity yielding both costs and benefits in order to achieve a socially optimal level of the activity;[7] or, in that criminal law punishes "stigmatic" offences, whereas "quasi-criminal"

---

[2] Indeed, the difference will be difficult to sustain even from a Kantian perspective, which must regard crime, not as a denial of pre-political rights (there being no realized ones), but as a denial of the general will's sovereignty; see Arthur Ripstein, 'In Extremis,' (2005) 2 *Ohio State Journal of Criminal Law* 415, 417; 'Authority and Coercion,' (2004) 32 *Philosophy & Public Affairs* 2, 32–5.

[3] *R v Woodrow* (1846) 153 Engl Rep 907; *Sherras v De Rutzen* [1895] 1 QB 918; *R v Ewart* (1905) 25 NZLR 709; *Proudman v Dayman* (1941) 67 CLR 536 (Aus. HC); *Sweet v Parsley* [1970] AC 132; *R v City of Sault Ste Marie* [1978] 2 SCR 1299. For criticism of the distinction, see Jeremy Bentham, 'Of the Influence of Time and Place in Matters of Legislation,' 1 *Works* (1843), 193; B Wooton, *Crime and the Criminal Law* (London: Stevens, 1963), 41–6; J Hall, *General Principles of Criminal Law*, 2nd ed. (Indianapolis: Bobbs Merrill, 1960), 337–42.

[4] *Sault Ste Marie*; F B Sayre, 'Public Welfare Offenses,' (1933) 33 *Columbia Law Review* 55, 65.

[5] *R v Beaver* [1957] SCR 531, at 539.

[6] Law Reform Commission of Canada, *Studies on Strict Liability* (Ottawa: Information Canada, 1974), 194.

[7] R Posner, *Economic Analysis of Law*, 6th ed. (New York: Aspen, 2003), 228; R Cooter, 'Prices and Sanctions,' (1984) 84 *Columbia Law Review* 1523.

law penalizes "non-stigmatic" offences;[8] or in that criminal law punishes actions bad in themselves (*mala in se*), whereas regulatory law penalizes conduct prohibited by legislation (*mala prohibita*).[9]

None of these criteria for distinguishing between crimes and public welfare offences succeeds in keeping the categories distinct. The criminal law would not protect individual interests in life, bodily integrity, and property if these interests were not also common to everyone; while the interests protected by public welfare statutes would not be public if they were not also the interests of discrete individuals. Further, whether laws "prohibit" or "regulate" depends on how broadly or narrowly one chooses to describe the targeted conduct. Thus, laws against theft, assault, and murder do not prohibit takings, coercion, or homicides outright; rather, they, together with justificatory defences, define the conditions under which such actions are thefts, assaults, and culpable homicides. Conversely, laws against speeding prohibit speeding outright. Inasmuch, moreover, as the interests protected by criminal and public welfare law—life, health, bodily integrity, the enjoyment of property—substantially overlap, it is difficult to see why one should be called "fundamental" and the other "non-fundamental".

Even seemingly more sophisticated grounds of distinction between crimes and welfare offences fail to withstand scrutiny. For example, the distinction based on prevention by harsh penalty versus rationing by prices likewise slips away, for some crimes can be prosecuted as summary offences punishable by fines (do these offences "price" harmless assaults or petty thefts?); and, while some regulatory fines are probably prices for permitted activity (overparking at a meter, for example), those protecting health and limb (for example, fines for speeding) cannot reasonably be viewed as such. From an economic perspective, moreover, preventing harmful activity with no redeeming social benefit and pricing activity carrying both costs and benefits are not so qualitatively different in aim as to demarcate different kinds of law; they are merely two techniques for achieving a single aim: efficiency. Where undesirable activity is concerned, the efficient level is zero.

Neither the distinction between stigmatic and nonstigmatic offences or between *mala in se* and *mala prohibita* fares any better. If by stigma is meant some level of empirical opprobrium directed by the populace against the convict, then it is impossible to draw a stable line between stigmatic and nonstigmatic offences; for the line will shift according to public opinion and political agenda, and judges will need to conduct opinion surveys to classify an offence as one or the other. If, however, stigma refers to the opprobrium objectively merited by the deed, then the distinction between stigmatic and nonstigmatic offences cuts across that between true crimes and public welfare offences. Selling tainted food in a chain of supermarkets seems more blameworthy than filching an apple from

---

[8] AP Simester, 'Is Strict Liability Always Wrong?' in AP Simester, ed., *Appraising Strict Liability* (Oxford: Oxford University Press, 2005), 23–4.
[9] Sir William Blackstone, 1 *Commentaries*, 55; 4 *Commentaries*, 42.

someone's orchard. Nor does the distinction between *mala in se* and *mala prohibita* quite map onto that between crimes and public welfare offences; for *mala in se* traditionally included consensual sexual practices considered harmful to the participants, while some regulatory laws prohibit activity that is blameworthy independently of a proscribing statute.

So what is the difference between true crimes and public welfare offences? I want to suggest that the source of the distinction lies securely in an articulation within the structure of human agency. Action presupposes a distinction between a capacity of the will freely to choose ends and the expression of this capacity in determinate choices actualizing a particular conception of the agent's welfare. The first element is formal, abstract, and common to agents, whereas the second engages the individual's particularity—that is, his or her preferences as shaped by upbringing, social influences, and so on. True crimes are actions that either pre-empt the capacity to choose ends through physical force or that interfere at the point of expression by threats imposing a narrow choice between acting for the threatener's ends or suffering a pre-emption or destruction of capacity. By contrast, public welfare offences are actions, omissions, or statuses made illegal because they are dangerous to a particular expression of the capacity in a widely shared preference or because they are dangerous to the agency goods necessary for any expression. Thus, while crimes are paradigmatically interferences with the capacity for choosing ends (or with the judicial apparatus for protecting the capacity), public welfare offences risk harm to the social preferences actually chosen or to the goods essential to action of any kind.

The distinction between social preferences and agency goods generates a division within public welfare offences between two broad types. One type consists of actions breaching statutes protecting a particular social preference or regulating activity directed at satisfying preferences. Another type consists of actions breaching statutes whose aim is to prevent harm to agency goods. Examples of the first type are infractions of greenbelt and heritage laws, hunting and fishing regulations, parking ordinances, traffic rules, and laws promoting economic competition. Examples of the second are breaches of statutes regulating the manufacture and sale of food, liquor, and narcotics, regulating environmental pollution, and enforcing standards of road, air, and industrial safety. In the category of actions harming agency goods also belong offences that, if committed with a form of subjective fault, would be a crime. So, causing death or bodily harm through a negligent failure to perceive a risk as well as assaults committed through an unreasonable mistake as to consent or through an unreasonable belief in the existence of justificatory circumstances can all be penalized as public welfare offences if the defendant lacked the culpable mind for the crime. We will see that different enforcement-constraining principles apply depending on whether a statute aims to regulate preference satisfaction or to protect an agency good.

So the difference between crimes and public welfare offences is firmly grounded in a natural division within the structure of human agency. That difference is no doubt obscured by the fact that crimes too usually cause or threaten harm to an agency good. But we have seen that crimes are first wilful interferences with agency (or against the public order enforcing rights of agency) and only secondarily (if at all) harms. Harming an agency good is neither a necessary nor a sufficient condition of criminal liability. Only if there is first a culpable transgression does a criminal become punishable for resultant harm; and he will be punished for the transgression even if no harm resulted. Even inchoate crimes, we have seen, are culpable wrongs to the extent that they publicly manifest a denial of agency rights. So the *gravamen* of crime is culpable interference (or attempted interference) with agency independently of harm, while that of public welfare offences is the imposition of an excessive risk of harm independently of an interference with agency.

2. Why is Subjective Fault not Required for Public Welfare Offences?

In Chapter 2 I argued that a choice to interfere with another's agency or to break the law is the level of fault alone permitting a right denial or a denial of law's authority to be imputed to the choice and hence alone ensuring that punishment is implicitly assented to by the recipient. So intention, advertent recklessness, or wilful blindness with respect to the interference or breach marks the fault threshold for liability to punishment for free persons. In legal parlance, any of these mental orientations toward (and going with) one's unlawful deed constitutes "subjective fault".

However, if this view is correct, we seem committed to the conclusion to which Jerome Hall was driven and from whose implications he refused to shrink: that all negligence offences are unjust even if the penal consequence of a breach is only a monetary fine, for fines are certainly penalties for lawbreaking.[10] This would entail the consequence that liability for public welfare offences must hinge on a knowing or reckless breach of the statute—a requirement that, by affording a defence to someone who failed to inspect his goods or equipment for risks, or who was ignorant of the law, would render the statute powerless to induce compliance with legal standards of care. Legislatures would thus be forced to rely on the suspension and revocation powers of licensing bodies to regulate desirable but risky activity, otherwise leaving the deterrence of excessive risk to the private enforcement of civil rights after the damage has occurred. The modern regulatory state would be impossible.

I shall not try to evade this implication by arguing, as some do, that the fines attached to public welfare offences are a kind of tax rather than a kind of penalty.[11]

---

[10] *General Principles of Criminal Law*, 351–9; 'Negligent Behavior Should Be Excluded from Penal Liability,' (1963) 63 *Columbia Law Review* 632.
[11] See Blackstone 1 *Comm*, 58: "But in these cases [that is, *mala prohibita*] the alternative is offered to every man; either abstain from this, or submit to such a penalty; and his conscience will

This will not do for a number of reasons. First, if penalties are distinguished from taxes by their aim of prevention as distinct from optimization, there is no reason why heavy fines could not serve a preventative purpose in some situations—for example, when the expected benefits of committing the offence are low (or the probability of apprehension is high) and when the most likely offenders are able to pay the amount sufficient to deter.[12] In those circumstances, fines will deter the activity outright rather than simply reduce it to an efficient level. Second, were a fine a tax on permitted conduct rather than a penalty for prohibited conduct, we could hardly justify our practice of increasing the penalty for a repeat offender who, by his repetition of the offence, merely indicated a willingness to pay the tax.

Most importantly, the claim that public welfare fines are a species of tax blurs an important distinction between regulatory purposes. Both fines and taxes are, to be sure, administrative techniques for regulating an activity thought to be in general desirable. There are, however, differences in the degree of liberty one might wish to leave those subject to regulation.[13] One might, for example, wish to curtail the general level of an activity (for example, alcohol consumption), while leaving to individual choice the time, manner, and place of doing it as well as the decision as to who will do it. The activity is then permitted subject to a price. Alternatively, one might wish to eliminate altogether a narrow, undesirable subcategory of the activity (for example, drinking while driving), taking away the element of choice with respect to that category; in that case the activity is prohibited by a penalty. We reflect the difference between these two regulatory aims (reduction and prevention) by distinguishing linguistically between taxes and fines. Were the latter reduced to the former, it is difficult to see how one could logically resist the further assimilation of imprisonment to heavy taxation.[14]

Nor can we avoid Hall's conclusion by pretending that fines are a kind of tort remedy rather than a kind of penalty.[15] Such an argument would be incoherent on its own terms. It becomes possible to view a penalty paid to the public treasury as a "tort fine", or an offence of negligence as a "public tort", only from a perspective that views tort law in general as penal—that is, as serving to deter excessively risky conduct in the public interest. From this standpoint, therefore, tort fines and tort damages are distinguished only as different strategies of deterrence, the former designed for activity that is undesirable simply, the latter for activity that is undesirable only when performed without due care.[16] However, if tort remedies in

---

be clear, which side of the alternative he thinks proper to embrace." See also Simester, 'Is Strict Liability Always Wrong?' 29.

[12] Posner, *Economic Analysis of Law*, 219–27.

[13] See G Calabresi, *The Cost of Accidents* (New Haven, Conn: Yale University Press, 1970), 113–19.

[14] Posner embraces this extreme conclusion but makes an exception for common-law crimes; see *Economic Analysis of Law*, 219–31.

[15] Posner, *Economic Analysis of Law*, 238. See also *R v Stephens* (1886) 1 QB 702, 708; *Sherras v de Rutzen*, 922.

[16] See S Shavell, 'Liability for Harm Versus Regulation of Safety,' (1984) 13 *Journal of Legal Studies* 357.

general are public sanctions, then we cannot escape our dilemma by labelling fines "tort fines", as if this meant that they were merely a form of private law remedy distinct from punishment. On the contrary, the conclusion that follows from viewing tort law in this manner is that negligence liability is unjust even in tort.

Nor, finally, can we adopt the justification typically given by judges for dropping the requirement of subjective fault from public welfare offences so as to force compliance with regulatory standards of care. These offences, they say, usually carry light penalties and incur little, if any, social opprobrium; therefore, the high level of blameworthiness represented by subjective fault is not required to deserve the comparatively slight consequences of a conviction.[17] Andrew Simester has elaborated on this view. He argues that culpability is required for stigmatic offences because otherwise convicts will receive the stigma that goes with a conviction for a named offence without deserving it; hence they will be mislabelled and defamed by the state. Because, however, this rationale for a culpability requirement has no application to nonstigmatic offences, the instrumentalist (deterrence, cost-internalization) arguments for strict liability meet no resistance from moral objections.[18]

This reasoning is flawed on two counts. First, the rationale for a culpable-mind requirement for crime cannot be that a culpable mind is needed to deserve severe penalties; for the law requires a culpable mind even for minor assaults and petty thefts, which may be punished with fines less severe than many we find in the regulatory context. For the reasons discussed in Chapter 2, subjective fault is rather the threshold level of fault for *any* punishment of a free agent. Second, the requirement of a culpable mind cannot be explained as providing the blameworthiness needed to deserve the opprobrium that comes with a criminal conviction; for this explanation treats a dependent variable as independent and vice versa. Opprobrium is not some independent reaction to a conviction to which a deserving level of fault must be fitted. Rather, opprobrium *hinges* on culpable wrongdoing and so cannot be identified as the reason for making a culpable mind an element of the offence. Indeed, Simester's "anti-defamation" rationale for a culpable-mind requirement makes sense only if we assume that crime typically requires a culpable mind for some other reason (and people know this), and then someone is atypically convicted in the absence of fault. But then the anti-defamation argument is one, not for a culpable-mind requirement for true crimes, but against wrongful convictions. Moreover, if opprobrium is not a good reason for attaching a culpability requirement to an offence, then neither can the absence of opprobrium be a good reason for eliminating that requirement.

How then can we avoid the apparent implication of our conclusion regarding the appropriate fault threshold for crime that a form of subjective fault must be a condition of penal liability for public welfare offences—that no one can be

---

[17] *R v Pierce Fisheries* [1971] SCR 5.
[18] Simester, 'Is Strict Liability Always Wrong?', 33–9.

guilty of such an offence unless he or she has knowingly broken the law or done so knowing, or being wilfully blind toward, the risk of breach?

We do so in the only manner possible—by denying the implication. It does not follow from our account of the culpable-mind requirement that public welfare offences should require subjective fault, because that account presupposed a narrow class of unlawful actions, to which its validity is therefore restricted. Let us briefly recall the main lines of that account. A knowing or consciously reckless interference with another's capacity for free choice implied a denial of rights of agency applying equally to the denier. Thus, any answering infringement of the criminal's right is implicitly self-willed and so compatible with his inviolability. An intention (or its equivalents) to interfere with agency was thus required as that without which there is no implied denial of agency rights that could rebound against the criminal; and the *actus* was essential as that without which there would be no claim of public validity for a right denial justifying its universalization. So, the account of punishment that revealed the necessity of a culpable mind assumed the transgression of a boundary demarcating a space reserved for the agent's freedom of choice. That account has no relevance, therefore, to penal sanctions for breaches of rules protecting not the capacity for free choice, but rather a particular societal choice about what conduces to happiness, or protecting agency goods against an excessive risk of harm whether or not a transgression occurs.

Because regulatory sanctions aim to prevent harm rather than to vindicate rights against denials of their existence, the language of "desert" and "punishment" is foreign to them. No account of regulatory offences could reveal a culpable mind as triggering a logical circuit between doing what the law forbids and liability to the penalty; for there is no such circuit. Apart from positive law, my intentional driving over 100 kilometers per hour on a highway implies no denial of agency rights and so no implicit denial of my own. And the same may be said of knowingly selling alcohol to a minor or engaging in a consensual transaction in narcotics. Such actions, if performed knowingly or negligently, are doubtless morally blameworthy; they reflect badly on the characters who perform them. But the blameworthiness of these actions cannot be said to deserve a response in the form of judicial coercion, for blameworthy behaviour deserves blame and censure, which could come from the press and the market, but not specifically state punishment infringing rights. Here, therefore, the reason for the official sanction is not to execute an antecedent nemesis but simply to deter excessive risk taking.

Because there is no logical connection between intentionally or negligently doing the deed proscribed by a regulation and liability to coercion, the rationality specific to regulatory sanctions is not the intrinsic rationality of desert but the instrumental rationality of means and ends. The regulatory sanction is justified, not by what the agent has done in the past, but by its suitability to the justified public goal it serves. This does not mean that regulatory sanctions are undeserved, but rather that (with a qualification I'll discuss momentarily) the idea of penal desert has no intelligible application in this setting, embedded as it is in the sphere of transgressions against agency. Thus, regulatory sanctions are neither deserved nor undeserved; they are rather efficacious or inefficacious. And since sanctions unmoored from desert cannot be called punishments, let us call regulatory sanctions noncriminal penalties, as we have done thus far. Here, then, is the justification for dropping the culpable-mind requirement from public welfare offences. The courts properly do so, not because of the supposedly lesser penalties or lesser stigma associated with these offences, but because the liberal theory of penal liability that reveals the necessity of the culpable mind also limits that necessity to punishment for deeds interfering (or attempting to interfere) with free choice.

However, to the foregoing remarks we must add the qualification already mentioned in Chapter 2. While regulatory sanctions are justified or not independently of desert, and while a culpable mind is thus unnecessary for liability, it is nevertheless possible to deserve punishment for a breach of a regulatory statute *if* one breaches with a culpable mind. For if one knowingly breaches a regulatory statute, one implicitly denies the authority of law under which alone rights are real, thereby conceptually exposing oneself to coercion, including even imprisonment for risking serious harm. Thus, the legal retributivist conception of punishment, while native to the sphere of transgressions against agency, can migrate to a small corner of the public welfare domain.

Observe that the foregoing account of why subjective fault is unnecessary for regulatory offences does not make crucial the difference between imprisonment and monetary fines. This is all to the good, since neither instrument is unique to a particular domain. However, the account explains the different public significance that fines bear in the two contexts, respectively; and so it explains why regulatory fines, though infringing a property right, do not require the same kind of justification as punitive fines. In the criminal context, a fine is a punitive invasion of a proprietary boundary *as if the right did not exist*—one that must be justified by a legitimating account of punishment specifically directed to the invasion and the indignity it signifies. Assent through the right denial implicit in subjective fault is that legitimation. In the public welfare context, the same factual taking of wealth has a different public meaning. Here the taking signifies not a punitive invasion of property, but a setback to welfare meant to shape incentives for a justified public purpose. True, the taking of wealth is still a taking of property; but because the taking expresses no *punitive disrespect* for the convict's property, the justification for it can take the same form as that for the police power generally. That justification would show how the right to property is qualified rather than absolute, hence capable of being overridden for a public end.[19]

It might be objected that, if regulatory fines are understood solely as a technique for shaping incentives and without reference to a punitive end, they become

---

[19] Though factual takings of wealth can have an insulting or benign significance depending on context, imprisonment insults whatever the context. Hence nothing but retribution for a right denial can justify it.

indistinguishable from taxes; and so, counterintuitively, the distinction between a penalty for prohibited conduct and a price for permitted conduct disappears. However, we have already seen that this is not necessarily the case. Viewed as a technique for shaping incentives, regulatory fines no doubt share with taxes a common genus; but they can be distinguished from taxes without reference to blame and censure by their aim of preventing undesirable, rather than pricing desirable, activity. The redundancy of censure to our account of regulatory penalties is all to the good, for otherwise innocuous breaches of rules regulating preference satisfaction would be troublesome. Of course, much conduct prohibited by regulation is blameworthy; but that does not mean the state-imposed penalty is meant to censure it or even that blameworthiness is a necessary condition of penalization.

3. What Principles of Penal Justice Apply to Public Welfare Offences?

The legal retributivist account of the culpable-mind requirement has vindicated the intuition of many judges that the traditional principles of criminal law "have but little application" to public welfare offences.[20] Indeed, it has vindicated the judicial distinction, so often disparaged, between crimes "in the true sense" and acts that are merely "prohibited under a penalty".[21] The real difficulty with this account of *mens rea*, therefore, is not that it makes the regulatory state impossible, but, on the contrary, that it gives the regulatory state carte blanche. For if the retributivist conception of punishment exhausts the content of penal justice, then penal justice consists solely in a requirement that punishment be deserved. Consequently, sanctions that are not "punishments"—whose justification is instrumentalist rather than desert-based—would be free of all right-based constraints. The only limits applying to them would be those generated by cost–benefit rationality. Thus, if the policy behind a regulation serves the general happiness, then efficacious coercive means are justified just in case they are necessary to further the policy and do not impose costs greater than their benefits. Liability rules cramping the enforcement of the policy would likewise be justified or not on a cost–benefit basis.

This is indeed the way in which strict liability for public welfare offences has typically been justified by courts and treatise writers. By strict liability I mean liability for a breach of a statutory rule or standard based on a voluntary act or omission but irrespective of whether the breach was non-negligent in the sense of occurring because of a reasonable mistake or despite all reasonable efforts to comply.[22] The case for strict liability has traditionally been that negligence-based liability would

---

[20] *Sault Ste Marie*, 1303.   [21] *Sherras v De Rutzen*, 922.
[22] In Canada, this form of liability is called "absolute", whereas strict liability refers to liability based on negligence; see *Sault Ste Marie*.

render public welfare statutes unenforceable because fault would be too difficult, costly, and time-consuming to prove. Because only a small percentage of infractions could be successfully prosecuted, the deterrent force of these statutes would be undermined. By contrast, it is argued, penalizing "innocents" is in this context a worthwhile cost of achieving an important statutory purpose, given that the penalties for breach are comparatively light and no stigma attaches to a conviction.[23]

Of course, such an unconstrained consequentialist reasoning could also justify dispensing with the voluntariness requirement of liability, a step that has been taken only in isolated cases.[24] That judges have balked at this logical move (if liability can be imposed despite the defendant's having done everything within reason to comply, why excuse him because he did not "do" anything?) indicates that the cost–benefit calculus by which they justify strict liability does not reflect a principled utilitarianism—indeed, it is unlikely that the judges who reason this way would extend the method to the criminal context. Rather, it reflects the normative void in which regulatory law operates as long as punishing in accordance with desert is thought to exhaust penal justice.

We have seen, however, that retributive justice does not exhaust penal justice because the formal agency paradigm to which it belongs does not do so. The deficiencies of that paradigm pushed us to a framework of justice ordered to public reason conceived as the real autonomy of the agent. And that framework, we will now see, generates not only an entitlement to the goods delivered by regulatory laws but also a fault proviso on penal liability for breaching them as well as a constraint on the type of sanction by which regulations are enforced.

The priority of autonomy over happiness

The principles of penal justice for public welfare offences vary depending on whether the aim of a statute is to regulate the pursuit of satisfactions or to prevent harm to agency goods. This is so because, whereas a simple priority rule setting up respect for autonomy as an absolute constraint on the enforcement of laws regulating the pursuit of happiness suffices for statutes of the former type, it does not work for those of the latter class; for these have as their own aim the protection of goods essential to autonomy. Here the agent's political entitlement to the conditions of autonomous action informs policy and constraint alike. So let us first deal with the principles applicable to statutes promoting a social preference or regulating the pursuit of satisfactions.

---

[23] Simester, 'Is Strict Liabilty Always Wrong?', 25–30. For a summary of the arguments supporting strict liability for public welfare offences, see Dickson J's judgment in *Sault Ste Marie*. See also J Edwards, *Mens Rea in Statutory Offences* (London: Macmillan, 1955), 76–86 and FB Sayre, 'Public Welfare Offenses,' (1933) 33 *Columbia Law Review* 55, 67–8.

[24] *R v Larsonneur* (1933) 24 Cr App R 74 (CA). On the apparent incoherence of the voluntariness requirement see Larry Alexander, 'Reconsidering the Relationship Among Voluntary Acts, Strict Liability, and Negligence in Criminal Law,' (1990) 7 *Social Philosophy & Policy* 84.

The real autonomy paradigm generates a duty on those claiming authority under public reason to facilitate, and equalize opportunities for, the satisfaction of right-respecting preferences. This is so, not because preferences have moral status by themselves, but because satisfying subjective preferences is the way agents realize their common potential for living according to self-authored ends. Utilitarianism, to be sure, treats preferences as having moral weight on their own, one that casts on others a duty to consider them in deciding on the right course of action. Yet utilitarianism gives no account of why idiosyncratic preferences should be an object of public concern; it merely takes their public standing as axiomatic. That individuals empirically do seek to satisfy their desires and aversions is no warrant for concluding that strangers ought to care whether or not they succeed, let alone ought to promote an impersonal sum of satisfactions at their own expense. Indeed, so far from elucidating the public significance of preference satisfaction, utilitarianism actually casts doubt upon it. For by abstracting preference satisfaction from the total concept of action wherein it belongs, utilitarianism must countenance the passive experience of, say, drug-induced euphoria as something a public authority ought to support.[25]

One who, by contrast, views preference satisfaction as the realized human potential for self-authored action has a plausible account, not only of the public standing of preferences, but also of autonomy as an absolute constraint on the enforcement of laws regulating the pursuit of satisfactions. Preference satisfaction is an object worthy of public concern because the realized potential for self-motivated action is a public end, and that potential is realized only in action pursuant to subjective ends. Put otherwise, the generic potential for action from self-authored ends would not be a potential were it not capable of realization, and realization inevitably engages the agent's particular ends. So a public authority directed to the public interest in autonomous action must also be concerned to facilitate and to regulate for everyone's benefit the pursuit of private satisfactions.

We can see, moreover, that this account of the public significance of preference satisfaction also establishes a priority rule with respect to autonomy and happiness. Because preference satisfaction is properly an object of public concern only as necessary to autonomous action, it follows that its pursuit must be constrained by respect for the autonomy that gives it public worth. It is impermissible, in other words, for a public authority to promote happiness by subordinating the very end under whose primacy happiness first rises to public significance. Were it to do so, its action would no longer be one of a public authority, for it would have sacrificed the public interest to particular ends. Accordingly, the principle of penal justice applicable to public welfare statutes regulating the pursuit of satisfactions is the priority of autonomy over happiness.

The priority of autonomy is reflected throughout the constitutional, statute, and common law of liberal legal orders. Thus the state's authority to promote the

[25] Robert Nozick, *Anarchy, State, and Utopia* (New York: Basic Books, 1974), 42–5.

satisfaction of preferences is constitutionally limited in many jurisdictions by respect for freedom of conscience and expression. Similarly, social preferences might congeal against certain forms of sexual expression, but the regulation of these practices is typically constrained by a duty to respect the free choice of mature agents acting in private. At common law, it is impermissible for A to expropriate B merely because a transfer will result in a net increase of happiness. The increase in happiness is permitted only with the consent of B. Indeed, even strict liability for public welfare offences is hardly ever *absolute* liability; for it is qualified by a requirement that the defendant have "acted" in breach, or have "permitted" the proscribed result, or have been voluntarily in possession of the outlawed matter (that is, have known of the fact of possession, though not necessarily of the unlawful character of the thing possessed), or have voluntarily adopted and kept the proscribed status—a half-hearted concession to individual control over penal liability.[26] The common theme of these examples is our assignment of a normative weight to individual autonomy such that respect for autonomy is due even if this means compromising the maximization of happiness or qualifying deterrence. Thus, respect for autonomy is not treated as one item in a mix of goods that maximizes overall happiness; rather it functions in legal reasoning as an indefeasible constraint on the pursuit of satisfactions.

The principle of autonomy's priority yields three conclusions with respect to penal liability for breaches of statutes protecting a social preference or regulating preference satisfaction. First, strict liability is unjust irrespective of whether the penalty for a breach is imprisonment or a fine, because strict liability means that the agent is vulnerable to a penal fate over which it has no control. No matter what care the individual may have taken to comply with the statute, he may find himself in breach because of some unforeseeable happenstance; hence to penalize him for the breach subordinates autonomy to the pursuit of satisfactions. The flaw in strict-liability offences is not that they penalize innocents or the morally blameless; for the concept of desert has no coherent role to play in the justification of regulatory sanctions. The problem, rather, is that strict-liability offences subordinate the public end of autonomy to the pursuit of private satisfactions; hence the statutes creating these offences are not the acts of a public authority to which free subjects can submit.

Cast in this light, the injustice in strict-liability offences can be remedied without introducing a subjective fault requirement that would kill the patient along with the disease. What is required is simply that the defendant be able to avoid liability by taking reasonable steps to comply even if, as luck would have it, he finds himself in breach. Accordingly, courts should interpret regulatory offences (as they do in Australia and Canada) as affording a defence of reasonable mistake or of due diligence, and they should invalidate under constitutional rights of due process public welfare statutes expressly creating strict-liability offences.

[26] *Robinson v California*, 370 US 660 (1962). *R v Larsonneur* is a counterexample, but it is almost universally criticized.

Second, the priority of autonomy determines that public welfare statutes potentially imposing imprisonment for a negligent breach of a regulation are unjust, because they too subordinate individual autonomy to the general happiness. Since depriving an agent of its freedom to act cannot (consistently with inviolability) be justified instrumentally as a deterrent needed to secure others' happiness, it must be justified on retributive grounds or not at all. Accordingly, it would be permissible to punish with imprisonment someone who knowingly breached a welfare statute, because the agent's loss of liberty can here be conceived as the logical implication of its denial of law's authority—hence as something self-willed. But imprisoning the negligent as a means of inducing general compliance with statutes regulating preference satisfaction promotes happiness at the expense of the end—autonomy—without whose priority happiness would not be a public goal.

It might be objected that a fine of great magnitude could have the same impact on the autonomy of a particular individual as imprisonment would have on every individual. This is certainly possible. Yet whatever accidental effect fines might have in particular cases, their purpose in the regulatory context is to threaten setbacks to individual happiness sufficient to outweigh the expected benefits of a breach. In general, therefore, regulatory fines do not subordinate autonomy to happiness, as nondeserved imprisonment does. Where they would do so in a particular case, however, specific measures are required to prevent this. In Canada, for example, no one may be imprisoned for failing to pay a fine if the reason for failure is inability to pay; and courts are obliged to consider ability to pay in setting a fine and to choose payment arrangements that will not reduce the convict to poverty.[27]

Accordingly, at the level of statutory interpretation, courts should construe a regulatory offence carrying a potential prison sentence as requiring subjective fault for a conviction; while at the constitutional level, they should treat as a violation of fundamental justice or due process a sanction of imprisonment where subjective fault is expressly excluded from the definition of the offence. A requirement of subjective fault for imprisonment need not undermine the deterrent force of regulatory penalties, since this requirement is for a distinct offence alongside the fine-backed offence based on negligence; it is not instead of the negligence offence. Moreover, a repeat offence or an offence subsequent to a warning by an inspector would place a heavy evidential burden on someone charged with the *mens rea* offence to prove lack of knowledge.

Third, because the injustice of strict liability for contraventions of statutes regulating preference satisfaction does not consist in punishing the innocent but rather in subordinating the public interest in autonomy to private ends, requiring the defendant to prove due diligence in excuse does not violate the presumption of innocence.[28] Because regulatory penalties cannot be deserved in the legal-retributivist sense by doing what the law proscribes or by failing to do what it

---

[27] Canadian Criminal Code, RSC 1985 c. C–46, ss. 734 (2), 736.
[28] *Wholesale Travel Group Inc. v The Queen* [1991] 3 SCR 154.

demands, no one can be either legally innocent of, or legally culpable for, the conduct made illegal by a statute. Rather, one either did or did not run afoul of the conduct elements of the offence. Of course, one may be *morally* blameless for a statutory breach (if it occurred despite one's best efforts), but this would be an argument against social censure, not against the state's imposing without censure a monetary penalty in the public interest. No doubt one could also be *morally* blameworthy for a breach, as where one negligently failed to take precautions when the public safety was at stake. But moral fault is accidentally, not essentially, related to breaches of regulatory statutes; not even an absent-minded failure to obtain a licence to fish can be said to deserve a penalty, while a blameworthy lapse endangering others correlates to blame but not to an exercise of the state's police power.

Accordingly, the defence of due diligence operates, not as a denial of guilt or of moral fault, but as a confession and avoidance. The defendant breached the statute, but if he has done everything one could reasonably expect of him to comply, any penalty would befall him as a fate beyond his power to avoid, and so the public good of autonomy would be subordinated to the satisfaction of preferences. Thus the public authority cannot penalize him without ceasing to be a public authority. Enforcement is blocked, not by the defendant's innocence or blamelessness, but by the effect enforcement would have on the integrity of the public legal order. But since a successful defence of due diligence does not mean that the defendant is innocent, to require him to prove due diligence on a balance of probabilities is not to require him to prove his innocence. This removes the concern that a defence of due diligence would impose too onerous a burden on prosecutors and so render public welfare statutes too difficult to enforce.

The noncontradiction proviso

The priority of autonomy principle constrains the enforcement of public welfare statutes embodying a social preference or regulating the pursuit of satisfactions. It cannot, however, constrain the enforcement of statutes, such as those protecting health and safety, which themselves aim to protect the physical conditions of living according to self-authored ends. Where real autonomy underlies both the policy of the statute and the constraint on its enforcement, something other than a priority rule is needed to arbitrate clashes between the public interest and that of the defendant.

One possibility is to say that strict liability and imprisonment for negligence are permissible where needed to maximize autonomy across individuals. The negation of the defendant's autonomy is justified to the extent that it is necessary to achieve a greater autonomy overall. But of course, this principle contradicts autonomy, for it is one by which agents may be deprived of their autonomy for the sake of the greater good of others, hence subjected to a rule they could not impose on themselves. It does not matter that the affected individual too may benefit from the law in the long run; for if the negation of autonomy may be justified by the greater autonomy it secures to the same individual over time, then it may in principle also be justified by the greater autonomy it secures for others even if the imprisoned individual receives no benefit. Since the justifying end is the net gain of autonomy, it cannot matter whether the beneficiary of the gain is the individual incarcerated or other members of society.

For statutes preventing harm to agency goods, the applicable principle of penal justice is one I'll call the noncontradiction proviso. This states that the public good of autonomy cannot coherently be pursued by penal means that secure autonomy for some by denying it to another, for these instruments turn the public good into a special interest. Thus, those claiming coercive authority under public reason cannot use these means without exceeding their authority.

Both strict liability and imprisonment for negligence are ruled out by the noncontradiction proviso. Strict liability is outlawed because the public goal of real autonomy cannot self-consistently be pursued against an agent through a liability beyond its power to avoid. Likewise, imprisonment (or ruinous fines) for negligent breaches is impermissible, for, absent an intentional breach implying assent to imprisonment, this penalty sacrifices one agent's autonomy to that of others, thereby contradicting itself as an instrument of the public welfare. Accordingly, the priority of autonomy and the noncontradiction proviso yield identical prescriptions for the same end: the integrity of public reason. The priority principle constrains the coercive regulation of preference satisfaction so that the latter remains a public end; the noncontradiction proviso constrains the use of penal measures to protect agency goods so that the public good does not dissolve in its realization into the interest of a part.

4. Ignorance of the Law

In this section, I discuss the modifications to the rule concerning ignorance of the law that are required in the public welfare context by the priority of autonomy and the noncontradiction proviso. I have already mentioned one such modification: where imprisonment is statutorily possible, a knowing breach of the regulatory statute is required to justify a pre-emption of liberty; hence ignorance of the law is here properly a defence, though it may also be an admission of liability for the lesser included offence punishable by fine.[29] But what of the latter? Can ignorance of the law ever excuse a regulatory offence punishable by a fine? Let me begin by juxtaposing the following scenarios.

---

[29] This principle condemns the NewYork Court of Appeals' ruling in *State v Marrero* 507 NE2d 1068 (1987) upholding the defendant's conviction for a weapons possession *felony* despite his good-faith belief that he, as a corrections officer, was included in the exempted class of "peace officers". For commentary, see Paul Robinson and Michael Cahill, *Law Without Justice* (Oxford: Oxford University Press, 2006), 28–35.

Suppose Polly and Esther (P and E) have an idea for combining two chemicals to produce a fibre hardier than any on the market. Before going into business, they check all the relevant statutes and regulations in their jurisdiction to make sure that what they want to do is legal and to see what regulatory requirements apply. A careful inquiry reveals no law prohibiting their planned enterprise, nor any regulation beyond those of which they were already aware. So P and E confidently open their plant and begin production. One day after they checked the regulations, however, a new one is issued and published making the combination of the two chemicals illegal without a special licence, because under certain conditions the combination can produce an explosion. Having no reason to inquire again so soon, P and E continue production until they are charged under the new regulation.

Under the positive law of most Commonwealth jurisdictions, P and E will have no defence, because ignorance of the law is no excuse for a breach. This will be so even in those jurisdictions (such as Canada) that have recognized a defence of due diligence for breach of a public welfare statute.[30] P and E obviously exercised due diligence in avoiding illegality, but because they were ignorant of the law's existence rather than of their noncompliance with a known law, they will be convicted. In some American states, by contrast, P and E would likely be excused, for there, ignorance of the law will excuse in the public welfare context if there was nothing to alert the defendant to the possibility of an infraction or if he took reasonable steps to ascertain the law.[31]

Now let's vary the facts somewhat. Suppose P's and E's research uncovered a law making the manufacture of chemical explosives an offence if done without a licence. Unsure of whether their enterprise could be classed as a "manufacture of chemical explosives", they consulted a lawyer, who informed them that there was no precedent deciding this question but that a judge could rule against them in the future. So, confident that no existing law stood in their way, P and E began production. At their trial for manufacturing explosives without a licence, the judge ruled that P's and E's activity was indeed the manufacture of an explosive, and so he convicted and fined them, pedantically intoning that ignorance of the law is no excuse even in a case of first instance.

Polly and Esther seem to have been unfairly penalized in both these cases, but I'll argue that the principles of penal liability for public welfare offences give them an excuse in the first case but not in the second.

In Chapter 2 I argued that legal retributivism vindicates the general (but not exceptionless) rule that ignorance of the law is nonexculpatory in the context of crimes. The thinking Agent in the defendant's position knows the wrongfulness of acts involving claims to liberty inconsistent with equal liberty, because it knows that claims to liberty can be validated as rights only by independent

---

[30] *R v Molis* [1980] 2 SCR 356.
[31] See, for example, *Long v State* 65 A2d 489 (Del 1949). For commentary, see Dan M Kahan, 'Ignorance of Law Is An Excuse—But Only For The Virtuous,' (1997) 96 *Michigan Law Review* 127, 149.

equals whose liberty is reciprocally respected. So it knows that claims to liberty unacceptable to an equal transgress a boundary demarcating valid rights. The Agent also knows (even without a statute) the punishability of an intentional or reckless transgression of the boundary, because it knows that practical denials of an agent's right to liberty render its own liberty insecure. And the thinking Agent's knowledge can be imputed to the defendant insofar as he is an agent.

Obviously, however, this rationale for the ignorance rule is limited to the criminal context. No one would say that the thinking Agent must know that catching undersized lobsters transgresses a person's boundary or that intentionally catching them is inherently punishable, for neither is true. And the same may be said for any imposition of a risk of harm that is not consequent on an interference with liberty or risk thereof. Here there is no connection of which the agent must know between knowingly doing the proscribed action or knowingly risking the harm and liability to coercion.

So the rationale for the ignorance rule must be different in the public welfare context. Here, I will suggest, ignorance of the law is no excuse because its excusatory force would be incompatible with the authority of law. The law would not be authoritative if its enforceability against an individual depended on his or her contingent awareness of the law's existence; for anyone could then escape the law's reach simply by holding himself in ignorance of its commands. Stated otherwise, the authority of law entails a correlative duty in the subject to obey the law; and since one cannot *obey* the law (though one can accidentally conform to it) without knowing it, the authority of law entails a correlative duty in the subject to know the law. But is this duty absolute or qualified?

Were the duty absolute, it would conflict with both the priority of autonomy and the noncontradiction proviso. This is so because an absolute duty to know the law (where the law is not knowable to reason) is a duty to know it even if it is impossible to know, such as when it does not yet exist. And if one had a duty to know a law that did not exist at the time one acted, then one's penal liability under it now when it does exist is a liability beyond the dutiful agent's power to have avoided. Such a liability contradicts the priority of autonomy if the law aims to regulate the pursuit of satisfactions; and it violates the noncontradiction proviso if the statute's aim is to prevent harm to agency goods. Since a violation of these principles negates the law's enforcement as a realization of public reason, imposition of the penalty cannot be a valid act of those claiming authority to coerce under public reason.

However, if liability under a retroactive law violates these principles, so does liability under a regulation that was signed into law before the defendant's breach but not published so that dutiful care could discover it. For here too the dutiful agent would be subject to an unavoidable penal fate. And if the duty to know the law does not extend to unpublished regulations because the dutiful agent cannot be expected to know them, then neither does it extend to published regulations that are so vague that no meaning can be attached to them, nor to those that (as in P's and E's first case) are frequently amended without public deliberation and of which the agent, though he acted dutifully, was unaware. For here again liability would expose the agent to a penal fate that even dutiful diligence could not have avoided. So P and E are entitled to an excuse in the first case. Though they breached the law, penalizing them would subvert the law as an expression of public reason; for it would subordinate the public interest in autonomy to private satisfactions or promote the autonomy of some at the expense of another's.

In the second case, however, the law under which P and E are penalized was published and known to them when they acted. What P and E did not know and could not have known was how the law would be applied to their particular situation. Had P and E consulted an official body authorized to apply the explosives law and been incorrectly told their activity was permitted, their reliance on that assurance would have been reasonable; for no more dutiful care was possible, and they would have acknowledged legal authority rather than relying on their own speculations. Hence penalizing them would have subjected them to a moral fate no more dutiful care could have avoided in a case where forbearing to exact the penalty would not have been inconsistent with law's authority.[32] But P and E had no such official assurance. They knew of the legal uncertainty and made a bet that their activity was permitted. Here, allowing their ignorance to excuse would be incompatible with law's authority, for it would mean allowing their guess as to how the law would be applied to displace the judge's application. Moreover, it cannot be said that penalizing them would subject them to an unavoidable moral fate, for they could have avoided liability by refusing the bet. Since they chose the risk of illegality, their autonomy is not compromised by penalizing them. That retroactive penalization might discourage lawful as well as unlawful activity is a consideration going to the wisdom of penalization but not in this case to its justice.

The somewhat paradoxical conclusion of these reflections is that ignorance of the law should excuse in cases where an excuse is required by the rationale for the doctrine that ignorance is no excuse. If the rationale is that an excuse based on ignorance of the law is incompatible with law's authority, then the rule must be qualified in cases where the failure to excuse would itself undermine law's authority as an expression of public reason. In this respect, there is no relevant difference between due diligence in complying with the law and due diligence in ascertaining it. Both ought to afford a defence to penal liability under a public welfare statute, although what counts as due diligence in ascertaining the law should be informed by the idea of law's authority (so heeding bad advice from a lawyer would not count, whereas heeding an official misstatement would). In both cases, the defence of due diligence operates as an excuse based on the state's lack of authority to convict. The defendant breached the law, but the state is barred from executing the law against him because doing so would transform the administration of justice under public reason into the enforcement of a particular interest. The defendant is not so much acquitted as the state's sword is stayed (see Chapter 7).

[32] *Levis (City) v Tetreault* [2006] 1 SCR 420.

The position of the American courts that recognize the distinctiveness of the public welfare context is thus the preferable one. The more rigid Commonwealth position extends a rule valid for the criminal context to the public welfare setting without appropriate qualification.

5. Conclusion

HLA Hart believed that all the exculpatory and excusing conditions recognized by the penal law could be explained by the principle that an agent should have had a fair opportunity to avoid penal liability.[33] This principle, he thought, embodied respect for individual autonomy, for only if the defendant could have avoided liability was liability under his rational control and his life plans thus protected against unforeseeable calamity. Moreover, Hart thought that individual autonomy was a good of sufficiently high value to warrant treating respect for it as a constraint on the forward-looking ends of punishment; and so for him the priority of autonomy took the place of desert as the limit on the state's pursuit of crime prevention, given that retributivism (which he identified with giving the morally wicked their just deserts) had, in his view, been discredited by reformist ideas.[34]

In this chapter I have argued that what Hart saw as the principle underlying all exculpation and excuse is really a principle valid for a limited domain—that of public welfare offences—in which the idea of penal desert has but marginal relevance. The priority of autonomy does not replace desert as a constraint on punishment, for the latter constraint remains valid for the sphere of criminal transgressions against agency. Indeed, if the priority of autonomy did replace desert, it would contradict itself. This is so because an autonomy constraint on the state's use of its penal power is satisfied by *any* fault requirement, including simple negligence. As long as the defendant could have avoided a violation of the law, punishing him for failing to do so is consistent with respect for his capacity to control his fate. But a negligence threshold of fault for crimes against agency or for offences carrying a prison sentence fails to connect punishment with the defendant's choice *where such a connection is possible.* And where it is possible implicitly to will one's punishment, punishing in the absence of the subjective fault from which alone assent can be implied violates the agent's autonomy. So, extending the priority-of-autonomy principle beyond the public welfare sphere where it is impossible (absent a statute) to will one's punishment violates the principle. Hart need not have jettisoned the idea of desert as a constraint on punishment just because giving the wicked their just deserts has no place in a progressive legal system; for the idea of desert is not tied exclusively to that undeniably unsuitable version of retributivism.

---

[33] *Punishment and Responsibility* (Oxford: Clarendon Press, 1968), 17–24, 35–53, 152–7, 177–85.
[34] Ibid, ch. VII.

6

Justification

1. Introduction

Almost no general statements about legal justifications are true.

If one says that legal justifications make wrongful actions exceptionally permissible, one is confronted by cases involving actors—police officers, for example—whose justification derives from a public duty and whose justified acts of force are therefore obligatory. Yet one cannot say that justifications always make otherwise wrongful actions obligatory, because no one is legally required to act in self-defence against an aggressor. Here justification gives a permission. However, if, with self-defence in view, one says that justifications confer a permission to do what is otherwise wrongful, one is immediately embarrassed by cases of putative self-defence—of a reasonable but mistaken belief in the existence of a wrongful threat. Here the mistaken actor cannot be said to have a permission to use force against an imagined assailant, because a permission implies no right in the victim to resist and no right in third parties to impede; and yet if the victim is an innocent, how could he have no right to resist someone who mistook him for an unlawful threat? How could a police officer have no authority to help him resist?

Some might say that the actor reasonably mistaken about the need for self-defence is excused from wrongdoing rather than justified, leaving the misinterpreted actor a right to resist unlawful force and others a right to assist him. This solution ends well (in an acquittal for both the mistaken and misinterpreted actors), and yet not all *is* well; for the mistaken actor could still justifiably complain about the expressive content of the verdict. "Why," he should protest, "if the truth of the matter was knowable only to a superhuman mind located in no particular place and suffering no limits on knowledge, should I, a finite, human agent, need an excuse? Excusing me presupposes that I have committed not simply a private wrong to this person (something I grant), but a criminal wrong, and this I vehemently deny." Moreover, if this complaint rings true when the wrongful threat is only apparent, how much more meritorious does it become when the wrongful threat is real and the defender is reasonably mistaken only about its lethal potential? Even were we inclined to deny that someone reasonably mistaken about the existence of a wrongful threat is permitted to use force against his imagined assailant, we might think differently if he used lethal force to repel a real wrongdoer he reasonably but mistakenly believed meant to kill him. Here we might think the lethal force justified despite the defender's mistake.

If justification is (sometimes) too strong and excuse too weak a defence of the reasonably mistaken defender, what about something in between? Perhaps we should say that the actor reasonably mistaken about the existence of a wrongful threat is "warranted" but not "justified" in using defensive force, or that he has an "agent-perspectival" but not an "objective" justification, or that he has a "qualified privilege" rather than a permission. Problems, however, cannot be solved by sweeping them under labels. The fact remains that the mistaken actor is granted a permission to use force subject to a permission in the victim (and all others) to resist him; this is the contradictory reality summed up by the labels. Yet how, apart from a judgeless state of nature, can such a contradictory legal situation exist? How can a permission in one actor coexist with a right to resist in the one acted upon? For a lawful condition, this seems an intolerable paradox.

If it is difficult to generalize about what a justification implies for the rights of others, it is impossible to say generally what conditions suffice for a justification or what conditions are necessary for one to exist. Return to the case of putative self-defence. While it was unclear whether a defender is permitted to use force against someone reasonably but erroneously believed to be an assailant, matters seem much more certain when the assailant is real but the threat is not. Suppose A points a gun at B demanding his money. A knows but B does not know that the gun is fake. Here it seems clear that B's reasonable apprehension of a threat, even if mistaken, gives him a permission to use force to avert the perceived threat; the true state of affairs is irrelevant. And yet, stating this as a truth valid for justification simply founders on the case of putative necessity. Suppose A, to save himself from death by freezing, tries to take shelter in B's home but B prevents his entry with force. B knows but A does not know that the temperature is about to rise and there is no real threat of death. Here it seems that only a true perception of a threat suffices to justify A's entry, for otherwise B's (an innocent's) rights are dependent on A's mistaken perceptions.

Similar problems exist with respect to unknown justification. With private necessity in view, one might conclude that what is necessary and sufficient for a justification is that justificatory circumstances really exist—that a ship will go down with its crew if its cargo is not jettisoned or that a runaway freight train will plough into a passenger train stopped at a station unless someone diverts it so as to destroy only property. Whether or not the defendant knew of the exigent circumstances and acted from a purpose to save lives seems irrelevant to his culpability for mischief (though relevant to his culpability for an impossible attempt), for necessity, as Glanville Williams tells us, removes culpability from the actor by removing it from the action: the defendant, though he violated property, did the right thing.[1] But then what shall we say about justifications claimed by public

---

[1] *Criminal Law: The General Part*, 2nd ed. (London: Stevens, 1961), 24.

officials such as magistrates, sheriffs, and policemen? Since what justifies otherwise wrongful acts by public authorities is a public *purpose* qualified to override agency rights and not otherwise achievable, it stands to reason that the acts must be done for that purpose.[2] Otherwise the actor, in pursuing a private end, is a private agent who (apart from self-defence and private necessity) has lost the justification for coercion the public office gave him.

Equally resistant to general description is the object of justification or what a justification justifies. With self-defence against a wrongful attacker in view, one might say that justifications give a permission to do what is generally wrongful but not wrongful in the particular case. On this view, justification justifies an act of coercion, not a wrong, for no wrong is done in repelling a wrongful attacker. But this generalization runs up against the case where one must defend oneself against an innocent threat—say, a falling human being transformed by the laws of gravity and impact force into a dangerous missile. Does this circumstance negate the wrong of defensive force in this case, or does it permit a wrong, or does it excuse a wrong? And what shall we say about a conflict between one agent's property right and another agent's life? Here a taking of property to save life is most commonly viewed as a justified *transgression*. That is, the right of necessity overrides rather than extinguishes the property right, so that the justification authorizes what remains a wrong. Nor, finally, can one say anything general about the reason for a justification. With necessity in mind, one might think that one is justified in choosing the lesser of two evils and that this is indeed the paradigm case of a justification.[3] But in a case of self-defence, it is by no means obvious that the repulsion of a wrongful attacker is an evil at all.

With all this diversity in the nature and consequences of a legal justification, it is not surprising that academic debate around justification has come to resemble the story of the blind men and the elephant. Everyone lays hold of a part and mistakes it for the whole. Some say justification is an all-things-considered negation of a prima facie wrong;[4] others say it gives a tragic permission to commit what remains a wrong.[5] Some say justifications entail that the victim has no right to resist and that third parties may assist the justified actor;[6] others say that a right to resist and no right to assist are compatible with justification.[7] Some say

---

[2] *R v Dadson* (1850) 169 ER 407.
[3] Paul Robinson, 'Criminal Law Defenses: A Systematic Analysis,' (1982) 82 *Columbia Law Review* 199, 214; Larry Alexander, 'Lesser Evils: A Closer Look at the Paradigmatic Justification,' (2005) 24 *Law and Philosophy* 611.
[4] Robinson, ibid, 272.
[5] George Fletcher, 'The Right and the Reasonable,' (1985) 98 *Harvard Law Review* 949, 978–9; John Gardner, *Offences and Defences* (Oxford: Oxford University Press, 2007), 77–89.
[6] George Fletcher, *Rethinking Criminal Law* (Boston: Little, Brown, 1978), 761–3; Robinson, 'Criminal Law Defenses,' 277–9.
[7] Kent Greenawalt, 'The Perplexing Borders of Justification and Excuse,' (1984) 84 *Columbia. Law Review* 1897, 1918–27; Hamish Stewart, 'The Role of Reasonableness in Self-Defence,' (2003) 16 *Canadian Journal of Law & Jurisprudence* 317, 329.

justification depends solely on objective facts,[8] others that it depends solely on reasonable beliefs.[9]

Part of my argument in this chapter is that both sides to these various disputes are partly right and partly wrong: right in that each side captures a part of the truth about justification, wrong insofar as each claims to describe justification simply. The important question, however, is whether there is a whole of which the competing views are parts or merely a plurality of separate justifications, each with its distinctive rationale and features. I offer an answer to this question, and it runs basically as follows.

It is impossible to generalize about the nature and rationale of justification because justifications divide themselves into two categories, each of which is further subdivided. The primary division is between justifications claimed by public officials and those claimed by private agents.[10] In the former category belong the legal authority to search, arrest, detain, punish (and penalize), and the public necessity to violate property or to override constitutional rights in general. Except insofar as this book as a whole is concerned with the substantive limits on the state's justified use of penal force, I say little in this chapter about this class of justifications; for my topic is the limit on the state's penal authority posed by the justified use of normally unlawful force by private agents. Thus, I deal here only with private justifications: self-defence, defence of others, defence of property, and justificatory private necessity and duress.

Even within this category, however, generalization is impossible. This is so because private justifications (like public ones) separate themselves into two groupings under two distinct frameworks of justice, each ordered to a particular conception of freedom. The justifications of force against a wrongdoer (self-defence, defence of others, and defence of property) belong to the formal agency paradigm of penal justice, whereas the justifications of force against an innocent (necessity and duress where they justify rather than excuse wrongful actions) reflect the interdependence of the formal agency and real autonomy frameworks. Each of these groups has a distinctive rationale and therefore distinctive limiting conditions. As a consequence, there is no such thing as a paradigm case of justification. Moreover, the answer to the question as to whether justifications negate wrongs in the particular case or justify abiding wrongs varies, as we'll see, for the different groups.

---

[8] Paul Robinson, 'Competing Theories of Justification: Deeds v Reasons,' in AP Simester and ATH Smith, eds., *Harm and Culpability* (Oxford: Clarendon Press, 1996), 45–70.
[9] Arthur Ripstein, *Equality, Responsibility, and the Law* (Cambridge: Cambridge University Press, 1999), 190–201; Stewart, 'The Role of Reasonableness,' 329–36; Malcolm Thorburn, 'Justifications, Powers, and Authority,' (2008) 117 *Yale Law Journal* 1070, 1110. Fletcher and Gardner say that legal justification depends on both—on doing the right thing for the right reason; see Gardner, *Offences and Defences*, 91–120; Fletcher, *Rethinking Criminal Law*, 565; 'The Right Deed for the Wrong Reason,' (1975) 23 *UCLA Law Review* 293, 310–11.
[10] For an argument that all legal justification is justification by public authority, see Thorburn, 'Justifications, Powers, and Authority.' For a rebuttal, see below, notes 36, 39.

However, while no single idea explains all justifications, the theory of justification is not fragmented. This is so because the two paradigms of justice to which legal justifications separately belong are united within a comprehensive whole that incorporates both paradigms as constituent elements. Each paradigm embodies not only its own ruling idea but also, incompletely, an underlying idea common to both. So it is neither true that there is a unitary theory of justification nor that there is a mere plurality of separate justifications. Rather there is a unified theory that embraces, without effacing, plurality. The idea that unifies all justifications is the idea that unifies the two paradigms of penal justice. Since one cannot say everything at once, I'll defer discussion of that idea until Chapter 9.

Despite the rather obvious dissimilarity between defensive force against a wrongdoer and aggressive force against an innocent in cases of necessity and duress, the prevailing tendency in theorizing about justification has been monistic. A single idea is typically put forward to explain all cases of justified force against a person. Two such ideas currently occupy the field: the lesser evil theory belonging to utilitarianism and the double effect theory belonging to classical natural law. Before presenting the theory of justification I believe best covers the legal terrain, I'll criticize these two unitary theories. Specifically, I'll argue that the lesser evil theory cannot give an account of justification, while the double effect theory is inappropriate to *legal* justification.

2. The Lesser Evil

Bentham argued that punishment ought not to be inflicted where the defendant's deed, though it produced a mischief, was necessary to avoid a greater mischief. The examples he gives are deeds performed "in the way of precaution against instant calamity" or in the exercise of legal authority.[11] Punishment in such cases of public necessity would be "groundless" because it would be irrational to deter welfare-enhancing actions; such actions, after all, are justified by the utility principle. Bentham treats cases of private necessity and self-defence somewhat differently. Here it may not be true that the evil avoided by the unlawful action is greater than the evil inflicted, but punishment would nevertheless be "inefficacious" because the evil of the threatened sanction would be outweighed in the defendant's mind by the immediate evil he faces.[12] Nevertheless, if, in a case of private necessity, the evil avoided were greater than the evil inflicted, Bentham would no doubt have said that the unlawful act was justified. And since unjustified offences against the person are by definition social evils, acts done with no more force than is necessary to prevent them must on balance be socially beneficial. Accordingly, the lesser evil theory of justification can easily encompass all

---

[11] *The Principles of Morals and Legislation* (Darien: Hafner, 1970), 172.
[12] Ibid, 174–5.

the justificatory defences known to the law: public necessity, legal authority, self-defence (defence of others, defence of property), and some cases of private necessity and duress.[13]

Paul Robinson has elaborated the Benthamite view of justification with exceptional clarity.[14] Penal codes, he argues, prohibit certain actions because in most cases these actions produce more harm to society than good. However, codes cannot provide for every situation, and so there is need for a defence that refines the code's generalizations by making exceptions for actions that, though nominally violating the rule, produce more good than harm in the particular case or at least produce no harm. Such actions are justified rather than excused, argues Robinson, because they do not come within the reason for the criminal prohibition, which is to prevent net social harm. Harmful actions require an excuse; harmless or beneficial ones do not.

Robinson admits that his theory of justification rests on the assumption that "harm is a prerequisite to criminal liability".[15] "As a penal code prohibits only harmful acts," he writes, "so does justification, in refining the application of the code, exculpate non-harmful acts."[16] Now, of course, Robinson is aware that if D injects V with medication against V's will, he commits an assault even if the drug is highly beneficial and riskless and even if V wants the benefit and would have accepted it had he not suffered from an irrational phobia of medication. So in what sense is harm a prerequisite of criminal liability? Perhaps Robinson thinks that there is harm in V's psychological experience of receiving the feared medication. But then will D's act be justified if its healing benefits exceed V's displeasure at being injected? Will V commit a wrong if he perversely resists D's ministrations with no more than necessary force? In utilitarian theory, perhaps, but not in law. Perhaps Robinson thinks that there is great harm in the psychological experience of another's disrespect for one's autonomy—a harm to one's dignity interest that outweighs any benefit of the medication. Yet we can imagine that V subjectively has no such interest because he is a follower of BF Skinner or has a slavish mentality. In law, this fact would have no relevance; D's act would still be an assault.

To save his harm principle from difficulties such as these, Robinson introduces the idea of a societal interest and a corresponding societal harm.[17] Whether D has harmed V is irrelevant, because, by injecting V against his will, D has harmed a societal interest in autonomy. But in this usage, society is either an aggregation of many units or an abstraction from them, neither of which mental constructs has interests

---

[13] The Model Penal Code, section 3.02 follows the balance-of-evil approach to justification, for it provides that "[c]onduct which the actor believes to be necessary to avoid a harm or evil to himself or another is justifiable provided that: (a) the harm or evil sought to be avoided...is greater than that sought to be prevented by the law defining the offense charged..." The Anglo-American theory of justification has traditionally been utilitarian; see Williams, *Criminal Law: The General Part*, 728–31.

[14] 'A Theory of Justification: Societal Harm as a Prerequisite for Criminal Liability,' (1975) 23 *UCLA Law Review* 266; see also Alexander, 'Lesser Evils,' 611–43.

[15] Robinson, ibid, 292.   [16] Ibid.   [17] Robinson, 'Criminal Law Defenses,' 214.

that can be harmed; while the natural individuals who compose society are like V in that they may or may not have a strong preference for autonomy. Is it then because a majority of individuals have an interest in autonomy that D will be punished? But majoritarian interest has a temporal and contingent quality that makes it a poor basis for the law of assault, the wrongness of which seems independent of transitory majorities. Would that wrong cease to exist in a society where only the ruling elite reported an interest in autonomy but represented their interest as "societal"?

It seems that Robinson must answer "yes" unless he thinks the representation true. But given that the representation is empirically false, it can be true only if the interest in autonomy can be imputed to human beings by virtue of their being agents with a capacity for free choice. And since this capacity is a condition precedent of having an interest in autonomy, pre-empting the capacity is an insult distinct from the harm it inflicts to the autonomy interest made possible by it. Although pre-emption of the capacity for free choice always also harms that interest, it cannot be identified with harming the interest, because the condition for having an interest in autonomy (or any other interest) cannot itself be reduced to an object of interest. Accordingly, Robinson's assertion that "harm is a prerequisite to criminal liability" cannot be maintained unless he thinks that the wrong of assault depends on a majority interest in autonomy. But if that assertion falls, then the theory of justification as refining the legislature's judgment that a certain type of action will produce net social harm falls with it.

Not only can Robinson not sustain a stable notion of wrongdoing unless he acknowledges the priority of agency to interests; he cannot sustain the notion of justification either. Apart from the priority of agency, harm is always harm to subjective interests. Take away the capacity for free choice as the human potential for autonomy and there is neither a public conception of welfare as the satisfaction of needs of autonomy nor a public conception of harm as harm to the interest in satisfying these needs. Hence there is nothing that could justify the use of force to promote one individual's interests over another's or even an interest shared by many over another's—nothing that could distinguish such coercive self-preference from what criminals (or criminal gangs) do. And yet, just this elevation of the subjective interests of some over others' is what, on the lesser evils theory, justificatory defences do. Normally unlawful actions are justified, according to this theory, if the benefit to the actor or to others exceeds the harm inflicted on the victim and cannot otherwise be obtained.

It might be thought that the proportionality and "cannot otherwise be obtained" provisos adequately distinguish the justified self-preferrer from the criminal, for they ensure that only self-preferrers who efficiently promote social welfare will be justified. But do these constraints truly make a moral difference? After all, we would not think it justified for the members of a ruling group periodically to force themselves upon their male subjects' wives as recompense for securing the husbands' property even if this arrangement produced a net surplus of satisfactions that could not be obtained otherwise. We would think the wives justified in resisting the force of a greater interest that was not theirs. The reason is obvious. The interest of others is greater only by virtue of accidental facts about numbers or about the strength of preferences. That the interest is factually greater is no warrant for concluding that it is entitled to subordinate the lesser and that others have an obligation not to resist its primacy. In leaping to this conclusion, the lesser evil theory of justification commits the naturalistic fallacy: it derives entitlement and obligation from fact. But this means that it fails to give an adequate account of *justification*.

Not only does the lesser evil theory fail to explain justification; it also dissolves the rule of law and subjects agents to a penal fate beyond their power to control. According to Robinson, the penal code embodies the legislator's judgment about what actions are so generally harmful as to require prevention. Justificatory defences allow judges or juries to fine-tune that legislative generalization in particular cases. But this means that the so-called law is really an heuristic presumption that the trier of fact is free to displace with its own judgment about the balance of evils in the case at hand. The only truly authoritative law, then, consists in the ad hoc decrees of triers of fact applied retroactively to the case. In effect, the justificatory defence as understood by the lesser evil theory embodies a principle of jury annulment of law.

It might be argued that annulment will be sufficiently exceptional to sustain the rule of law, because, in deciding whether to leave a justificatory defence to a jury, a judge will have to consider the social effects of an acquittal based on a jury's judgment that the defendant did more good than harm. A successful justificatory defence might encourage others contemplating crimes to apply their own judgment about the balance of evils in the hope that a jury will agree. But considerations such as these only make matters worse for the rule of law. For if the defendant's guilt or innocence depends not only on the circumstances surrounding his action, but also on a wide-ranging analysis of the costs and benefits of an acquittal, then he is subject to no law that he could know beforehand; again, the rule of law has become a series of retroactive decrees. To avoid this result, judges may become rule- rather than act-utilitarians, deciding that rule following is more beneficial in the long run because ad hoc discretion removes all the well known benefits of fixed and knowable laws. But such a move would abolish justificatory defences as they are understood by the lesser evil theory.

Finally, the lesser evil theory of justification distorts the role that the justificatory defence of necessity plays in law. That role is exceptional and affirmative. What remains a wrong is justified in the exceptional case by *necessity*. Necessity does not extinguish the victim's right but rather gives the actor a permission to transgress.[18] A right is infringed, and so compensation for damages is due, but the *infringement* (not simply the action) is exceptionally justified, and so there

---

[18] *Vincent v Lake Erie Transportation Co* 124 NW 221 (1910); German Civil Code (1871), s. 904; Fletcher, *Rethinking Criminal Law*, 776–7.

is no culpability. If necessity did extinguish the right, there would be no need for an affirmative defence—that is, for a defence that affirms an overriding circumstance rather than denying an essential element of culpability. Yet in law, the defence is recognized as affirmative: a transgression has indeed occurred, but it is justified *qua* transgression.

For the balance-of-evils theory, however, necessity is neither exceptional nor affirmative. It is not exceptional because it amounts to nothing more than a particular application of the harm principle that standardly determines illegality. As Glanville Williams has written from this perspective, "the whole law is based upon social necessity".[19] No doubt, necessity refines or corrects a generalization, but a refinement and correction does not make an exception; rather, it applies better the principle underlying the generalization. Nor is necessity affirmative on this theory. Since prohibited actions are those that in general produce more harm than good, a plea that in this case there was no net harm is not a plea in the affirmative. Harm has been done but no net harm, and the action's presumptive illegality was based on its normally producing net harm. The defendant's action meets the letter of the offence but not the reason for its being an offence. So, for the lesser evil theory, a plea of necessity is a denial of what is essential to illegality, not an affirmation following an admitted offence.

3. Double Effect

To the question whether one may kill another in self-defence, Aquinas answers:[20]

Nothing keeps one act from having two effects, one of which is in the scope of the agent's intention while the other falls outside that scope. Now, moral actions are characterized by what is intended, not by what falls outside the scope of intention, for that is only incidental, as I explained previously.

Thus from the act of defending himself there can be two effects: self-preservation and the killing of the attacker. Therefore this kind of act does not have the aspect of "wrong:" on the basis that one intends to save his own life, because it is only natural to everything to preserve itself in existence as best it can. Still an action beginning from a good intention can become wrong if it is not proportionate to the end intended.

Consequently, if someone uses greater force than necessary to defend his own life, that will be wrong. But if he repels the attack with measured force, the defence will not be wrong. The law permits force to be repelled with measured force by one who is attacked without offering provocation. It is not necessary to salvation that a man forgo this act of measured defence in order to avoid the killing of another, since each person is more strongly bound to safeguard his own life than that of another.

---

[19] 'The Defence of Necessity,' [1953] CLP 217.
[20] St Thomas Aquinas, *Summa Theologica*, 2–2, Q 64, A 7, quoted in Germain Grisez, 'Toward a Consistent Natural-Law Ethics of Killing,' (1970) 15 *The American Journal of Jurisprudence*, 64, 73.

But since it is wrong to take human life except for the common good by public authority, as I already explained, it is wrong for a man to intend to kill another man in order to defend himself.

A noteworthy feature of this discussion is that the permission to kill in self-defence is not by its logic limited to wrongful attackers. By "wrongful" I do not mean "culpable". A culpable wrongdoer is one who may be punished for his wrong because he has the *mens rea* required for punishment. It is uncontroversial that the legal permission to use defensive force is not limited to situations where the aggressor knowingly or recklessly interferes with another's agency, having the capacity to know right from wrong. The permission extends, for example, to delusional attackers, to children, or to those who use force under an exculpatory mistake of fact. Though nonculpable, such people are still wrongdoers because their mistaken belief in permission is a mistake as to the boundary of their permissible action; and so the mistake implies a claim of permission inconsistent with the defender's right to exclude at the true boundary.

However, Aquinas's permission of deadly force, because it hinges solely on the distinction between an intended and an incidental effect, extends to situations where the threatener is not even a wrongful attacker, say, because his motion is involuntary, as in the case of a homicidal sleepwalker. A threatener of that sort is not a wrongdoer because, there being no subject of bodily motion, no belief in permission is implied in the imminent boundary crossing; hence the factual crossing will not contradict (infringe) the right of the person threatened. Yet in these situations too, the person immediately threatened is justified, on Aquinas's account, in killing the threatener if lethal force is necessary and if he intends only to preserve himself.

I'll call "innocents" agents who cross a boundary involuntarily or with consent, or who cross a boundary in justified self-defence against a wrongful attack (or with any other recognized justification), or who do not cross a boundary at all. Now if nothing in Aquinas's permission of self-defence requires a *wrongful* threat, then there is no logical necessity that the victim of defensive force be a "threat" either; all that is required is that one not be able to preserve oneself without killing another. Thus, the innocent bystander whom you know will certainly be killed if you repel an attacking tank gunner with the force (an anti-tank grenade) necessary to do so cannot rationally be distinguished from the person blown by a gust of wind from a skyscraper and about to crush you unless you vaporize him (you cannot move aside because your coat is caught in a car door). Provided your aim is only to preserve yourself, the double effect doctrine says you may take necessary steps even if that will mean incidentally killing the bystander. Killing the bystander is not simply excused; it is permissible.

But further, if rightful self-defence does not require that the victim be a threatener, then its logic is not even limited to situations of *defence*. Thus, if the continued life of one agent is incompatible with the continued life of another, it would seem that each may kill the other provided that he intends only to preserve himself. The standard example features two miners trapped in a caved-in mine and competing for scarce oxygen. Both will die soon if the oxygen is shared, but one may live long enough for help to arrive if the other dies. Now it is true that, according to the doctrine of double effect, one who uses evil means to an intended good end intends the means as well as the end. Thus a contract killer who kills for the money to feed his family cannot say he intended only to support his family and that he regretted the killing; since he used the act of killing as a means of attaining his end, he intended also the means. Means are never beyond the scope of one's intention. Accordingly, it might be objected against the trapped miners example that, if either of the miners were to kill the other to preserve oxygen for himself, he would be killing as a means of preserving his life and so would be intending the other's death, which is forbidden. And yet how is this situation distinguished from justified self-defence against an attacker? Aquinas apparently does not believe that the person who kills an attacker by an act intended to save himself intends the death of the attacker as a means of preserving himself. Why?

Germain Grisez explains that an agent intends an evil effect as a means to achieving a good end only if the means is an action distinct from the action whose meaning is determined by the good intention. He writes:

> [A] good effect which in the order of nature is preceded in the performance by an evil effect need not be regarded as a good end achieved by an evil means, provided that the act is a unity and only the good is within the scope of the intention. Means and end in the order of human action do not necessarily correspond to cause and effect in the order of nature, because a means must be an integral human act.[21]

By this Grisez apparently means that an act producing an evil effect but for which the aimed-at good effect could not have been achieved is not a means to the good end if it is integral to the action whose description is determined by the good intention; such an act is a means to the end only if it constitutes a separate action. This is so because acting for an end and acting as a means of achieving a further end are distinct actions, each having its own unity; they cannot belong to the same action without destroying the distinction between means and end. I don't move my fingers as a means of striking a match; I simply strike the match.[22] Similarly, I don't kill an attacker as a means of saving myself; I simply act to save myself, and the attacker (expectedly) dies. By contrast, I torture someone as a means of saving the regiment, because the act of torturing to obtain information has a unity distinct from the act of transmitting the information to save the regiment. Provided the action is unitary under a good intention, the evil effect is incidental and not intended as a means.

Let us grant, *arguendo*, this separation between acting for an end and acting as a means to achieve a further end. Let us even grant that one intends an evil effect as a means to a good end if the evil effect belongs to a separate act but not

[21] 'Toward a Consistent Natural-Law Ethics of Killing,' note 20 above, 90.
[22] Ibid, 88.

if it is integral to the act whose aim is the good. And let us now return to the two trapped miners. Is one miner's killing the other a means to saving himself, or is it part of a unitary act of saving himself? Since choking the other stops his consumption of oxygen, it would seem that one could describe the act as "saving oxygen"; that the other dies is an incidental effect. Even clearer is the example of two twins joined at the head, both of whom will die soon unless the stronger is severed from the weaker, who will die once separated. Here one and the same act saves one and kills the other. By contrast, Dudley's and Stephen's killing the cabin boy for the purpose of consuming him so as to preserve their lives is a case of intending evil means to achieve a good end, because (as Grisez says) killing and eating are distinct actions.[23] So, provided only that the evil effect is not produced by an act distinct from the act shaped by the good intent, killing to preserve oneself would seem to be justified under the doctrine of double effect even if the killing were done out of "necessity" rather than in self-defence. It is in this sense that the double effect doctrine provides a unitary theory of justification.

The double effect doctrine is far more permissive than Anglo-American law, which does not treat killing to save oneself in a situation of necessity as justified but rather, at most, as excused culpable wrongdoing.[24] It is not even clear that the positive law will treat the foreseen killing of an innocent bystander as justified by self-defence; such a homicide too is at best excused.[25] Of course, this gap between double effect theory and legal practice would not in itself argue decisively against the former. However, I'll argue that the gap is symptomatic of a fundamental disjunction between justification as it must appear to an ethics focused on the goodness of the individual soul and justification as it must take shape within a juridical practice focused on what free agents owe each other as participants in a coercive public order. Drawing attention to this disjunction would be unnecessary if moral philosophers did not often think that the ethical conception of justification should guide the legal one.

In law, justification is a relational concept. It denotes a privilege that affects the legal position of the person in relation to whom the justification is claimed. Thus, leaving putative self-defence aside for the moment, a right of self-defence entails that the person against whom the right is claimed has a correlative obligation not to resist the defender's force; hence someone who assists the defender has made a juridically determined choice, not an arbitrary one between two morally equivalent rivals. It is because legal concepts like justification are relational that they must be shaped from a public standpoint that is impartial as between the parties to the juridical relationship. If affording D a justification means imposing an obligation on V, then the justification must be shaped by a reason neutral as between D and V, so that both, as thinking Agents, could accept it.

---

[23] Ibid, 90.
[24] *R v Dudley and Stephens* (1884) 14 QBD 273; *United States v Holmes* (1842) 26 F Cas 360.
[25] Model Penal Code, 3.09(3).

Contrast to the juridical conception of justification Hobbes's view. For Hobbes, every person has an absolute and inalienable right to self-preservation such that defenders are not privileged over attackers, nor even law enforcers over criminals.[26] Even in a civil condition, a right of self-preservation in a defender does not cancel the right of the attacker to defend himself in turn against the one he attacked, with the result that there is no normative closure to violence: endless war has the *imprimatur* of natural right. This is the antithesis of a juridical conception of justification, for it is entirely nonrelational and anarchic: a permission in one person does not affect the legal position of others. It is as if each person were enclosed within a self-contained moral space of which it is the sole occupant. But this, I'll argue, is just the situation created by the double effect doctrine.

For Aquinas, the permission to kill another in self-defence depends on the premise that "it is only natural to everything to preserve itself in existence as best it can".[27] However, both attacker and defender have this natural inclination to prefer one's own existence to another's when they come into conflict. Since wrongdoing is irrelevant to determining who has the permission to pursue his inclination, there is no reason for an impartial judge to prefer the defender to the attacker. Thus if the defender has a permission to defend, the attacker has a permission to repel the defender, as Hobbes too believed.

It will be objected that Aquinas explicitly limits the permission to kill to cases of *unprovoked* attack, because provoked attacks are justified by the provocation. By "provocation" Aquinas must mean attacks that would justify defensive force, for if the provocation were by taunts or insults, the provoked party's self-preservation would not be at stake, and so there would be no reason to take away the provoker's permission to defend. The provoked party would intend not to preserve himself, but to avenge the insult. So, by limiting the right to use force in self-defence to cases of unprovoked attack, Aquinas seems to imply that a permission to defend against a provocation engenders a correlative duty in the provoker not to respond in turn.

However, I want to argue that the limitation of the right of self-defence to cases of unprovoked attack is incoherent within the double effect doctrine. It is incoherent because, if threateners need not be wrongdoers (if they can be involuntary threats), then there is no reason why threateners must be provokers—why they cannot be defenders instead. If I am justified in using defensive force against innocent threats, then I am justified in using defensive force against those who innocently defend themselves against my provocation. There can be no morally relevant difference between someone who is innocent because he is moving involuntarily and someone who is innocent because he is responding to an attack. If I am justified in defending against the former, I must also be justified in defending against the latter provided that my purpose is to preserve myself and not to kill

---

[26] *Leviathan* (Oxford: Blackwell, 1957), 142.   [27] Note 20 above.

the other. Thus the double effect theory of justification collapses into a Hobbesian right of self-preservation against provoked and unprovoked attacks alike.

The double effect theorist might respond that I am justified only in defending myself with force against *unjustified* threats. Though not a wrongful threat, someone falling through space is nevertheless an unjustified threat in the sense that there is no justification—no justifying reason—for it.[28] By contrast, a threat in response to my provocation is justified because there is a justifying reason for it, namely, the provocation. Accordingly, double effect doctrine (one might argue) does seem able to distinguish between innocent, unprovoked threats I can resist and innocent threats I have provoked, which I cannot resist. There is normative closure to violence.

However, the terminology of "unjustified threat" is disingenuous here. After all, a rock hurtling through space is also an unjustified threat in this sense—there is no justification for the threat. Since neither the rock nor the falling man is an unjust (wrongful) threat, it would be better to say that both are nonjustified rather than unjustified—that is, neither justified nor unjustified but morally neutral. So the man falling from a skyscraper (Falling Man) is a nonjustified threat to the one about to be crushed, whereas someone responding to a provocation is a justified threat to the provoker. Both are innocents in the sense that neither are wrongdoers. But the double effect theory says I can defend myself with lethal force against the innocent nonjustified threat (Falling Man) but not against the innocent justified threat (Provoked Man). This distinction ostensibly makes sense, because a nonjustified threat imposes no obligation on the person threatened not to resist it, whereas a justified threat, one might think, does.

However, it is not the case that all justified threats preclude a right of self-defence in the person threatened. Suppose D attacks V because A threatened D with death if he did not kill V. Here D has a justifying reason for threatening V, namely, his self-preservation, but V has a right to defend himself against an attack he did not provoke. So the idea of a justified threat does not by itself distinguish cases of permissible and impermissible self-defence.

Nor does a justified threat necessarily foreclose a right of self-defence in the person threatened even where the person threatened himself gave the threatener his justifying reason. This becomes evident as soon as we ask whether Falling Man can shoot Man on the Street defending himself (say, by aiming a ray-gun at Falling Man) against the threat of being crushed. Since Falling Man is an innocent, there is nothing to distinguish the threat he poses to Man on the Street from the threat Man on the Street poses to him except that Falling Man's threat came first. But the fact that Falling Man's threat came first cannot affect the parties' rights, for if Man on the Street had not come to the spot on which he is

---

[28] Suzanne Uniacke, *Permissible Killing: The Self-Defence Justification of Homicide* (Cambridge: Cambridge University Press, 1994), 74–81; Jeremy Horder, 'Self-Defence, Necessity, and Duress; Understanding the Relationship,' (1998) 11 *Canadian. Journal of Law and Jurisprudence* 143, 146.

now standing, Falling Man would not be a threat to him, and he would not be a threat to Falling Man. Factually speaking, both are nonjustified causes of the other's being threatened, and so each has a right to resist the other's force even though the defensive force of each is a justified threat to the other. The right to self-preservation that gives Man on the Street a permission to vaporize Falling Man also gives Falling Man a permission to shoot Man on the Street to avoid being vaporized.

If a justifying reason for a threat does not necessarily preclude a right of self-defence in the person threatened even where the person threatened is the source of the threatener's justification, is there anything special about provocation as a justifying reason that would preclude a right of self-defence in the provoker? There is not. For if wrongdoing does not identify a provoker, then only temporality can. But then Falling Man is a kind of provoker, and yet he could resist the defensive force of the Man on the Street he provoked. Yes, it will be objected, but Falling Man was an involuntary provoker and that is why he could not be said to have unilaterally caused the threat to Man on the Street. Voluntary provokers are different because they do unilaterally threaten the people they provoke.

But do they? Again, we must analyse the causal situation apart from wrongdoing, for the double effect right of self-defence does not hinge on wrongdoing. Like Falling Man, the voluntary provoker can claim that the provoked party is no less a provocation to him than he is to the provoked party, because the latter's allowing himself to be provoked constitutes a nonjustified threat to him. No doubt the provocation caused the reaction of being provoked, but, as in the case of Falling Man, causation is reciprocal as between the parties; but for the reaction of being provoked, the initial act would not have amounted to an act of provocation. Thus, remove wrongdoing from the equation, and the two parties' effects on each other are symmetrical: each is a nonjustified threat to the other, and so each may repel the other's threat *ad infinitum*. Anyone who comes to the aid of the provoked party is not an enforcer of law but an ally of a particular interest, who thus may also be resisted.

Accordingly, Aquinas's limitation of the right of self-defence to unprovoked attacks is incoherent within the double effect doctrine. For that doctrine, there is nothing intrinsic to a justification that changes the moral position of the person in relation to whom the justification is claimed; justification in one does not entail no-justification in the other. But this means that someone's being justified in repelling a provoker does not preclude the provoker's being justified in repelling the defender, provided his purpose is only to preserve himself. The double effect doctrine's right of self-defence operates as promiscuously as Hobbes's.

The symmetry of double effect justification is even more evident in the necessity case. In the example of the trapped miners, miner A has a permission to stop miner B's consumption of oxygen and vice versa. Here too the root cause of symmetrical justification is the irrelevance of wrongdoing. Once eliminate wrongdoing from the right of self-defence, and there is nothing to distinguish the right of self-defence from the right of necessity.[29] Both are cases of competing inclinations for self-preservation, and there is no principled basis for preferring one person's preservation to the other's. Were necessity distinguished from self-defence on the basis that the latter presupposes a wrongdoer whereas the former does not, some other impartial basis for preferring one agent's interest to another's in necessity cases would have to be found. I'll suggest such a basis in section 5.

Why the double effect doctrine of self-defence should dispense with wrongdoing and focus entirely on the defender's purpose may be gleaned from Grisez's explanation of the doctrine:

> In this nonutilitarian moral outlook, whether or not another person's death is admitted within the scope of our intention is extremely important. A difference of intention can relate identical behavior in quite different ways to our moral attitude, and to the self being created through our moral attitude. If one intends to kill another, he accepts the identity of killer as an aspect of his moral self. If he is to be a killer through his own self-determination, he must regard himself in any situation as the lord of life and death. The good of life must be rated as a measurable value, not as an immeasurable dignity. Others' natural attitudes toward their own lives must be regarded as an irrational fact, not as a starting point for reasonable community. However, if one intends not the death of another but only the safety of his own life, then one need not identify himself as a killer. One's attitude toward human life itself and toward everything related to it can remain that of a person unwilling to take human life.[30]

Thus, wrongdoing is irrelevant to the justification of defensive force, because the wrongdoer is a human being whose life is inviolable. The fact that he is a wrongdoer is a problem he has for his own wellbeing, not a factor relevant to how we may treat him. To intend a human death, whether of an innocent or a wrongdoer, is to incorporate the identity of killer of inviolable human life into one's self. It is thus to constitute oneself as the supreme arbiter of value in the universe. Accordingly, the essential thing in a situation of self-defence or necessity, where two lives of immeasurable worth are mutually incompatible, is to kill without becoming a killer. And this is possible only if one keeps the other's death separate from one's purpose, while acknowledging through regret the continuing force of the moral reason not to kill. Provided one does both, one may preserve one's own human life at the expense of another's.

Even if one were to regard this conception of justification as the guide for one's conduct most conducive to wellbeing, one could still consider it unsuitable to legal

---

[29] Uniacke rests the distinction on that between creating or exacerbating a threat and exposing someone to an independent threat, while Horder distinguishes self-defence and necessity on the basis of a difference between active and passive threats. Neither, however, explains why, assuming the involuntariness of the human threat, these factual distinctions should make a normative difference between having no right to resist self-defensive force and having a right to resist force justified by necessity. Moreover, if no such normative distinction exists (if there is a right to resist in both cases), to what point are the factual distinctions? See Uniacke, *Permissible Killing*, 164–77; Horder, 'Self-Defence, Necessity, and Duress,' 154.

[30] 'Toward a Consistent Natural-Law Ethics of Killing,' 76.

ordering. This is so, not only for the reasons discussed in the conclusion to Chapter 4, but also because a conception so focused on the integrity of the individual soul is powerless to order the relations *between* souls who are involved in nonconsensual transactions. We have seen that the consequence of dispensing with wrongdoing as a determinant of justified self-defence is the symmetry of justification. One implication of symmetry is that justifications are mutually inconsistent, so that it becomes impossible for a court to determine rights coherently in disputes involving violent transactions. A, reasonably anticipating an imminent attack from B, pre-emptively attacks B who fends off A with measured force, inflicting injury. A sues B for damages from assault and B countersues A for assault. A loses because B was justified in meeting force with force, but B loses his countersuit because A was justified in his pre-emptive strike. Thus, the double effect doctrine of self-defence gives birth to a legal monster: parties in the right lose and parties in the wrong win. Another consequence of symmetry is a condition of legalized anarchy when lives conflict—that is, a condition of justified nonstop violence, where an aggressor has a claim equal in strength to that of a victim of aggression, and where a right of necessity is a right of lawless war. For Hobbes, at least, this situation was a brutish state of nature that natural law commands us to quit. The proponents of the double effect doctrine, insofar as they urge it as a guide to legal practice, would return us to that state.[31]

4. Justification against Wrongdoers

Legal justifications for private actors can be divided into justifications against wrongdoers and justifications against innocents. The former include self-defence, defence of others, and defence of property, while to the latter category belong some cases of necessity and duress. Since the justification of defence of others is parasitic on the defender's own justification, I will not deal with it separately. Self-defence and defence of property I'll treat together as the right of a private agent to use defensive force against a wrongdoer in order to realize the right infringed by the wrong. All private justifications against wrongdoers are justifications of defensive force, but not all private justifications of defensive force are justifications against wrongdoers. Some acts of defensive force are justified against innocents by necessity. However, since a right of necessity is not logically limited to the case of defensive force (whereas a right against a wrongdoer is), I'll use phrases like "right to use defensive force" and "right to self-defence" to mean the right to use force against a wrongdoer.

To repeat, justifications against wrongdoers are not justifications against culpable wrongdoers only or even against at-fault (including both culpable and

---

[31] Since we have Hobbes's and Aquinas's views of the right of self-defence as symmetrical, I would not go as far as Fletcher in saying that it is in the nature of justification to be asymmetrical (*Rethinking Criminal Law*, 767); but it is in the nature of a fully juridical conception of justification to be asymmetrical.

negligent) wrongdoers only; they are justifications against an agent who, through a voluntary motion and without consent, crosses a boundary delimiting a sphere wherein another agent's choices rightfully rule.[32] Whether the agent knows it lacks permission or acts under a reasonable but mistaken belief in permission is irrelevant, because the mistaken claim to permission itself suffices to challenge the victim's true boundary; and coercive force is justified precisely as necessary to realize the right to free choice within a certain boundary against acts inconsistent with it. Thus, defensive force may be justified against those acting under insane delusions, against children, and against those who attack under a reasonable but mistaken belief in justification (for example, that they are being attacked).[33] Voluntary motion and lack of consent are necessary to trigger a justification based on right realization, because involuntary motion implies no claim of permission inconsistent with the right, while a consented-to boundary crossing implies no *mistaken* claim to permission. Only voluntary boundary crossings without consent transgress the boundary. Because acts of defensive force against involuntary boundary crossers (such as Falling Man) cannot be justified as necessary to realize the defender's right, they either fall into the category of excused culpable wrongdoing (to be discussed in Chapter 7) or are justified on the principles (discussed in the next section) governing a conflict of agency interests between innocents.

The justification for defensive force against a wrongdoer authorizes a voluntary boundary crossing without consent. That is to say, it authorizes what would normally be a transgression. We'll see, however, that it does not authorize a *transgression*. Rather, self-defence against a wrongdoer resembles the defence of consent in that it negates as a transgression what would be a transgression in its absence. Thus the self-defender using necessary and proportionate force to repel a wrongful attacker need not compensate the attacker for the harm he causes him. No wrong is done the attacker, and so the attacker has no justification based on right realization for using defensive force in turn: the justification of defensive force against a wrongdoer is asymmetrical and finite. The questions for discussion in this section are: what theory of the right to self-defence explains the asymmetry of that right in a civil condition? How well does the explanation of asymmetrical justification account for the usual limitations on the right to use defensive force in the positive law?

Real justification

We begin with the case where the defender is faced with a real threat of wrongful force; for this is the only case where the justification of defensive force properly

---

[32] Model Penal Code, s. 3.11(1).
[33] Some writers illogically dispense with wrongdoing as a determinant of justified self-defence on the basis of the irrelevance of culpable wrongdoing. See Horder, 'Self-Defence, Necessity and Duress,' 144–6.

comes into play. As we'll see, a different (nonjustificatory) theory of exculpation applies to cases where a wrongful threat is apprehended but unreal, and I'll deal with this kind of case (putative justification) in the next sub-section.

The typical parameters of the right to use defensive force in Anglo-American law and that require a theoretical derivation are the following. First, there must be an antecedent unlawful attack or entry or threat thereof. Second, the unlawful attack or entry must be under way or imminent. Third, the attack must have been unprovoked by the victim. Fourth, defensive force must be limited to what is necessary to repel or prevent the attack or entry; force in excess of what is necessary is unlawful. Fifth, lethal or seriously harmful defensive force must be confined to cases where the defender reasonably apprehends an unlawful threat to his life or bodily integrity; this is the proportionality requirement. Sixth, the defender has no duty to retreat except as a condition of using lethal force or unless he was the aggressor and is now defending against disproportionate defensive force.[34]

Because there is value in theoretical parsimony, it is tempting to view the right of self-defence so circumscribed as an application of the retributive theory of punishment.[35] The defender has the right to use force against his assailant, one might think, because the assailant has authorized coercion by his own right-denying action; and the defender's use of force against him vindicates the right-affirming legal regime the assailant challenged. In effect, the defender acts as an ad hoc agent of the public legal order, just as he does when he makes a citizen's arrest.

Though tempting, this approach is mistaken. First, punishment aims to set the criminal wrongdoer back from his position of equality with other agents. By turning the right-denying implication of the criminal's wilful interference with agency back on him, punishment demonstrates the unreality of a claimed right to unlimited liberty and vindicates the basis of stable rights in mutual respect for liberty. However, for this setback to the criminal wrongdoer to be a vindication of universal rights rather than the satisfaction of a particular interest, it must be the impersonal act of the public custodian of rights, not a retaliatory act of the victim; otherwise it is a personal act of revenge mixed up with passion and self-interest, hence construable as another wrong, against which self-defence is symmetrically permissible (*ad infinitum*). The individual immediately threatened by wrongful force is a poor representative of the public authority just because his personal interest is engaged by the threat. This is why he may not punish.[36] Instead, to maintain its distinction from wrongful revenge, self-defence must be

---

[34] See Model Penal Code, s. 3.04 (2)(c); Canadian Criminal Code, RSC 1985 c. C–46, ss. 34(2)(b), 35(c).
[35] As Robert Nozick did; see *Anarchy, State, and Utopia* (New York: Basic Books, 1974), 62–3.
[36] This is also why, *pace* Thorburn, the threatened party cannot be conceived as exercising the public authority to enforce the law in defending himself nor as drawing justification from that authority. A private actor can make a citizen's arrest, but he can defend *himself* only as a private agent. His justification comes from his own individual right, not from the political sovereign. Thorburn's view obliterates the self in self-defence while corrupting the public in public authority; see 'Justification, Powers, and Authority,' 1107–10.

pre-emptive rather than retaliatory; and it must be directed solely to *preventing* a setback to the person threatened rather than to setting back the attacker; hence the theory of punishment is inapplicable.

Second, the "punishment" theory of self-defence does not fit the law, for, as we have seen, wrongdoers need not have the culpable mind that signifies a right denial inviting punishment; indeed, they need not even be negligent or blameworthy at all. It is enough that they voluntarily transgressed a boundary—that is all that is meant by "unlawful".[37] So we must look outside the theory of punishment for a justification of defensive force against a wrongdoer.

The formal agency paradigm of justice provides the theoretical framework one needs to understand all the limits on the right to use defensive force in the positive law. That framework rests ultimately on the agent's right to command respect for the end-status involved in its capacity for free choice. The right to respect is specified, as we have seen, in a right against pre-emption of the capacity through forcible restraint or killing, against interference with the capacity's exercise through threats of pre-emption, and against another's meddling with the things under the exclusive sway of an agent's capacity for choice. Crucially, however, the right to respect for end-status is not a right to self-preservation. One's biological existence may be threatened—for example, by an involuntary attacker—without this involving a show of disrespect for one's agency. Because agency rather than the body is the bearer of rights, the right to act in defence of one's right will be engaged by a threat if and only if the threat has a bearing on agency's dignity—which is to say, is wrongful. This is the key to the possibility of an asymmetrical right, for rightful defenders of their dignity also threaten bodies; they do not wrong ends.

Now given that a right is an objectively valid claim of end-status in relation to something (my body, my acquired things), its notion contains an authorization to realize it objectively—to enforce the right in the world—against challenges to its reality by actions inconsistent with it. Because a recognizable right embodies an inherently valid claim to dignity, it entails an authorization in the right bearer to give the claim actual validity by enforcing it against challenges; for if the right were powerless against actions inconsistent with it, it would be invalid, unreal, and hence self-contradictory as a right. This is why Kant says that "right" and "authorization to use coercion" mean the same thing, and it is why Hegel says that "abstract right is a right to coerce".[38]

Since the notion of a right to act from ends one chooses entails an authorization to use force to realize it, force circumscribed by the requirements of right realization is justified by the right and therefore negated as a further transgression. Here, though, the justification wipes out rather than overcomes the wrong that force normally is, because, whereas force normally interferes with a freedom

---

[37] Model Penal Code, s. 3.11(1).
[38] Immanuel Kant, *The Metaphysics of Morals*, trans. Mary Gregor (Cambridge: Cambridge University Press, 1991), 58; GWF Hegel, *Philosophy of Right*, trans. TM Knox (Oxford: Oxford University Press, 1967), para. 94.

of choice the victim was permitted to exercise (hence its wrongfulness), here force realizes a right against interference—against an exercise of freedom to which the victim had no permission. This is why there is no legal duty to compensate the trespasser, though morality may require expressions of regret if the wrongful interference was unintentional.

In order that a right (of life, bodily integrity, property) may gain the objective reality involved in its notion, it must be enforceable not only after it has been infringed but also pre-emptively. A right against interference with liberty or property would be self-contradictory were it enforceable only by an after-the-fact remedy; for then compensation would amount to a forced sale of the plaintiff's permission, and punishment (assuming the wrongdoer is punishable) would address the general significance of the wrong but not the particular—in either case the remedy would fail to actualize the individual agent's right. So a right to liberty or property must by its idea be enforceable pre-emptively, and both the legal remedy of injunction and the state's duty to protect its citizens obviously reflect this conceptual requirement. Where recourse to these means is possible, there is a duty to adopt them, because valid rights to liberty and property presuppose a public authority instituted to adjudicate rival right claims impartially. Where, however, it is unfeasible to obtain a restraining order from a court or protection from the police, the right to liberty and property requires a right of self-help to repel an infringement.[39] Provided the force used in self-help is limited to what is required to realize the threatened right, it draws justification from the right it realizes. Therefore, it is not another transgression against which the aggressor would have his own right of defence.

Still, the right of self-help does not betoken a suspension of the civil order. Were that the case, the "right" would be no more than a subjective claim of right against which the attacker would have an equal and symmetrical claim. No, the right of self-help is a right *within* the civil order. This is shown by the right's limitation by rules about necessity and proportionality, breach of which renders the defender liable to judicial punishment. It is conceptually possible, in other words, to exercise the right of self-defence wrongfully—something impossible in a state of nature, where each is judge of what is necessary and proportionate. But then it is also possible to exercise the right validly, and so the right can be asymmetrical.

From this account of the right to use defensive force, we can derive the contours of the right acknowledged by positive law. First, because the justification rests on a right to realize end-status against an action inconsistent therewith *and not on a*

---

[39] Is the right of self-help a delegated power of public law enforcement analogous to the police officer's power to make a warrantless arrest when application to a magistrate is unfeasible? Or is it the temporary recovery by the individual of a private right he must be conceived as having surrendered for the sake of an authoritative determination of rights? The former view, held by Thorburn ('Justification, Powers, and Authority,' 1107–10), is inconsistent with a right of self-defence, because if the defender is acting as a civil servant, his legal power is subject to enforcement discretion by superiors, who may decide that his use of force against a minor assault, though proportionate, was against the public interest, in which case he would have done wrong.

right to self-preservation, it presupposes an antecedent wrong (unlawful act), not simply (or necessarily) an antecedent threat of harm. There must at least be a voluntary, unconsented-to boundary crossing, for (as we saw) involuntary crossings, however threatening of harm, imply no mistaken claim of permission—hence no mistake about where the boundary is—inconsistent with the right embodying worth. Thus Man on the Street has no right of self-defence to vaporize Falling Man (though he may be excused from his culpable wrong).[40] But voluntary crossings do imply such a mistake, and so nothing more faulty than volition is needed to trigger the justification. Moreover, if involuntary boundary crossers give no right of self-defence, then *a fortiori* those who cross no boundaries at all. Thus, there is no right of self-defence against someone whose mere existence is threatening (he is consuming scarce oxygen or his weight is too much for the lifeboat), or whose imminent death is threatening (he is attached to someone by tissue or by a mountaineer's rope), or who stands in the way of one's preservation from a threat (he is stuck in the only exit from a cave), or whose injury will inevitably ensue from one's repelling a wrongful threat (he is an innocent bystander).[41] In the next section, we'll see that there is no right of necessity in these cases either, and so the only road to acquittal is through excuse.

Second, the wrongful attack must be under way or imminent. It need not be actually under way, because having a right entails having a right to defend the right pre-emptively; otherwise one would have to allow a violation. So there must be temporal room reflecting a right to pre-empt a violation, and the permission to repel an imminent attack is that room. Since having a right entails having a right to pre-empt an infringement, an imminent attack is itself a right infringement, for it crosses into the temporal zone that buffers the right. At the same time, the attack must be at least imminent, because defensive force is justified as necessary to realize the right of self-actuation against actions inconsistent with it, not as necessary for the defender's peace of mind. Thus even if an attack is practically inevitable, a pre-emptive strike in advance of imminence is not justified (though it might be excused), and so the attacked party may resist, whereas the attacker may not.

What does "imminent" mean? How long must someone under threat wait before responding with force? Because a pre-emptive right of self-defence in the one threatened excludes the threatener's right to defend himself in turn, the temporal buffer zone protecting the defender's right must reflect the mutual recognition of the parties as ends, allowing both to accept it. Thus it cannot be drawn at the point

---

[40] But he has no coercive duty to confer a benefit on Falling Man either. If he could free his coat, he may stand aside and let Falling Man hit the pavement. For the same reason, one may "duck" to allow a bullet to hit someone behind. Moreover, Man on the Street has a right of necessity to use *harmless* force to prevent Falling Man from crushing him, say, by deflecting him onto a safety net; see section 5 of this chapter.

[41] Contrast Judith Thomson, who says it is permissible to kill Falling Man but not an innocent bystander, yet provides no moral reason to distinguish them: 'Self-Defense,' (1991) 20(4) *Philosophy & Public Affairs* 283–310. She says she has a good reason for thinking that agency is not required for a right violation but does not tell us what it is (302). Does a falling rock violate rights?

beyond which this particular threatened individual would feel insecure in his ability to defend, for this boundary would allow one individual's appetite for security to determine another's right to defend himself against attack. But neither can the temporal line be drawn at the point beyond which someone with full knowledge of all relevant facts and equal in strength with the threatener would actually be insecure, for this line pays no regard to the defender's actual situation or finite perspective; hence it is incompatible with his right of self-defence. To reflect mutual respect, the boundary must be drawn at the point where this particular threatened person *reasonably* believes it could not successfully defend its right if pre-emption were further delayed. Accordingly, an imminent threat is not necessarily a temporally immediate one. Observe, however, that the wider the time frame for permissible pre-emption, the less likely it is that a right of self-help exists, for that right depends on the nonfeasibility of recourse to public law enforcement.[42]

Third, one may use defensive force only against an attacker whom one did not provoke by a wrongful threat (or against a provoked agent whose defensive force is disproportionate), for a provocation of that sort challenges the right of the provoked party, hence gives him a justification to use defensive force to realize the right, one that negates the wrongfulness of his defensive force; hence the provoker is not justified in resisting the attack he provoked. Here we see that the formalist paradigm explains (as neither Hobbesian natural right nor the double effect doctrine can) the qualification on the right to use defensive force that is really the crux of juridical justification, reflecting as it does the asymmetry and closure of justified force in defence of rights. Provocation is not simply a factual threat of harm along a causal two-way street; it is a *wrongful* threat that triggers a justification in the provoked party and precludes a reverse justification in the provoker.

Fourth, the defensive force must be no greater than necessary to repel the attack, for unnecessary force obviously falls outside the scope of the justification based on right realization. But a more subtle point lies behind this requirement. The force must be no more than necessary to repel, regardless of whether the wrongdoer

---

[42] Alas, this point has been lost in some prominent cases of self-defence involving women in physically abusive relationships. In *Lavallée v The Queen* [1990] 1 SCR 852, the Supreme Court of Canada reasoned that construing the imminence requirement as one of temporal immediacy involves a male-centered interpretation of "reasonable apprehension of death" based on an assumption of equal physical strength as between men. It thus relaxed the temporal requirement for a battered woman, holding that she was justified in killing her abusive partner as he walked away from her after threatening her with death once guests left if she did not kill him first. On the facts in *Lavallée*, it is not difficult to conclude that the deceased's verbal threat to kill the defendant after house guests departed amounted to an assault and left no reasonable time to call the police. But the court's flexible interpretation of "imminence" coupled with its concession to the psychological infirmity of battered women now creates the possibility of justified pre-emptive killing to remove a threat the defendant sees as otherwise irremovable once and for all, though it is avoidable in the short term by recourse to the police. But this is to justify killing for the sake of peace of mind, which is to justify symmetrically and anarchically (if a physically abusive husband awoke to find his wife aiming a gun at him, would anyone question his right to resist her with force?). Cases of battered women who kill their partners because they do not see public law enforcement as a permanent solution to their problems are best analysed under the rubric and limits of provocation.

is a nonculpable psychotic (child, non-negligent trespasser) or a sadistic rapist. Because the right realization specific to self-defence takes the form of preventing a transgression rather than punishing a transgressor, the requirements of prevention determine necessary force, not what the transgressor deserves.[43] Further, the meaning of necessity is shaped in the same way as the meaning of imminence. Because the line between necessary and excessive force determines the legal position of both defender and attacker, it must be drawn intersubjectively. Hence necessary force is not what the defender thinks is necessary nor what an omniscient observer would know to be necessary; rather, it is what a reasonable agent viewing the world from the defender's finite perspective would regard as necessary.

However, if defensive force is justified only as preventive, what are we to make of the requirement that the force be proportionate to that of the attacker? At first sight, this constraint seems at odds with the preventive rationale, for it requires the defender to forgo a defence of his property if nothing but lethal force will repel the thief. Indeed, George Fletcher thinks that the proportionality requirement is out of place in a coherent law of self-defence—that it either belongs to a punitive theory or else imposes a duty of ethics on the defender to moderate enforcement of his strict right for the benefit of the attacker.[44]

But this is not so. The defender is not justified in using lethal force to repel a challenge to a property right even if no lesser force would succeed, because personhood is the capacity for property and so cannot be subordinated to a particular item thereof without denying the possibility of the right the defender seeks to realize. Lethal force is justified only as necessary to repel lethal or seriously harmful force. Observe that the requirement of proportionality between response and attack is not a desert-based constraint. Just as the attacker's fault is irrelevant to the justification of defensive force, so is the proportionality of the response unrelated to the attacker's fault. The point is not that the attacker must receive no more than he deserves, for this requirement is specific to punishment. The point is rather that the force used to defend the right cannot assert an order of ends (property over personality) that denies the possibility of rights. This is why the positive law measures the proportionality of a response by what the defender believes and thus intends rather than by what is objectively the case. Lethal force is proportionate if the defender *reasonably believes* his life is in danger, whether or not it actually is.[45] Surprisingly, a disproportionate response negates justification by reintroducing the publicly manifested right denial that constitutes crime.

It follows that necessary force is not disproportionate just by virtue of its inflicting more harm than the harm inflicted or threatened. The harm the wrongdoer inflicted is an irrelevant measure; for, inasmuch as self-defence is preventive

---

[43] George Fletcher, 'Punishment and Self-Defense,' (1989) 8 *Law and Philosophy* 207, 208.

[44] Fletcher denies that proportionality is a requirement of self-defence, because he equates proportionality with a requirement of desert. 'Punishment and Self-Defense,' 210. See also Fletcher, 'Proportionality and the Psychotic Aggressor,' (1973) 8 *Israel Law Review* 367–90.

[45] Canadian Criminal Code, s. 34(2)(a).

rather than punitive, the defender is entitled to the force necessary to prevent a further attack even if what is necessary and proportionate to the threat (in the abovementioned sense) will inflict much more harm than the wrongdoer already inflicted. But further, if wrongdoers threaten death, the number of deaths they threaten is also an irrelevant yardstick of proportionate force; for, as an absolute end, personality's worth cannot vary inversely with the denominator of a fraction. Thus, force necessary to prevent one wrongful death is not disproportionate just by virtue of its causing many more deaths than the wrongdoers threaten. If some*one* is threatened with imminent death by a gang, he may kill all the gang members. Nor is necessary lethal force in self-defence disproportionate if it accidentally kills many innocents and proportionate if it kills but a few. In either case, the killing is wrongful (though potentially excusable) as the killing of innocents long before we arrive at the question of proportionality. Whether the wrong itself is justifiable is discussed in the next section.

Finally, the defender has no duty to retreat before an unprovoked attack, because the right of self-defence is a right, not to what is necessary to avert bodily harm, but to what is necessary to realize a right to respect for end-status. The right to respect for one's agency (juridical honour, in Kant's phrase) entails a right to stand one's ground. Hence it is a right to *repel* simply, not a right to repel as a last resort. There is, however, one qualification. The same rationale that underlies the proportionality constraint also demands that (unless the victim of aggression is at home) lethal force be applied to repel wrongful lethal force only if escape is impossible.[46] Just as the capacity for property cannot be subordinated to a particular item thereof, so the capacity for rights cannot be subordinated to a particular exercise of rights. Only when killing a wrongdoer is necessary to preserve capacity can one kill without dishonouring the priority of agency that makes a right to coerce in self-defence possible.[47]

Putative justification (is exceptionally a justification)

Legal scholars have been greatly vexed by the problem of putative justification for defensive force against apparent wrongdoers—that is, justification based on a reasonable but mistaken belief that one is being assaulted.[48] Nathan learns

---

[46] Model Penal Code, s. 3.04(2)(b)(ii).

[47] Yet one is not required to retreat from one's home, for otherwise a retreat from a mortal threat would be a surrender rather than an affirmation of rights.

[48] I shall take putative justification for defensive force to refer to justified force against an apparent wrongdoer who is really innocent but not to justified force against a real wrongdoer who cannot accomplish his purpose (e.g. his gun is empty) or carry out his threat (e.g. his gun is fake). Against real wrongdoers, there is always a real justification. Several writers view the latter situation as a case of putative justification for defensive force in general rather than as a case of putative justification for lethal force in particular, and then base the sweeping claim that a reasonable but mistaken belief in justificatory circumstances justifies defensive force on such a case; see Ripstein, *Equality, Responsibility, and the Law*, 193; Stewart, 'The Role of Reasonableness,' 317–26. This

of Riff's plan to kill him. While Nathan is sitting at a bar, Riff's twin brother, Mack, walks in carrying a 19th-century Bowie knife he wants to show off to his friend, the bartender. Nathan, reasonably believing that Mack is about to stab him, rushes Mack, grabs his arm, and tries to wrest the knife from him.

Currently, the prevailing Anglo-American view is that Nathan is justified in using defensive force against Mack.[49] This view is supported, moreover, by several legal theorists.[50] In particular, those who think that legal justification is parasitic on moral justification will regard Nathan's defensive actions as legally justified, for they will see justification as depending solely on the valid justificatory maxim or reason informing one's action; how circumstances in the external world fortuitously turn out does not affect the moral quality of the will nor, therefore, the moral worth of the action. Alternatively, one might see the idea of reasonableness as fairly allocating the risks of mistake in a world of uncertainty.[51] Mack's right to resist cannot depend on Nathan's subjective beliefs, but neither can Nathan's right to defend depend on facts knowable only to an omniscient observer. On this view, then, a reasonable belief in the existence of justificatory circumstances suffices for a valid justification even if the belief turns out to have been mistaken.

Yet this view is not without problems and detractors.[52] In particular, to regard Nathan as justified in using defensive force against Mack is to sacrifice asymmetry and closure; for surely Mack, an innocent, is justified in resisting Nathan's threat, while Nathan, if he was justified in the first place, must be justified in resisting Mack, and so on. This is indeed the position of the Model Penal Code, which, after treating putative justification as justification simply, nevertheless gives a "privilege" to the party mistakenly believed to be an aggressor to resist.[53] Not only does this position sacrifice asymmetrical justification; it also blurs the border between justification and excuse, for both can now exonerate the actor without affecting the legal position of other parties.[54]

And yet the contrary position seems equally problematic. According to that position, Nathan is excused rather than justified for trying (as he sees it) to disarm

confusion stems from viewing the right of self-defence as a right to defend against threats of harm (which may be unreal even though the threatener is a real wrongdoer) instead of as a right to defend rights (which may be infringed though no harm is possible).

[49] *R v LaKing* (2004) 185 CCC (3d) 524 (Ont CA); Model Penal Code, s. 3.02(1); JC Smith, *Smith and Hogan Criminal Law*, 10th ed. (London: Butterworth, 2002), 245.

[50] Greenawalt, 'The Perplexing Borders,' 1918–25; RA Duff, 'Rethinking Justifications,' (2004) 39 *Tulsa Law Review* 829, 836–842; Joshua Dressler, 'New Thoughts About the Concept of Justification in the Criminal Law: A Critique of Fletcher's Thinking and Rethinking,' (1984) 32 *UCLA Law Review* 61, 92–5; Stewart, 'The Role of Reasonableness,' 317; Thorburn, 'Justification, Powers, and Authority,' 1110.

[51] Ripstein, *Equality, Responsibility, and the Law*, 190–201.

[52] Robinson, 'Competing Theories of Justification,' 45–70; Fletcher, *Rethinking Criminal Law*, 762–8; John Gardner, 'Justifications and Reasons,' in AP Simester and ATH Smith, eds., *Harm and Culpability* (Oxford: Clarendon Press, 1996), 103–29; Uniacke, *Permissible Killing*, 39–41.

[53] S 3.04(1). Stewart also accepts reciprocal justification; see 'The Role of Reasonableness,' 329.

[54] Greenawalt, 'The Perplexing Borders,' 1915–25.

Mack; and, since excuse presupposes a wrong, Mack can resist and the bartender can help him.[55] This no doubt saves asymmetry (and the distinction between justification and excuse); but if Nathan's mistake was reasonable and the truth could have been known only to an omniscient observer, it seems unjust to require Nathan to rely on excuse, for excuse (an affirmative defence) presupposes *culpable* (criminal) wrongdoing, and Nathan's wrong was surely nonculpable. How, after all, can we expect Nathan to have exercised a cognitive capacity no human agent possesses?

In response, John Gardner argues that it is "perfectly possible" for actions to be wrongful and yet to cast the person in a "not unfavourable light"; and this state of affairs, he claims, is just "the equilibrium which a valid excuse...establishes".[56] Perhaps so. But whatever one might think of this account of excuse in general (see Chapter 7), it is not a good theory of mistaken belief in justificatory circumstances; for whereas in cases of excusing necessity or duress the defendant chooses an arbitrary sacrifice of another's life to his own and so must properly rely on excuse, here no such arbitrary self-preference is intended. Though Nathan intended a show of force, he acted under a belief which, had it been true, would have justified his self-preference. Thus he made no culpable choice. True, he wronged Mack and is liable to him civilly. But he did not wrong Mack culpably; *a fortiori* if his mistake was justifiable. But then why, in a criminal court, should he have to rely on excuse?

Further, in cases involving altruistic conduct, the excuse theory produces a contradiction between legal right and moral good that ethical life as a whole cannot bear. Say the bartender, acting on the same reasonable belief as Nathan's, comes to Nathan's "rescue" by wrestling Mack to the ground. Because the moral worth of actions depends on the goodness of the reasons animating them rather than on contingent facts about the world, we would say that the bartender's actions were morally praiseworthy despite their having produced an unintended result. But this means that the excuse theory requires us to say that the bartender's actions were morally praiseworthy yet legally culpable (though excused). Now, of course some disjunction between legal guilt and moral blame is inevitable (as I have been arguing). For example, one's outward actions can be consistent with another's right and yet, because improperly motivated, morally blameworthy. They can also, as we have seen, be morally blameless yet legally culpable, as in murder under duress. In both cases, legal and moral judgment diverge because they apply to different ethical precincts (right and virtue), but they do not contradict each other. In the first case, morality demands more than legality, and in the second case legality demands more than morality, but in neither case do they demand contradictory things.

They would demand contradictory things, however, were it possible for an action to be morally praiseworthy all things considered and yet culpable, for then morality would look with favour upon an action that right condemns. So, if the

---

[55] Robinson, 'Competing Theories of Justification,' 47–8; Fletcher, *Rethinking Criminal Law*, 762–8.
[56] 'The Gist of Excuses,' (1998) 1 *Buffalo Law Review* 575, 578.

ethical universe is coherent, it must be impossible to deserve moral credit and judicial punishment for the same action. But this is what the excuse theory comes to in cases of noble rescue under a reasonable misperception of an unlawful threat. The rescue is at once morally laudable and legally culpable, albeit excused. Accordingly, it seems that we are faced with our own choice of evils: either to call Nathan's act justified and so acknowledge the possibility of symmetrical and mutually inconsistent justifications; or to call it excused and so wrongfully require someone to rely on an excuse for a nonculpable (and, for the rescuer, praiseworthy) action.[57]

Some theorists have sought to dissolve this dilemma by introducing a nuance into the idea of justification. Nathan's self-defensive action is justified both if Riff is really attacking him and if Mack is apparently attacking him, but in different senses. Suzanne Uniacke distinguishes between "objective justification" and "agent-perspectival" justification;[58] RA Duff distinguishes between self-defensive actions that are "right" if the defender's belief in the existence of justifying circumstances is true, and those that are "wrong" but "warranted" if the defender's belief is false but reasonable;[59] while Heidi Hurd would say that, whereas Nathan would have been both epistemically and morally justified in attacking Riff, he was morally unjustified but epistemically justified in attacking Mack.[60] The supposed advantage of these distinctions is that they enable us to explain how the following propositions can both be true at once: Nathan is justified in applying force to Mack (and anyone with Nathan's beliefs can help him); Mack is justified in resisting Nathan (and anyone who, like Mack, knows the true situation is justified in helping Mack).

It is difficult to see, however, how verbally distinguishing between two senses of justification or (in Duff's case) between "right" and "warranted" solves the substantive problem at the heart of putative justification. The problem, once again, is the symmetrical permission of violence and the relapse of a condition of civil peace into a state of war that it signifies. One symptom of this anarchy can be detected if we imagine that the saloon has been transformed into a court and the bartender into a judge. The judge knows that Riff has vowed to kill Nathan but that Mack, not Riff, has entered his court; he also realizes that Nathan has quite

---

[57] Arthur Ripstein's solution is to treat reasonable mistakes of identity as never justifying but at best excusing, because the victim did nothing he ought to have known was menacing; *Equality, Responsibility, and the Law*, 197–201. He thus assumes that, for all other mistakes, the reasonableness of the defender's mistake implies the unreasonableness of the victim's action and so justifies defensive force. But he does not explain why someone who makes a reasonable mistake of identity is culpable and thus in need of an excuse. Moreover, there is no reason to suppose that only mistakes of identity can give rise to the symmetrical reasonableness of defender's mistake and victim's action. Suppose Nathan was reasonably mistaken that Riff was out to kill him (Riff had previously uttered death threats against him) and Riff walks into the bar showing off his newly acquired knife, having no reason to believe Nathan is there.
[58] *Permissible Killing*, 15–23.   [59] 'Rethinking Justifications,' 841.
[60] 'Justification and Excuse, Wrongdoing and Culpability,' (1999) 74 *Notre Dame Law Review* 1551, 1563–5.

reasonably mistaken Mack for Riff (assume a liberal judicial notice rule!). Now suppose that, when Nathan approaches Mack aggressively, Mack hastily petitions the judge for an injunction restraining Nathan. Under a lawful condition, there must be a univocal answer to Mack's suit; "granted and denied" is not an option. But on the nuanced view of justification, what other result can the judge deliver?

Accordingly, the problem that makes the classificatory choice between justification and excuse in cases of putative justification a choice between evils cannot be averted simply by distinguishing between two senses of justification. There is, however, another solution.

The Gordian knot comes easily undone with the theory of *mens rea*. Someone who transgresses a boundary under a sincere but mistaken belief in the existence of justificatory circumstances has chosen nothing from which a denial of rights may be inferred. Therefore, his transgression is not a culpable one justifying punishment. Nevertheless, it is still a transgression, for, as there was really no action inconsistent with the defender's right, his force was not justified by right realization. Therefore, Mack has a right both to resist Nathan and to recover from him civilly (though only nominal damages for trespass if Nathan's mistake was reasonable); and Nathan, though a tortfeasor, is exculpated from crime. This is the intuitively correct result—reached without sacrificing asymmetry of justification or requiring Nathan to rely on excuse. Nathan is exculpated rather than excused, but exculpation comes, not from justification, but from the absence of a culpable mind.[61] No doubt, Nathan has chosen to interfere with Mack's agency, and normally a denial of rights of agency would be imputable to this choice. But if Nathan believes, reasonably or not, that his act is justified by self-defence, then, provided his mistake is one of fact ("I thought he was attacking me") and not of law ("I thought I could use force today to prevent his attacking me tomorrow"), the thinking Agent in his shoes chooses an act justified by right realization; and so no denial of right can be imputed to Nathan's choice in this case. Thus justification can be reserved for real justification (and the distinction between justification and excuse preserved) without having to excuse the nonculpable.[62]

---

[61] *R v Williams (Gladstone)* (1983) 78 Cr App R 276 supports this view. Defendant assaulted complainant, who was chasing a thief, believing the complainant was assaulting the thief. Held, honest belief in justificatory circumstances constitutes mistake of fact negating mental element; a reasonable belief is unnecessary. This view was upheld by the Privy Council in *Beckford v The Queen* [1988] AC 130.

[62] Does our conclusion that correctness of belief alone justifies force in self-defence entail the incorrectness of the "reasonable and probable ground" standard for justifiable arrest by police officers? No. The arrest power belongs not to the defence of rights against wrongdoers in general, but to the process of law enforcement through the punishment of criminal wrongdoers in particular. Since the truth of the matter of guilt is a legal truth that results from a trial, there is, at the moment of the decision to arrest, nothing but a reasonable or unreasonable belief in guilt (the belief cannot be mistaken). Moreover, asymmetry of justification is here secured by the authority of a public official acting on the only truth available at the time. In the case of defence of rights, however, there is a truth of the matter at the point of decision as to whether A is wrongfully invading B's boundary, since "wrongfully" means only voluntarily and without consent. Because no judgment of culpability is required, truth is not mediated by due process. No doubt a court will determine whether A's

We are left with the case of a reasonable but mistaken belief in the existence of a lethal threat from a real wrongdoer. Suppose it is actually Riff who saunters into the bar with the Bowie knife in his belt. On seeing Nathan, Riff approaches him menacingly but without intent to kill. Nathan, reasonably believing that Riff means to kill him, steps backward as far as he can and then draws a gun. Riff stops and retreats, but Nathan advances, pointing his gun at Riff. Riff then pulls out a gun and shoots Nathan.

Most, if not all, Anglo-American jurisdictions permit the use of lethal force to someone who reasonably (not just correctly) apprehends a wrongful threat of lethal force, provided he reasonably believes no escape is possible.[63] This (intuitively sound) view embarrasses the unqualified assertion that putative justification is no justification. Nevertheless, our earlier remarks about proportionality show how counting putative justification as justification in this exceptional case avoids the symmetrical permissions that make putative justification legally absurd as a justification *tout court*.

One of the rules of proportionality, we saw, is that the defender may use lethal force against a real or apprehended threat of unjustified lethal force only as a last resort; for only under that condition is the capacity for rights (agency) prioritized over a particular exercise of rights. So, the defender (Nathan) may use lethal force against a wrongful aggressor whom he reasonably but mistakenly perceives as a lethal threat only after he has retreated to the wall. Likewise, the wrongful aggressor (Riff), though he may use defensive lethal force against a disproportionately lethal response to his attack, may do so only if he has retreated as far as he can.[64] But if Riff is obliged to retreat when Nathan's permission crystallizes (after he has exhausted his alternatives), the permission to use lethal force is not symmetrical. And yet Riff is not legally helpless, because Riff's retreat ends Nathan's permission to use force of any kind and puts both parties back to their legal position before the confrontation. If Nathan persists with a real threat of lethal force, he is now the wrongdoer, and so Riff may use lethal force against him, while Nathan may not resist (though he will). Thus permission remains asymmetrical throughout.

---

boundary crossing was voluntary and without consent; but the truth of these matters is here ascertained by the court, not produced by it.

Thorburn argues that reasonable belief is sufficient for justification because justification takes hold at the moment of decision rather than after trial, and the defendant can only be expected to act on evidence available at the time of decision ('Justification, Powers, and Authority,' 1110). But this is a *non sequitur*, for it does not follow from the inevitability of epistemic uncertainty that reasonable belief justifies; the same consideration can point to excuse. The sufficiency of reasonable belief for justification follows not from the unavailability of evidence, but from the unavailability of truth. But truth is unavailable at the point of decision only in matters of legal culpability.

[63] Model Penal Code, s. 3.04(2)(b); Canadian Criminal Code, s. 34(2).
[64] Canadian Criminal Code, s. 35.

Unknown justification (is exceptionally not a justification)

What about putative nonjustification (or unknown justification)? Suppose the twin in the bar is really Riff about to kill Nathan, but Nathan thinks Riff is Mack only showing off a new knife to the bartender. Nevertheless, Nathan, seeing an opportunity to settle an old score with Mack, wrestles Riff to the floor. Is Nathan guilty of an assault?

For those who, with morality or practical reasoning generally in view, treat all justification as depending on the conformity of one's motive with the objective reason for justification, Nathan will have no justification and so will be guilty of an assault.[65] So too for those whose theory of justification generalizes from the case of justification for public officials, who must certainly act for the justifying public purpose if they wish to cloak themselves with the justification of public authority.[66] Moreover, the prevalent common-law position (which generalizes from the case of a public official) seems to be that the defendant's knowledge of the objectively existing justificatory circumstances is a necessary condition of a valid justification.[67]

However, those who hold this position must explain why someone with failing sight who enters a house marked "open house, all welcome" believing he lacks permission is not guilty of trespass, while someone who thwarts a real attack believing there is none is guilty of assault. That consent obviates the need for justification, while coercion requires it, is not an answer; for self-defence is a legally recognized reason for publicly permitting a coercive act that would otherwise be wrongful, just as consent is a legally recognized reason for permitting a boundary crossing that would otherwise be wrongful (for a right to exclusive possession entails a presumption of no consent). In neither case, therefore, is the transaction illegal; just as the factual crossing of the threshold is no legal trespass, so the factual coercion is no legal assault.[68] So how can it be permissible for the state to punish someone for an assault that did not in fact occur? It seems

---

[65] Gardner, *Offences and Defences*, 91–120; Fletcher, *Rethinking Criminal Law*, 565; 'The Right Deed for the Wrong Reason,' 310–11.

[66] Thorburn, 'Justification, Powers, and Authority,' 1110.

[67] *Dadson*, note 2 above; *Thain* (1985) 11 NI 31; *Smith and Hogan Criminal Law*, 37. But s. 34(1) of the Canadian Criminal Code makes no mention of knowledge or belief. Only s. 34(2), which deals with proportionality, allows lethal force on condition that the defendant reasonably believes (a) he is being threatened with death or serious bodily harm and (b) no other avenue is available. Further, *Dadson* was a case involving a public official. The account presented here supports (and draws support from) the Canadian position.

[68] This leads Duff to conclude that "deeds theorists" are talking not about affirmative justification, but about denials of criminal wrongdoing, while "reasons theorists" are properly talking about justification for 'presumptive wrongdoing'; *Answering for Crime* (Oxford: Hart Publishing, 2007), 277–84. This is puzzling. Both deeds theorists and reasons theorists believe that justification of any sort negates *criminal* wrongdoing at the end of the day. Both also think that justification overcomes a presumptive criminal wrong in that the defendant's action is an assault unless justified. So Duff cannot argue that reasons theorists alone are talking about true justification without assuming what needs to be argued: that legal (like moral) justification must justify persons rather than actions alone.

clear that Riff could not successfully sue Nathan for assault, for Nathan's subjective beliefs cannot transform Riff from a wrongdoer to an innocent victim. But if Riff cannot pursue Nathan for assault, how can the state punish him for assault?

It might be argued that, because criminal verdicts express evaluative judgments of defendants—because they condemn and hold safe from condemnation—justification in criminal law must work differently from justification in tort law. Specifically, it must be attuned to the way the concept of justification works in ordinary practical reasoning and in morality.[69] And in these discourses, for a *person* to be justified in an action for which reasons exist against performing it requires not only that there be a reason *pro* that defeats all the reasons *con*, but also that the person act for the justifying reason. The person is not justified unless both these conditions are satisfied.

Yet this argument is hoist on its own petard. For if justification in criminal law is indeed distinct, why should a concept of justification taken from the realm of practical reasoning in general dictate to a legal realm specifically concerned with drawing the parameters of legitimate public coercion?[70] Principles of practical reasoning are maxims by which one must guide oneself if one wishes to perform well the activity to which the maxims apply. If I wish to be a decent human being, I will guide all my actions by the principles of morality; if I wish to be a good general, I will guide my campaigns by the principles of military strategy; and if I wish to be a true agent of the public authority, I will keep within the constraints of constitutional law applying to my role. Successfully guiding myself by the principles is the way to ensure that I can validly claim justification for my action (though it might have had an undesired effect), for it was the sort of action that an exemplary role-incumbent could have performed. Here, in other words, what is or is not justified is the self—the subject of the action—and the self's justification is just its conformity with the ideal actor in the role. So, if I trap the enemy while intending a premature retreat or attack a felon not knowing him to be one, I have acted in a way unbecoming a good general or outside my authority as a policeman, and so *I* cannot claim justification for the action. In this context, then, for someone to be justified in an action, it must be the case, not only that there were good and sufficient reasons to perform the action, but also that it was performed for those reasons.

However, Nathan is a private citizen, and what has his excellence or incompetence in morality or practical rationality to do with whether his action has violated someone else's right? To have a right, after all, is to have a claim against others that is valid independently of their foibles, frailties, subjective beliefs, or motives. So whether Riff has a right that Nathan not attack him (or Nathan a permission to attack) cannot depend on Nathan's motives, good or bad. It can depend only on

---

[69] See Joseph Raz, *Practical Reasons and Norms*, 2nd ed. (Oxford: Oxford University Press, 1999), 15–19; Gardner, *Offences and Defences*, 95.
[70] A point also made by Stewart in 'The Role of Reasonableness,' 329.

whether Riff is wrongfully attacking Nathan. Since he is, his right is forfeit. No doubt, in everyday moral discourse we will say that *Nathan* was not justified in wrestling Riff to the ground, and we will blame him for it. But in criminal law discourse, we will say that, because Nathan can be judicially punished for assault only if he does something amounting to an assault, he cannot be punished for assault where a wrongdoer's attack justified his *action,* nullifying it as assault. Against this position it cannot plausibly be maintained that having a legal permission to X and being blameable for X are incompatible; for the case of Shylock shows that this is not generally true, nor is it true in Nathan's case. Why should a condition of moral justification (knowledge of justifying circumstances) negating blameworthiness automatically apply to legal justification, whose only effect is to negate coercibility?

For those who think that justification is bifurcated into some variation of the objective/agent-perspectival distinction, there is once again no determinate answer to the question whether Nathan is guilty of assault; for since Nathan has done a right thing for the wrong reason, his act is in one sense justified and in another sense unjustified. By contrast, the viewpoint of right realization yields an unequivocal verdict. Nathan's right against coercion was in fact threatened, and so Nathan had a right that his right be enforced against Riff. That right cannot depend on anyone's subjective beliefs, including Nathan's, for if it did, it would be nonsensical as a right.[71] Had Riff attacked Nathan in the mistaken belief that Nathan was attacking him, Nathan's right to use force in self-defence would be unquestioned. But if mistaken beliefs are irrelevant to Nathan's right of self-defence when they are others' beliefs, they are no less irrelevant when they are Nathan's; for the reason they are irrelevant is just that they are *beliefs.*

Accordingly, legal (as distinct from moral) justification for private actors requires the existence of justificatory facts alone; with a nuance I'll come to presently, it does not require that the agent act for the justifying reason (here self-defence), and so Nathan is not guilty of assault. However, given his criminal intention, he is possibly guilty of attempted assault, depending on whether an observer could have reasonably interpreted Nathan's action as taken in self-defence (see Chapter 3). If so, Nathan, though wicked in character and sinful at heart, is not guilty of any crime.

Suppose, however, that Nathan knows Riff is about to assault him but does not know that Riff intends to kill him. Nevertheless, to secure his peace of mind for the future, Nathan intentionally employs lethal force against Riff and kills him. Here our account of the proportionality requirement determines that Nathan must indeed act in the knowledge or belief that Riff intends him death or serious bodily harm in order successfully to plead a justification for a homicide. Recall that a breach of proportionality negated justification because it implicitly asserted

---

[71] The opposing view gives rise to the following *non sequitur*: "Because defensive force is only justified as a way of protecting rights, it only justifies force when the person using it is aware of the justifying circumstances." Ripstein, *Equality, Responsibility, and the Law,* 217. Does lack of awareness of rights entail forfeiture of rights?

an order of ends (property over personhood) destructive of the right of personality the defender was alone justified in defending; that is, it transformed the meaning of the defensive act from one of right realization to one of right denial. The same reasoning applies when the defender intends a response the law would regard as disproportionate were the circumstances as the defender believes them to be. Thus, someone who kills an assailant not knowing that the latter intends him death or serious bodily harm makes a choice to which a culpable denial of the possibility of rights is imputable. He is therefore a criminal deserving punishment; and since he intentionally caused death, he is responsible for a homicide in the degree known as murder.

It is true, of course, that the defender's lethal force was *in fact* proportionate. But this is irrelevant here, because the legal point of the proportionality requirement, we saw, is not to match force to the assailant's desert but to preserve the public meaning of the defender's choice as one of right realization rather than right denial. And so if the defender chooses what, given his beliefs, is a disproportionate response, then he chooses culpably regardless of the true state of affairs. Here the happenstance of proportionality does not negate the wrongfulness of the homicide (as the happenstance of defending against a wrongdoer negates the wrongfulness of force) because in this context absence of proportionality is not an element of wrongful killing (whereas absence of a situation permitting self-defence is an implicit element of wrongful force); rather it makes for the right denial constitutive of a culpable mind.[72] Further, that lethal force was *in fact* necessary to avert death is also irrelevant, for we saw that necessity is determined from the standpoint of the reasonable agent positioned within the defender's finite perspective. Thus, if the defender reasonably but mistakenly believed his life was *not* in danger, he cannot claim that murder was legally impossible.

The upshot is that, whereas his knowledge of the imminence of a transgression is irrelevant to whether the party assaulted is justified in disabling the transgressor (the fact alone matters), his knowledge of the existence of a lethal threat is necessary to justify lethal force. Indeed, belief is enough, for what matters here is not whether force *is* proportionate (this is not punishment) but whether the victim acts for a reason consistent with the priority of personhood and the possibility of rights (the reason alone matters). Still, the belief in the existence of a lethal threat must be reasonable, for otherwise the defender used unnecessary force, which is beyond the scope of his justification.[73]

Accordingly, the controversy in self-defence theory as to whether justification hinges solely on objective facts or solely on reasonable beliefs stems from a false generalization of claims valid for a limited domain. Both sides are partly right,

---

[72] So someone who believes that a simple assault justifies lethal force in response makes a culpable mistake, whereas someone who uses lethal force under an unreasonably mistaken belief that his assailant means to kill him makes an exculpatory mistake. See *R v Owino* [1996] 2 Cr App R 128.

[73] This configuration is precisely the position of the Canadian Criminal Code, ss. 34(1) and 34(2).

and so both are wrong in their unqualified claims. The private actor's justification for defensive force *simpliciter* turns solely on whether the target is in fact a wrongdoer: here putative justification is not a justification, and the unknowingly justified actor is justified. However, a reasonable belief in the existence of a lethal threat from a real wrongdoer is both necessary and sufficient for the justification of lethal force. Thus the fact/reason controversy is resolved not through the triumph of one view over the other, but through the limitation of each view to its proper sphere.[74]

5. Justification against Innocents

In the case of defensive force against wrongdoers, otherwise wrongful force is rightful because it serves not the defending agent's subjective interest in security, but a right to liberty or property belonging to the aggressor no less than to the defending agent. To the extent that defensive force is circumscribed by the requirements of legal self-defence, it realizes rather than violates the right to freedom.

However, in cases where someone is compelled by a third party (duress) or by circumstances (necessity) to coerce an innocent, the justificatory rationale of right realization is unavailable. Recall that by "innocent", I mean someone who would not be liable in tort for a trespass—someone who crosses no boundary or whose nonconsensual boundary crossing is involuntary or justified by wrongdoing. Since the innocent victim has committed no wrong, there is nothing to trigger a justification based on right realization; hence the compelled actor's self-interested use of force is itself the only wrong here. This will be so even if the only necessitous circumstance is a wrongful attack one cannot repel without coercing an innocent, as in the case of the human shield or innocent bystander, or is a threat posed by the innocent victim himself, as in the case of Falling Man or a homicidal sleepwalker. Since neither the innocent shield, bystander, nor involuntary threat contradicts a right, preventive force pre-empting their agency cannot be justified by right realization. Thus the justification legally known as "self-defence", which is structured around right realization, is inapplicable. But if coercing an innocent cannot be transfigured into a rightful act, then it must be justified, if at all, as a wrongful one. The innocent victim's right has been infringed, but if certain requirements are met, the right infringement is justified.

This is indeed how the positive law views the matter. Anglo-American law regards justified force against an innocent as a privileged transgression for which compensation is still due rather than as a negation in the particular case of what is generally a transgression.[75] Moreover, whereas the requirements of legal

---

[74] On this argument the Gardner–Fletcher position that legal justification depends both on there being justificatory facts and on the defendant's acting in light of them is valid only for the case of public officials.

[75] *Vincent v Lake Erie*, note 18 above.

self-defence screen out all coercion not required by right realization, those of legal necessity and duress (insofar as they are justificatory defences) specify what is conceptually required for a right infringement to be justified, or, in other words, for a liberty or property right to be overridden. Our task in this section is to find the theory of justification that can account for the idea of a justified transgression and to derive from this theory the requirements of a valid defence. Again, I'll confine my discussion to the case of justified force against an innocent by a private actor.

The mutual subordination of right and welfare

We should begin by observing that the formal agency paradigm that explains legal self-defence so well is powerless to explain justified force against innocents. This is so because, for this framework, public reason is identified with mutual respect for the capacity for free choice; there is no public reason beyond this. But coercing an innocent is obviously incompatible with mutual respect for free choice, and if there is no public reason beyond the formalist one, there will be nothing to justify a right infringement by a private actor—nothing by which a right to liberty or property might be conceptually overridden. All coercion of innocents by private actors, no matter for what reason, will be interpreted as the self-interested use of force against an agent, which is crime itself.

This will be true, moreover, whatever the balance of interests. Not even the violation of property to save life will be justified, for the equation of public reason with respect for free choice presupposed the subjectivity of all interests, including the interest in life. For the formalist paradigm, life is animal life embroiled in causal determinism, and the capacity for free choice is precisely the capacity not to be bound by the natural interest in self-preservation.[76] That interest is thus treated as a contingent one—something an agent can choose either to promote or to renounce, to cling to or to risk, as it subjectively decides. But then someone's violating property to save his life is an infringement of public right to serve a private interest, and of course there is no reason why such a violation should be privileged. No wonder, then, that Kant's only view of necessity is that it affords, not a justification, but a stay of prosecution where no threat of punishment could have deterred the wrongdoer.[77]

Though the formalist paradigm cannot by itself countenance transgressions in cases where rights bar action needed for self-preservation, it possesses a theoretical momentum toward a framework that can. We saw that formalism equates public reason with respect for free choice because it regards all material ends as

---

[76] Kant, *Metaphysics of Morals*, 40.
[77] Ibid., 60. Cf. *London Borough of Southwark v Williams* [1971] 2 All ER 175, in which the English Court of Appeal rejected homelessness as a justification for trespass. Lord Denning relied on Hale for the view that, if necessity could justify theft, "men's properties would be under a strange insecurity, being laid open to other men's necessities, whereof no man can possibly judge, but the party himself". (179).

subjective. We also saw that the capacity for choice supports a claim of dignity or absolute worth because, as the possibility for acting from optional ends valuable to the agent, it is itself a necessary end valuable without qualification. Further, a claim to end-status based on the capacity for free choice is a claim to others' respect for one's freedom to act according to ends one chooses. However, a claim to respect for end-status is not yet an objective right. The claim becomes objectively valid as a right only if it can be accepted by other agents without loss to the independence that qualifies them to give an objective validation. But claims to liberty can be accepted by other agents without self-loss only if the claimant gives a reciprocal recognition to the like claims of others. Accordingly, the mutual recognition of capacities for choice is the ground of all valid claims to others' sufferance of one's actions. Permissions to act issue from this relation; hence they presuppose limits internal to the permission in the sense that one has a right only to as much liberty as can be accepted by other free agents.

If rights are valid claims to worth obliging all agents, one would think they are absolute or indefeasible. Since rights are products of mutual recognition, they already presuppose all the limits they require for validity. The final product would thus seem to be subject to no further limits consistent with the right. For example, a civil right to free speech is internally limited by the time, place, and manner regulations ensuring equal freedom of speech. Were speech satisfying these limits further limited by content censorship favouring some opinions over others, we would say that the right has been violated rather than further specified; otherwise the idea of a right as a moral boundary against others' self-interested action would dissolve. Accordingly, it would seem that any limit on liberty beyond what is required to ensure equal liberty must deny the right and hence contradict the individual worth the right embodies.

However, not all limits on valid rights have this partisan meaning; some are for purposes just as public as the capacity for free choice. Because the right is borne by an abstraction indiscriminately assuming the subjectivity of ends, asserting it in cases where the right collides with another's need for an agency good will produce an outcome inconsistent with equal human worth even though the assertion is a valid exercise of the right. For example, if the permission to acquire unowned things as exclusive property is absolute, then some may end up in a position where they must either starve to death or sell their labour to those in a position to dictate terms unilaterally—to treat them as a means to the realization of their projects without symmetrically serving any project of the labourer's. True, the master would serve the labourer's animal interest in bare existence, but he would not serve any autonomous purpose of the labourer's that could make existence valuable to him; for the labourer could not bargain for anything but subsistence. Such an unequal relationship, however, violates the norm of mutual recognition internal to formalism itself. Moreover, since free agents have come to a fork between death or servitude through mutual respect for freedom of choice, respecting choice cannot be enough to respect equal human worth. On the contrary, a conception of public reason as mutual respect for free choice has led, when intransigently realized, to the dissolution of public reason in the special worth of the propertied.

Because the cause of this dissolution was formalism's equating the interest in life with a subjective inclination toward a biological end, the downfall points to a new conception of public reason unburdened of this error. Public reason is now equal concern for the conditions (including security of subsistence) of all agents' realizing their potential for acting from self-authored ends. In light of this conception, the right to property in a particular thing is justifiably overridden where another's life is threatened—overridden for the sake of the equal human worth the property right reflects but which the right absolutized would itself upset in this case. Since an exclusive possession in some that is compatible with the starvation or servitude of others is not an institution an absolute end can accept, the only avenue consistent with equal human worth is a taking subject to a duty to compensate the owner when compensation becomes feasible.

Observe that, on this account of justification by necessity, property is overridden for its own sake as well as for the sake of the person in peril. Because property turns into privilege in the face of destitution, its override in favour of the destitute is necessary to its preservation as a right. Thus, not only does the starving man have a permission to take the baker's loaf of bread; the baker has no right in property to resist. Justification is once again asymmetrical and closed. Observe also that property is overridden only in circumstances where its intransigent enforcement would contradict its own foundational end, and where an override is necessary to reinforce the equal human worth the property right itself embodies, though incompletely. Because the override is justified by equal human worth, the property owner can accept it along with the trespasser.

It will be objected, however, that what I have described is not an override of the property right but a more concrete, all-things-considered, determination of the final right. Because equal human worth underlies both the property right and the exception thereto, the only valid property is one that is consistent with everyone's guaranteed subsistence. Formalist right, one might argue, has simply merged into a paradigm protective of genuine rights to real autonomy; and so, when the starving man takes the baker's loaf, he commits no transgression requiring affirmative justification or compensation.

Reinforcing this objection is the fact that formalist public reason came to grief when confronted with destitution because it indiscriminately treated all goods as subjective and contingent. Its collapse shows that there are after all universal conditions for enjoying rights of liberty—conditions to which formalism was blind. But then if formalism was partially blind, why is it not folded into the full-sighted real autonomy paradigm? It would seem, in other words, that the real autonomy framework is sufficient by itself to secure the conditions of human worth. Were that so, individual rights would result from a global determination as to what will secure the conditions of an autonomous life for all. They will not be generated independently of that reasoning and so will require no override by the public welfare. Necessity would thus afford a right to take without compensation rather than the qualified privilege granted by positive law. It would justify a taking, but not a wrongful taking, for there would be no independent right to infringe.

The response to this objection will provide our first glimpse of the idea that unifies the paradigms by incorporating both as constituent elements of its own self-realization. If rights were simply conclusions of the public welfare (understood as real autonomy), they would no longer embody the individual agent's independent end-status; they would instead reflect the exclusive end-status of the public welfare. But if, in realizing itself, the public welfare submerges the individual's independent worth, then it contradicts itself as the public *welfare;* for welfare is here understood as the individual's realized potential for self-directed action. The real autonomy paradigm too is agent-centred: it came forward to protect the agent's actualized potential for autonomous action, given that the formal agency framework lacked the resources to do so. Thus, if the intransigent realization of formalist property secures individual worth without equality, that of the real autonomy paradigm secures equality without equal *worth*. But if treating each paradigm as self-sufficient contradicts its own end, then, for the sake of its own self-consistency, each must acknowledge the other's independence as something it requires. Each must, for its own sake, accept the other as a limit, asserting itself within bounds consistent with the other's independent existence. And if each paradigm requires the other's independence, then each is part of a larger whole formed by the interdependence of their respective ends, namely, individual worth and the public welfare. This means that the individual agent's final right to liberty or property is the product of neither paradigm taken alone but of their mutual recognition.

Implications for a right of necessity

That individual rights issue from the mutual recognition of the two paradigms yields the following implications for a right of necessity. First, a threat to life, whether emanating from impersonal circumstances or from another agent, gives the imperilled agent a permission to take or destroy another's item of property when a taking is necessary to avoid the danger. Property in a particular thing reaches its limit in collision with another agent's dire need for a good essential to living according to self-authored ends; hence the owner has no right to resist *vis-à-vis* the taker.[78] But the permission to take is limited by a requirement that the permission be consistent with the independent existence of the property right—that is, with its existence outside the public welfare; hence the taker's permission

---

[78] The qualification "*vis-à-vis* the taker" is required because of the duress situation. The victim (and everyone else) is surely entitled to treat the coerced agent as an instrument of the coercer and therefore to resist the *coercer* through his instrument. Factually, he resists the coerced agent, but his right to resist (and others' right to help him) is a right against the agent who coerces; hence justification remains asymmetrical.

is qualified by a duty to compensate the owner when the taker is able to.[79] Thus (to take Aristotle's example), no one may resist the ship captain's efforts to jettison cargo if that must be done to save lives; but the captain must compensate the owner afterward, for he committed a wrong, albeit a justified one.[80]

Second, the permission to infringe a right arises only in situations of genuine conflict between property and life, when the threat to life is immediate and no lawful means of avoiding the threat are available: for otherwise the property right is yielding, not to public reason as equal autonomy, but to the particular interest of the taker. Since the owner is not a wrongdoer challenging a boundary reflecting worth, infringing his right is justified only as a last resort.

Third, the defendant's prior fault in bringing about the necessitous situation should not preclude a justification. Once a conflict arises between one agent's negative right to an exclusive sphere of choice and another's positive entitlement to an agency good, the solution sanctioned by a public reason both could accept is that there is a permission to take subject to a duty to compensate. How the conflict came about is irrelevant to the defendant's culpability for his intentional interference with property, though it bears on his liability for an included public welfare offence (if one has been legislated).

Fourth, justification by necessity settles a conflict between the property right of one person and the welfare of another by subordinating to each other the right to exercise the capacity for free choice and the entitlement to the means for realizing the potential for autonomy the capacity implies. The logic of justification thus applies only to situations where the *mutual presupposition* of formal right and the public welfare can close the conflict in a principled and neutral way acceptable to both parties. It does not apply to conflicts that no agent-neutral principle can adjudicate and wherein justification must therefore be symmetrical and lawless. Thus no justificatory defence exists in a situation where one individual can save his life only by taking an innocent's life, not even if the innocent is involuntarily shielding a wrongful aggressor or is himself the involuntary source of the threat to the other; for there is no neutral reason for preferring the threatened person's agency good over the innocent's. Nor (generally) is there a justification for destroying another's property to save one's own, for there is no neutral reason for preferring the taker's property to the victim's unless the taker will otherwise be reduced to destitution. In these cases, therefore, the wrongdoer must rely on excuse.

Fifth, the viewpoint from which to determine whether the circumstances were sufficiently perilous to life to justify a taking is the objective one of a detached observer, for what is at stake is the limit of an objectively valid right. Where right realization against a wrongdoer was at issue, necessary force had to be

---

[79] The right to compensation for justified right infringements is embodied in s. 904 of the German Civil Code of 1871. See Fletcher, *Rethinking Criminal Law*, 776–7.

[80] *Nicomachean Ethics*, 1110a in R. McKeon, ed., *The Basic Works of Aristotle* (New York: Random House, 1941).

determined from an intersubjective standpoint rooted in the finite perspective of the right bearer. Requiring the defender to be omniscient would have been inconsistent with *his* right of self-defence, hence with the idea of right realization itself. Accordingly, necessary force was force the defender reasonably believed was necessary. However, where the overriding of an innocent's valid right for the sake of another's agency good is at issue, a standpoint that privileges the finite perspective of either party is one-sided. Here the only impartial standpoint is that of the omniscient observer. Accordingly, a mistaken belief in necessitous circumstances, even if reasonable, cannot justify an infringement precluding a right to resist, for otherwise valid rights are overridden by invalid opinions. As with self-defence, however, a mistaken belief in justificatory circumstances negates a culpable mind, provided the mistake is one of fact ("I didn't know help was otherwise available") rather than of law ("I thought I was justified in killing an innocent if I could not otherwise preserve my life"), for here a mistake of law is culpable (because arbitrary) self-preference itself.

Sixth, the same objectivist reasoning telling us that putative necessity is not necessity also tells us that unknown necessity is. A taking that is objectively justified but not known to be justified by the taker (say he believes, mistakenly, that help is available from a rich uncle) is justified nonetheless, for whether the owner's right to property is validly overridden (precluding his right to resist) must be determined independently of the taker's subjective beliefs; otherwise the owner's rights are self-contradictorily at the disposal of the taker. In this case, the taker is guilty, not of theft, but of attempted theft.

Paradigmatically, justification by necessity settles conflicts between one agent's property right and another's need by means of the logical interdependence of private property and the public welfare. But the idea of resolving conflicts of interest between innocents by means of neutral principles can be extended to problems outside the paradigm case. Take, for example, an involuntary threat to one's life or bodily integrity from, say, a sleepwalker or an extremely intoxicated individual. Against such a threat, there is no right of self-defence in the strict legal sense because no right of agency is challenged by the threat. Moreover, could the defender protect his agency goods only by harming those of the innocent threatener, no neutral principle acceptable to the threatener could give the defender a right of necessity to do so; here the defender must invoke excuse. Nevertheless, the individual threatened has a right of necessity to repel with *harmless* force, for in this case he can protect his agency goods without pre-empting the free choice of the threatener. Provided no serious harm is inflicted, no wrong is done the threatener even though he is an innocent, for there is no active volition to pre-empt. Here the neutral principle that both parties could accept is that one may protect one's agency goods against an innocent human threat where this involves no wrong or harm to the other.

The neutral principles method for resolving conflicts of interest can also be extended to the public welfare domain. In particular, the principles constraining enforcement of public welfare statutes developed in the previous chapter can resolve conflicts between individual welfare and laws promoting the general happiness or protecting agency goods. Thus, the priority of autonomy over happiness determines that laws regulating the pursuit of satisfactions (stop on red, go on green) can be broken when necessary to protect an agency good (life or health) and when no threat to others' safety is involved; and the noncontradiction proviso determines that laws (speed limits) promoting agency goods for all can be broken when necessary to preserve an agency good for an individual, provided the risk to others is minimized.

Finally, our account of justificatory necessity allows us to say something about the controversy in criminal law theory as to whether a stable distinction exists between answers to a criminal accusation negating the crime and those admitting the crime but affirming a defence (or between no-offence and defence).[81] Once again, generalization is impossible. We'll see in the next chapter that there is a rock-solid distinction between no-offence and excuse, for excuse presupposes culpable wrongdoing. Whether there is also a distinction between no-offence and justification is more complicated. In one sense, there is not, because (unknown justification of public officials excepted) justificatory circumstances negate the *culpability* of the action (*actus reus*), an element of the offence; after all, if I am permitted to perform the action, then the action cannot, all things considered, be an *actus reus*, even where it remains a compensable transgression.[82] However, some justifications (e.g. self-defence) negate the underlying transgression itself, while others (e.g. necessity) do not. The former, since they make no confession of wrongdoing, may be said to negate an implicit element of the offence; the latter, because they have the structure of confession ("I intentionally interfered with an innocent's freedom, which is wrong") and avoidance (the wrong is justified), may be said to constitute true defences.

No doubt, denials of *mens rea* also negate the culpability of an abiding wrong. But what distinguishes affirmative justifications from denials of *mens rea* is that the latter deny a violation of the framework of formal right as a whole, whereas the former admit such a violation but argue that formal right must be overridden in this case by a public purpose external to it, lest formalism's commitment to equal human worth fall into contradiction. Absence of *mens rea* signifies that no right denial is implicit in the defendant's infringement of *this* individual's right. Justificatory necessity signifies that no right denial is implicit in the defendant's violation of the rights paradigm. Thus justificatory necessity is affirmative, not because it admits a particular wrong, but because (like excuse) it admits a violation of the whole category of (formal) right.

---

[81] See Glanville Williams, 'Offences and Defences,' (1982) 2 LS 233–56; Gardner, *Offences and Defences*, 77–89, 141–53; Alan Norrie, *Punishment, Responsibility, and Justice* (Oxford: Oxford University Press, 2000), 145–65; Fletcher, *Rethinking Criminal Law*, 552–5.

[82] *Beckford v The Queen*, note 61 above. *Dadson* appears inconsistent with this, but it is distinguishable as a case involving a public official.

Hegel's right of distress and the lesser evil theory contrasted

The foregoing account of justification by necessity is an elaborated version of Hegel's terse account of the "right of distress" in his *Philosophy of Right*.[83] Is it just the lesser evil theory dressed up in fancier language? After all, the lesser evil doctrine would also justify takings of property in a life-threatening emergency. Moreover, if Hegel's account of necessity would justify taking an item of property to save life, it would *a fortiori* also justify breaches of regulatory laws (running a red light, for example) to save life or to prevent lasting bodily harm; for the capacity to act from preferences is prior to the satisfaction of any particular set. And, of course, the lesser evil doctrine would reach the same result.

However, these are just coincidental convergences of vastly different accounts. The divergences of result are more telling. For example, the lesser evil approach would justify destructions of property of lower value to save property of higher value.[84] But there is no public reason that both owners could accept for preferring the property of higher value, for that value belongs only to one of them. On Hegel's account, no item of property can be privileged over another, whatever their difference in value; only the sustained capacity to own can be privileged over the ownership of something in particular. Thus, if a private agent destroys someone's house to stop a fire from consuming many houses, he is at best excused.

What of a conflict between one agent's right against interference with bodily integrity and another agent's interest in sustained life? Suppose Lucy needs a blood transfusion to avoid death, and among all those with Lucy's blood type, only Seward is near enough to save her. But Seward refuses to donate a small quantity of his blood even though he could do so at no risk to himself. Can others forcibly take some of Seward's blood and give it to Lucy?

The lesser evil doctrine must say yes,[85] but Hegel's account would, I think, say no.[86] The right to subject a particular thing to the exclusive rule of one's choices yields to the preservation of the condition for exercising the capacity for choice in general. That capacity is not bound up with any of its particular expressions: divesting the agent of this piece of property does not touch his capacity to own. However, the body is indissolubly linked to the capacity for freedom, since that capacity exists only in a living body. True, taking a half-litre of blood will not harm Seward, but the reason we speak of a right to bodily integrity is that the body is an organism whose unifying life is in every part. Hence injuring it in a part injures the whole, and injuring the body as a whole injures the capacity for freedom. But there is no impartial reason to prefer Lucy's capacity to Seward's. By contrast, things external to the body are also external to each other. Thus, provided one does so for a right-affirming reason, one can take a single item of property without taking "property".

---

[83] Paras. 127–8.   [84] Model Penal Code, s. 3.02 commentary 1, 3.
[85] Model Penal Code, s. 3.02, commentary 1.   [86] *Philosophy of Right*, para. 48.

Finally, the lesser evil approach would view as legally justified the killing of one innocent person to save many in any of the variations of that scenario depicting the range from moral evil to moral heroism. Thus it will justify harvesting organs from one person to save the lives of several, diverting a mortal threat (say, a runaway train) from many to fewer, or hastening the already imminent death of some (say, the passengers in a hijacked plane transformed into a ballistic missile) to avert the mortal threat they innocently pose to thousands of others. On Hegel's account, none of these homicides is justified, for there is no agent-neutral reason that the person(s) sacrificed could accept for losing its—an innocent's—right to defend itself against deadly force. The "greater" good here is nothing but the many discrete goods of separate others. Accordingly, the altruistic murderers in all these scenarios must plead excuse, to which we now turn.

7

Excuse

1. The German Constitutional Court and the *Luftsicherheitsgesetz*

In June 2004, the German Bundestag enacted the *Luftsicherheitsgesetz* (Air Security Act) in order to prevent terrorist attacks of the kind suffered in New York and Washington on September 11, 2001. Section 14(3) of the Act empowered the Minister of Defence to order the Air Force to shoot down a hijacked commercial airplane full of passengers if he concluded that the plane would be used to kill human beings and if no less drastic means would prevent an imminent catastrophe.

In February 2006, the German Constitutional Court invalidated section 14(3) both on federalist grounds and as a violation of the right to life and human dignity enshrined in the Basic Law.[1] The Court's reasons rang with Kantian tones. The state, it said, was prevented by the Constitution from sacrificing some innocent lives to the salvation of others, for it was barred from treating autonomous subjects as means and objects for others' ends. Extinguishing some human lives for the sake of others "objectifies" (*verdinglicht*) those lives and therewith deprives them (*zugleich entrechtlicht*) of their right-bearing status.[2] Against this principle of inviolable human dignity no numerical calculation of net lives saved could avail as justification, for many lives are discrete lives, each with absolute value.[3] Nor did it matter that the innocents on board the plane were doomed to die shortly if the plane were not shot down and that the cost of minimizing deaths was thus only a few minutes of harrowing life for each of the passengers. Inseparable from the freedom on which dignity rests, human life is inviolable, said the Court, whatever its likely duration.[4] Matters would stand differently, it argued, if the plane were occupied only by those intending to use it as a bomb, for then the state would be justified in killing the terrorists by its duty to defend its citizens against wrongful threats. In this scenario, the terrorists would not be treated as selfless objects, for by initiating the unlawful attack, they would themselves have been responsible for whatever proportionate response they invited.[5]

---

[1] *Bundesverfassungsgericht* (BverfG), 1 BvR 357/05 vom 15.2.2006.
[2] Ibid, para. 124.   [3] Ibid, paras. 119–121.
[4] Ibid, para. 132.   [5] Ibid, para. 141.

We can see that the Court approached the question before it, as it was compelled to do, solely from the standpoint of whether the state was *justified* in violating the right to life of some in order to save the lives of more. As a matter of constitutional law, states are either justified in infringing rights or they are not; there is no other way of saving right-violating legislation. States cannot be constitutionally *excused* for violating rights, for an excuse already presupposes the invalidity of the legislation, all things considered, and so cannot count as a reason for a court's upholding it. Perhaps a "notwithstanding clause" of the Canadian type, which empowers the legislature to declare a law operative despite its constitutional invalidity, might be conceptualized as permitting a government to plead a constitutional excuse in the political arena; but strictly speaking, for a court to give force to the excusing reason would be to suspend the constitution, not to apply it. Even if the reason could count in criminal law as an excuse for an individual, it would not be a reason the constitution could recognize as saving right-violating state action.[6]

It is no wonder, then, that the Constitutional Court expressly declared the criminal law to be irrelevant to the *Luftsicherheitsgesetz* case.[7] To be sure, the idea of a justified right infringement is hardly foreign to the criminal law; on the contrary, the limits on the authority to punish as well as on the defences of self-defence, defence of others, justificatory necessity, and duress all depend on a theory of the conditions necessary and sufficient to justify a wrong or what would otherwise be a wrong. However, on the topic of justification, criminal law cannot teach constitutional law anything it does not already know. Unknown justification aside, the principles of justification for right violations are the same whether the wrongs are committed by private individuals or by public officials: valid reason, necessity, proportionality. The sole unique contribution that criminal law can make to the ghastly choices people face in scenarios contemplated by the *Luftsicherheitsgesetz* lies in its concept of *excusing necessity*. And yet, where the validity of legislation purporting to authorize a right violation is in question, this concept has no purchase.

Suppose, however, the Minister of Defence took it upon himself to order the Air Force to shoot down a hijacked commercial airplane about to crash into a civilian target. The order is carried out, and both the Minister and the executing pilot are indicted for the murder of the passengers and crew. Section 35 of the German Penal Code of 1975 provides a defence of excusing necessity to murder only to someone whose own life or whose close relative's or intimate's life is imperilled. Suppose the defendants challenged the constitutionality of this section on the ground that its exclusion of those who kill to save strangers (altruistic murderers, as I shall call them) permits punishing the morally innocent, hence using them as objects, in violation of their constitutional right to dignity. The constitutional question would then be, not whether public officials (in the name of the state) can authorize subordinates to

---

[6] Hence the Supreme Court of Canada has refused to scrutinize the government's reason for invoking the notwithstanding clause; see *Ford v Quebec* [1988] 2 SCR 712.

[7] BverfG, 1 BvR 357/05, para. 130.

sacrifice some civilian lives for others, but whether the state can punish as murderers those who do so. To the resolution of this question, criminal law theory can make a unique contribution, and this chapter seeks to provide one.

2. Exculpation and Exonerating Excuse

In Chapter 2 we briefly encountered the distinction between exculpatory and excusing conditions. Though frequently given short shrift by criminal law theorists, this distinction is, I believe, well entrenched in Anglo-American criminal law.[8] Perhaps this claim will be vigorously disputed, for judges rarely convey the distinction in exactly these words. Instead, they say that excuses are pleas in the affirmative. Or they say that, whereas some answers to a criminal accusation deny an essential element of the criminal offence (*actus reus* or *mens rea*), excuses admit the "offence" and put forward a "defence".[9] My claim that the law recognizes a distinction between exculpation and excuse is neither more nor less than a claim that it recognizes a clear distinction between a denial of the offence and a plea of excuse.

Now it is true that some theorists—John Gardner and George Fletcher, for example—adhere to the law's distinction between no-offence and excuse without acknowledging a distinction between exculpation and excuse; and so one might think the latter distinction superfluous. Not so. For one cannot conflate exculpatory and excusing conditions without having the distinction between no-offence and excuse slip through one's fingers. Gardner, for example, equates the distinction between no-offence and excuse with that between no-wrongdoing and no-fault.[10] But a denial of *mens rea* also concedes wrongdoing, while denying fault, and yet no Anglo-American lawyer thinks that a denial of *mens rea* is a plea in the affirmative.[11] To keep affirmative excuses apart from denials of *mens rea*, one

---

[8] Hart and Fletcher lump them together under their respective theories of "excuse"; see HLA Hart, *Punishment and Responsibility* (Oxford: Clarendon Press, 1968), 152; George Fletcher, *Rethinking Criminal Law* (Boston: Little, Brown, 1978), 799–802, *The Grammar of Criminal Law* (Oxford: Oxford University Press, 2007), 309–12. Fletcher's conflating of nonjustificatory exculpation and excuse under "accountability" or "excuse" is an example of the very "holistic thinking" about criminal liability he decries and erroneously attributes to Hegel; *The Grammar of Criminal Law*, 56–8. Gardner too treats the completely excused as nonculpable, though he does not see all nonjustificatory exculpating conditions as excusatory; for him, the only nonjustificatory exculpating conditions that make excuse unnecessary are those negating responsible agency (which, remarkably, he sees as the gist of the insanity defence even supposing fitness to stand trial); see John Gardner, *Offences and Defences* (Oxford: Oxford University Press, 2007), 110–13, 131–2, 177–83. Duff too sees excuses as exculpatory; see RA Duff, *Answering for Crime* (Oxford: Hart Publishing, 2007), 284–96. For an explicit distinguishing between exculpation and excuse, see Model Penal Code, ss. 2.02, 2.09; *R v Ruzic* [2001] 1 SCR 687.
[9] *R v Howe* [1987] AC 417; *R v Hibbert* [1995] 2 SCR 973.
[10] *Offences and Defences*, 150–3.
[11] Gardner calls this a "logical puzzle", which he tries to solve by calling the wrong-with-*mens rea* a further wrong distinct from the "strict" wrong, one which may itself be excused; ibid, 151–3. But the "strict wrong" is not a criminal offence. Indeed, it is not even an *actus reus*, which in law

must say that a plea of excuse concedes, not just wrongdoing, but wrongdoing that manifests a culpable choice.

Nor can the distinction between no-offence and excuse correspond, as Fletcher would have it, to one between no-wrongdoing and no-attribution.[12] Like Gardner's, Fletcher's division would place all denials of culpability (except those of voluntary motion but including pleas of reasonable mistake) on the side of excuse, leaving nothing on the offence side except wrongdoing, which may or may not be culpable. But nonculpable wrongdoing is not a criminal offence. It is not even an *actus reus*, for, as the law tells us, *actus non facit reum nisi mens sit rea*. Nonculpable wrongdoing is civil wrongdoing. Thus, an excuse denying culpability could not be a plea in the affirmative, for there would be no fully constituted offence to excuse. To make sense of the affirmative nature of excuse in the positive law, one must say that a plea of excuse concedes, not just wrongdoing, but culpable wrongdoing.[13]

So I shall press forward with the distinction between exculpatory and excusing conditions as the only way to maintain a grip on the positive law's distinction between no-offence and excuse; and I shall endeavour to give a theoretical account of that distinction, one that shows how a criminal law can fully excuse the culpable without falling apart.

A taxonomy of answers to a criminal accusation

First, however, a brief taxonomy. Answers to a criminal accusation invoke either exculpatory or excusing conditions. Exculpatory conditions, moreover, are either completely or partially exculpatory. Completely exculpatory conditions are those whose presence means either that the defendant did no wrong (consent, self-defence), or that he lacked the self-conscious agency underpinning basic responsibility and making culpable choices possible (involuntariness, infancy, some cases of insanity), or that he in fact made no culpable choice (mistake of fact, legal insanity, colour of right)—that is, no choice to which a denial of rights or of law's authority can be imputed—or that his wrong was justified (justificatory necessity). The consequence is that (unknown justification aside) the defendant is undeserving of judicial punishment of any severity. For this reason he will be exonerated, by which I mean (in what follows) fully released from the burden of punishment. Partially exculpatory

---

presupposes a *mens rea*. How then can excusing a strict wrong be excusing an *offence*? Moreover, if the fault external to strict wrongs can be built into more complex wrongs, why stop the progression at *mens rea*? Why not treat cowardly killing as an even more complex wrong than intentional killing? Unless there is no end to excusing conditions, we must eventually arrive at a wrong for which there is no excuse (absolute wrong?), all negations of excuse having been internalized to the wrong. In such a wrong the distinction between no- wrong and no-excuse disappears.

[12] *Rethinking Criminal Law*, 798–807; *The Grammar of Criminal Law*, 49–55.

[13] It is thus no wonder that, without a distinction between exculpation and excuse, that between no-offence and defence becomes an object of scepticism; see Glanville Williams, 'Offences and Defences,' (1982) 2 LS 233–56; Alan Norrie, *Punishment, Responsibility, and Justice* (Oxford: Oxford University Press, 2000), 145–65.

conditions are those that, without affecting the defendant's culpability for wrong, reduce his responsibility for the harmful result of the wrong (because he did not choose the harm) and so entitle him to a criminal label and sentence range reflecting that lesser degree of outcome responsibility. Here belong intoxication and the diminished responsibility of the legally sane but mentally ill defendant.

By contrast, conditions that excuse crime presuppose culpable wrongdoing as well as the defendant's full responsibility for the harmful result (he chose it). Etymologically, "excuse" derives from the Latin *ex causa*—for a reason. The defendant pleads, in effect, "guilty with an explanation". Sometimes the explanations the court is willing to hear have no bearing on any generalizable criterion of exoneration or mitigation but simply point to individuating circumstances relevant to the deterrence, reformative, and expressive aims governing sentencing discretion within the deserved range prescribed by statute. For example: "the defendant, fatigued and under great financial stress, acted out of character." To the mitigating force of this kind of explanation the defendant has no right, because this reason for leniency may be outweighed by other reasons for severity. Sometimes, however, the explanation, without affecting the degree to which the outcome is imputable to the defendant's choice, points to a nonidiosyncratic emotional disturbance—one that even a self-composed person could have experienced had he or she faced the same triggering event. This kind of explanation provides (in Raz's terms) a protected reason for reducing the severity of punishment; that is, it yields a partial or mitigating excuse—called provocation when the triggering event is a wrongful act or insult—to which the defendant is entitled by law if the law has otherwise excluded the force of mitigating explanations by imposing a mandatory sentence.

However, not all explanations of criminal wrongdoing are like this. Sometimes the explanation is of a kind that, without affecting either the defendant's culpability for wrong or his responsibility for harm, warrants (if not deserves) the same total exoneration from punishment to which a completely exculpatory defence leads. Of such a kind are explanations that invoke necessity, duress, and entrapment. The challenge for a theory of excuse is to identify the gist (or gists, as it will turn out, for entrapment belongs to a class apart) of this kind of explanation in a way that integrates, without effacing the border between, exculpation and excuse. Put otherwise, the challenge is to devise a theory of excuse that, without blending it into exculpation, avoids condoning crime.

The tension between law's authority and exonerating excuse

The challenge is not easily met. Since it is generally agreed that an exonerating excuse such as necessity has as its object the actor rather than his or her unlawful action, the only exculpatory defences with which excusing ones need to be harmonized are those that negate culpable mind: mistake of fact, legal insanity, colour of right. Now consider the famous case of *R v Dudley and Stephens,* in which two shipwrecked seamen in a lifeboat consumed a third in order to avert starvation;[14] and recall the theory proposed in Chapter 2 explaining why the abovementioned defences exculpate. They remove criminal desert, I argued, because they preclude an inference from what the defendant chose to do to a denial of agency rights. By agency rights I mean rights to act on ends of one's own choice free of interference (restraint, threats of force) from other agents. If applicable to his case, exculpatory defences mean that the defendant has not *knowingly* interfered with another's free agency or knowingly risked doing so; hence he has made no choice to which a denial of agency rights may be imputed. And because he has not implicitly denied rights, he has not implicitly authorized his own coercion nor given the state a reason to vindicate the authority of rights against him.

Now, it cannot seriously be argued that Dudley's situation placed him within this rationale for exoneration. He consumed the cabin boy for the sake of his own preservation—as clear an example of using a person for one's own ends as there can be. He thus made a choice to which a denial of agency rights may indeed be imputed. By doing so, he implicitly authorized the public authority's treatment of him as right-less; and the public authority was in general duty bound to punish him in order to realize the authority of rights to equal liberty that he denied. Necessity or not, Dudley was guilty of murder (as the court held) according to the legal conception of culpability; and so it would seem that to exonerate him (his life sentence was commuted to six months) is to set aside that conception. But to set aside the legal conception of culpability, one would think, is either to admit its inadequacy as a conception of criminal desert or to condone a murder.

Everything just said about a situation of necessity can also be said of situations of nonjustificatory duress. D participates in the killing of V, an innocent, under a believable threat of unavoidable death from T if he does not. As in the necessity scenario, D, when faced with a choice between killing an innocent and dying, chose to save himself at V's expense. Whether the threat to D comes from impersonal circumstances or from a human source is irrelevant to D's culpability, for V's right against coercion entails that T's holding a gun to D is D's misfortune, not V's. By intentionally killing V for the sake of his self-preservation, D implicitly denied V's right and, since V's right claim rests on his agency, exposed himself to right-vindicating punishment. Thus D comes squarely within the legal conception of criminal desert, duress or no.[15] If we nonetheless think that D has an exonerating excuse, then the conditions that excuse from criminal liability stand in apparent tension with the principles of culpability. We thus ostensibly admit the failure of the legal conception of guilt to provide a full account of criminal desert. From this *aporia* comes the urge to recast the whole theory of guilt and exculpation in light of a theory that explains why necessity and duress exonerate—whence the character theory of culpability as well as Hart's "fair opportunity to exercise choice" account.

[14] (1884) 14 QBD 273.
[15] Hence the antipathy of many writers and courts to the defence. See James Fitzjames Stephen, *A History of the Criminal Law of England* (London: Macmillan, 1883), II, 108; *R v Howe* (denying that duress is a defence to murder). The Canadian Criminal Code defence of duress is inapplicable to a wide range of offences; see s. 17.

It might be argued that it is not obvious that the actor who kills under threat of death to himself merits exoneration (after all, Dudley's commuted sentence was an exercise of executive clemency and Anglo-American common law denies a defence of duress to murder) and that the necessity and duress cases where the inclination to acquit is stronger may not run counter to the legal principles of culpability. For example, the *Luftsicherheitsgesetz* case is very different from that of *Dudley and Stephens*. It is more like Judith Thomson's variation of the famous trolley problem, in which a switchman diverts a runaway train from a track to which five people are tied to one on which one person is trapped, there being no other options.[16] As in the German case, the actor is not himself threatened but observes an impending disaster and acts conscientiously to minimize the number of deaths. His act is therefore altruistic rather than directed at his own preservation. Or suppose the actor will die in any event but acts heroically to minimize deaths, as in the case of a pilot who manages to divert a plummeting airplane away from an urban area and onto a farmhouse (we can suppose he then miraculously survives to face justice). One can also easily imagine analogous duress cases. Suppose D is ordered by T to kill A under a believable threat that T will otherwise detonate a bomb likely to kill hundreds, but not D. Do such situations place the killers outside the rationale for, and legitimating conditions of, judicial punishment?

At first sight, it may seem odd to say that someone acting to minimize the cost in lives of an inevitable catastrophe is in the same position with respect to criminal desert as someone who, to save himself, takes innocent life. Yet a moment's reflection will reveal that this is indeed the case. As the German Court's decision makes clear, anyone who shoots down a commercial airplane to save lives knowingly sends innocent passengers and crew members to their deaths to satisfy the interests of others. He thus makes a choice to which a denial of rights of agency may be imputed. And because agency is distinct from the sensible matter that is alone amenable to quantification, it makes no difference that the innocents will die shortly anyway. What then could be the basis for exculpation?

The only plausible suggestion is that the defendant (say, a military pilot) acted out of a moral duty to save as many lives as possible. In this situation, however, the moral duty to minimize deaths conflicts with the public, legal order of rights proscribing the subordination of some to others' ends. We know this conflict exists, because, if the passengers could prevent their being shot down by firing at the military pilot, they would have a self-defensive right to do so; they would have no coercive duty to allow themselves to be sacrificed for the numerically greater lives of others. Since, however, the moral duty on the military pilot conflicts with the public order of rights, it obligates him, if at all, as a private individual concerned with his own moral excellence, his own self-perfection or flourishing as a

---

[16] Judith Jarvis Thomson, 'The Trolley Problem,' (1985) 94 *Yale Law Journal* 1395. See also Philippa Foot, *Virtues and Vices and Other Essays in Moral Philosophy* (Oxford: Oxford University Press, 2002), 23.

human being.[17] Yet to raise the inward self's moral excellence above the public order of rights is to claim a permission to pursue one's private good in a manner inconsistent with the order of equal freedom secured by law—the very thing that criminals do. Even if the moral duty were characterized as a duty to advance an impersonal principle (such as the greatest overall good) indifferent to one's good, the pilot would still be elevating a private opinion about what duty requires above the public order of equal rights and their correlative duties not to sacrifice some to others; and that would be to arrogate to oneself a power over life and death just as all murderers do. Since, however, the moral necessity the defendant pleads shades into the principle of crime, it can hardly count as an exculpatory reason. If we nonetheless think that exoneration in these cases is in order, do we not admit the bankruptcy of the legal conception of guilt and exculpation?

I shall argue that we do not. It is true that, if situations of nonjustificatory necessity and duress exonerate from punishment, they do so despite the presence of all the conditions of criminal desert identified by the legal conception of culpability. This is why we must distinguish between exculpation and excuse; and it is why there cannot be a unitary theory of complete defences in which exculpation and exonerating excuse are blended.[18] It does not follow, however, that there can be no unified theory of defences. That exculpation and exonerating excuse are differently explained leaves open the prospect of a theory of excuse by which exonerating excuse is reconciled with the legal conception of culpability and thereby harmonized with the exculpatory defences. The burden of the rest of this chapter is to show the possibility of such an account. The immediate question for discussion is: given that neither compulsion by circumstances nor compulsion by human threats removes either the legitimacy of, or the reason for, punishing, how can its exonerating force be harmonized with the principles of culpability? More simply, how can exonerating the culpable be rendered compatible with the state's general duty to punish the culpable? Since entrapment belongs to a class of excuse (of which officially-induced error and due diligence are the other members) distinct from the dyad of necessity and duress and requiring a separate account, I'll leave it for section 5.

3. Why Should Excusing Necessity and Duress Exonerate?

I shall begin by considering and rejecting some possibilities for reconciling exculpation and exonerating excuse. In general there are two types of unsatisfactory solution, though not all extant theories fall neatly into one category or the other.

---

[17] Tatjana Hörnle characterizes the duty as a "weak duty of general solidarity... towards fellow human beings in distress..." See 'Hijacked Airplanes: May They Be Shot Down?' (2007) 10 *New Criminal Law Review* 582, 594. Put that way, the duty could hardly (as she sees) justify killing other human beings in distress.

[18] So Horder errs when he says that I wish to extend the theory of exculpatory mistake "to almost all existing excuses, even when they involve deliberate wrongdoing..." Jeremy Horder, *Excusing Crime* (Oxford: Oxford University Press, 2004), 64, n.66.

On the one hand, we have theories of excuse that reconcile exculpatory and excusing defences by denying their difference—that is, by blending them under a single explanatory idea. The character and fair-opportunity-for-choice theories of excuse belong in this category, but since I dealt with these in Chapter 2, I'll say no more about them here. Bentham's idea of conditions rendering punishment inefficacious as a deterrent is another homogenizing theory, but since this idea has been well criticized by others, I'll consider its force spent.[19] Instead I'll focus on two examples of this type propounded, respectively, by George Fletcher and John Gardner: the "moral involuntariness" theory of excuse and the "conformity-with-human-moral-potential" account.[20] On the other hand, we have theories of excuse that respect the difference between exculpation and excuse but not the difference between an exonerating excuse and a partial one calling for mitigation of sentence. Into this category falls the "concession-to-human-frailty" thesis favoured by courts.[21] Finally, we have Kant's theory of necessity, which is *sui generis* and inadequate for reasons peculiar to it.

Moral involuntariness

In *Rethinking Criminal Law,* George Fletcher proposed that excusing conditions exonerate to the extent that they render otherwise culpable wrongs involuntary in the sense that they cannot be regarded as expressions of the actor's free choice.[22] Of course, the defendant acted voluntarily in the usual sense that his bodily motion was consciously willed. "Normatively", however, the action was involuntary, because, committed under coercion or under extraordinary pressure of circumstances, it was not freely chosen by the actor and so is not justly attributable to him. In *Perka v The Queen,* the Supreme Court of Canada adopted this theory:[23]

The lost Alpinist who on the point of freezing to death breaks open an isolated mountain cabin is not literally behaving in an involuntary fashion. He has control over his actions to the extent of being physically capable of abstaining from the act. Realistically, however, his act is not a "voluntary" one. His "choice" to break the law is no true choice at all; it is remorselessly compelled by normal human instincts. This sort of involuntariness is often described as "moral or normative involuntariness".

We can see that the moral involuntariness account seeks to integrate exonerating excuse with exculpation through an analogy between severely constrained choice and inoperative capacity for choice. If the involuntariness produced by unconsciousness or physical force exonerates by negating the capacity for choice, involuntariness in the normative sense exonerates by removing the possibility of choosing autonomously. In either case, according to the argument, the legal

---

[19] See Hart, *Punishment and Responsibility,* 18–21.
[20] Fletcher, *Rethinking Criminal Law,* 802–7; Gardner, *Offences and Defences,* 121–39.
[21] For example, *Perka v The Queen* [1984] 2 SCR 232.   [22] pp. 802–7.
[23] Note 21 above, at 249, *per* Dickson, J. See also *Ruzic,* which extended this reasoning to the defence of duress.

judgment is the same: the action is not imputable to the defendant's agency.[24] If this is the correct understanding of exonerating excuse, then the altruistic murderer will rarely be able to tell an excusing story, for he is more likely to have killed regretfully from principle than compulsively from instinct.

But is nonimputability the correct basis of excuse? If so, the moral involuntariness theory integrates exonerating excuse with exculpation by assimilating the reason for excuse to a reason for exculpation: the absence of free choice or basic responsibility. The capacity to choose freely is, after all, the precondition for choosing culpably. The moral involuntariness theory thus obliterates the distinction between excuse and exculpation, for if necessity and duress really negate the action's imputability to the actor, the defendant deserves exculpation; he has no need of excuse. Indeed, "excusing" him does him an expressive injustice, for it implies his culpability for wrong. Accordingly, the moral involuntariness theory fails to account for the specificity of exonerating *excuse*. Relatedly, it fails to account for the status of exonerating excuses in positive law as affirmative defences presupposing the elements of a culpable wrong.[25]

It may be objected that the positive law is mistaken to regard necessity and duress as affirmative defences—that the mismatch between the moral involuntariness theory and the law reflects badly on the law rather than on the theory. This is possible. But the theory's problems run deeper than the issue of fit. The deeper problem concerns the analogy between narrowly constrained choice and inoperative capacity for choice.

Consider the case in which someone kills an innocent victim as the only alternative to dying himself. Here the moral involuntariness theory gains plausibility from the fact that the defendant's choice, as Aristotle pointed out, is in one sense free and in another sense unfree.[26] It is free in the purely formal sense that the agent's capacity for undetermined choice—for doing otherwise than he did—is present and unimpaired. No doubt the pressure of the instinct to survive was, given the immediacy of the peril, exceedingly powerful—much more powerful than the appetites human beings are ordinarily called upon to control. However, we must dismiss as rhetorical exaggeration Justice Brian Dickson's remark (quoted above) that self-preserving actions performed under necessity are "remorselessly compelled by normal human instincts"—that inordinately pressing instincts can negate the formal capacity for free choice; for inasmuch as this capacity consists precisely in choice's freedom from determination by instinct, quantitative considerations are beside the point. The will cannot literally be compelled by powerful desire unless it is compelled by desire simply, in which case we are committed to a

---

[24] See Martha Shaffer, 'Scrutinizing Duress: The Constitutional Validity of Section 17 of the Criminal Code,' (1998) 40 *Criminal Law Quarterly* 444.

[25] An ironic result for Fletcher, given his efforts to keep separate the elements of offence and defence; see *Rethinking Criminal Law*, 552–5.

[26] *Nicomachean Ethics*, 1110a in R. McKeon ed., *The Basic Works of Aristotle* (New York: Random House, 1941).

philosophical determinism with which the institution of punishment (as distinct from threat management) is obviously incompatible.

On the other hand, the defendant's choice was doubtless unfree relative to a more robust sense of freedom. According to this conception, freedom requires not only that the agent have the capacity for free choice, but also that the potential for acting from self-authored ends inherent in the capacity be fulfilled in the capacity's exercise—that, in other words, the capacity be exercised in the deliberative choice and achievement of a valued end. This is, of course, freedom in the sense of real autonomy. Whereas the opposite of freedom in the formal sense is determinism, the opposite of freedom in the robust sense is heteronomy—the free choice of ends given externally rather than self-originated. Now, in situations of necessity and duress, the actor acts unfreely measured by the conception of freedom as autonomy, for neither of the options available to him are ones he would choose if he could choose what he values. Those options—kill or be killed—are externally imposed by circumstances beyond his control, and he detests both. Thus, while he exercises his capacity for free choice, the potential for autonomy borne by the capacity is frustrated rather than realized in the capacity's exercise.

The question, however, is whether the absence of autonomy precludes the attribution of act to actor in the way that the absence of the capacity for free choice does. There are good reasons to think that it does not. First, autonomy is a moral achievement. Acting from reflectively endorsed ends rather than from those given by impulse, social opinion, unconscious drives, etc. is not something that comes with personhood, though the potential does. Thus, if we were to say that heteronomy precludes attribution, we would have to say that those who act in ways incompatible with others' rights because they act on impulse or to gratify strong physical appetites cannot be held responsible for their actions. I trust no one will say this. The formal capacity for choice is sufficient for attribution, because it signifies that the agent's will is causal—that *it* chooses the end it acts on even if the end it chooses is given by biology independently of reflection. Whether the agent chooses to act from ends given to it or acts from self-authored ends, it is the chooser. Indeed, we can say that it itself chooses whether to act impulsively or deliberatively.

Further, it is doubtful whether autonomy is really the sense of freedom relevant to criminal desert in the positive law. None of the exculpatory defences operate by negating the possibility of an agent's fulfilling its potential for acting from self-authored ends. Involuntariness in the usual sense negates the capacity for choice as such, either because the will is asleep or because it is moved by an external physical force. Mistake of fact, legal insanity, and colour of right negate the culpability of a *particular* choice, which may or may not have been an autonomous choice (the agent who by nonreckless mistake kills a man having autonomously chosen to hunt and shoot a deer is exculpated).[27] This is as it must be, for if the

---

[27] No doubt, the legally insane person acted heteronomously, but this is not why he is exculpated (though it is why he can be detained though innocent; see Chapter 9). He is exculpated

gist of criminal wrongdoing is that the wrongdoer impliedly claims a right to a liberty inconsistent with equal rights under law, then it is completed by a choice to which an actor's challenge to law's authority may be imputed, whether or not that choice is made approvingly or reluctantly. Criminal wrongdoing does not require that the particular choice be endorsed by the agent, because whether the object of choice is desired or resignedly accepted as a necessary means of satisfying an aversion, the implication is the same: the law is subordinated to the primacy of the agent who is the subject of desire and aversion.

Accordingly, criminal law cannot coherently admit as a ground of exculpation the fact that a choice was heteronomous. Nor, therefore, can constitutional law shield an individual from the state's general duty to punish the culpable on the basis that his choice to break the law was "morally involuntary".[28] To be sure, this gap between heteronomous choice and exculpatory reason might leave space for exonerating excuse, if only exoneration because of heteronomous choice could be coherently integrated with the gist of exculpation and so rendered compatible with the state's general duty to punish the guilty. But it cannot be, as the following example shows.

Suppose that, owing to the combined circumstances of his birth, upbringing, natural endowments, and a depressed economy, Clyde is faced with a choice of either receiving social assistance or embarking on a criminal career. No other alternative to starvation is available. Clyde regards neither of these options as desirable but despises a life of crime less than the humiliation he would feel in going on welfare. He therefore chooses crime. With respect solely to whether Clyde's choice is morally involuntary, this situation seems structurally identical to that in which someone must either take innocent life or die. In both scenarios, neither of the available options is valued or self-endorsed; neither would be chosen by the agent if he could choose an object of desire. Inasmuch as Clyde can choose only between evils imposed on him by circumstances, his choice of crime is morally involuntary.

Now, granted Clyde's obvious culpability, were he nonetheless excused because of moral involuntariness, he would be excused incompatibly with the state's duty to punish the culpable; for nothing in his explanation addresses the criteria of culpability or brings him within the spirit, if not the letter, of exculpatory reasons. Clyde chose crime as a means of satisfying an aversion. He thus implicitly claimed a permission inconsistent with rights under law and with the authority of the public legal order. To excuse him would be to *ratify* his claim of permission and the denial of law's authority it implies. So, not only is moral involuntariness unassimilable to the reason for exculpation; its excusing force is discordant with the rule of law.

Furthermore, the foregoing example shows that moral involuntariness cannot be the reason for exonerating in a true case of necessity or duress either. If the person

because (and to the extent that), given his mistaken beliefs, no right denial can be imputed to his choice.

[28] Though the Supreme Court of Canada did so; see *Ruzic*, note 8 above.

who kills under threat of death is excused but the person who steals rather than accept social assistance is not, it cannot be because the action of the first is morally involuntary while that of the second is morally voluntary. Both choices are heteronomous—partly free and partly unfree. If one is excused and the other is not, it can only be because we expect Clyde to overcome his aversion to social assistance in this case, whereas we regard with understanding the killer's failure to overcome his aversion to death. The choice he made was one that a person of ordinary or reasonable fortitude would likewise have made (for now I leave the standard ambiguous).

However, this places excusing necessity and duress on a theoretical footing entirely different from that of moral involuntariness. Whereas the latter denies "real" imputability, the law of necessity and duress concedes imputability and measures the defendant's action against a standard of moral strength we can fairly expect him to have met: in choosing culpably, the defendant did not display less fortitude than we can fairly demand of him in his situation.[29] Accordingly, the focus now shifts from the legal culpability of the defendant's external choice to the moral merit of the inward disposition manifested in the choice. Legally speaking, the defendant acted culpably; nevertheless, the political community of which the law is a part ought not to punish him, because it cannot expect him to have shown more self-forgetfulness than can realistically or reasonably be demanded of beings who are not only interchangeable agents but also determinate characters with names.

Of course, we still need to specify the appropriate meaning of "realistically" and "reasonably". Does "realistically or reasonably" imply a standard of ordinary or mediocre courage involving a concession to typical human frailty? Or does this phrase imply an ideal of courage of which human nature is capable—a standard above what most people achieve but below angelic purity? Still, we can already see that, by distinguishing between culpability before the law and punishability by the political community, this account will succeed in keeping exculpation and excuse distinct. The question, however, is whether, by revealing a good reason for exoneration despite culpability, this account subverts the legal conception of culpability or whether it can be integrated with that conception.

Excuse as concession to human frailty

One version of the plea that "I displayed no less fortitude than can fairly have been expected of me in the circumstances" is: "I exhibited a weakness of will to which a person of ordinary fortitude would likewise have succumbed." In *Perka*, Justice Dickson put the argument this way:[30]

---

[29] This is the theory of excuse on which the Model Penal Code rests the defence of duress; see s. 2.09.
[30] *Perka*, p. 248. See also *R v Baker and Wilkins* [1997] Crim LR 497 at 497–8. This is also the gist of Tatting's judgment in L Fuller, 'The Case of the Speluncean Explorers,' (1949) 62 *Harvard Law Review* 616, 626.

[The defence of necessity] rests on a realistic assessment of human weakness, recognizing that a liberal and humane criminal law cannot hold people to the strict obedience of laws in emergency situations where normal human instincts, whether of self-preservation or of altruism, overwhelmingly impel disobedience... Praise is indeed not bestowed, but pardon is, when one does a wrongful act under pressure which, in the words of Aristotle... "overstrains human nature and which no one could withstand".

I'll call this the "concession-to-human-frailty" or "compassion" account of excusing necessity and duress. On this account, to excuse a culpable wrong committed under threat of death or serious harm to oneself is to bestow humane compassion ("pardon") on someone who only exhibited a weakness that we—judge and jury—might also have displayed in the same situation.

If the compassion theory is the correct account of excusing necessity, then the altruistic murderer is once again bereft of excuse. Someone who kills as the only alternative to dying himself might be thought to exhibit an understandable weakness evoking compassion; but what of the head of government who, upon solemn reflection, orders the shooting down of a civil airplane transformed by hijackers into a bomb and about to kill thousands? It seems wrong to judge his act as exhibiting weakness of will—quite the contrary, we are more likely to admire his moral strength rather than condescend to his frailty.

Yet the compassion theory too must be rejected. First, it fails to explain why duress and necessity should exonerate from punishment rather than provide a reason for mitigating sentence. That the defendant exhibited an understandable *weakness* is, after all, no reason to acquit a culpable agent, though it is perhaps a reason for tempering the severity of punishment and, where sentencing discretion is precluded, for offering a statutory mitigation to liberate discretion. Indeed, according to positive law, the defence of provocation likewise rests on an understandable failure of self-control, and yet it is only a partial excuse reducing murder to manslaughter. So, the concession-to-frailty account elides the difference between exonerating and mitigating excuse. It also fails to provide an exonerating reason suitable for a court as distinct from one appropriate for the executive in exercising its prerogative power of clemency. If, as Justice Dickson argued, pardon is the appropriate response to crimes committed through understandable weakness of will in the face of overpowering instinctual pressures, then surely it is for the head of state to set justice aside, not the court.

Furthermore, the concession-to-frailty account exonerates for a reason that is incompatible with the state's duty to realize public reason by punishing the culpable. Its reason is that we (judge and jury) have no standing to convict because, placed in the same situation, we might have exhibited the same moral weakness and done the same thing.[31] This reason bears a resemblance of sorts to a true exculpatory reason, in that it signifies that the defendant, though he transgressed a boundary, did not set himself apart from the public community. Just as the

---

[31] Sanford Kadish, 'Excusing Crime,' (1987) 75 *California Law Review* 257, 273.

noncriminal tortfeasor believes he is acting within the order of rights and so does not set himself against it, so does the wrongdoer who gives in to extraordinary instinctual pressure act within the custom of humanity (or way of the world).[32]

Yet the resemblance is obviously superficial. The custom of humanity may or may not coincide with the standard of public reason; and so to judge the defendant by the former standard is to deny practical authority to the latter. Accordingly, if someone were charged with speeding, no one would think it a good reason to bar conviction that everyone, including the judge, is frequently guilty of the same offence. No doubt, the judge might feel a twinge of hypocrisy in convicting, but his inner integrity is maintained so long as he is ready to accept the same penalty he imposes on the convict.[33] Besides, the judge enrobed is distinct from the man wearing the robe. As "animate justice", his individuality is nothing but a conduit of law's judgment; it is no longer regarded as the immediate or natural individuality of Brian, Antonin, etc. (hence it is not unbecoming a free man to call him "Your Honour", "My Lord").[34] Thus, barring corruptibility (including susceptibility to blackmail) or bias that might disqualify him or her from that honourable role, the private individual's inner failings do not touch the judge's standing to convict; and the same may be said for a jury member screened for bias and sworn to duty.

Excuse as conformity with human moral potential

Another version of the plea that I exhibited the fortitude that could fairly have been expected of me is that, though I acted culpably according to the legal conception of culpability (I made a right-denying choice), I nonetheless acted blamelessly or even virtuously in the moral sense; for I demonstrated no less righteousness or courage than the appropriately righteous or courageous man would have displayed. Forbearing to kill some in order to save thousands more would have shown a fanatical adherence to justice in the face of untold suffering that the righteousness of the character of practical wisdom (that is, the character who demonstrates complete virtue) does not demand; while forbearing to kill to save myself or a loved one would have called for an angelic impartiality as between one's own and a stranger's interest that moral courage does not demand. For lack of a better expression, I'll call this the "conformity-with-human-moral-potential theory of excuse".[35] According

---

[32] Or "common run of humankind" as Kadish says: ibid, 266.
[33] Joshua Dressler, 'Exegesis of the Law of Duress: Justifying the Excuse and Searching for its Proper Limits,' (1989) 62 *Southern California Law Review* 1331, 1369.
[34] Aristotle, *Nicomachean Ethics*, 1132a, note 26 above, 1009.
[35] Thus John Gardner writes; "The gist of an excuse...is precisely that the person with the excuse lived up to our expectations...Did she manifest as much resilience, or loyalty, or thoroughness, or presence of mind as a person in her situation could properly be asked to show? The character standards which are relevant...are not the standards of our own characters, nor even the standards of most people's characters, but rather the standards to which our characters should, minimally, conform." *Offences and Defences,* 124. Other adherents are: Horder, *Excusing Crime*, 104; Kadish, 'Excusing Crime.'

to this theory, "realistic or reasonable" fortitude means the fortitude that beings composed of both body and rational agency can be expected to possess. Though in the passage from *Perka* quoted above, Justice Dickson invokes Aristotle in support of the compassion theory, it is the conformity-with-human-moral-potential theory that is truly Aristotelian; for the "human nature" that a duty of selflessness would have "overstrained" is human nature in the sense of human moral possibility.

The conformity-with-human-moral-potential theory is free of most of the difficulties afflicting the compassion theory. It can apply to altruistic as well as self-preferring criminal conduct, for the reluctant, altruistic murderer may have acted with the intelligent righteousness of the character of practical wisdom, while the reluctant, self-preferring one may be said to have displayed no less courage than would have been shown by the ideally courageous character, from whom selflessness is not expected. The theory also provides a reason for exonerating rather than simply for mitigating; for inasmuch as the character who conforms to human moral potential is blameless, he or she ought to be freed, not punished less severely. The theory even explains why excuse is appropriate for a court rather than for the executive. If the defendant is morally blameless, he *ought* to be exonerated; there is room neither for discretion or clemency.

Yet here is a case where too much success might mean failure. This is so because the very success of the conformity-to-human-moral-potential theory on the foregoing dimensions makes it problematic as a theory of *excuse* supplementary to the legal theory of *exculpation*. As a supplement, after all, excuse as explained by virtue theory could lead to a verdict of guilty but with an absolute discharge signifying no moral stigma. But why, the moralist might protest, should the moral conception of innocence take a back seat to the legal one? Why should someone who acted virtuously or blamelessly require an excuse from culpability? The fact that moral theory explains so well a duty to exonerate someone legal thought holds culpable seems to make it a rival rather than a supplement to the legal conception of guilt and exculpation. It seems to point to a shortcoming of the legal conception (which would inculpate a morally blameless person) and promises an account of guilt and innocence that covers more of our moral experience. So the theory of excuse brought in to complete the legal conception of culpability actually threatens to subvert it.

It is no wonder, then, that some theorists have sought to extend the conformity-to-human-moral-potential theory of excuse into a general, moral-character theory of defences for which excuse is second best, not to exculpation (of which it is a form), but to justification. John Gardner is one of these theorists.[36] A defendant is exculpated, on his view, if, though he committed a wrong, he either acted for a reason that justified the wrong (in which case he was justified), or he acted unjustifiably under a mistake or from a motive that the agent of reasonable virtue in his shoes could have made or acted upon (in which case he is excused).

[36] Gardner, *Offences and Defences*, 91–120.

A main theme of this book has been that the moral conceptions of blameworthiness and blamelessness, when raised to a general theory of criminal liability and exculpation, *conflict* with most of our moral experience—at least with that significant part of our moral experience reflected in the criminal law. In particular, such a theory demotes the *actus* requirement from an essential element of culpability to a piece of relevant information about moral character (so overall good character exculpates while bad character alone inculpates if dangerous), fails to connect right-infringing judicial punishment in particular (as opposed to censure in general) to moral blameworthiness, and, contrary to agent inviolability, deprives free persons of their liberty pursuant to the discretionary and fallible judgments of other individuals as to the inward state of their souls. But on top of all this, the moral theory of defences can be criticized internally as extinguishing the category of exonerating excuse.

When made part of a general moral account of the defences, the conformity-with-human-moral-potential theory of excuse renders the idea of exonerating excuse extinct. This is so because, within a moral theory of defences generally, excuse must fight a two-front war against annexation by justification and by the partial excuses. According to Gardner, the difference between a justification and an excuse is this: the justified actor acted for what was in fact an undefeated reason to do wrong, whereas the excused actor acted for what he *justifiably* but mistakenly believed was an undefeated reason.[37] In the case of a justifiably mistaken belief in circumstances which, had they existed, would have afforded a justification (for example, putative self-defence), this view would excuse what Gardner concedes is a nonculpable wrongdoer. Why, one wonders, should this individual need an excuse? Yes, he has done wrong, but he is not blameworthy for his wrong, and this, according to Gardner, is exactly the position of the justified actor, who, he believes, is always justified in a *wrong*.

Gardner's answer is that the excusable actor has erred, albeit justifiably, in his practical reasoning; and this error constitutes a shortfall from "perfect success as a rational being".[38] And since, he argues, rational beings must strive for excellence in rationality, the shortfall is cause for regret. This may be true, but when one considers the paragon relative to whom the error represents a shortfall, the justified actor too falls short, for his success was a matter of luck rather than perfect rationality. Both excused and justified actors are, after all, rational beings limited by spatial and temporal horizons. Since the excused actor erred, not through fault, but through the same epistemic limitations faced by the justified actor, all that distinguishes the two actors is morally irrelevant luck (this is implied by the justifiability of the mistake). The justified actor was merely fortunate that the world was in fact as he reasonably thought, whereas the excused actor was merely unfortunate. But for the law to depreciate the excused actor relative to the justified one simply because he unluckily though faultlessly erred is to judge the finite human being by

---

[37] Ibid, 108–13. [38] Ibid, 272.

the standard of an infinite Being with perfect knowledge, while giving the justified actor a windfall credit. And even were it rational (as Gardner believes it is) for a rational being to aspire to an epistemic infallibility to which its human condition renders it incommensurate, still, no secular court could fairly hold a human being accountable to that standard. Accordingly, from the standpoint of human moral possibility, excuse based on putative justification merges with real justification.

On the other front, the excuses not swallowed up by justification are consumed by the category of partial excuse. Where, counterfactually, the action would have been justified in the world as reasonably but mistakenly perceived by the defendant, Gardner would "excuse" completely. Where, as in the case of provocation, the action would not have been justified even in the world seen through the defendant's justified anger, Gardner would excuse partially.[39] Where does this leave nonjustificatory necessity and duress when the actor's perceptions are correct? In a case of killing as a means of saving oneself, the action would not have been justified even in the world seen through the defendant's justified fear. This places excusing necessity and duress on all fours with provocation. Thus, on the moral theory of defences, the category of partial excuse annexes nonjustificatory necessity and duress.

So the question becomes: if the conformity-to-human-moral-potential theory of necessity and duress cannot be generalized (consistently with the freedom and equality of persons or even the stability of exonerating excuse) into a complete account of criminal liability and exculpation, can it nevertheless be coherently integrated or harmonized with the legal conception of guilt and exculpation so as to provide a *legal* theory of excuse? I shall return to this question after examining Kant's theory of necessity.

Excuse as suspension of law's threat

In Carneades's famous example, two shipwrecked sailors are swimming for a plank that will support only one of them. Sailor A wins the race, but sailor B, who will otherwise perish, wrests the plank from A, who drowns. Kant has no doubt that the surviving sailor is criminally culpable for murder; indeed, he calls it "a strange confusion" that jurists regard necessity as exculpatory of homicide, apparently unaware of the common-law tradition on this point.[40] Nevertheless, he presents an argument purporting to show why, despite his culpability, the survivor is entitled to exoneration from punishment.

The argument rests on Kant's conception of the relation between law and ethics. As Kant conceives them, the legal order and the realm of ethics are each defined by excluding what is essential to the other. While right-based duties are common to both spheres, the obligation to conform to the duty is grounded

---

[39] Ibid, 155–72.
[40] *The Metaphysics of Morals*, trans. Mary Gregor (Cambridge: Cambridge University Press, 1991), 60.

differently in each. In the sphere of ethics, the individual obeys the moral law purely for the sake of the autonomy inherent in legislating for oneself the dictates of practical reason. The moral obligation is thus the obligation to will the law disinterestedly, as an impartial judge would, divorced from all considerations of private advantage. In the legal order, by contrast, the basis of the obligation to obey the moral law concretized in positive law is the coercive threat posed by the general will's executive sword. Thus, to say there is a legal obligation to conform one's conduct to law is to say no more than that one will suffer unacceptable penal consequences if one disobeys.

Kant's point here is not simply that legal authority rests on the threat of overwhelming force only from the perspective of the bad man inclined to break the law; nor is it simply that legal norms, applying as they do only to external actions and not to inward dispositions, *need* not rely on virtue as an incentive for obedience. Kant's deeper point—or rather assumption—is that the legal order is by its nature an external power, because it is the order through which the moral law obtains effective force among persons naturally inclined to self-love—to partiality toward their own interest. Because self-love is natural, the moral law can gain effective public authority only as an external, threat-backed command that uses the fear of disadvantage to secure compliance. But this means that autonomy *must* be a matter of private virtue and not the political virtue of the self-governing citizen (Kant's legislative sovereign is not democratic and has no enforceable duty not to wrong its subjects).[41] In moral obligation, accordingly, there is no trace of external compulsion but also no trace of self-love; in legal obligation, there is abundant room for self-love but no place for autonomy.

Now if the purely legal obligation to obey the moral law concretized in positive law rests on the threat of unacceptable penal consequences for disobedience, then in the situation of the drowning sailor, there is no obligation known to positive law to forbear from violence. This is so because, in that situation, no threat of future and uncertain punishment could overwhelm the present fear of imminent and certain death; and so the law is toothless in that situation. No rationally self-interested agent in the sailor's position would be deterred by the threat of punishment. Hence, although there has doubtless been a violation of right for which punishment is deserved, no actual court can pass sentence on the accused—or as Kant puts it, "no judge can be appointed to the task".[42] As the agency through which the moral law obtains force among rationally self-interested persons, the court finds its jurisdiction circumscribed by the limit of law's power to shape incentives. In the legal order, if the moral law cannot operate by threat, it cannot operate at all.

Here we seem to have satisfied all the desiderata of an adequate account of legal excuse. True, the account will not excuse the official who, in the safety of his office, orders the shooting down of a commercial-airplane-become-lethal-missile (or any altruistic murderer); but the account might seem sound enough on other

---

[41] Ibid, 125–6.   [42] Ibid, 60.

dimensions to persuade us to accept that implication as correct.[43] We have a clear distinction between exculpation and excuse, an account of why excusing necessity should exonerate from punishment and not simply mitigate, as well as an apparent reconciliation of exonerating excuse with the principles of culpability. Kant's account of a complete legal excuse suggests no defect in the theory of culpability, for the defendant (in his view) is not legally culpable despite having acted virtuously; rather he has fallen short of moral excellence as well. The surviving sailor is not so much acquitted of murder as the state is barred from proceeding against someone on whom the positive law could have exerted no *ex ante* compulsion; or we can say that the sailor is not so much acquitted as the court proceedings against him are stayed. We will presently see that the idea of a stay of penal proceedings against a guilty person in order to preserve the legal order's essential nature does indeed underlie the other set of complete excuses mentioned at the outset of this chapter—the set of which entrapment, officially induced error, and due diligence are the members. However, the essential nature to be preserved is not the one identified by Kant.

For all its apparent virtues, Kant's theory of excusing necessity must be rejected; for it is incompatible, first, with his own idea of the moral necessity of the rule of law and second, with his own retributive theory of punishment.

Kant's account of why necessity exonerates from punishment cannot logically be confined to situations of necessity. It extends to other situations where the rationally self-interested agent in the circumstances of the prospective lawbreaker is undeterrable from crime. Let us not overstate this objection. As his defenders have argued, Kant's understanding of an impotent threat is conceptual rather than empirical.[44] An impotent threat is one that cannot shape the conduct of a typical actor, not one that could not, as it happens, shape the conduct of this particular defendant. Thus, Kant's reasoning in the necessity case does not extend to, say, the insane agent who delusionally believed he was protected by a cosmic shield against the penal consequences of an action he knew was wrong;[45] nor does it apply to the murderer who planned but then failed to commit suicide after his crime. Because the excuse is a general, legal one binding on the court rather than an individualized one going to discretionary mitigation, it must rest on objective features of a situation knowable to everyone rather than on individual idiosyncrasies; and it must presuppose an ideal actor—the rationally self-interested person—rather than gearing itself to the preferences of this or that defendant.

---

[43] Ripstein tries to extend the Kantian analysis to this kind of situation by arguing that the criminal law cannot rightfully deprive the imperilled person of his rescuer, hence cannot threaten the rescuer. This is an unsuccessful argument. If the innocents have a right against being killed to save another, the law can surely protect that right against a rescuer—or what does the right mean? See '*In Extremis*,' (2005) 2 *Ohio State Journal of Criminal Law*, 429–33.

[44] Dennis Klimchuk, 'Necessity, Deterrence, and Standing,' (2002) 8 *Legal Theory* 339; Ripstein, '*In Extremis*,' 421–2.

[45] *R v Abbey* [1982] 2 SCR 24.

So the question is whether the rationally self-interested agent placed in the *real* circumstances of the defendant would have been deterrable by the law.

In the case of the delusional or suicidal agent, the answer is "yes," and so any plea for excuse must be one for individualized mitigation. But what of the Mafia godfather whose minions have so thoroughly infiltrated law-enforcement agencies, or who has so successfully intimidated or corrupted their officials, that he is rationally undeterrable by the threat of punishment? His situation is no more particular or idiosyncratic than that of the rational agent about to drown in the sea unless he dislodges his rival for life from the plank. His real situation is, let us say, just as he perceives it to be; and that situation, like the drowning sailor's, renders the threat of punishment empty. So, having rendered himself undeterrable from crime by intimidation and bribery, the Mafia don will, on Kant's theory of excuse, be rewarded with a stay of conviction on a murder charge by the only judge he has failed to corrupt.

Obviously, something is wrong here. Moreover, something is wrong from the standpoint of Kant's own doctrine of Right. One of the postulates of that doctrine (the "postulate of public Right")[46] is that there is a duty based on the innate right of humanity to move from a lawless condition in which rights are "provisional" because hostage to private opinion to a rightful condition in which rights are actualized under the effective rule of public justice.[47] The situation of the drowning sailor resembles the state of nature (hence the saying "necessity has no law") inasmuch as, in both situations, no one can count on the other's being restrained by law, and so no one has a duty of self-restraint.[48] Accordingly, were a court within an established civil condition to stay law enforcement in a situation calling for the actualization of Right merely because the defendant was undeterrable, it would hold the rightful condition hostage to the state of nature, subordinating it thereto. It would thus also violate the "postulate of public Right", namely: "When you cannot avoid living side by side with all others, you ought to leave the state of nature and proceed with them into a rightful condition..."[49]

Kant's theory of necessity also presupposes a view of punishment inconsistent with the retributive view for which he is famous. Specifically, it assumes a Hobbesian conception of punishment as sustaining the empirical conditions—namely, universal fear of unacceptable consequences for violence—needed for everyone rationally to renounce self-help to a public authority and thus to bring a rightful condition into existence. No doubt Kant says many things in line with this view.[50] On his retributivist theory, however, punishment is necessitated by the idea of "judicial authority" under universal laws.[51] That is, it is contained in the notion of the judicially actualized authority of Right. On this view, it would make sense to punish even if no empirical advantage in sustaining an actual rightful condition were to come from it.

---

[46] *The Metaphysics of Morals*, 121. [47] Ibid, 121–2, 124. [48] Ibid, 60, 122.
[49] Ibid, 121–2. [50] Ibid, 122. [51] Ibid, 143.

Now, of course Kant is notorious for having espoused just this view. There is, he writes, a "categorical imperative" to punish a murderer, one that holds even if a society is about to disband and thus nothing of any empirical advantage can result from punishing.[52] But if there is a duty to punish a murderer even if no benefit in sustaining law's threat can be gained from it, why is the murderous sailor entitled to a stay of penal proceedings just because the law could not intimidate him when he acted? After all, if any crime is committed, specific deterrence has failed; the *ex ante* threat did not work. If there is nonetheless a duty to punish, and if this duty would hold even if no advantage in sustaining deterrability could come from it, then the purpose of punishment can only be to actualize the Right. But this purpose would be served even in the case of the undeterrable sailor. And if, as Kant says, retributive punishment inheres in the idea of judicial authority under universal laws, then surely a judge can be appointed to carry out the assignment. Accordingly, if punishment is retributive, undeterrability (even conceptual undeterrability) is no excuse.

4. Excuse as Moral Analogue of Legal Exculpation

Let us now return to the suggestion I offered earlier—that the idea of moral blamelessness might be integrated with the legal conception of exculpation so as to provide a legal theory of excuse resulting in acquittal. Without such an integration, there is no reason why the defendant's blamelessness could not be reflected in a mandatory absolute discharge following a guilty verdict. After all, if there can be moral stigma without criminal wrongdoing (as in the case of the slothful or self-indulgent character), why could there not be criminal wrongdoing without moral stigma? Integrating moral blamelessness with legal exculpation requires three steps: first, it requires showing why the legal theory of culpability leaves room for nonexculpatory but fully exonerating excuse; second, it requires showing how excuse is sufficiently *like* exculpation to be compatible with the state's duty to punish the guilty; third, it requires explaining why admitting morality within the sphere of excuse is consistent with the reasons for excluding it from the rest of the general part.

Nonmoral culpability and moral innocence

Step one requires a reprise of the remarks made in the concluding section of Chapter 4. There I argued that the criteria of criminal culpability as well as for distinguishing grades of responsibility for harm are necessarily impersonal and nonmoral. They are impersonal in the sense that they refer to the individual as an abstract agent rather than as an individuated character; they are nonmoral in the sense that they refer to external actions rather than to the inward self. As a

---

[52] Ibid, 141.

consequence, the criteria of legal culpability are detached from the standards (of self-control, uprightness, courage, etc.) by which we judge the virtue of full moral characters in everyday life as well as in literature and drama. They are *necessarily* impersonal and nonmoral, I argued, because judgments of culpability and responsibility leading to deprivations of liberty are consistent with the freedom and inviolability of the person only if they can be conceived as self-imposable by all agents whatever their opinions about what makes conduct more or less wicked or whatever their opinions about other people's views of their moral character. And this means that the agents whose assent to punishment alone matters are those stripped of all qualities but those they necessarily share as agents, namely, their capacity for free choice and their potential for real autonomy. The thinking Agent who represented empirical agents before the ideal court of criminal justice and whose willing or nonwilling of punishment was imputed to them in actual court personified that abstraction.

However, I also argued that, though nonmoral criteria of culpability and responsibility are essential to a punishment consistent with freedom, their very abstractness renders them partial or incomplete as criteria for deserving punishment in all cases. Because they focus exclusively on external choice and ignore the full moral character, they will sometimes provide an incomplete picture of how empirical defendants ought to be ethically judged for what they have done. And this, as we have seen, creates the possibility of a defendant who is at once legally culpable (deserving of punishment) and morally blameless.

So the nonmoral theory of culpability advanced in Chapters 1 to 4 explains why there can be a category of nonexculpatory but fully exonerating excuse. Because the legal conception of culpability is a partial conception of ethical desert, it requires supplementing from the moral viewpoint it has excluded in order to avoid inequity in the cases that reveal its one-sidedness. That is to say, it requires the concept of an exonerating excuse despite culpability and so distinct from exculpation. Yet this supplementing will complete the legal conception of desert rather than subvert it only if it can be rendered coherent with that conception. So let us now consider how this might be possible.

Excuse appeals from the legal norm to the political community

According to the legal conception of culpability, an empirical agent deserves judicial punishment if and only if a denial of equal agency rights can be imputed to its actual choice. By this denial, the agent lays claim to a liberty in respect of all other agents in excess of that which free others could recognize as valid. It thus sets itself against, and so apart from, the common will—that is, against the public framework of valid claims to respect for the liberty of abstract agents. And it is only this implicit self-separation that justifies the punishment that casts the agent out explicitly; for it signifies its assent to that moral fate. If, despite his transgression, the wrongdoer acted under a mistaken belief within which his choice was to respect free agency, then he is exculpated of crime; for his action implied no denial of rights, hence no surrender of the right to complain of a violation of his.

Now in the case of murder by necessity (or under duress), the agent satisfies the legal conception of self-separation from the common will without, however, deviating from the public standard by which whole human beings—agents individuated as living characters—are judged by their actions as righteous or unrighteous, courageous or cowardly by their co-participants in a political community sufficient for *all* dignitary needs. The idea of a political community sufficient for dignity connects with the juridical idea of excuse in the following way.

If a political society ordered to mutual respect for free choice and mutual concern for real autonomy were sufficient for human dignity, no room would exist for fully exonerating excuse, for there would be no public reason beyond the common will and the public welfare to which the intentional transgressor lacking justification could appeal as of right; all excuse would be a matter of discretionary mitigation or clemency. However, these frameworks are insufficient for all dignitary needs, for while they actualize the metaphysical worth of the abstract agent, they do not recognize the moral worth of the concrete character—of that unique organization of aims, values, loyalties, talents, dispositions, habits, and roles that bears a proper name. Invisible to these frameworks, characters are recognized and valued in families, cultural and religious groups, collegial associations, and in the political communities (through public honours) that incorporate these associations together with the justice and welfare systems. Political societies dedicated solely to realizing the metaphysical worth of abstract agents, taking no interest in civil associations, presuppose morally self-sufficient persons who treat political authority as a means to the protection of their pre-political dignity. By contrast, political communities devoted to satisfying the whole man or woman—the character in whom agency is individuated not less than the agent—are ends for the individual because they reciprocally take the full satisfaction of dignitary needs as their end.

Now because the political community so understood is the community sufficient for dignity, it embodies a public reason more comprehensive than that of the common will and the public welfare, whose institutional ministries form parts of that larger whole. It is therefore possible for an action unjustifiably to violate the public reason uniting abstract agents without denying the authority of the comprehensive public reason of the self-sufficient community. This is so, moreover, both in the case of self-preferential murder and in that of altruistic murder, as we shall now see.

In the case of self-preferential murder by necessity, the legal conception of desert holds the individual culpable because it requires him (in this case) to be impartial as between his life and that of another agent when both cannot live, forbidding him from treating his life as having more importance than that of another agent equal in dignity to himself. That is, the law does not merely require him, as it does in the usual case (where law can threaten), to act *in accordance with* the principle that their lives are equally important, never mind his motivation. In this case (where law cannot threaten), the law requires him to act forgetfully of self-interest and in light of the impartial standpoint, just as if he were a disinterested judge observing his dilemma from a perch outside it. Here we see the grain of truth in Kant's analysis of necessity. Because the drowning sailor is not compellable by the threat of punishment, his forbearance from (attempted) homicide could issue only from such a self-transcending impartiality.

From the moral point of view, however, this self-transcendence requires an angelic selflessness that, however godlike if shown, is not demanded of embodied agents with proper names; for inasmuch as the good is understood as the good life of the whole human being, the individual is permitted to care for his or her life for the sake of the good life and to prefer it over a stranger's in a conflict.[53] Moreover, if, as Aristotle and Hegel taught, the good life is possible only within a political community embracing subordinate communities and sufficient for all dignitary needs, then at least some virtues of the exemplary human being (for example, rectitude, courage, self-control, self-respect, civic-mindedness) are political virtues, not simply interior, motivational ones. They are the virtues of someone who excels in the familial, economic, and citizenship roles constitutive of the life sufficient for dignity; and so their outward signs in dutiful actions, whether other- or self-regarding, merit formal public recognition. Accordingly, if (giving him the benefit of the doubt) the murdering sailor preferred his life over a stranger's for the sake of the good life and not merely for the sake of biological life, then he did not fall below the public standard by which embodied agents bearing names are judged courageous or cowardly by their fellow citizens. He showed no less fortitude or self-restraint than the character of reasonable firmness and self-love would have shown.

The same conclusion follows from Kantian no less than from Aristotelian ethics. Whereas the Aristotelian standard of virtue is the moral possibilities of the *zoon logikon*, the Kantian standard is the moral possibilities of *homo noumenon*. From the standpoint of *homo noumenon*, the sailor's disinterested forbearing from attempted homicide would have been praiseworthy; for if nonmoral adherence to law (that is, adherence from fear of punishment) is morally neutral, deserving neither credit nor blame, then moral adherence (adherence for the sake of the law) is praiseworthy. But since adherence to law in the necessity situation must be praiseworthy moral adherence (the agent being undeterrable by the threat of punishment), it follows that nonadherence to law in this situation is morally neutral; it deserves neither praise nor blame. And this means that the self-preferential murderer in the necessity situation has not deviated from the public standard of acceptable ethical conduct.[54] From the standpoint of the best embodied agent,

---

[53] St Thomas Aquinas, *Summa Theologica,* trans. Fathers of the English Dominican Province (New York: Benziger, 1947), 2–2, Q 64, A 7. Cf. Horder, *Excusing Crime,* 60. Since self-preference is here permissible rather than praiseworthy, no contradiction between moral and legal judgment arises.

[54] See Klimchuk, 'Necessity, Deterrence, and Standing.' However, if he foreseeably put himself into a position (for example, by joining a criminal gang) where he might be coerced into crime, then he is morally blameworthy for his subsequent act under necessity or duress and so loses the excuse. He is then culpable for his intentional act, not for his negligence.

258   *Excuse*

his action was morally permissible; from the standpoint of *homo noumenon*, his action was morally indifferent.

Let us now consider the case of altruistic murder by necessity. Here we must distinguish between the private agent—for example, a pilot who shoots down the civil airplane/missile on his own initiative—and the statesman. Law requires the pilot to act as the agent impartial toward persons would act; and this agent would neither count the numbers (for, as no person experiences welfare in the aggregate, the greater welfare is just the particular welfare of discrete others, of no more importance than the welfare of the one sacrificed), nor measure the duration of lives cut short (for each person is considered only as an agent). Bracketing calculations of human suffering and suppressing compassion as a motive for action, he would let the airliner run its deadly course.

However, morality considers justice in the sense of treating equals equally as only one of several virtues comprising complete virtue.[55] It regards appropriate compassion also as a virtue—call it the mean with respect to the emotion of pity between callousness and sentimentality; and so it requires the whole human being to balance within itself the virtue of justice as equal respect for abstract agents with the virtue of compassion for the suffering of determinate individuals. Moreover, morality requires the individual to achieve this balance while avoiding the *hubris* of deciding life and death according to a free discretion unconstrained by natural fate; for it is unbecoming a finite human being to assume a divine power of life and death over its equals. Thus, hastening an already imminent doom is morally different from redistributing a malign fate from some to others. And whereas (because of its focus on external choice) law can make no distinction between purposely producing an outcome and foreseeing it as a certain but regrettable side-effect of one's action, morality attaches great importance to this nuance as reflecting different degrees of self-identification with the outcome. Accordingly, though it is, as Aristotle says, "difficult sometimes to determine what should be chosen at what cost",[56] the pilot might reasonably conclude (though he is not morally obliged to do so) that, all things considered, the action most becoming a human being would be to bring about a quick and painless death to those whom fate has determined will presently die in order to avoid untold suffering for many others, provided that their death is a regretted side-effect of defending others against a wrongful attack.[57]

---

[55] *Nicomachean Ethics*, 1131a.   [56] Ibid, 1110a.

[57] Observe that this principle will not excuse the surgeon who kills one person in order to distribute his organs to several others, because it is unbecoming a human being to assume the role of lord over life and death by redistributing natural threats according to his free discretion. In the airliner case, the defendant does not decide who will live and who will die independently of natural fate's decree. The passengers' deaths are imminent, and he *defends* many lives against a threat of which the passengers are part rather than freely choosing the beneficiaries of someone's death. In Thomson's version of the trolley problem, the detached switchman redirects a malign fate from many to one just as the surgeon does; his action too is an assumption of the power of life and death over the universe unbefitting a finite human being. In the plummeting airplane case (and in the

Of course, we can see the havoc the moral view would play with the public order of rights if the criterion of what is "most becoming a human being" were generalized into a comprehensive theory of justification. Rights would be at the disposal of everyone's moral virtuosity. Law can accept the exonerating force of virtue only on terms consistent with the reality of rights—which is to say, only as an excuse for the guilty. Indeed, as a theory of justification (hence exculpation), morality is inconsistent even with itself. This is so because, when asserting itself as a justification for wrongdoing, morality shades into evil, for it makes the individual moral conscience the lord of right and wrong, of who shall justly live and who shall justly die. Confined, however, to the peripheral role of excuse, morality supplements without subverting the legal conception of criminal desert; while, in preserving the authority of the legal norm, it also preserves its own nature.

For the statesman, too, justice as respect for equal agency is part of the complete virtue of practical wisdom, which, Aristotle says, is the capacity to deliberate well about what conduces to the good life in general.[58] In its liberal interpretation, the good life in general is the life sufficient for dignity; and the political community is the human association directed toward all constituents of the dignified life, of which the administration of justice enforcing respect for formal agency is but one. If this community were threatened with destruction, the statesman could validly claim a justification for intentionally violating agency rights were this necessary to save the polity, because the political community is the logically prior condition for there being fully realized rights at all. Since, however, we are assuming a threat short of that magnitude, the logic of justification, by which rights are overridden for their own sake, is not available.

Nevertheless, the ethics of excuse is. Inasmuch as the political community is the self-sufficient community—the community lacking in nothing of what is required for a dignified life—the statesman might reasonably conclude (though he is not obliged to) that the dignified life as a whole would be best served by preventing an attack on the state even at the cost of innocent lives, provided that the killing were a regretted side-effect of pursuing this end and so removed from his identity. Though not necessary for the state's preservation, such an action might nonetheless display wise judgment in weighing the harm avoided to the polity against the harm inflicted on innocents whose death is, in any case, imminent. So, while the statesman here opposes the common will (legal norm), he may do so without opposing the community sufficient for dignity, of which the legal norm and its realization are a part. In that case, he does not deny the authority of the legal norm outright; he denies its indefeasible authority (though without the justifying necessity that defeats it), while recognizing the comprehensive public reason of the self-sufficient

---

original trolley problem), fate has already decreed that *either* these many *or* these few will die, and so here the choice of the lesser evil is virtuous because it operates within the limits of natural fate rather than presuming to redistribute its impact.

[58] *Nicomachean Ethics*, 1140a.

The parameters of valid excuse

The account of legal excuse as the moral analogue of legal exculpation determines the contours of a valid claim to exonerating excuse. In contrast to the case of justificatory necessity, where the necessitous situation must really exist and the unknowingly justified private actor is legally justified, the conditions of excusing necessity are satisfied if and only if the defendant reasonably believed in the existence of a threat to life leaving no alternative but murder. He must believe the emergency existed, for if he killed believing that killing was unnecessary to save his or others' lives, there is no virtue in his action to excuse his crime even if killing *was* the only alternative to his or others' dying. But he must also reasonably believe in the emergency, for otherwise his action failed to display the self-composure and prudence that would have made his action blameless and his condition an analogue of legal exculpation. If he acted rashly or in panic, then his action might have evinced understandable moral fault in circumstances where even the best character would have found self-composure difficult; but this is grounds for mitigation, not exonerating excuse. Still, reasonable belief is enough, for necessity here excuses the actor without justifying the action. Inasmuch as the action remains impermissible, no problem of inconsistent rights as between aggressor and victim arises. Finally, in contrast to justificatory necessity, where a stringent rule of proportionality applies to favour life over property, excusing necessity relaxes the proportionality requirement. Up to a point, the embodied agent under a moral duty to live as the best character would live may prefer his (or his intimates') life to that of many strangers, while the altruistic murderer acts in a morally permissible (and legally excusable) way only if, without freely redistributing natural threats, he chooses the lesser evil.[59]

Summary of the argument

My argument, then, is that the conditions for moral blamelessness excuse crime completely because they are analogous to the conditions for legal exculpation. In cases of murder under necessity or duress, the criminal denies the final authority

---

[59] Result-oriented lawyers may now object: if the lesser evil doctrine that was earlier rejected as a theory of justification is now resurrected (with qualifications) to excuse altruistic wrongdoers, and if both kinds of defence result in an acquittal, why was all the effort necessary? First, it makes a great ethical difference whether the lesser evil doctrine works to negate rights or to preserve them, to annul the rule of law or to keep it intact; second, it makes a great expressive difference whether a court publicly tells an accused he did the right thing in killing or that he is excused for having committed murder. Third, it makes a great practical difference whether the lesser evil defence is or is not allowed to affect the permissions of victims and third parties.

of the legal norm without the agent-neutral reason that could justify overriding it; but he acknowledges (or does not deviate from) the public reason of the self-sufficient community of which the legal norm is a constituent element. The self-sufficient community is the political community that not only enforces the rights and entitlements of interchangeable agents but also promotes the good of individual characters by supporting the civil associations wherein they are recognized as valuable ends. As the community sufficient for dignity, the political community embodies a public reason more comprehensive than the common will and the public welfare, which value individuals only as abstract agents; and it is to this inclusive public reason that defendants appeal when they rely on excuse. This is how exonerating excuse can be distinct from exculpation, yet be compatible with the authority of public reason and with the state's duty to punish deniers of that authority. The defendant is *exculpated* if, though he transgressed a boundary, his choice implicitly acknowledged rather than denied rights of formal agency; he is *excused* if, though he chose what for the thinking Agent in his shoes was a denial of rights, he acted as the embodied agent concerned with his own good in political community would have acted. True, he acted against the legal norm when nothing internal to the equal worth of abstract agents defeated it, and this why he cannot rely on necessity as justification. Nevertheless, he acted conformably to the public ethics of the life sufficient for dignity, balanced participation in whose goods is virtue. Hence he can rely on necessity as excuse.

Observe that making room for virtue within the confines of excuse is consistent with the reasons for excluding it from the rest of the general part, because moral character does neither the inculpatory nor exculpatory work we criticized earlier. Because wickedness does no inculpatory work, no one is punished by the state pursuant to others' opinions of his or her character; and no one can be punished unless his or her actus externalized a culpable choice. Because virtue does no exculpatory work, its role cannot imply that bad character inculpates, nor does excuse merge with justification. Further, the proposition that some virtues are political and their action-tokens deserving of public recognition does not entail that character is similarly knowable and can be the object of fair punishment by finite beings; for what is excused is only the single outward action that is open to the light of day and that may or may not reveal the settled character that remains shrouded in darkness.

The account of exonerating excuse as the moral analogue to legal exculpation satisfies all the requirements of an adequate account of legal excuse. Inasmuch as the excusing conditions of necessity and duress *simulate* exculpatory ones, the distinction between exculpation and excuse is maintained and therewith the idea of excuse as an affirmative defence pleaded after the elements of guilt have been proved. Inasmuch as excusing necessity and duress simulate *exculpation,* the account explains why necessity and duress exonerate rather than mitigate, why they lead to an acquittal rather than an absolute discharge following a guilty verdict, and why exoneration is appropriate for judgment by a court rather than for clemency by the executive.

In that they simulate exculpatory defences, complete excuses confer what may be called a quasi-right to an acquittal that a court ought in equity to recognize just because the legal conception of culpability necessarily abstracts (because of its penal consequence) from a full picture of ethical desert. By calling it a quasi-right, however, I do not mean that the juridical force of an excuse is weaker than that of an exculpatory defence or that the excused defendant is not "really" innocent. Rather, I mean that an excuse, while signifying that the defendant is morally blameless, presupposes rather than negates his legal culpability and so leaves the authority of the legal norm intact. The accused is culpable before the law but innocent before the political community; hence his entitlement to an acquittal is only like, not identical to, the right afforded by an exculpatory defence. "Legally guilty but morally innocent" is the verdict that best expresses the juridical situation. Yet the effect of both types of defence is the same: complete exoneration.

It is possible, however, that a common-law court might hesitate to recognize without external prompting a complete defence that comes from outside the law. In that case, it is for the legislature, as the agent of the self-sufficient ethical whole, to create a statutory excuse binding on courts. Such an excuse would exonerate the defendant if, though a denial of rights is imputable to his choice, he nevertheless showed the uprightness, courage, compassion, humility, or practical wisdom that the appropriately law-abiding, courageous, compassionate, modest, or statesman-like character would have shown.[60] And since the basis of excuse is conformity to virtue rather than moral involuntariness, understandable frailty, or the impotence of law's threat, there is no rational basis for excluding the altruistic murderer aware of his human finitude from the benefit of the defence. On the contrary, given the unavoidable limitations of the legal conception of exculpation, such an exclusion permits the unconstitutional punishment of the morally innocent.

5. Excuse as Staying the State's Sword

Kant thought the criminal had a right to a stay of penal proceedings if punishing him would destroy the nature of the legal order as compelling obedience by the threat of superior force. In this he assumed a positivist conception of legal authority and obligation in tension with his view that the duty to enter and sustain a lawful condition rested on the "concept of Right in external relations", which concept justified whatever force was needed to actualize the Right.[61] Nevertheless, the idea that some excuses can be founded on the criminal's right to a stay of penal proceedings where punishing him would subvert the rule of law is worth exploring.

---

[60] Because such a character deserves an acquittal because of his moral blamelessness, the presumption of innocence implies that the defendant should carry no burden of proving necessity or duress as excuse.

[61] *The Metaphysics of Morals*, 122.

But how, one might wonder, could punishing a guilty person ever subvert the rule of law the punishment supposedly actualizes? If "rule of law" means the rule of an unlimited personal sovereign through published general commands backed by threats, then punishing a lawbreaker could never subvert the rule of law except, perhaps, in the way Kant suggested. But if "rule of law" means constitutional rule under a conception of public reason instantiated in positive laws, then punishing even a culpable wrongdoer could subvert the rule of law if it fragmented the public reason under which rule claims legitimacy, corrupting it into a private interest. On this view, a criminal would have the right to a stay of penal proceedings if, despite his culpability, punishing him would so pervert law enforcement into an instrument of private power that official coercion would be external violence rather than self-imposable punishment consistent with freedom. In the idiom of courts, a criminal would have that right if prosecuting him would "bring the administration of justice into disrepute".[62]

Entrapment

Certainly, British and Canadian courts understand the defence of entrapment in exactly this way. Both the House of Lords and the Supreme Court of Canada agree that the defence of entrapment consists in the claim that, though the defendant is guilty as charged, prosecuting him would so abuse the court's process that the court could not convict him without suffering a loss of its "purity" or essential nature.[63] Thus, instead of an acquittal by the jury, the defendant receives a stay from the court. This position stands opposed to that of the United States Supreme Court, for which entrapment is a substantive defence negating guilt (hence for the jury to decide) because it signifies that the police seduced an otherwise "innocent" person into crime.[64] For the US Court, accordingly, entrapment occurs only when law enforcement officers instigate someone to commit a crime who was not already predisposed to do so—that is, only if, but for their inducement, the crime would not have occurred. On this view, the defendant's predisposition is the focus of the inquiry, not the conduct of the police.

British and Canadian courts (as well as dissenting American judges) have rightly seen that the entrapment defence has nothing to do with the defendant's culpability and that the focus on the defendant's predisposition is inappropriate to the abuse-of-process rationale.[65] Even had the defendant not been predisposed

[62] *R v Latif* [1996] 1 WLR 104, 112; *R v Mack* [1988] 2 SCR 903, paras. 77, 81.
[63] *Mack*, para. 81; *R v Loosely* [2001] 4 All ER 897. Australian and New Zealand courts deal with entrapment by excluding improperly obtained evidence: *Ridgeway v The Queen* (1995) 184 CLR 19; *Police v Lavalle* [1979] 1 NZLR 45.
[64] *Sorrells v United States* 287 US 435 (1932); *Sherman v United States* 356 US 369 (1958); *United States v Russell* 411 US 423 (1973); *Hampton v United States* 425 US 484 (1976); *Jacobson v United States* 503 US 540 (1992).
[65] For dissenting American views, see Roberts, J in *Sorrells*, 457–9; Frankfurter, J in *Sherman*, 380–5.

to commit the crime, his seduction by the police cannot negate his culpability, for he knowingly committed the unlawful act, and there would be no doubt about his guilt had the person who seduced him been a private agent. Nor does the inquiry into the defendant's predisposition make sense as a test for procedural abuse, since it would permit egregious police incitement of the crime as long as the defendant was predisposed to commit it.

Nevertheless, the so-called objective test of entrapment that British and Canadian courts have substituted is no real improvement. According to this test, entrapment occurs when police pressure is such that a hypothetical person of average firmness, not already predisposed to the crime, could have yielded to it.[66] Put otherwise, could the police conduct have seduced the average person into crime? The argument favouring this test is that it is more consistent with the procedural rationale for the defence, since it screens out the objectionable police conduct that the "subjective" or factual predisposition test might permit. However, defenders of the subjective test rightly reply that if, as the objectivists agree, what is objectionable is police instigation, manufacture, or causation of the crime, then the subjective test is the right tool for ferreting it out; for what does it matter that the average person was not predisposed to commit the crime if the defendant was? His predisposition is the answer to the question whether the police produced a crime that would not have occurred but for their encouragement. The answer is no; he would likely have done it anyway.

The problem here is that a narrow meaning of the word "entrapment" is driving the analysis on both sides of the dispute, and yet this meaning is too confining a vessel for the defence's rationale. Advocates of both subjective and objective tests take for granted that the entrapment defence is directed at police instigation of a crime that would likely not otherwise have occurred. Entrapping is thus equated with seducing an innocent character into crime. If that is the only target, the factual predisposition test is probably the best weapon for hitting it. However, that target is too narrowly drawn, given that the defence is supposed to bar a prosecution that would corrupt the court's essential nature as actualizer of law's rule. If that is the purpose, then any police conduct that would constitute counselling or inciting crime if done by a private person should warrant a stay of proceedings; for then an accomplice to a crime has donned the mantle of public prosecutor to convict and punish his accomplice, using the court as his intrument. Thus, causation or manufacture is much too high a bar. If law enforcement officers incited the defendant to commit the crime, then their using the court to punish him perverts the court into a party to an internecine war between co-conspirators.[67] Thus, it should not matter whether the defendant was predisposed to commit the

---

[66] *Mack*; *Loosely*; Model Penal Code, section 2.13(1)(b).

[67] On this view, the state's distancing itself from the offending conduct by prosecuting the police officers is no solution, for the state cannot disown the conduct while intentionally putting it to use.

crime, nor even whether a nonpredisposed person of average firmness would have succumbed to the pressure; the proper target is incitement, not seduction.

Lowering the bar in this way need not unduly hamper undercover police work, for creating the opportunity for a suspect to commit a crime would still be permissible. No one commits a crime by setting a stage apparently favourable to one (leaving a safe open, for example), by offering to purchase, as any customer would, a legal substance from someone suspected of selling it illegally, or by posing as someone open to an offer for sale of an illegal substance.[68]

Officially induced error and due diligence

It may seem strange to group officially induced error and due diligence together with entrapment. An official's unintentional misleading of an inquirer regarding a point of law hardly rises to the level of abuse of court process, nor does fining someone for faultlessly breaching a regulation. Nevertheless, I shall argue that these defences do belong together, not only because they are all exonerating excuses presupposing legal guilt, but also because they are all excuses warranting, not an acquittal, but a stay of proceedings to preserve the court's integrity.[69]

Suppose a cinema operator receives permission from an official Censor Board to show a film and then, upon showing it, is charged with violating an obscenity law. Assume that a breach of the obscenity law is a noncriminal offence for which the penalty is a fine. That is, no one who, absent a statute, knowingly shows films appealing to a prurient interest deserves on that account alone judicial punishment from a secular court. Thus, there is no question of the cinema operator's deserving retribution, and hence there is no need for fault to deserve it. The law's purpose, let us say, is to promote the public welfare by prohibiting the showing of films portraying the degradation of women for no artistic or documentary end. Because that purpose is served by penalizing the external conduct alone, the defendant (absent statutory language to the contrary) is presumptively guilty of the offence just in case his action matched the conduct elements of the offence. Fault is not an offence element, for there is no retribution to deserve. Consequently, any plea that the defendant acted non-negligently is relevant, not to negating the offence, but to excusing an admitted offence. Accordingly, the pleas of officially-induced error and due diligence are affirmative excuses coming after the prosecution has proved the offence—in positive law as well as in theory.[70]

---

[68] Thus (short of a constitutional wrong) random virtue testing is overzealous and overintrusive law enforcement for the political process to correct, not a crime disentitling the public prosecutor from a conviction of a guilty defendant. *Contra: R v Barnes* [1991] 1 SCR 449. But random virtue testing may be a (rebuttable) sign of improper motive, which would corrupt the court's process.

[69] At positive law, Anglo-American courts view officially-induced error in this way, but not due diligence.

[70] *R v Sault Ste Marie* [1978] 2 SCR 1299; *Levis (City) v Tétreault* [2006] 1 SCR 420; *Proudman v Dayman* (1941) 67 CLR 536.

Are they excuses like necessity and duress in that they signify that the defendant was morally blameless for the breach and so deserves an acquittal? At first sight, they appear to fall into this category, for the individual who took all reasonable steps to comply with a statute or who sought out and reasonably relied on an official statement of the law has shown the law-abiding disposition that the reasonably upright character would have shown. His conduct is indeed ethically spotless. And yet, how can it be relevant that the defendant was blameless if his liability did not turn on culpability? How can it be relevant that he does not deserve the penalty if the penalty cannot be deserved? Since the point of the penalty is prevention rather than retribution or the vindication of law's authority, the defendant's moral blamelessness has no more significance than his legal non-culpability. Here, excuse as moral blamelessness cannot supplement legal exculpation, because there is no exculpatory reason of which it can be an analogue. So, while the cinema operator is no doubt blameless, this cannot be the reason for exonerating him. Indeed, the positive law admits as much in holding that the burden of proving reliance on official error or due diligence can be placed on the defendant without violating the presumption of innocence.[71]

The reason for exonerating the cinema operator is that conviction and penalization would corrupt the public reason under which he was charged. In Chapter 5 I argued that the conception of public reason underlying public welfare statutes is real autonomy—the agent's actualized potential for shaping a life according to self-authored plans. I also argued that laws justified by this conception cannot coherently be enforced with penalties that befall the agent as an uncontrollable fate, for this would promote the autonomy of the many at the expense of that of the defendant. The public reason that justifies law enforcement would thus be fragmented into a particular interest, to which the court would be allied. Now someone who takes all reasonable steps to comply with the law regulating his activity or who reasonably relies on an official statement of the law has done everything within his power to comply short of abstaining from his enterprise, which the law does not seek to stop. Accordingly, if he is penalized despite his best efforts to obey, his penalty was an unavoidable fate incompatible with his autonomy. It thus fragments the public reason justifying the statute's enforcement and therewith delegitimates the court. So the defendant who took reasonable care to comply or who reasonably relied on an official statement, though guilty as charged, is entitled to a stay of prosecution to prevent a private taking of his resources.

Observe how different this account of a due diligence defence is from one that highlights the defendant's moral blamelessness. When we, having normal capacities, negligently breach public welfare statutes, we are not punished *for* our negligence, however morally censurable our negligence may be in the court of public opinion. Indeed, we are not *punished* at all. Rather, we are penalized in order to deter breaches of the law serving a public goal, but a negligence requirement (and

---

[71] *Wholesale Travel Group, Inc v. The Queen.* [1991] 3 SCR 154.

hence a due diligence defence) is a constraint ensuring that the agent remains in control of its legal destiny. Conversely, a due diligence defence is not a claim that, though guilt has been proved, it would be morally repugnant to convict someone who is blameless because he did the most that could be expected of him. Rather, it is a claim that the state exceeds its rightful authority as agent of the common good of autonomy in applying a penal sanction whose incidence was beyond the individual's power to avoid. Of course, the accused *has* done all that we could expect, and it *would* be morally repugnant to penalize him. But a court cannot excuse someone on this basis from a penalty that does not have the denunciation of blameworthy conduct as its end. Accordingly, a due diligence defence works, not as an affirmation of moral blamelessness by the defendant, but as a stay on the state's sword for the sake of the integrity of the public legal order.

6. Partial Excuse as Moral Analogue of Partial Exculpation

Partial defences are either partially exculpatory or partially excusing. Partially exculpatory defences can be explained in light of the plural paradigm theory of the criminal law as follows. These defences leave the defendant's culpability for wrong intact because he still chose that (for example, an assault) from which a denial of agency rights is imputable to his choice. Nevertheless, they affect the degree of his responsibility for the harmful outcome of the wrong by reducing the degree to which the outcome is imputable to his choice as distinct from chance. The defendant is thus punishable as a criminal, but he deserves a specific criminal label and attendant severity of punishment that reflects the participation of accident in the harmful result. Classically, intoxication and the mental illness of the legally sane defendant are the conditions that might mitigate guilt on this basis. Thus drunkenness negating a specific intent to bring about a certain harmful outcome (for example, death) leads to a conviction for a lesser included crime (for example, manslaughter instead of murder) reflecting the degree of responsibility for the outcome known as foreseeability. Similarly, mental illness falling short of legal insanity might negate the specific intent to kill required for murder and lead to a conviction for manslaughter.[72]

Of course, there is no reason why drunkenness could never negate the intention to interfere with agency (general intent) and hence exculpate completely from crime.[73] After all, neither the intention to get drunk nor recklessness in getting drunk is a good substitute for the intention to assault someone; at most, it warrants conviction for a separate offence of criminally negligent intoxication. Nor is there any good reason for limiting the defence of diminished responsibility owing to mental illness to murder. Any crime of specific intent should be reducible to a

---

[72] *More v Queen* [1963] 3 CCC 289 (SCC).
[73] Contrast *DPP v Majewski* (1976) 62 Cr App R 262 (HL) and *R v Daviault* [1994] 3 SCR 63.

conviction for foreseeably causing the proscribed harm if the defendant did not in fact intend the proscribed harm. Perhaps deterrence considerations extrinsic to desert motivate these half measures; or perhaps adverse judgments of moral character are infecting legal principles of criminal desert.[74]

Since intoxication negating specific intent and diminished responsibility owing to mental illness simply lead to a conviction for the result crime for which the defendant is responsible according to the legal scale of imputability, they are not mitigating conditions in the strict sense.[75] They are, rather, partial exculpations—partial because (in contrast to involuntariness or mistake of fact) they go to responsibility for harm rather than to culpability for wrong, hence to measure of punishment rather than to punishability. Truly mitigating conditions give rise to partial excuses. These presuppose that the defendant chose that from which a right denial may be imputed to his choice and that he also chose the harmful result of his right-denying choice, so that he is fully responsible for it (the result was not an accident). They also presuppose that the crime is inexcusable because the defendant's conduct fell below the standard of self-control demanded of embodied agents. So where, one might ask, is there room for partial excuse?

The partial excuses form a family with two branches. One branch consists of failures of self-control due to disabilities of character (mental disease, youth) for which the defendant is not to blame; the other consists of failures to channel or control morally appropriate emotions such as righteous anger or reasonable fear. On the first branch belong the defences of diminished or undeveloped capacity to live up to human moral possibility;[76] on the second belong provocation, excessive or disproportionate force in self-defence, unjustified recourse to self-help, as well as panicky misperception of facts which, if true, would excuse completely on the ground of necessity or duress. In contrast to the partial exculpations, the partial excuses are not ones to whose mitigating force the defendant has a right, for, as we saw, they presuppose full legal responsibility for the harm caused. Nevertheless, they are defences to which the defendant has a quasi-right, because they signify that the defendant is morally less blameworthy than other inexcusable murderers. Just as the complete excuses are moral analogues of the complete exculpations, so the partial excuses are moral analogues of the partial exculpations. Or so I shall now argue with particular reference to provocation.

Standing apart from the partial defences based on diminished responsibility for the outcome, provocation is rather a variation on the moral theme underlying excusing necessity and duress. Words or acts amounting to legal provocation (but

---

[74] One may object: if morality is allowed to supplement legal desert for the benefit of the accused, why not for the benefit of society? The reason is that a supplemental excuse can be logically confined to the periphery of the criminal law, whereas a supplemental inculpation cannot be.

[75] In the UK, diminished responsibility refers to a diminished capacity for self-control rather than (as in Canada) a lower degree of imputability of outcome to choice. This would put diminished responsibility into the category of partial excuse along with provocation. See *R v Smith* [2001] 1 AC 146.

[76] Horder, *Excusing Crime*, 125–37.

not to the provocation that would justify defensive force) reduce murder to manslaughter, not because the killer did not intend or foresee death, but because he lost self-control in circumstances where the "ordinary person" (Canadian) could have done so too or where the "reasonable man" (British) would have been similarly moved to great anger or indignation.[77]

Ordinary vice

The "ordinary person" standard of Canadian law suggests an excuse based on a compassionate concession to human frailty, which would normally go to sentencing discretion but which requires a statutory mitigation where, as in murder, a life sentence is mandatory. On this understanding of the defence, problems arise in holding the defendant to an objective standard of ordinary self-control, for the compassion rationale naturally bursts its dikes. How, for example, can one coherently divest the ordinary person of the past experiences and emotional state (for example, depression, low self-esteem) of the defendant that help explain, not only the gravity of the provocation, but also his particular over-reaction to it?[78] After all, a compassion rationale naturally makes relevant all the circumstances of the defendant that make his reaction understandable as a momentary lapse that anyone in his shoes might have suffered.

And yet, if the person of ordinary powers of self-control is given the defendant's biography and frame of mind, it no longer serves as a critical standard for the defendant's conduct; for what the defendant did is the best evidence of what the person of mediocre temperateness would have done in the same situation. Thus, the compassion rationale naturally leads to the thoroughly subjectivized test of *R v Smith:* did the defendant kill in the heat of anger caused by something the victim said or did that could have deprived anyone in the defendant's frame of mind of his or her power of self-control?[79] However, if this test is used, how does one filter out "ordinary" prejudices (for example, homophobia or racist attitudes) that led the defendant to react as he did and that the law ought not to countenance?[80] And why single out anger as the only mitigating emotion? Why not "ordinary" avarice and lust in the context of long deprivation or impoverished upbringing? This, I suggest, is an inescapable dilemma for the compassion theory of provocation. It arises because, once one abandons the objective standard of moral expectation rooted in human moral possibility, there is no lower objective standard to fall back to. The defendant *is* the ordinary person. Accordingly, one might as well

---

[77] Canadian Criminal Code, RSC 1985 c. C–46, s. 232; UK Homicide Act 1957, s. 3.

[78] Accordingly, this version of provocation shades into a diminished capacity defence without, however, distinguishing between impairing factors for which the defendant may be held responsible and those for which he may not.

[79] Note 75 above; see also *R v Thibert* [1996] 1 SCR 37.

[80] See Mayo Moran, *Rethinking the Reasonable Person* (Oxford: Oxford University Press, 2003), 230.

simply ask whether the defendant killed in the heat of passion; and why should that excuse even partially?

Further, the compassionate-concession-to-infirmity version of the provocation defence fails to interpret it in a way that makes provocation a reason for mitigation that is properly protected against other, perhaps outweighing, reasons for severity. On this view, accordingly, there would be nothing wrong with a judge's using his liberated discretion to give the provoked manslayer the same sentence as the mandatory sentence for murder, nor even with abolishing the provocation defence altogether. On the compassion-for-infirmity rationale, provocation is not a defence to which the defendant has a quasi-right.

The gentle character

The "reasonable man" standard of British law embodies a different interpretation of the provocation defence, one illuminated by Jeremy Horder's excellent book on the subject.[81] Like excusing necessity and duress, provocation in British law exemplifies the marginal relevance of moral character to judgments of criminal desert, given the need in some cases to supplement the impersonal, agency-based focus of the legal criteria of culpability and responsibility. Thus provocation reduces murder to manslaughter despite the defendant's having intended death if the outrage driving the action was justified or appropriate, albeit the expressive action itself was over-reactive and so indicative of a blameworthy intemperateness. Outrage is justified if the reasonable character, who is neither short-tempered nor diffident but displays the mean (gentleness) between these extremes, would also have been provoked to express outrage (though not by killing) had he or she been placed in the defendant's body and other outward circumstances. Because the over-reaction is blameworthy, there is no reason to exonerate someone whom the legal criteria of desert would punish. But because the provocation would have stirred even the virtuous character to outrage, the loss of self-control is partially excused. Here the justifiability of the outrage does the excusing work that impaired capacity does on the other branch of the family tree. The parental idea is that the circumstances making self-control unusually difficult were not ones themselves reflecting a blameworthy deficiency of moral strength.

So understood, partial excuses are moral analogues of partial exculpations, for both signify diminished fault for a wrongful outcome. The difference is that, whereas partially exculpatory conditions diminish fault in the *external* sense of lowering the degree to which an outcome is imputable to choice as distinct from chance, partially excusatory conditions diminish fault in the *inward* sense of reducing the disparity between the defendant's conduct and that of the ideally temperate character. Someone too drunk to intend death is less responsible for

---

[81] Jeremy Horder, *Provocation and Responsibility* (Oxford: Clarendon Press, 1992); see also Horder, *Excusing Crime*, ch. 4, Gardner, *Offences and Defences*, 155–76.

the death in the legal sense than someone who chose it. Someone who lost self-control in circumstances that made self-control objectively difficult and that do not themselves reflect moral weakness is less blameworthy relative to the moral standard of the gentle character than someone who coolly intended death or than someone who, though a sane adult, reacted angrily because of ego-fragility.

Because it holds onto an objective standard of morally justifiable anger, the virtue-based rationale for the provocation defence avoids the dilemma besetting the compassion theory. In particular, the *Camplin* distinction between characteristics of the defendant relevant to the gravity of the provocation (which the jury may consider) and those going to his powers of self-control (which they may not) makes sense on this rationale.[82] For if the gentle character with the relevant (racial, physical) characteristic would not have been moved to great anger by what the victim did or said, that is an end of the matter; and if he or she would have, the jury may still consider whether the gentle character would have experienced strain in successfully controlling violent inclinations such that the defendant's failure to control them was a failure to accomplish the objectively difficult. If the gentle character would not have experienced strain, then the defendant's over-reaction was due not to the objective difficulty of self-control, but to the defendant's idiosyncratic and fully censurable intemperateness.

Nevertheless, the reasonable anger standard faces problems of its own. Inevitably, that standard gives rise to all the problems in application that the abstract legal criteria of criminal desert are structured to avoid. Once we move away from the objectivity of the agency-based criteria and into the sphere of moral judgment of the inward character, all sorts of controversial assumptions and cultural prejudices are bound to infiltrate the moral standard—prejudices the defendant might not share. Are the reasonable character's sentiments concerning marriage and domestic relations conservative or avant garde? Thus, is a husband's murder of his estranged wife upon learning of her liaison with another man an over-reactive expression of virtuous anger or of male possessiveness? Are the reasonable character's sentiments around homosexuality religious or secular? Thus, is the defendant's killing someone in response to a homosexual advance an excessive expression of appropriate indignation or of bigotry? These problems give a taste of what is in store if the conformity-to-human-moral-potential theory of desert were to move from the margin of the criminal law to the centre, determining all questions of criminal desert. Imagine if one's liability to punishment for an assault depended on a judge or jury's opinion as to whether one exhibited anger under the right circumstances, with the right person, in the right way, and at the right time.[83]

Still, the porosity of the moral standard to variable sensibility is not a reason for eliminating the supplementary role the provocation defence plays in mitigating

---

[82] *DPP v Camplin* [1978] AC 705.
[83] A paraphrase of Aristotle's description of the gentle man. *Nicomachean Ethics*, 1125b.

murder, as some argue.[84] Rather, it is a reason for judges to exert control over its consideration by the jury by filling in the axiological indeterminacy of the standard with values drawn from legal norms. In particular, whether the defence is based on compassion for infirmity or on a morally principled mitigation for an unjustified expression of justified outrage that is less vicious than most other inexcusable murders, it seems appropriate for judges to allow legal norms of equality and nondiscrimination to inform judgments of what is appropriate anger and of what is worthy of compassion. Thus passions rooted in racist, misogynist, and homophobic attitudes the law elsewhere discourages ought not to be legally recognized as grounds for partial excuse; judges should rather exclude (or be statutorily directed to exclude) from jury consideration provocation pleas based on these attitudes. More is at stake here than the internal consistency of a liberal legal order. Screening provocation pleas for discriminatory attitudes also goes some way toward reconciling sentencing decisions based on judgments of the defendant's moral character with the freedom and inviolability of the person. For inasmuch as the legal norm of nondiscrimination is by definition acceptable to all agents considered as free and equal, it gives a negative moral judgment on the defendant the feature of self-imposability it would otherwise lack.

[84] Horder, *Provocation and Responsibility*, 192–7.

8
Detention after Acquittal

1. Requiem for a Defence

'Automatism' is the legal term for a temporary psychological disorder characterized by mind–body dissociation. The body moves, but the conscious mind does not direct the movements. Tokens of automatism are sleepwalking, epileptic seizures, and dissociated states triggered by extreme intoxication, hypoglycaemia, or by physical or psychological trauma. The legal effect of automatism in a criminal case is the same as that for involuntary bodily movement generally. Provided the defendant did not engage in risky activity knowing he was prone to such episodes, the condition negates the basic capacity for free choice that is the precondition of making a culpable choice. Hence the condition is completely exculpatory; the defendant does not deserve punishment at all.

Since the mid-20th century, however, the evolution of the defence of automatism in the common-law world has been the story of a gradual slide toward extinction. Whereas in 1955, an English judge could put the defence to a jury in a case where the defendant had beaten his son with a hammer during an unconscious episode caused by a cerebral tumour, the same case decided today would almost certainly result in an instruction to the jury solely on insanity.[1] Why this is so is not difficult to determine. Because a successful defence of automatism means that the accused has not acted, it leads to an absolute acquittal. The worry has been that someone who inflicts harm while in an automatic state will be able to circumvent the restrictions (the reverse onus) and consequences (continued detention) of the defence of insanity and that someone prone to recurrent unconscious behaviour would thus go free, perhaps to inflict harm again. For reasons of social protection, therefore, common-law courts have increasingly limited the availability of automatism as an independent defence, forcing defendants to rely on a defence of insanity if they wish to bring forward evidence of unconscious motion.

Disease of the mind: a disordered concept

The principal strategy by which courts have limited access to a defence of automatism has been to draw a distinction between sane and insane automatism. Sane

---

[1] *R v Charlson* (1955) 39 Cr App R 37. For an approving commentary on this development see JLJ Edwards, 'Automatism and Criminal Responsibility,' (1958) 21 MLR 375.

automatism is unconscious behaviour that is unlikely to recur or (which comes to the same thing) that is caused by an extraordinary external event such as a blow to the head or a psychological shock severe enough to cause an automatic reaction in a person of ordinary constitution. Insane automatism is unconscious behaviour attributable to a disease of the mind. If the evidence suggests that the defendant's automatism was of the latter sort, then the judge will instruct the jury only on insanity.

Requiring the defendant to rely on the defence of insanity where the evidence for automatism plausibly points only to mental disease is in itself unobjectionable. However, common-law courts have defined very broadly the term "disease of the mind" so as narrowly to restrict access to the defence of sane automatism. In *Bratty v Northern Ireland*,[2] Lord Denning defined disease of the mind as "any mental disorder which has manifested itself in violence and is prone to recur".[3] And such disorders might well include not only psychological illnesses but also diseases of a purely physical or neurological nature such as a brain tumour, arteriosclerosis, epilepsy, or diabetes.[4] In *R v Burgess*, the English Court of Appeal held that even somnambulism might be a disease of the mind, with the result that someone who behaves violently while sleepwalking and who might sleepwalk again must accept a defence of insanity if he or she wishes to plead involuntariness.[5]

The strategic manipulation of the concept of mental disease has been carried even further in Canada. In *R v Rabey*, the Supreme Court of Canada expanded Lord Denning's definition of the concept, declaring that any subjective disposition to which an automatic episode could be attributed constituted a diseased mind whether or not the psychiatric profession would consider it pathological.[6] In that case, the subjective disposition was an adolescent infatuation. Moreover, in *R v Stone*, the same court took the logic of social protection to the limit by articulating two propositions that render the defence of sane automatism now practically inaccessible.[7] One is that an automatic episode is itself a mental disorder, and so it creates a presumption of a diseased mind, rebuttable by evidence that the episode had a wholly external cause. The other is that, in assessing the likelihood that the violent episode will recur, the judge is to consider, not only the psychiatric history and emotional make-up of the defendant, but also the likelihood that the external triggering event will itself recur.[8]

Taken together, these two propositions effectively submerge the category of sane automatism into that of automatism from mental disease. This is so because, according to the first, any case of unconscious behaviour by definition evinces a diseased mind unless an external cause can be identified; and, according to the second, even if an external cause can be identified, there may nonetheless be

---

[2] [1963] AC 386 (HL).   [3] Ibid, at 412.
[4] See *R v Kemp* [1956] 3 All ER 249; *R v Sullivan* [1984] AC 156 (HL); *R v Hennessy* [1989] 2 All ER 9.
[5] [1991] 2 QB 92.   [6] [1980] 2 SCR 513.
[7] [1999] 2 SCR 290.   [8] Ibid, at 440.

disease of the mind if it is likely that the external cause will recur and irrespective of whether there is evidence of a peculiar susceptibility in the defendant. Thus, if *Rabey* decided that a disease of the mind need not be a disease, *Stone* decided that it need not even be predicable of a mind.

Clearly, the definition of mental disease elaborated by common-law courts in the aforementioned cases bears little resemblance to any that a psychiatrist might proffer. It is a legal rather than a medical definition—one carefully crafted with a view to a policy of controlling persons thought to be dangerous.[9] This definition ensures, first, that any defendant who, at the time of the attack, lacked the capacity for conscious choice because of a dangerous and potentially recurrent disorder or event will not go free but will be subject to continued detention and confinement after acquittal. Obversely, it ensures that only those whose lack of conscious choice was caused by an external and probably nonrecurrent event will have the benefit of a defence leading to an absolute acquittal and a return to society.

However, structuring the automatism defence with a view to a policy of controlling the dangerous has produced a law of automatism that, I'll argue, unjustifiably violates the right to liberty of those found innocent of crime. Because this approach has led to a concept of a diseased mind having nothing to do with mental pathology, it can result in the prophylactic and paternalistic detention of innocents who are capable of autonomous action and for whom the diminished respect implied by such treatment is therefore unwarranted. Suppose, to take an extreme example, that a perfectly healthy rugby player inflicts harm during an unconscious episode resulting from a blow to the head suffered during a match. If, as *Stone* decided, the unconscious episode itself raises a presumption of mental disease, and if the external cause cannot dislodge the presumption because of the high likelihood of its repetition, then the only defence is insane automatism unless the player intends to retire. True, there is little prospect that this individual would actually be confined to a mental hospital once acquitted. Nevertheless, he has been stigmatized as not guilty because of insanity, detained even though innocent pending review, and subjected to the indignity of a review for dangerousness whose reservation for the insane shows that we think it unfitting for the mentally competent.

The extreme inflation of the concept of mental disease represented in *Bratty*, *Rabey*, and *Stone* should prompt a fresh approach to the question as to when detention following an acquittal is justified. Such an approach should rest on a more principled understanding of the concept of a diseased mind than that hitherto shown by the courts; and it should accomplish the policy objective of the present law without unjustifiably violating the agency rights of the innocent. In this chapter, I shall suggest such an approach.

---

[9] See *Bratty*, 410, Lord Denning: "Suppose a crime is committed by a man in a state of automatism or clouded consciousness due to a recurrent disease of the mind. Such an act is no doubt involuntary, but it does not give rise to an unqualified acquittal, for that would mean that he would be let at large to do it again. The only proper verdict is one which ensures that the person who suffers from the disease is kept secure in a hospital so as not to be a danger to himself or others."

The law of insanity at the border of two paradigms

To see what is needed, however, we must first understand how the present law unjustifiably violates rights. It does so, I'll argue, by forcibly detaining persons found innocent of crime for reasons of social protection and their own welfare in the absence of the only justification for giving force to these reasons consistent with their right to liberty. That justification is the diminished respect owed persons who, while possessing the capacity for free choice underlying right-bearing as well as criminal capacity, lack capabilities for autonomously motivated choice warranting *unqualified* respect for their right-respecting choices. A satisfactory criterion of insane automatism will reflect this justificatory reason for detaining the innocent and will afford as much protection from dangerous persons as a legal order founded on the inviolability of the person permits.

Inasmuch as the valid reason for detaining an insane person who has been exculpated of crime is different from the valid reason for exculpating him, the criminal law of insanity further exemplifies the plural paradigm theory of the penal law I am presenting. According to this theory, the formal agency paradigm is the theoretical framework for understanding and justifying the criminal liability of the insane, whereas the real autonomy framework provides the justificatory reason for detaining the acquitted insane for their own good and that of others. Thus, unless the mental disorder is so extreme as to render the sufferer a nonagent (in which case he is unfit for trial), the reason why the legally insane accused is acquitted after trial is that he was labouring under a delusion within which his choice was not one to which a right denial is imputable (see Chapter 2). By contrast, the only reason (consistent with his right to liberty) that can justify detaining him after acquittal on grounds of dangerousness is that he lacks the capabilities for acting from self-authored ends that warrants the state's full respect for the (right-respecting) choices he makes.

The fact that different reasons apply to exculpating the insane and to holding them liable to prophylactic detention after acquittal places a strain on a defence of insanity that must perform two distinct functions with one legal formula.[10] One is the criminal-law function of identifying the nonculpable; the other is an administrative-law function of identifying the nonculpable who are eligible for therapeutic and preventive detention. The original M'Naghten rules cracked under the strain. In that they specified only the conditions for the exculpatory force of insanity, they left the acquitted insane person in the normative void we have seen elsewhere when the formalist paradigm is thought to exhaust the constraints on state power.

---

[10] This problem will remain undetected as long as legal insanity is thought to exculpate because the defendant lacked the responsible agency prerequisite for a judgment of guilt; for, as responsible agency is the capacity for rights, the defendant's lack thereof is also a legitimate reason for detaining him though he is not guilty. But the M'Naghten rules do not test for responsible agency (for which a clinical diagnosis would suffice); they test for culpable agency.

Because of this vacuum, people exculpated by reason of insanity could be held as a result of a single past transgression "until the pleasure of the Crown was known" and then committed to a psychiatric hospital indefinitely without an inquiry into their present or continuing dangerousness. In this way, the verdict of not guilty by reason of insanity was indistinguishable in its legal effect from that of guilty but insane.[11] Indeed, not only could the legally insane individual justifiably complain that he was being punished for a past deed in the absence of a culpable mind; he could also claim that, with an indeterminate period of confinement, he was being punished with a severity out of all proportion to his transgression.

I shall argue, however, that the Canadian revision of the M'Naghten rules, coupled with a reformed regime for the disposition of those found not guilty because of mental disorder, fills this legal vacuum with a criterion of therapeutic detainability supplied by the real autonomy framework. This revision allows the M'Naghten rules to perform reasonably well the dual role of identifying those mentally ill agents who are undeserving of punishment and distinguishing those who, though undeserving of punishment, are eligible for detention for paternalistic and prophylactic reasons. What remains to be done, however, is to revise the common-law criteria for insane automatism so that they too can perform this dual function.

2. Why is Detention of the Innocent Insane Permissible?

To see what is wrong with the current law of automatism, we have to ask more generally what, if anything, justifies continued detention of those acquitted of criminal wrongdoing because of mental disorder; and then we have to inquire whether the current law of automatism prescribes criteria for detention meeting this justification. Obviously, a justification is needed. After all, those found not guilty by reason of insanity are subject to coercion by the state for reasons that would not be considered valid for most people. Having been found undeserving of punishment, they are nonetheless forcibly confined for their own good as others see it and to protect others from what they might do in the future. In a society of free and equal persons, such treatment of a sane individual would be regarded as an unjust deprivation of liberty, because by coercing him for our good or to implement our conception of his good, we violate a duty of respect owed to his capacity to act on ends he freely chooses.

To be sure, punishment also protects us from convicts for a time and affords us an opportunity to reform them according to our conception of their best interests. However, if the criteria of culpability and responsibility discussed in Chapters 2 to 4 have been satisfied, then punishment respects the convict's agency; for if he

---

[11] Traces of this perspective still linger in the courts; see, for example, Justice McLachlin's judgment in *R v Chaulk* [1990] 3 SCR 1303, in which she says that an acquittal on grounds of mental disorder is not a true acquittal.

has chosen that from which a denial of agency rights is logically imputable to his choice, then he has implicitly authorized the state to coerce him according to a measure proportioned to his responsibility for the harmful outcome. By choosing to interfere with another's agency, the convict has licensed his own coercion, and so he cannot complain if, within the context of a public vindication of rights, he is subjected to the good and good intentions of others. If, however, an accused has not chosen to interfere with another's agency, then coercing him for the sake of our interests is externally imposed force difficult to distinguish from crime itself. Accordingly, no one would think that, absent a threat to its existence, a liberal state could confine someone of sound mind who had neither committed nor attempted a crime simply because the authorities were of the view that he had dangerous proclivities or that he would be better off without his liberty. Yet such a fate routinely befalls the insane. How can it be justified?

Two possibilities suggest themselves. One is to deny that detaining the innocent insane violates their right to liberty; another is to argue that a violation is justified in their case. A denial of a violation might be supported by three distinct lines of argument. One could argue that coercing the innocent insane does not violate their rights because, lacking a capability for autonomously motivated action, they do not have rights. Second, one could argue that coercing the innocent insane does not violate their agency right, because if they knew what we know about the risks they pose and possessed full powers of deliberation and judgment, they would consent to being held in custody for their own and others' safety. Call this the argument from constructive consent.[12] Alternatively, one could argue that, though not criminally culpable for any danger he might now pose, someone found not guilty by reason of insanity may nonetheless pose a threat of serious harm against which coercive prevention in defence of others is permissible.

No right is violated

If the capacity for rights rests on a capacity (or developing capacity) for choice undetermined by the causal laws governing matter, then there is no reason to think that people who act on fixed delusional beliefs engendering irrational fear, anger, confidence, guilt feelings, etc. lack the capacity for rights. The capacity for undetermined choice is an undemanding criterion for respect. It is given by a simple and rudimentary awareness of self as differentiated from the desires and emotions the self experiences—as the subject of these desires and affects. Thus, to have the neurological potential to say "*I* want" is sufficient to indicate a capacity for rights. Now, perhaps some mental disorders are so severe as to collapse the self into the body—I do not know. But surely most impair higher-order functions *of* the self. Specifically, they impair the agent's ability autonomously to form a

---

[12] See J Woodward, 'Paternalism and Justification,' in W Cragg, ed., *Contemporary Moral Issues*, 3rd ed. (Toronto: McGraw-Hill Ryerson, 1992), 398.

set of fundamental values, to act from ends calmly evaluated for their coherence with those values; or they impair the agent's ability to form realistic beliefs about the environment on which his choices are premised. These disorders can certainly undermine the agent's ability to realize the potential for self-determination its capacity for undetermined choice carries. But because the capacity for rights depends on the capacity to choose freely and not on the ability to live autonomously, mental disorders impairing autonomy have no bearing on the agent's capacity for rights.

What of the argument from constructive consent? The point of this argument is to justify coercion of the innocent insane in a way that takes their agency rights seriously as a constraint on the societal pursuit of values external to those of the person coerced. The argument is that we can pursue these values only if the individual against whom force is used would, if he knew what we know, consent to the force. Of course, we are already familiar with the idea of constructive consent to the application of force from the retributivist legitimation of punishment defended in Chapter 1. According to that account, consent to coercion is inferred from a choice which, for the thinking Agent in the empirical actor's shoes, is a choice to deny rights of agency. Yet there is an important difference between the constructive consent of a culpable wrongdoer to punishment and the supposed constructive consent of an innocent schizophrenic to prophylactic confinement.

In the retributivist argument, no claim is made that the constructive consent of the thinking Agent is a valid *substitute* for the actual consent of the empirical agent. On the contrary, the justification of punishment (as we saw in the Introduction) must presuppose the empirical agent's nonconsent; for the empirical agent is forbidden to alienate his right to liberty in general for some particular and contingent end. This is why punishment is always deemed coercive and why a justification of punishment must be a justification of a wrong. By contrast, the argument now under consideration relies on the idea that, for one incompetent to consent, we may substitute consent by the same person hypothetically considered as competent. The claim is that the empirical agent has, in effect, granted power of attorney to his hypothetical rational self to authorize others to confine him against an inauthentic expression of his will given while he was incompetent to consent. Here, in other words, constructive consent to forcible confinement is posing as a valid substitute for actual consent.

A variation of an example given by John Stuart Mill shows how such a device might succeed within a narrow band of cases. If a blind man is unwittingly about to walk into the path of an oncoming truck and there is no time to warn him, applying force to stop him can be justified by an argument from constructive consent, since he would assent to such a trivial interference if he knew that it was necessary to save his life. As Mill puts it, there is no interference with liberty, because liberty consists in the freedom to do as one desires, and the blind man does not desire to die.[13] Of course, if a seeing man aware of the risk resisted your

---

[13] J S Mill, *On Liberty* (New York: Crofts, 1947), 97; Woodward, ibid, 400.

efforts, further force would constitute a battery. But if a blind man, unaware of the danger and thinking you were a mugger, resisted, continued force would be permissible on the theory that, had it been put to him, he would have authorized you in advance to save him against himself in that kind of situation.

This example works because one must assume that an agent wills its continued agency. However, the further we get from a situation of imminent and certain harm to life and limb, the more strained and artificial does the argument from constructive consent become.[14] This is so because, short of that extreme situation, the point at which someone might prefer protection against a *risk* of harm to his or her freedom of movement involves a subjective weighing of values that varies from one individual to another. If, within the area of reasonable diversity of preference, we simply impute to the insane person the values we hold or consider rational to hold, then obviously our respect for the agency constraint on the pursuit of our values is a sham.

We could say, however, that coercing the insane is justified only if the insane person would have consented in advance given the relatively enduring content and configuration of his own values and commitments; and we might thus require substituted consent from someone intimately familiar with those values. Yet, given the separateness of persons, substituted consent is almost always fictional consent. Cases of imminent harm aside, the impossibility of projecting oneself into another's schedule of values so as to decide as he would have decided, as well as the high risk of bias in doing so, means that the argument from constructive consent—and the device of substituted consent in particular—is a mere figleaf for a consequentialism freed of effective constraints. Indeed, our practice of confining the innocent insane acknowledges this, for it places no reliance on the substituted consent of intimates as a legitimating precondition for confinement. It simply confines them.

Accordingly, the argument from constructive consent will justify coercion of the innocent insane only in a very narrow range of cases involving imminent and practically certain harm to interests crucial to anyone's conception of welfare. Needless to say, our present practice of confining the insane is not limited to such cases; it extends to cases of risk. So let us try out a third argument for the claim that no agency right of the insane is violated by this practice—the argument from the legitimate defence of others.

A liberal state's rightful authority to defend agents within its territory against wrongful threats is ultimately derived from the right of the threatened party to self-defence. Officers of the state have a right (indeed, a duty) to lend assistance only because the person threatened is the holder of an agency right that will be infringed if he or the public defender of rights does not protect it. So let us ask whether the people on whose behalf the state acts in detaining the innocent insane would have a right of self-defence against them were state help unavailable.

While the instinct for self-preservation might motivate our policy of maintaining control over those acquitted of crimes because of mental disorder, the right of

---

[14] This was recognized by Mill; see *On Liberty*, 98.

self-defence will not lend its normative stamp to the gratification of this instinct. That right justifies the use of necessary and proportionate force only against a wrongdoer. As we saw in Chapter 6, the wrongdoer need not be culpable for his wrong (for punishment and self-defence are distinct responses to wrongdoing), and so an assailant's legal insanity is no bar to justified force in self-defence or defence of others against him. However, since the right of self-defence derives from the right of agency it realizes, there must be a threat of imminent interference with agency by a voluntary actor—that is, a palpable threat and not a merely speculative one. Speculative threats, even if the conjecture is based on good evidence, are insufficient to trigger a right of self-defence derived from a right of agency, because the possibility of a wrong is not yet a wrong. Rather, the threatened interference must be imminent in the sense that the defender must reasonably believe that further delay will prejudice his ability successfully to defend his right. Those found not guilty by reason of insanity, however, do not normally pose a threat of the required imminence, and those that do can be lawfully restrained as wrongdoers rather than as inchoate threats. Thus, the state's rightful authority to defend its subjects against wrongful threats cannot justify our present practice of confining those found not guilty by reason of insanity because of a likelihood that they will pose a wrongful threat in the future.[15]

The agency right of the insane is justifiably infringed

It appears, then, that if our practice of coercing the innocent insane is to be legitimated, this must be done not through a denial that the practice violates their agency right, but by a claim that the admitted violation is justified in their case. Such a claim might be supported by either of two lines of argument. One could argue, from a eudaemonist point of view, that the violation of right is justified by the social goods it produces, namely, public safety and the improved wellbeing of the person held in therapeutic custody. Alternatively, one might argue—as I will—that the agent's right to respect for its formal capacity for free choice is justifiably overridden for the sake of the public interest in autonomy only if its ability to exercise the capacity in autonomous choices is radically impaired; for then the reason for the state's unqualified duty to respect the agent's *specific* right-respecting choices—that they are self-determined choices—has no application. In these circumstances, the state may intervene to prevent choices harmful to goods essential to exercising the capacity for choice. On this dignity-based view, while the paradigm of formal agency governs the insane defendant's liability to punishment, that of real autonomy governs his vulnerability to prophylactic detention after acquittal.

The eudaemonist line of argument is unpromising, because any social good that may be obtained by violating the rights of the insane will also be obtained by violating the rights of the sane. We have just as much reason for indefinitely

---

[15] Nor can our practice rely on the excuse of necessity based on morally reasonable self-preference (see Chapter 8) as long as there is time to act when the potential danger materializes.

incarcerating a dangerous convict whose prison term has expired as we do for confining someone innocent but dangerously insane. Indeed, the same eudaemonist argument that will justify confining the innocent insane for the general welfare will also justify imprisoning someone we know intends a crime but who has yet to act upon his intent or whom psychological testing has revealed as a latent sociopath. Similarly, if we can violate the rights of the innocent insane for their own good, why can we not also violate the rights of the innocent alcoholic or cigarette smoker? Accordingly, the first line of argument bears implications incompatible with the inviolability of the person. Besides, although rights can be overridden by some goods, they cannot coherently be overridden by another's good or by another's opinion of one's own good; for to have a right of free agency is precisely to have a moral protection against interference for reasons of that sort. Such reasons cannot override the right; they can only destroy it. To be compatible with rights, overrides must be for reasons that realize the dignity claim underlying the right but that an absolute right itself upsets.

This brings us to the dignity-based justification. The reason the state may coerce the innocent insane, on this view, is that they lack the empirical capabilities for real autonomy that ground a right to unqualified respect for their rights-respecting choices. By real autonomy I mean the realized potential of free beings to act from self-authored ends rather than from those given immediately by passion and to actualize those ends in works that adequately reflect them (so that one is author of one's life, more or less). Realizing this potential requires powers of planning, deliberation, evaluative judgment, foresight, and reality apprehension. In short, it requires adequate empirical equipment. Those equipped to realize the agent's potential for autonomy have an unqualified right to respect for their right-respecting choices, for the ends driving these choices proceed authentically from the self that, as freedom from causal necessity, commands respect in the first place. However, those unable to act from self-authored ends have a right to respect for their right-respecting choices only to the extent that those choices will not harm goods (life, physical health) essential to exercising their capacity for choice; for respect for an agent's choices is properly limited by a concern for its good if (and only if) its choices reflect no autonomous conception of its good precluding interference. Further, respect for an agent's capacity for free choice is permissibly limited by a concern for others' agency goods if the agent, though it has committed no crime, is dangerously inclined *and* lacks equipment for living autonomously; for if the agent has no empirical capability for autonomy to respect, then the public interest in the conditions of autonomy is not reduced to a private interest by his or her preventive detention for the sake of others' autonomy. Call this the argument from diminished respect.

The argument from diminished respect may have an unattractive ring, but there is at least one element of the insanity defence for which it provides an attractive explanation. I refer to the presumption of sanity and the corresponding burden on the defendant to prove legal insanity should he wish to plead it. Since the result of a successful plea of mental disorder is that the defendant is innocent of criminal wrongdoing, the reverse onus violates his right to be presumed innocent until proved guilty beyond a reasonable doubt. However, this violation is justified in a free society, one might argue, because an acquittal on grounds of legal insanity exposes the individual to consequences that would be degrading to a free person, and we need more than a reasonable doubt about the defendant's sanity before we subject him to those consequences. Even if the defendant prefers therapeutic custody as a diminished human agent to conviction as a full one, the inalienability of the agent's right to respect requires that he prove the condition for diminished respect, at least on a balance of probabilities. Here, then, the reason for limiting the right to be presumed innocent is consistent with the norm of respect for persons underlying the right itself.

How *M'Naghten* selects for impaired autonomy

Let us assume that an argument from diminished respect is needed to justify detention of the innocent insane for prophylactic and paternalistic reasons. A question now arises as to whether all those who have disease of the mind lack the capability for autonomous action that grounds a right to undiminished respect.

Here again we must distinguish between two senses of freedom. The latter can mean a formal capacity for uncaused choice in the presence of which we can always say that (metaphysically speaking) an agent could have done otherwise than it did, no matter how powerful the emotions or distorted the perceptions that drove it to act in a certain way. It seems clear that, with the exception of a transient episode of automatic behaviour or an advanced stage of dementia, no mental disorder can vitiate freedom in this weak and formal sense. This is why insanity justifies at most a diminished respect for agency rather than a total withdrawal. Because he is an agent, the insane accused is, unlike the infant, entitled to stand trial if he is fit to answer the charge; and he is entitled to be judged guilty or not guilty on the same formalist criteria of culpability (did his action publicly manifest a choice to which a right denial is imputable?) that apply to the sane. Put otherwise, unless he is demented, the insane accused is entitled not to be treated as an infant lacking the responsible agency prerequisite for making a culpable choice.[16] He is also entitled, on acquittal, to a review within a reasonable time (and periodic reviews thereafter) to determine whether his continued custody is justified by his present dangerousness. And even if he has been deemed dangerous to himself or others, he is still entitled to—and under our positive law generally receives—as much respect for his choices as is consistent with his own and the public's safety.[17]

However, the idea of freedom can also denote the richer capability I have been calling real autonomy—the ability to act from self-authored ends and to produce

---

[16] Contrast RA Duff's view of the insanity defence; *Answering for Crime* (Oxford: Hart Publishing, 2007), 38–43, 285–7.
[17] Canadian Criminal Code, RSC 1985, c. C–46, ss. 672.54 and 672.55.

through the sum of one's actions a life pattern reflecting those ends. It is reasonable to assume that mental disorder could seriously impair freedom in this fuller sense, if only because it might pervasively distort information about the environment that one needs in order to author ends and accomplish what one chooses to do. If my life revolves around a single purpose I have formed because of a delusional belief in persecution and the fear generated by this belief, I cannot be said to live according to ends I have reflectively and spontaneously chosen and can affirm as my own. If I want to behead a snake that is attacking me but instead decapitate a person who appears to me as a snake, I do not act autonomously in the larger sense, for I do something and face consequences I did not choose. And if, as a result of an underlying pathology, I suffer from these delusions frequently, then my overall capability for autonomous action is fundamentally damaged.

There is, however, no reason to think that mental disorder necessarily effects such a radical diminution of one's capability for autonomy, and so we need to distinguish between those disorders that justify diminished respect for autonomy and those that do not. Of course, the rules governing insane defendants formulated in *M'Naghten's Case* did not address this distinction at all. A pure-blood child of the formalist paradigm, they focused solely on whether the accused did or did not, as a matter of fact, intend the prohibited action or intend it within an imagined world where the action would not have been wrong. Because they specified nothing but the conditions under which insanity exculpates, the M'Naghten rules left the acquitted insane vulnerable to an administrative detention unlimited by law, so that they could be confined indefinitely without even a determination of continuing dangerousness. This situation produced intolerable contradictions. For one, administrative detention was indistinguishable from the punishment for a past action they had been found not to deserve. For another, having been found to possess the agency required to stand trial and to give full answer and defence, they were nonetheless treated, once acquitted, as nonagents subject to despotic power.

The insanity provisions of the Canadian Criminal Code fill this legal void in a reasonably adequate (though still imperfect) way. Though its revision of the M'Naghten rules is slight, section 16 accomplishes what *M'Naghten* did not: it defines legal insanity with a view to the conditions of both exculpation and eligibility for continued detention for safety reasons alone. It does this by employing a formula that, embodying the formalist and real autonomy frameworks at once, does double duty as a criterion of nonculpability and a proxy for impaired autonomy warranting diminished respect. Section 16 states that "no person is criminally responsible for an act committed... while suffering from a mental disorder that rendered the person incapable of appreciating the nature and quality of the act... or of knowing that it was wrong." That the accused *did not* appreciate what he was doing renders him innocent of criminal wrongdoing because he lacked the culpable mind for the offence; that is, he made no choice to which a right denial may be imputed. That he did not appreciate because he *could not* means that he is generally incapable of fully autonomous action, hence less worthy of respect than those with full capability, hence subject to continued detention (if detention is warranted) even though innocent. Similarly, that the accused did not know his action was wrong negates criminal intent in the same way that colour of right negates guilt for theft. That he was *incapable* of knowing means that he is chronically subject to delusions that lead him to mistake criminal actions for ones that are justified or excused. Because he did not know, he is innocent of crime and undeserving of punishment; because he could not know, he has a diminished capability for autonomy and for *that* reason is detainable for the safety of himself and others.[18]

The statutory provisions relating to fitness to stand trial can be understood in a similar way. Someone "unable on account of mental disorder to conduct a defence... and, in particular, unable to... understand the nature or object of the proceedings... the probable consequences of the proceedings, or communicate with counsel" is excused from trial, because the fairness of the trial would be seriously compromised by the defendant's inability to mount a defence or to provide counsel with the information needed to mount one for him.[19] But the same criterion that selects those unfit for trial also selects those whose mental disorder is so extreme as to render them incapable of functioning as autonomous agents. And it is because they are incapable of so functioning that they can be indefinitely confined without a trial by virtue of their dangerousness alone.

Accordingly, the Canadian Criminal Code provisions on mental disorder can be reasonably interpreted as carefully selecting those who are subject to state coercion for public safety and paternalistic reasons even though innocent of crime (or not yet proved guilty) on the basis of a diminished capability for autonomy. Although incapacity to appreciate consequences and to know right from wrong, along with past violent conduct, strongly indicate a dangerous person, it is clear from the overall structure of the Code provisions on mental disorder that dangerousness is not the criterion for the court's remitting the innocent insane to state custody. Where dangerousness becomes the key consideration is at the post-trial disposition hearing, at which the court (now reconstituted as an administrative body) or Review Board is instructed by law to impose the least restrictive order consistent with public safety and the welfare of the mentally disordered individual.[20] At this stage, a full inquiry is conducted into the *present* dangerousness of the acquitted person—an inquiry that would be redundant if the criteria of legal insanity were interpreted as providing predictors of violence. Moreover, the

---

[18] The use of one formula to perform two separate functions is an imperfect solution, because it can detain for review for present dangerousness an innocent whose insanity at the time of the offence was temporary (i.e. who was incapable then but not now). A better solution is to pose two questions to the jury serially, one asking whether the defendant was legally insane at the time of the offence, the second asking whether, if so, he is generally incapable of understanding the nature and consequences of his actions. If he was legally insane then but capable of normal cognitive functioning now, he walks out of the courtroom; if he is incapable of normal cognition now, he is detained for review for present dangerousness.

[19] Canadian Criminal Code, s. 2. [20] Ibid, s. 672.54.

criterion of unfitness to stand trial—inability to conduct a defence—is not even loosely connected with a propensity for violence, nor is the suspected commission of an unlawful action, which may not have involved violence at all.

For these reasons, section 16 and the fitness provisions are best viewed as providing (besides criteria for exculpation and trial legitimacy, respectively) eligibility criteria for determining which innocents will be vulnerable to state coercion for reasons of dangerousness rather than as themselves providing *indicia* of dangerousness. So interpreted, these provisions are fair because, by selecting for coercion for social protection and paternalistic reasons only those innocents who, lacking a capability for full autonomy, command diminished respect for their agency, they constitute a justified limit on the defendant's right to liberty.

3. Divergence of the Criteria for Insane Automatism and Diminished Respect

Compare with these provisions the common law of automatism. The centerpiece of that law is the judge-made distinction between sane and insane automatism by which defendants pleading involuntary behaviour are routed by judges into the defence of insane automatism if the episode has led to violence and is bound to recur. Once within the legal contours of the insanity defence, the defendant will be acquitted or not depending on whether he knew what he was doing and that it was wrong. If the jury believes he committed the unlawful deed while in an automatic state, he will be acquitted under the M'Naghten rules and detained in the manner of all those found not guilty by reason of insanity.

This merger between the law of automatism and the defence of insanity produces, however, a rather glaring disharmony. Although someone acquitted of a crime because of insane automatism will have been acquitted because he was incapable of appreciating the nature and quality of his act and will be subject to the process governing those acquitted because of mental disorder, he will not have been channeled into this process under the same criterion as others acquitted under the M'Naghten rules. Whereas those who acted voluntarily are detained after acquittal because of a general cognitive incapacity due to mental disorder to appreciate the consequences of their actions, those who behaved unconsciously are detained simply because their involuntary episode was attributable to an internal disposition likely to lead to a recurrence. Under the common law of automatism, therefore, dangerousness rather than a diminished capability for autonomy selects the innocents destined for continued detention. Such detention is unjust, however, because it involves the coercion of someone who is innocent of crime and who is generally capable of autonomous action in order to satisfy ends external to his own. It thus violates the agency right of someone who has neither authorized such a violation through criminal conduct nor justified a diminished respect for his autonomy through severe mental disorder.

It might be objected, however, that the criterion of insane automatism, no less than the revised M'Naghten rules, does double duty as a test of culpability for wrong and of diminished autonomy, so that no one worthy of full respect will be detained after an acquittal because of insane automatism. Anyone who falls into an automatic state and commits a violent act from a mental disorder that is likely to recur is, one might argue, as lacking in real autonomy as the person who, though acting voluntarily, was incapable of appreciating what he was doing or of knowing that it was wrong. Yet a consideration of some actual cases will reveal this assurance as naïve.

In *R v Kemp*, the defendant struck his wife with a hammer causing a serious wound.[21] There was strong medical evidence that, at the time of the attack, the defendant was not conscious of picking up the hammer or of striking his wife with it. Two doctors also testified that the defendant's loss of consciousness was probably caused by an inadequate supply of blood to the brain, in turn attributable to arteriosclerosis. Much of Lord Devlin's judgment is taken up with a discussion of whether arteriosclerosis is a disease of the mind so as to warrant an instruction on insanity rather than involuntariness; and of course, once the issue is framed in these terms, the conclusion is inevitable that a mental disease might have a physical as well as a purely psychic cause. Concluding that the defendant was indeed suffering from a disease of the mind, Lord Devlin left only insanity to the jury, which accorded Mr Kemp the dubious benefit of an acquittal on that ground.

It is not, however, enough to ask whether an episode of automatism is attributable to a disease of the mind. Since an acquittal because of insanity leads to detention despite innocence, one must also ask whether the mental disease was of a nature and extent that would justify the diminished respect for autonomy implied by that fate. The facts of the case relevant to such an inquiry are mentioned by Lord Devlin only in passing. They are that the defendant, as Lord Devlin described him, was a man "of excellent character" and that he and his wife had "always been thought to be a devoted couple".[22] Moreover, two doctors testified that, although arteriosclerosis might lead to a massive degeneration of brain cells amounting to disease of the mind as they understood the term, Kemp's condition had not yet nearly progressed to that point. What had occurred, according to these witnesses, was a temporary interference with the normal supply of blood to the brain, akin to that which occurs during a concussion. Since the cause of that interference was an underlying physical disease, it is reasonable to assume that the violent behaviour could happen again. Yet Kemp was far from exhibiting the kind of mental deterioration that alone justifies the diminished respect for autonomy signified by detention following acquittal and by the possibility of indefinite confinement because of dangerousness alone.

---

[21] Note 4 above. [22] Ibid, 251.

The case of *R v Quick* likewise illustrates the divergence of the criteria for insane automatism and diminished respect, although in this case the court reached the right result by refusing to follow the logic of Lord Devlin's position.[23] The defendant was a nurse who assaulted a paraplegic patient causing serious bodily harm. The evidence revealed that the defendant was a diabetic, that he had taken insulin on the morning of the assault, and that he had consumed little food but a considerable quantity of alcohol during the day. There was also evidence that on 12 previous occasions, the defendant had been admitted to hospital either unconscious or semi-conscious from hypoglycaemia, a condition produced by too low a level of blood sugar. A doctor also testified that Mr Quick's ingestion of insulin combined with his having consumed little food and much alcohol could have produced hypoglycaemia, in the advanced stages of which the sufferer may become unconscious and violent. On this evidence the trial judge ruled that the defendant's only defence was insanity, whereupon the defendant pleaded guilty and appealed.

Applying Lord Denning's definition of mental disease (any mental disorder that has manifested itself in violence and is prone to recur) to this case, the conclusion is inescapable that the trial judge's ruling was correct. Unconsciousness produced by hypoglycaemia is no different than unconsciouness produced by an epileptic seizure or by arteriosclerosis. Moreover, the disorder had manifested itself in violence and was likely to recur. Nevertheless, the English Court of Appeal resisted the pull of this logic in the name of common sense. What, after all, would be the point of sending Quick to a mental hospital? Since, however, one could ask the same question about Kemp, Lord Lawton needed a principle to stop the logic of Lord Devlin. The one he devised drew a distinction between unconsciousness produced by an external factor (such as a blow to the head or the ingestion of a drug) and that caused by an internal one. The former, which is a transitory and likely isolated incident, gives rise to a defence of sane automatism; the latter, which is more likely to recur, supports only a defence of insanity. In this case, said Lord Lawton, the defendant's automatic state was produced by an external factor—the injection of insulin.

From the standpoint of Lord Denning's dangerousness criterion, however, the external/internal dichotomy is unstable, because unconsciousness may be produced by an external factor working upon an internal susceptibility. A thin-skulled person may be just as prone to unconsciousness from minor blows to the head as an epileptic is from internal causes. A sleepwalker is less able to cope with the psychological effects of external stresses than an awake consciousness. Quick himself took insulin only because he was a diabetic. Thus to say that his unconsciousness was produced by an external factor ignores the internal condition that ensures the regular repetition of the external cause.[24] Were its logic pursued relentlessly, therefore, the dangerousness test of insane automatism would detain and

---

[23] [1973] 3 All ER 347.
[24] Nevertheless, Quick was reaffirmed in *R v Roach* [2001] EWCA Crim 2698.

possibly confine indefinitely an innocent whose brittle skull, or diabetes, or tendency to somnambulism made him a risk to others.[25] Neither a brittle skull, nor diabetes, nor somnambulism, however, fundamentally impairs autonomy. And if it is objected that this logic need not concern us, because no purpose would be served by placing a diabetic, etc. in a mental hospital, the reply is simple: if the point is public safety, why must it be a mental hospital or, indeed, even a hospital?

The breakdown of the external/internal dichotomy is the theme of *Rabey*, the leading Canadian case on psychological blow automatism.[26] There the defendant was a somewhat introverted university student who had conceived a romantic interest in a woman with whom he shared various student activities. One day he found a letter she had written to a friend in which she declared a sexual interest in someone else and described the defendant as a "nothing". The next time the defendant saw her, he inquired as to her feelings about him, and when told that she regarded him simply as a friend, he fell (or so he said) into a semi-conscious state and began striking her with a rock and choking her. When he realized what he was doing, he stopped. At trial, the defendant raised the defence of sane automatism, claiming that the psychological shock received on reading the letter induced a dissociated state that was not a disease of the mind nor symptomatic of any underlying pathology. The trial judge accepted the defence psychiatrist's view that the defendant was not insane and acquitted him on the ground of sane automatism. The Crown successfully appealed and the defendant then appealed to the Supreme Court of Canada.

A majority of the court dismissed the defendant's appeal on the following reasoning. It drew a distinction between a malfunctioning of the mind caused primarily by factors internal to the defendant and one attributable to an external cause. Where the event triggering a dissociative episode is a psychological blow, one must inquire into the nature of the trauma in order to locate the primary cause of the malfunctioning. If the shock was sufficiently extreme to precipitate the same reaction in an ordinary individual, then the cause is the external shock, and the appropriate plea is sane automatism. However, if, as in this case, the triggering event is part of the ordinary stresses and disappointments of life, then the primary cause is the defendant's unusual emotional sensitivity, and the only defence is insane automatism. Justice Ritchie, writing for the majority, found the key to the defendant's extreme reaction in his introversion and inexperience in amorous relationships, in which psychological setting the infatuation with the woman created an "abnormal condition" amounting to disease of the mind.[27]

In *Rabey*, accordingly, the logic of the likelihood-of-recurrence test that was resisted by Lord Lawton in the case of an insulin injection for diabetes was pursued in the case of a psychological shock working on an unusual susceptibility. The result was that introversion, inexperience with the opposite sex, and an

---

[25] The logic *was* pursued relentlessly in *Hennessy* (diabetes) and *Burgess* (somnambulism).
[26] Note 6 above. [27] Ibid, 521.

infatuation were held to indicate a diseased mind for which the defendant could be detained despite having been found innocent of criminal wrongdoing. Although the Crown's psychiatrist testified that a dissociative episode was itself a mental disorder, there was no evidence in Rabey of any underlying pathology, either psychological or organic, that would warrant the diminished respect for autonomy implied by detention of an innocent for paternalistic and prophylactic reasons.

It is true, of course, that Rabey would now likely be set free under the provisions permitting an absolute or conditional discharge of someone found by a Review Board to be no longer dangerous. However, this assurance misses the point. The mere detention of an innocent for the purpose of assessing his dangerousness as well as his subjection to a procedure that makes his liberty conditional on predictions of harm all involve affronts to human dignity for which some threshold justificatory condition must be met. Public safety cannot itself be that justification, because detention for prophylactic reasons alone is precisely the thing to be justified. Nor can it be an answer to the offence to dignity implicit in the very process of administrative review for dangerousness that the person acquitted may at the end of the process be set free.

4. Toward a New Legal Definition of Disease of the Mind

The cases of *Kemp, Quick,* and *Rabey* amply illustrate the possibility of divergence between the common-law criterion of insane automatism and that for diminished respect for autonomy. Both the continuing-danger test and the internal-cause test (which is itself ultimately concerned with dangerousness) will routinely lead to the detention and confinement of innocent persons who exhibit no marked impairment of cognitive and deliberative powers and who, though they may suffer periodic episodes of semi-conscious behaviour, are as generally capable of autonomous choice and action as anyone without their infirmity. For these people, the disrespect for their autonomy implied in continued detention for paternalistic and prophylactic reasons involves an unjustified violation of their agency rights, for nothing in their condition warrants it.

Accordingly, we need a new definition of disease of the mind to distinguish insane from sane automatism. Like the present one, this definition should be a legal rather than a purely medical one, because its work is normative rather than diagnostic. Its purpose is to screen those innocents whose right to liberty the state may justifiably override for the good of others or for their own good as others see it. Though novel, the definition should nonetheless be indigenous to the legal tradition, akin to the criterion of incapacity recognized in other statutes governing the civil capacity of the mentally incompetent. The definition I propose is this: a disease of the mind is any impairment of the powers of cognition, foresight, deliberation, and judgment that renders the individual generally (and not merely episodically) incapable of appreciating the reasonably foreseeable consequences of his or her actions or of understanding information relevant to forming and carrying out a life plan. Those whose condition satisfies this definition of mental disease command a diminished respect for autonomy, because they will habitually produce outcomes and face consequences they did not choose.

Several objections to this definition may be anticipated. First, if the criterion of insane automatism were narrowed to mental impairment destructive of real autonomy, many more people would win absolute acquittals whose dissociative episodes are likely to recur and who thus pose a continuing danger to others. This could not only increase the risk of harmful behaviour but also undermine public confidence in the administration of justice, which will be seen to favour the rights of the defendant over the security of the public. Second, it might be argued that the proposed definition, with its requirement of a general and not merely episodic disability for autonomous action, would counter-intuitively exclude those whose automatic episodes occur frequently as well as those whose severe psychiatric disorders are normally controllable by medication. These people, it seems, would go free if found not guilty of the crime charged. Third, the proposed definition of mental disease is arguably too inclusive, for everyone knows somebody whose plans always seem to misfire through lack of judgment and foresight.

To the first concern there are at least two responses, one that staunchly invokes principle and one that meets the concern for public safety on its own ground. The principled and sufficient response is that any decrease in public safety that might result is in itself no argument against the narrower criterion, for a society of free and equal persons is entitled only to as much public safety as is consistent with its moral foundations. From a public safety standpoint, there is as much reason to subject every convict whose prison term has expired to a review for likelihood of recidivism as there is to hold innocent people in custody under the present criterion of insane automatism. Yet we would all recognize such a practice as inconsistent with a liberal legal order. Moreover, if public opinion ridicules the administration of justice for being true to its principles of freedom and equality, then, as Justice La Forest observed in *R v Parks*, the opinion may be discounted.[28]

However, there is also a response that more directly meets the concern for public safety and confidence and that, realistically, a legislative body responsible to the public is entitled to offer. The risk of freeing the dangerous can be lowered without any compromise of principle if those knowingly prone to unconscious episodes were charged with criminal negligence causing harm if they failed to take reasonable precautions for others' safety, and if the evidentiary burden on the defendant to raise a reasonable doubt about the voluntariness of his actions were appropriately toughened. The natural presumption that human beings act voluntarily is, after all, a strong one and should not be capable of being easily rebutted. Accordingly, trial judges could be instructed by legislation on the considerations that weigh against putting automatism of any kind to the jury. For example, an

---

[28] [1992] 2 SCR 871, at 908.

expert witness adds little to the defendant's bare assertion of involuntariness if he or she simply testifies to the plausibility of the defendant's account of events and to the general nature and aetiology of dissociative states rather than to the actual psychiatric condition and history of the defendant. If there is no witness to the event to corroborate the defendant's account, then the absence of personalized expert testimony should be fatal to any plea of involuntariness. Also, the fact that the defendant had an obvious motive for the assault or that the victim was the very person whose insult triggered the alleged dissociative episode casts serious doubt on a claim of involuntariness, since we would expect violent acts committed while reason is asleep to be inexplicable in terms of clear and evident motives.

The second objection voices a concern that, under the proposed definition of mental disease, those who have frequent periods of automatic behaviour, or who generally control their severe symptoms with medication, will go free once acquitted. The response is that they will go free only if their illnesses do not seriously interfere with their ability to form and carry out life plans. Someone who experiences automatic episodes that occur (or that are expected to occur) so frequently as to significantly impair his overall capability for autonomy will not go free under the proposed definition, nor will someone who repeatedly neglects to take his medication. Of course, it is impossible to determine with precision the frequency of unconscious behaviour at which someone may be said to suffer from a general disability for self-directed action, but indeterminacy of this kind is no stranger to the law, and juries are well enough equipped with common sense to deal with it—or so we assume. Finally, we need not be concerned that the proposed definition of mental disease will sweep in every ne'er-do-well, since it requires an incapacity to execute a life plan rather than a mere failure to do so—one attributable to a severe impairment of mental faculties.

Adopting the proposed definition of mental disease (or one like it) would have implications for a problem that has arisen ancillary to the one concerning the criterion of insane automatism: whether the defences of sane and insane automatism should be conjunctive or mutually exclusive. As long as a policy of controlling the dangerous underlies the definition of insane automatism, there will be an impetus to ensure that the category of insane automatism is inescapable for those who qualify for it. Thus, in *Bratty*, the House of Lords ruled that once the jury has rejected a plea of insane automatism, the defendant cannot plead sane automatism on the same evidence.[29] This ruling, however, bore implications embarrassing for the courts. Since the burden of proving insanity is on the party raising the issue, while the burden of proving involuntariness (an element of the *actus reus*) is on the prosecution, the rule in *Bratty* meant that the jury, having rejected the defendant's insanity defence, would be forced to convict even if it had a reasonable doubt about the voluntariness of the defendant's conduct. This, however, would violate the defendant's right to be presumed innocent and (since the trial judge has withheld from the jury a defence logically open to him) his right to a trial by jury.

[29] Note 2 above.

The violation of the defendant's right to be presumed innocent and to a trial by jury is the end point of a law of automatism based on a policy of controlling the dangerous. If an impaired capacity for autonomy rather than dangerousness were the criterion of *insane* automatism, there would be no need for mutually exclusive pleas. No policy would be subverted and no principle violated if a jury, having decided that the defendant probably did not evince a mental disorder warranting diminished respect, nevertheless acquitted because they held a reasonable doubt as to whether the defendant's behaviour was voluntary.

5. Conclusion

In their concern for controlling dangerous persons, common-law courts have produced a law of automatism that massively violates agency rights. Not only does it deprive acquitted persons of their liberty without the sort of justification that is consistent with their right to liberty; it also runs a high risk (given the inescapability of the reverse onus) of punishing the innocent.

Failing action by courts, therefore, legislation is needed to put the law of automatism on a principled footing independent of a policy of controlling the dangerous. This is all the more possible where, as in Canada, public safety concerns are given full play where they belong—in a legislative scheme for the disposition of those found not guilty by reason of mental disorder.[30] The Canadian regime's principal innovation is a post-trial hearing to determine what disposition of the acquitted individual—indefinite hospitalization, conditional discharge, or absolute discharge—is appropriate in light of his present dangerousness to himself and to others. Since the detainee's continuing dangerousness is decided on all the evidence at the post-trial hearing, the law of insane automatism can focus exclusively on the question of principle, namely, who among innocent persons is eligible for detention and confinement for public safety and paternalistic reasons alone? The answer, I suggest, is: those whose capacity for autonomy has been severely impaired by disease.

I would therefore propose that the law of automatism be reformed along the following lines. Where the defendant raises sufficient evidence to render a plea of automatism plausible, the judge should put the defence of insane automatism to the jury if and only if he concludes that, if believed by a jury, the evidence for the unconscious episode would warrant a finding that the defendant was probably suffering from a mental disorder that renders him generally incapable of appreciating the reasonably foreseeable consequences of his actions or of understanding information relevant to forming and executing a life plan. It would be irrelevant

---

[30] Canadian Criminal Code, ss. 672.54 and 672.55. In the United Kingdom, the Criminal Procedure (Insanity and Unfitness to Plead) Act 1991 gives judges flexibility in disposition depending on present dangerousness.

whether such a disorder had a psychic or physical origin. It would then be for the jury to determine whether they had a reasonable doubt that the action was voluntary, and, if so, whether the episode probably manifested a mental disorder of the required severity. If they find the action was voluntary, the accused is guilty. If they have a reasonable doubt about voluntariness but there is insufficient evidence to establish mental disorder on a balance of probabilities, the verdict is not guilty, and the acquitted person walks freely from the courtroom. If they have a reasonable doubt about voluntariness and conclude that the defendant probably has a disease of the mind in the sense proposed, the verdict is that the defendant is not criminally responsible because of mental disorder, whereupon he is remitted to the administrative procedures for determining dangerousness.

Under this scheme, there would be no mutual exclusivity between the pleas of insane and sane automatism. Whenever insane automatism is put to the jury, a verdict of sane automatism would also be available; for the jury may doubt whether the defendant behaved voluntarily but not be persuaded that he suffers from a disorder of the severity needed to justify diminished respect.

9

The Unity of the Penal Law

1. Introduction

In the Introduction to this book, I promised to exhibit the general part of a liberal penal law as a complex unity of plural frameworks of justice. I have not yet delivered on that promise. So far, I have displayed the penal law's general part as a togetherness of two frameworks—one ordered to freedom understood as a capacity to act from optional ends (formal agency) distinguishing agents from things, the other based on freedom conceived as the actualized potential for acting from self-authored ends (real autonomy) distinguishing autonomous agents from those who thoughtlessly choose ends given by nature or custom. However, I have not yet shown the unity of the frameworks. But of course without such a demonstration, the penal law looks more like a patchwork than a whole.

The impression of a patchwork is strengthened when we review the main conclusions of the discussion thus far. With its exclusive concern for protecting agents (including wrongdoers) against interference with their capacity for free choice, the formal agency paradigm yielded the threshold requirements of criminal culpability for wrongdoing in the abstract and hence for judicial punishment of any severity. But it could not on its own generate a determinate scheme of punishments for crimes of varying harmfulness, nor could it yield any constraints on punishability for the harmful consequences of criminal wrongs once the threshold of criminality had been crossed. For such a scheme and such constraints we had to move to a framework of penal justice ordered to the agent's actualized potential for self-determined action. In treating real autonomy as the end of law, that framework recognizes harms to agency goods of varying importance as punishable harms of varying seriousness, protects the agent's authorship of its life against an unlimited vulnerability to moral fate, and ensures that its rightful vulnerability is structured in accordance with the degree to which the harmful result of its culpable wrong is imputable to its choice as distinct from chance.

Nor could the formal agency paradigm account for the highly populous class of offences known as public welfare offences or (given the inapplicability here of penal desert) provide any moral constraints on state coercion within this sphere. Aimed at preventing harm to agency goods or at facilitating the pursuit of self-authored ends, public welfare laws belong to the real autonomy framework, which, for the sake of autonomy, disallows unavoidable (strict) liability as well as imprisonment for negligence.

The affirmative defences to a criminal accusation likewise appeared as a hybrid product of two frameworks. Thus, while the formalist paradigm sufficed to explain the contours of the right to self-defence against wrongdoers, only the interaction between formalist and real autonomy frameworks could explain justified force against innocents; and only the real autonomy framework could explain the excuse of due diligence for breaches of public welfare statutes. Further, the formalist paradigm explained the role of mental disorder as an exculpatory defence, but only the framework of real autonomy could explain why it is permissible to detain for prophylactic and paternalistic reasons someone acquitted of a crime by reason of insanity. And, as if this confusion of frameworks were not enough, neither of the two paradigms could explain the excuses of necessity, duress, and provocation, for an account of which we had to admit an idea of moral blamelessness insofar as this idea could be viewed as simulating the exculpatory conditions generated by the formalist framework.

In self-defence against this lengthy indictment, I will say that showing in detail the togetherness of the paradigms is essential to revealing the penal law as a complex whole. For one cannot exhibit the penal law's general part as a complex unity without first showing that it is complex in the way that an organism can be complex—as comprising a plurality of subsystems ordered to distinctive ends.

Indeed, it is this plurality that explains the puzzling features of the penal law's basic structure that awoke our curiosity in the Introduction. In particular, it explains why causing or risking harm is inessential to liability to judicial punishment *simpliciter* but is nevertheless an aggravating factor relevant to an appropriate measure of punishment; why subjective fault is normally required at the threshold of criminal culpability but not for punishability for results; why risking harm is inessential to criminal liability but determinative of liability for a public welfare offence; why harm is inessential to criminal liability but comparisons of harm inflicted and harm avoided determine whether an accused has an affirmative defence to liability; why blameworthy character is neither necessary nor sufficient for criminal desert but blameless character in the face of extraordinary pressures excuses from punishment. The penal law has these features, not because it is a chaotic jumble of historical accretions, but because it reflects a plurality of internally coherent theoretical frameworks ordered, respectively, to formal agency, real autonomy, and (peripherally) moral virtue.

Having shown the complexity of the penal law, however, I must now make the case for its unity. For to leave the law in this patchwork state would be to open the door to rule-of-law sceptics who argue that law generally, and the penal law in particular, is fraught with "dialectical contradiction" or is nothing but a battleground for rival political ideologies (libertarian, egalitarian, communitarian)—one on which public reason is the first fatality. Such a result would spell defeat for a liberal legal order claiming to reconcile punishment with freedom; for it would mean that punishment is an instrument, at worst, of the politically dominant liberal sect, at best, of a contingent coalition of competing sects. What it would *not* be is self-imposable by all recipients regarded as free and equal. To avoid this result, I must show that the frameworks form parts of a whole. This requires that I introduce a further idea distinct from the ones separately governing the paradigms, and that I show how the paradigms respectively ordered to formal agency, real autonomy, and moral virtue reflect in diverse ways this more comprehensive idea, of whose organized body of law they are constituent and mutually complementary systems.

The further idea is revealed by the interdependence of formal agency and real autonomy regarded as conceptions of the freedom that supports a claim of human dignity. We show this interdependence by demonstrating that, when either conception of freedom is made the penal law's fundamental end (either ignoring or subsuming the other), it produces a self-contradictory outcome—that is, an outcome in which the dignity borne by the conception is contradicted rather than realized. In that way, we show that each conception needs the other's independent ordering for the sake of its own self-consistency—that the order governed by each complements and completes the other. Once this argument is made, it will remain to grasp the nature of the idea revealed by the mutual complementarity of the paradigms and then to show how the paradigms are particular examples of that idea.

2. The Interdependence of Formal Agency and Real Autonomy

Formal agency and slavery

Little more needs to be done to show the dependence of a claim to human dignity invoking formal agency on a legal framework ordered to real autonomy; for this dependence was already shown in the argument for the transition to the real autonomy paradigm in Chapter 4. Let me briefly recapitulate the argument.

When we treat the bare capacity to act from ends one freely chooses as the penal law's fundamental end, we arrive at the result that slavery is consistent with freedom. This is so because, strictly speaking, the only ways in which that capacity can be disrespected are (a) through the unprovoked application of overbearing physical force so as to move or restrain from movement another agent, (b) through the unprovoked destruction of the capacity, and (c) through threats of wrongful force. Not covered by any of these actions, however, are voluntary contracts of servitude.

Why, one might wonder, do threats of force pre-empt free choice? Certainly, if someone, against my will, lifts me up and sets me down at a different spot, he has prevented the exercise of my capacity for directing my body according to ends *I* choose. In effect, he has reduced me to a natural object whose motion is causally determined by external forces. But if someone pointing a gun at me says "your labour or your life" and I give him my labour for an indefinite period, then it looks as though I have expressed my capacity for undetermined choice (for I could have chosen otherwise), albeit in a way that frustrates the potential for self-determination the capacity carries (for I now act in obedience to another's ends rather than from those proceeding from my own capacity for originating ends). Accordingly, one might argue, if what we mean by respect for freedom is respect for undetermined rather than for self-determined choice, then enslaving someone by threats is consistent with respect for freedom. This is why Hobbes, for whom freedom is just the absence of physical impediment to motion, could think that a promise made under threat of death—even a promise to hand over money to a gunman—creates an obligation unless the laws of the commonwealth say otherwise.[1]

The rejoinder, however, is that where one agent imposes on another a choice between destruction of the capacity for freedom (i.e. death or serious physical injury) and service to its ends, the capacity is not respected, because threatening a wrongful pre-emption of the capacity unless the victim does one's bidding is equivalent to pre-empting the capacity. Factually, it is true, I could have done otherwise than accept slavery; but because the "otherwise" would have been a wrongful pre-emption of my freedom of choice, formalist right cannot recognize it as a possible option. But with one of the only two available choices off the table, there is no choice, and so the agent "acts" as if moved from without.

Suppose, however, the threat to life comes not from another agent, but from circumstances of destitution within a private property regime; and suppose that, to avoid starvation, the agent submits indefinitely to the ends of someone who provides subsistence in return. Because starvation is a choice a free agent can factually make (he is not instinctually *compelled* to avoid it), the capacity for choice is undoubtedly exercised here; the agent chooses slavery rather than starvation. And since starvation would have violated no norm of formal right, it is not legally excluded either. So there was a choice between two live options. But if the agent is here bound to a master only by a desire for life that he, as a free agent, is not compelled by nature to satisfy, then it would appear that the slave is self-enslaved, chained to a master by virtue of his own chosen attachment to life. Were he to renounce the attachment (as he can), he would die a free man. If, therefore, the agent's freedom consists solely in the capacity freely to choose ends, we would be forced to conclude that a person who submits to another's mastery to avoid death by starvation has chosen freely and that its free choice is respected by the master. This is perhaps why Roman law, which seems to have been ordered exclusively to respect for formal agency, could recognize slavery and personhood as two equally possible legal statuses for a human being.[2] Unlike the Greek slave, who was considered a slave by nature, the Roman slave was a slave by choice, having (typically) preferred slavery to death in military combat. Thus, he was not a thing in the true sense, for he had chosen a status defined by having duties but no rights; true things—nonagents—have neither.

---

[1] *Leviathan* (Oxford: Blackwell, 1957), 91.
[2] Hegel saw Roman law as ordered exclusively to respect for formal agency; see *The Philosophy of History*, trans. J Sibree (New York: Dover, 1956), 278–9, 316–18.

How did a conception of human dignity come to countenance a condition antithetical to human dignity? The root problem with formal agency as a conception of freedom is that it treats the agent's particularity—the particular body in which the agent is alive as well as the subjective ends of its motion—as necessarily belonging to the animality of the agent, forming no part of its freedom. With this equation of particularity with biological particularity, the freedom to choose ends must be conceived as a possibility of detachment from particularity as such—as the capacity *not* to be compelled by particular ends or as the capacity always to have chosen some end other than the one chosen. Freedom thus becomes simply a capacity to renounce every end, with the result that all specific ends actually chosen, including self-preservation, are subjective values one may either have chosen to further or not. In this way, freedom becomes identical to arbitrariness, since no principle is yet available for deciding how to choose. But this means that we now have a dichotomy between a contentless capacity for nondetermination generic to agents and the subjective ends of the individual, all of which are possible objects of choice. Since no particular choice is inconsistent with the capacity for choosing, no disrespect for the capacity is implied in recognizing the choice of slavery over nonwrongful death as a possible option for human agents.

I assume it is common ground that no conception of human dignity can be adequate that treats slavery as consistent with it. That freedom as the negative capacity for nondetermination is consistent with a condition in which the agent is an object for another's ends shows that freedom must be conceived more robustly so as to rule slavery out as a possible manifestation of it. Specifically, it must be conceived as actualized potential for self-determination or as living according to self-authored ends. On this view, then, the particular life and subjective ends of the individual have rational (not just biological) significance as the medium through which the generic *purposiveness* of the agent (i.e. its capacity to set ends *for itself*) is necessarily expressed. The particular agent is not a ghostly self inhabiting a natural body independent of it; rather it is a generic capacity for acting purposively that is individuated in a body moulded to its purposes and executing its self-authored ends.

Only if human dignity rests on a conception of freedom as actualized potential for self-determined action is slavery normatively impossible for human agents. For now there are some ends the agent cannot validly choose to renounce, because renouncing them would be inconsistent with its dignity adequately conceived—with the dignity that commands (up to a limit) respect for its choices. For example, the agent cannot renounce its life (except for a worthy end), because freedom as self-determination is actual only in a living body directed to a self-authored purpose. Nor can it (except in anticipation of incompetency) renounce or alienate to another agent the power to choose the ends of its life, for actualized potential for self-determination means living according to self-authored ends. Thus just as, under the former conception, the agent could not choose, consistently with respect for its freedom, that someone kill or maim it, so now it cannot validly choose that others choose the ends of its action. Contracts of servitude are thus normatively impossible.

Further, because a living and whole body is the indispensable medium through which the potential for self-determined action becomes actual, life and bodily integrity are common, agency goods rather than widely shared preferences; and so a legal order founded on public reason as real autonomy must be concerned with protecting freedom, not only against interference with its exercise, but also against harm to agency goods, and not only against the harm consequent on interferences, but against harm to agency goods generally. Finally, because ownership is also essential to self-determination as delimiting a range of selfless objects over which the agent's purposes are sovereign, property too is an agency good, even if this or that item of property is an object of preference.

Not only, however, does freedom as actualized potential for self-determination generate a distinction between subjective ends and agency goods (and so between legally irrelevant and legally cognizable harms); the actualized potential for acting from self-authored ends is itself a human good. Indeed, within a legal framework ordered to actualized potential, it is the fundamental human good—the good through which things necessary to self-determination are judged to be necessarily good for everyone. Whereas the bare capacity for free choice cannot be called a good because it is simply an ontological fact about a certain kind of being (one with self-consciousness), actualized potential for self-determination is a good, because it is a perfection one may or may not achieve. Choosing *undetermined* by external causes is something a conscious human agent necessarily does, but acting according to *self-authored* ends is something an agent may not do, for this requires the integration of biological and customary ends into more fundamental and autonomously chosen life goals. Hence it requires the cultivation of powers of moral independence, reflection, deliberation, foresight, self-control—in short, what the ancients called *phronesis* or *prudentia*. But if real autonomy is a goal to be achieved rather than a given fact, then a legal paradigm ordered to it is one ordered, not simply to individual liberty, but to a common good.

Accordingly, the self-contradictory realization of a conception of human dignity based on formal agency shows that a paradigm of penal justice ordered to formal agency requires one ordered to real autonomy to supplement and complete it. Without such a framework, slavery would be a normatively possible choice for free beings, while varying punishments for interferences with freedom according to the harm inflicted on an agency good would be logically impossible—hence practically possible only at the price of incoherence. Within the formal agency framework taken alone, there is only one crime—the public manifestation of a right denial—and only one punishment—the infringement of the criminal's right.

Real autonomy and the rule of others' autonomy

But now the obvious question arises: if the only coherent conception of freedom is the actualized potential for self-determined action, why do we need a legal framework independently ordered to formal agency at all? Surely, a framework ordered to real autonomy must also protect the capacity for choice against pre-emptions of, and interferences with, the capacity's exercise; for a basic precondition of acting from one's own ends is that one be free to act. So, the real autonomy framework must incorporate all the protections against coercion generated by the formalist paradigm within its more expansive guarantees against an unlimited vulnerability to fate. Moreover, we have already admitted that the formalist paradigm rests on an inadequate view of public reason—that its viewing the bare capacity for choice as the only public thing stems from a mistaken equation of all interests with subjective interests; and that this impoverished conception of the public left it powerless to fit the notion of harm coherently into the penal law. But if all this is so, why not let the common good of real autonomy singly and exclusively order the penal law?

Let us see what happens when it does so. If real autonomy were the fundamental end of the penal law, then the latter's general part would exhibit the following features. Since real autonomy is the fulfilment of a potential rather than a mere possibility to have chosen otherwise, the end of penal law would be a goal rather than a capacity for choosing goals. Hence all judicial coercion would be justified instrumentally as a means of promoting the goal—as serving the common good of self-determination. Therefore, the retrospective idea of desert would have no justificatory role to play anywhere in the penal law, not even within the sphere of "true crimes". Indeed, the distinction between true crimes and public welfare offences would no longer be viable, for all judicial coercion would aim at the public welfare understood as actualized potential for self-determination. The border between crimes and infractions would thus have to be redrawn along the line separating offences endangering agency goods from those against statutes embodying social preferences.

Once all crimes become public welfare offences, however, the nature of judicial coercion undergoes a fundamental transformation. From the backward-looking punishment of wrongdoers it becomes the forward-looking management of human threats. Preventing harm rather than vindicating rights of formal agency becomes the aim of criminal law no less than of regulatory law. This means that the dangerous character rather than the criminal agent becomes the object of penal law and its sanctions, which become instruments honed to the aim of incapacitating him, preferably before he can strike. Thus, inchoate offences, once an apparent anomaly in a regime of punishment, become the norm in a regime of threat control, yet (as we shall see) without the robust *actus* requirement imposed by a law of punishment. Moreover, where the aim of penal law is to defend against human threats rather than to punish the guilty, there is no need for a presumption of innocence, which can only interfere with prosecuting the aim and which, if desert is no constraint, becomes pointless anyway. Thus, the reverse onus that is the hallmark of the regulatory offence spreads throughout the penal law.[3]

---

[3] According to Markus Dubber, this dystopia actually describes the state of criminal law in the United States; see *Victims in the War on Crime* (New York: New York University Press, 2002), chs. 1–3.

The fact that a public goal rather than desert would legitimate judicial coercion would not, however, entail an unconstrained consequentialism. It would not mean that the factually innocent or nonresponsible could be forcibly confined if incapacitating them were necessary to achieve the goal; for (as Hart showed) whatever role the outmoded idea of desert played in reconciling punishment with freedom could now be taken up by the idea of autonomy itself. Thus, the gist of the defendant's answer to a criminal accusation would not be "I don't deserve to be punished for this"; rather, it would be "to punish me would be to impose a fate I could not reasonably have avoided and so had no reasonable possibility of controlling. It would thus undermine the very autonomy the penal law is supposed to promote."

Nevertheless, the obsolescence of the idea of criminal desert would mean the loss of the retributivist rationale for a requirement of subjective fault at the threshold of criminality; and since the real autonomy framework provides no substitute rationale, the subjective fault requirement would disappear. True, promotion of the forward-looking aims of punishment must be constrained by respect for individual autonomy, but this can be done (as Hart advocated) with a negligence standard of fault that takes into account the defendant's capacity to have conformed to the law; for to say that the defendant negligently broke the law is just to say that he failed to comply though it was within his power to do so. A higher, subjective standard of fault would subvert the preventive aim of the law (by giving negligent mistakes exculpatory force and by making proof of responsibility more onerous and uncertain), yet would be unnecessary for an individual's control over his penal liability. Thus, a claim that one had exercised due diligence in trying to comply with the law would become the paradigmatic defence to crime. Indeed, all exculpatory conditions would be reinterpreted from this standpoint (as they were by Hart) as conditions under which the agent lacked a fair opportunity to avoid penal liability. But this means that the severe sentences required by a regime aimed at incapacitating human threats could be meted out on the basis of ordinary negligence.

The *actus* requirement of penal liability would likewise assume a new shape under a regime ordered to real autonomy. Within the formal agency framework, the rationale for the *actus* requirement is retributivist. According to that rationale, recall, the *actus* is needed to give the right denial implicit in the criminal's intention a show of public validity, without which there is no conceptual impetus to generalize his principle so as to bring him under it. On this view, the *actus* has an intrinsic importance for liability distinct from that of the culpable mind; for its role is to externalize, not corroborate, criminal intent. But if all judicial coercion is justified instrumentally (subject to a controllability constraint), then the retributivist rationale for the *actus* goes by the board. And since the retributivist rationale is (to my knowledge) the only one that gives the *actus* requirement an intrinsic importance, the necessity for an *actus* also atrophies under the new regime.

This can happen in either of two ways. One could say that the point of the *actus* is simply to give evidence of a firm disposition to harm or endanger others. Thus, the role that an *actus* requirement plays is to select for incapacitation those who are really dangerous from the many who might innocuously harbour felonious thoughts now and then. But of course evidence of dangerousness might be available from other sources—for example, from previous convictions, from psychological tests of a prisoner whose term for a crime has expired but who still poses a threat, from previous episodes of violent automatic behaviour by someone whose defence to a crime is involuntariness (no act), or from the confession of someone whose preliminary steps toward executing his criminal design were minimal and could be interpreted innocently. Alternatively, one could say that the point of the *actus* requirement is to ensure that agents are punished only for their choices, hence only for offences under their control. But, as Douglas Husak has shown, agents can control many things besides their acts; they can control their omissions, their statuses, and even the length of time they play host to a dangerous thought.[4] The result in either case is that the *actus* ceases to have intrinsic importance for criminal liability; it becomes a stand-in for some other requirement, which can be satisfied in other ways. Hence it withers away.

Of course, the question we must ask is not whether a penal regime exclusively ordered to real autonomy would be true to a subjectivist conception of fault or to an intrinsically important *actus* requirement; rather, we must ask whether it would be true to its own ideal of individual autonomy. Yet a moment's reflection will reveal that it would not.

Retributive punishment, at least in its legal version, is itself the condition of respecting someone's autonomy even in depriving him of liberty. Only when the conditions of culpability generated by legal retributivism are met can the convict be said to have implicitly authorized his moral fate. Those conditions are the making of a choice to which a right denial can be imputed, and the doing or omitting to do something publicly manifesting that denial. But since the basis of criminal liability under the real autonomy regime is negligence—the failure to avoid the proscribed conduct or to take the required precautions when one reasonably had the opportunity and power to do so—the right to liberty is no longer lost by implication of one's deed. Because no logical circuit connects negligently doing the proscribed deed and liability to coercion, we can no longer say that the punishment the convict receives is implicitly assented to. But this means that, if he is judicially coerced, the convict is deprived of his liberty in order to secure the agency goods of others. In other words, he is used violently as a means.

Because, moreover, judicial coercion promotes the autonomy of some by denying it to others, the good served by the institution of punishment is no longer a common good—a public reason for coercion. Hence it is no longer capable of free endorsement by the thinking Agent in advance of any particular administration of punishment. Punishment is thus externally imposed violence both

---

[4] 'Does Criminal Liability Require an Act' in RA Duff, ed., *Philosophy and the Criminal Law* (Cambridge: Cambridge University Press, 1998), 77–90.

in its generality and in its application. It would seem, therefore, that the rigorous actualization of real autonomy as the penal law's fundamental end engenders heteronomy with respect to official coercion.

Now the fact that, when separately actualized as fundamental ends, both formal agency and real autonomy produce self-contradictory outcomes shows that each needs the other's independent ordering for its own internal coherence. The dignity resting on the capacity for free choice collapses unless certain factually possible choices (slavery) are normatively ruled out for free beings. But this is possible only under a regime ordered to real autonomy, which treats certain values (e.g. civil independence) as nonrenounceable agency goods distinguishable from renounceable wants. Likewise, the dignity resting on the actualized potential for autonomy collapses unless judicial punishment is a fate one authors. But authorizing one's vulnerability to coercion is possible only within a penal framework that legitimates punishment retrospectively, by what the criminal has implied by his choice, rather than prospectively, by a common good. Punishment conceived as the logical nemesis of the criminal's principle is embedded in a goodless normative framework; that is its home. Such a conception is impossible in a teleological or good-based paradigm; for if punishment is justified as serving the common good, it cannot coherently be hobbled by a requirement that it be nothing but the nemesis of an intentional or advertently reckless act of coercion.

Accordingly, instead of ousting its rival for supremacy, each conception of public reason, in order to preserve itself, must apply itself with a moderation that preserves the other as a distinctive ordering principle. Thus, the real autonomy framework must pursue the good subject to nondefeasible (except in constitutional emergencies) requirements that judicial punishment be deserved by a publicly manifested right denial and that negligent lawbreaking be distinguished from "crimes" and be deterred only with noncustodial penalties. For its part, the formalist paradigm must allow itself to be supplemented with a requirement that criminal liability for consequences be constrained by, and proportioned to, the degree to which the consequence is connected to the criminal's choice; and it must accept the existence of a separate penal regime ordered to the public welfare—one within which the idea of desert plays but a marginal role.

And yet, as long as each conception of freedom claims to be fundamental, this mutual tolerance of paradigms will appear as an incoherent compromise between antagonistic principles—an intellectually shabby, albeit practically necessary, pluralism of frameworks. And this pluralism will be the soil in which contemporary rule-of-law scepticism grows, with its claim that law is, at best, the outcome of a reasoned but ultimately discretionary balancing of competing values, at worst, a maze of truce lines between warring ideologies—individualism and collectivism—leaving judges free to draw the lines where they please.

Yet, once we see how contemporary rule-of-law scepticism originates, we also see that it cannot be the final truth of the matter. For if each principle needs the other's distinctive rule for its own self-consistency, then neither can be the fundamental end of the penal law. And since there is no logical imperative to push to their extreme conclusions principles whose validity is not absolute, there is no necessary incoherence in their mutual accommodation. On the contrary, logic *requires* their accommodation, because the interdependence of formal agency and real autonomy as conceptions of human dignity shows that the fundamental end of the penal law is neither one nor the other but the whole of which both are constituent and mutually complementary parts.

However, the next question is: what is the nature of the whole revealed by the interdependence of formal agency and real autonomy? How precisely are we to understand it? We know that it somehow synthesizes the other two principles, but we do not yet know what new conception of public reason emerges from this synthesis. To grasp this idea we must formulate a theory of the relationship between individual free agency and the common good of self-determination that makes conceptual sense of their already revealed interdependence. So far, we have learned that the two principles of the penal law are interdependent by conducting thought experiments in which we treated each as self-contained. Now, however, we must understand their relationship in a way that puts their interdependence in the foreground, treating each element as part of a whole.

3. Public Reason as Dialogic Community

The conceptions of public reason ordering the two justice frameworks thus far considered both presupposed an atomistic agent—an agent standing outside of political association. Public reason is the bare capacity to choose ends if all material ends are assumed to be the preferences of separate individuals. Public reason is content-neutral concern for living from self-authored ends if all substantive commitments are the contingent life-plan choices of individual agents. In both cases what is implicitly rejected is the idea that there are public substantive ends—basic constituents of the good life that must figure in the life plans of all dignity-claiming beings whatever the otherwise variable shape of those plans. No doubt, public reason as real autonomy brought to the fore agency goods necessary for realizing the potential for self-determination. But these goods—life, health, a secure income, and so forth—are all goods one needs to *support* a self-determined life plan; they are not themselves constitutive parts of the good life for free agents. Where public reason is real autonomy, no law can proscribe or support activity for the reason that it is inconsistent with, or required by, a life fulfilling for a free agent; for public reason as real autonomy presupposes that there are no substantive life choices that are necessarily good for everyone.

The idea that makes conceptual sense of the interdependence of formal agency and the common good of self-determination implies a supersession of atomism. This is so because the interdependence of individual agency and a common good is the idea of a political community that is alive in the civic-mindedness of free agents and of free agents whose dignity rests on active citizenship. This idea raises to a public interest (as opposed to a personal preference) a committed relationship between the individual agent and its political community—a relationship that must figure into the conception of the good of any being claiming dignity. I shall call this relationship dialogic community. We can gain an understanding of it by contrasting a relation of domination with one of friendship.

The form of dialogic community

Imagine someone who has a very high opinion of his worth—who thinks, as the expression goes, that he is "god". Now being god solely in one's own estimation must be very unsatisfying, because one would then have a nagging sense that one's incomparable worth is a mere subjective conceit—a fantasy lacking objective reality. So one might then feel an urge to obtain objective confirmation of one's exalted self-image. There are a number of ways one could do this. One way would be to subjugate another person and to force him by threats to acknowledge that you are the god you think you are. Yet this strategy would not yield satisfaction either, because your subjugating activity shows that you need confirmation from someone other than yourself, and yet you are still manipulating the object from which you seek confirmation. Hence what you receive is no confirmation at all; it is just your own voice asserting your greatness over again. What you desire is that the other person acknowledge your worth spontaneously, with no interference from you.

Suppose that he does. Suppose that he repeats day after day that you are god, you are magnificent, exalted, etc. and that he is a speck of dust by comparison. Suppose that he even translates these words into action by serving your every need and whim with no expectation of reciprocity. Would that be a satisfying confirmation of your opinion of self-worth? Probably not, because in order for the other's recognition effectively to confirm your self-worth, it must not only come freely; it must also come from someone who *remains* free in his submission to you, for otherwise he loses the otherness or independence that qualifies him to confirm your self-worth objectively and that therefore makes his opinion valuable to you. Someone who abases himself, who denies his self-worth, has ceased to be a self existing for himself and so has ceased to be the other being who alone can deliver objective reality for your claim of worth. This suggests that a person can receive satisfying proof of his or her self-worth only if that worth is freely acknowledged by another person who remains free in his submission. But one can remain free in submitting to another person's worth only if the other person reciprocally submits to the first. Accordingly, a satisfying confirmation of self-worth can issue only from a relation of mutual recognition between free and equal persons.

The same reasoning applies to the relationship between a political community and an individual agent. A political community cannot actualize its claimed authority over individual agents by forcibly subjugating them, because it would then appear as a violent force rather than as a valid authority. The authority-claim of a political community is objectively validated only insofar as those over whom it claims authority accept the claim from their own conative standpoint, freely choosing submission for their own good as they conceive it. Therefore, the community must submit for confirmation of its authority-claim to the free, deliberative activity of the agent who aims at a self-authored conception of its good. It must defer to that activity, for it can receive confirmation of its authority only through the free recognition of a morally self-determining being; and because the political community must defer to the agent for the sake of its valid authority, the agent comes to its dignity—its rational importance—in active citizenship.

What does it mean for the political community to defer? Most generally, it means to address citizens with reasons for its authority the citizens can accept from their own good-seeking standpoint. It thus means to communicate with citizens as with rational beings, providing procedural scope (for example, through democratic institutions and open trials) for moral persuasion to public norms, for answering to the community for alleged wrongdoing, and for free, thoughtful recognition of communal authority. For its part, the individual agent can now reciprocally submit *qua* citizen to political authority as to that whose need for confirmation first dignifies the independent agent and so endows it with rights of formal agency and real autonomy. Because the political community must guarantee these rights for the sake of its own valid authority, the thinking Agent can accept that authority without loss to its independence. It can regard its moral fate—to be subject to a political authority—as self-authored and self-endorsed. In sum, the form or structure of dialogic community is a relationship between ends through which each freely acknowledges the end-status of the other as a condition of the other's independently validating its own claim of worth.

Dialogic community, solidarity, and restorative justice

Must we then regard the idea of a mutual recognition between individual citizen and political community as the fundamental idea of a liberal penal law? If so, the legal frameworks whose instability on their own led us to dialogic community will become immersed in a new paradigm of penal justice carrying revolutionary implications for liberal legal institutions. This paradigm—call it communal solidarity—will be ordered to a conception of freedom that no longer assumes the fixed reality of the monadic agent, of the agent abstracted from political association. Rather, it will be ordered to freedom understood as willing membership in a political community respectful of the liberty and moral self-determination of its citizens. Like the previous paradigms, this one will generate its own justification of punishment and therefore its own constraints on just punishment.[5] These can be described as follows.

---

[5] For elaborations of the criminal-justice implications of this model, see John Braithwaite and Philip Pettit, *Not Just Deserts* (Oxford: Clarendon Press, 1990), 86–136; RA Duff, *Punishment,*

Whereas punishment is retributive within the formalist framework and instrumental within the real autonomy model, in the solidarity paradigm it is expressive, communicative, and restorative. Here the penal law's purposes are to announce communal norms, to allow those accused of breaching them to answer the accusation, to censure unjustified and unexcused breaches, and to invite the penitent return of the guilty to community as well as the forgiving return to wholeness of his victim. The primary aim of penal force, accordingly, is neither to punish the deserving, nor to minimize crime, but rather to restore the community's integrity as a moral unit by providing opportunity for defence, reprobation, repentance, restitution, forgiveness, and reintegration. Penal justice consists in repairing the relationships of mutual recognition that have been damaged by the crime—those between wrongdoer and community, and between wrongdoer and victim as equal members of the community.[6]

The aim of restoring wholeness determines the form of punishment unique to the framework of communal solidarity. Whereas retributive punishment is paradigmatically a restraint of liberty, and instrumentalist penalization aims at a setback to welfare, restorative punishment takes the form of shaming.[7] The feeling of shame is the experience of alienation from the communal fellowship, and the pain felt teaches the consequences of one's self-separation as well as the social basis of one's wellbeing. By shaming wrongdoers within a process that simultaneously values their contrition, the community preserves its moral solidarity, while the shamed members learn the value of the social bonds they have broken. Sometimes the only way to bring home to offenders the seriousness of their wrongs is to exclude them physically from the rest of the community, for that is the most vivid symbol of their moral self-estrangement. Yet imprisonment is an exceptional punishment within this framework, for the goal of restorative justice is not to isolate offenders but to reintegrate them into relationships of mutual recognition with their victims and with the political community.

Accordingly, the central institution of restorative justice is not punishment but the meeting. Surrounded by their respective support groups, wrongdoer and victim engage in face-to-face dialogue. The offender hears from his victim what physical and emotional suffering he has caused. He feels shame and remorse. He acknowledges wrongdoing and apologizes. All discuss what penance might be appropriate—perhaps enrolment in counselling or community service, perhaps monetary or other reparation for the victim. If all goes well, the wrongdoer repents

---

Communication, and Community (Oxford: Oxford University Press, 2001); RA Duff, *Answering for Crime* (Oxford: Hart Publishing, 2007).

[6] RA Duff, 'Restorative Punishment and Punitive Restoration,' in Gerry Johnstone, ed., *A Restorative Justice Reader* (Portland: Willan, 2003), 390–1; Duff, *Punishment, Communication, and Community*, 79–130; Wesley Cragg, *The Practice of Punishment: Towards a Theory of Restorative Justice* (London: Routledge, 1992), 138–65.

[7] John Braithwaite, *Crime, Shame and Reintegration* (Cambridge: Cambridge University Press, 1989); Braithwaite and Pettit, *Not Just Deserts*, 88–90.

his defiance of communal norms as well as his wrong to the victim, while the victim lets go of vindictive aims in forgiveness of the wrongdoer. Community representatives welcome the defector back to the fold. Perhaps they even acknowledge their responsibility for whatever social conditions contributed to his choice to offend.[8]

The meeting, however, is not a trial. In a trial, ascertaining the truth about what occurred in the past is constrained by the need to legitimate a process that may culminate in the confinement of a defendant whose right against external constraint is inviolable. Truth is thus subordinated to the requirements of publicly justifying coercion to the defendant—in particular, to the presumption of innocence, the right to counsel, the noncompellability of the defendant, the right against self-incrimination, and, in general, to an adversarial procedure. Where, however, the individual's dignity rests on fellowship *rather* than on his capacity as a monadic agent for free choice, and where punishment is in any case shaming rather than physical restraint, there need be no such impediments to fact finding. Thus the aim of the meeting is not the public justification of coercion but reconciliation through the unfettered airing of truth.[9]

Some advocates of restorative justice go so far as to urge its supplanting of courts, trials, and retributive justice, which they see as "stealing conflicts" from parties, as leaving victims without voice or satisfaction, and as making offenders suffer for no pedagogical end.[10] For its radical theorists, restorative justice is the lost treasure of pre-modern and aboriginal societies, buried by the West's centralizing of adjudication and coercion in a universal state separated from, and opposed to, particular communities. Yet the time for recovering it has come, they say, for it promises psychological satisfaction for victims, empathy-learning for offenders, as well as healing for families and communities—benefits the retributive model cannot deliver. Evaluating retributive punishment as a therapeutic regimen for the social ills of victimization and recidivism, the critics unsurprisingly conclude that it has been a colossal failure; and so, having judged a fork to be an inferior knife, they now, like a character in an Aesop fable, wish to dispose of the fork and replace it with a knife.[11]

Others, however, have more limited aims. They see restorative justice as playing a supplementary role in compensating victims of crime as well as in structuring diversionary programmes for groups, such as juvenile and aboriginal offenders, with justified claims to special treatment.[12] They also see a place for restorative

---

[8] Alan Norrie, *Punishment, Responsibility, and Justice* (Oxford: Oxford University Press, 2000), 14.
[9] See J Llewellyn and R Howse, 'Institutions for Restorative Justice: The South African Truth and Reconciliation Commission,' (1999) 49 (3) *University of Toronto Law Journal* 355.
[10] Nils Christie, 'Conflicts as Property,' (1977) 17(1) *British Journal of Criminology* (January), 4.
[11] See Howard Zehr, *Changing Lenses: A New Focus for Crime and Justice* (Scottdale, Pa: Herald, 1990), 1–15.
[12] See Jim Dignan, 'Restorative Justice and the Law: The Case for an Integrated, Systemic Approach,' in L Walgrave, ed., *Restorative Justice and the Law* (Portland, Or: Willan, 2002), 168–90; Gordon Bazemore and Colleen McLeod, 'Restorative Justice and the Future of Diversion

justice procedures in post-trial sentencing hearings that allow victims to tell of their suffering, offenders to apologize for their wrongs, and judges to fine-tune sentences to the particular nature of the offence. Finally, moderate advocates see restorative justice as appropriate for projects of national reconstruction following serious crimes committed on a large scale over a long period by a ruling group against a subject group. For reasons I shall try to articulate, the moderates are right to assign restorative justice a role so circumscribed.

To treat restorative justice as the whole of penal justice rather than as a supplementary element thereof would be to actualize the idea of dialogic community in a self-contradictory way. Dialogic community is a certain conception of how individual autonomy and political authority are reconciled. The individual agent freely accepts communal authority as that which reciprocally defers to its liberty and moral self-determination as vehicles for its confirmation as the common good. As a conception of freedom within political community, dialogic community is also a conception of the public reason that distinguishes state coercion from private violence: coercion is legitimate when used to realize communal norms in ways that address the offender's reason and encourage his spontaneous reintegration. Yet, when dialogic community is actualized solely as communal solidarity, public reason becomes a private interest and civic autonomy becomes subjection to external violence.

This turnabout occurs because the community here recognizes only those who acknowledge solidarity as the basis of their dignity; it withholds recognition from the defiant. Those who commit crimes and resist integration reject the fellowship that is here regarded as the sole source of their rights. So the only thing to do is to banish them, whether by stripping them of their membership, isolating them in prisons, or executing them. Where, however, justice is exclusively restorative, there are no justice constraints on the term or manner of expulsion when restoration fails. Within restorative justice, punishment is constrained by what is necessary to restore. Outside that process, there are no limits, for the idea of punishing a social rebel in accordance with his just deserts has been supplanted. True, a political community dedicated to its citizens' civic freedom will have reason to minimize invasions of liberty. However, this reason will not rule out the disproportionate punishment of those who have rejected citizenship in order to secure the liberty of responsible citizens against an incorrigible offender.

Accordingly, where restorative justice is complete justice, the recalcitrant offender stands in a normative void. Restorative justice has nothing to say against vastly disproportionate punishments for the unrepentant—punishments that, since they now reflect the victim's input and are imposed by the offended community rather than by an impartial judge, are thoroughly tainted by

and Informal Social Control,' in Elmar Weitekamp and H-J Kerner, eds., *Restorative Justice: Theoretical Foundations* (Portland, Or: Willan, 2002), 143–76.

vengefulness and hatred. Any constraint must come from an ad hoc and vestigial retributivism.[13]

Further, because the political fellowship fails to recognize the defiant, it can only assert its authority violently *against* the defiant; it neither seeks nor gains a spontaneous validation for its authority from the mouth of the adversary as adversary. Because it does not value its adversary, restorative justice is not structured with a view to preserving his distance, so that the community's judgment might obtain an independent validation from the reasonable agent in his shoes. On the contrary, every effort is made to submerge distance in solidarity. Thus there is no judge in restorative justice, for the judicial role presupposes a dispute between offender and community requiring impartial adjudication. Here rupture is acknowledged, but dispute is denied. The people shame, censure, criticize, yet the target of all this condemnation is supposed not to dispute—though his censors are, like him, fallible human beings. He is meant only to nod and repent. Of course, he may refuse, but (assuming criminal courts and retributive justice supplanted) that is the way into the void.

In restorative justice, accordingly, the offender's independent agency as *outsider* is effaced. Indeed, he is not even accorded the right to enter a curt plea of guilty, by which the offender grants legitimacy to his punishment while maintaining his separate dignity. Rather, he is expected to confess guilt from his heart in supplication of acceptance or *else* suffer punishment. Moreover, reconciliation is achieved, not by integrating the adversary *as adversary*, but by eliminating him as adversary. Thus confessions are encouraged without independent counsel and without an intentional waiver of a right to remain silent; and they are accepted even though induced by an offer of a choice between extreme leniency or outright pardon, on the one hand, and severe punishment, on the other. Moreover, there is no presumption of innocence entailing a high standard of proof, such that a reasonable adversary, even if innocent, could accept an adverse judgment as humanly fair.

Because the communal fellowship does not value the adversary, it cannot attract the adversary's loyalty. Hence restorative justice fails on its own terms: it fails to integrate what has opposed itself to community. Moreover, if no validation of the communal norm is forthcoming from the adversary in his position as adversary, then the communal norm is a private reason *vis-à-vis* the adversary's, and its penal force is the violence of an external agency. Faced with a social rebel, the communal solidarity breaks up into a moral majority (or perhaps an oligarchy of elders) dominating a moral or cultural dissident. Dialogic community, when exclusively actualized, is neither dialogic nor a community.

We have a fascinating literary portrayal of the failure of restorative justice as complete penal justice in JM Coetzee's novel, *Disgrace*. Its protagonist is David

---

[13] See Andrew Ashworth, 'Responsibilities, Rights and Restorative Justice,' in Gerry Johnstone, ed., *A Restorative Justice Reader* (Portland, Or: Willan, 2003), 426–37. Life imprisonment for a third felony ("three strikes and you're out" provisions) may be understood in light of the normative void created by the communal solidarity paradigm; see e.g. California Penal Code s. 667.

Lurie, a 52-year-old professor of Romantic poetry who has an exploitative affair with a 20-year-old female student. The distraught student lays charges of harassment, and Lurie appears before a university committee at which a student representative is present. He is urged to confess, repent, and take counselling, in return for which, after taking a discreet leave of absence, he will be permitted to continue his career. Lurie, however, finds the whole process demeaning. He is prepared to plead guilty and take his punishment, but the committee will not accept a perfunctory guilty plea. It demands contrition. It also demands that he acknowledge the larger social wrong of which his is an instance. Lurie refuses and is dismissed. Later he says that he stood up for a principle—the freedom to remain silent. He has a superficial and self-indulgent understanding of the wrong he has done—he sees himself as a "servant of Eros"—until what he did to the student is done to his daughter. Only at that point does he undergo a change and spontaneously seek reconciliation with the family of the woman he used.

What do we learn from the potential for tyranny in restorative justice? It is not that dialogic community is an inadequate conception of public reason. It is rather that communal solidarity is an inadequate expression of dialogic community. Community is genuinely dialogical—genuinely respectful of the individual agent's independence—only in awaiting spontaneous recognition from the individual who, standing outside the communal solidarity, lays claim to dignity as a monadic agent. And conversely, the agent's independence is preserved in submission to community only if the community to which it submits makes room for spheres of penal justice ordered to the dignity of the monadic agent. Put otherwise, dialogic community must practise what it preaches. Dialogic community would contradict its own nature if, in seeking validation of its authority as Law, it subdued all rival conceptions of public reason to its undifferentiated solidarity. To be self-consistent, dialogic community must defer to those rival conceptions—conceptions asserting the dignity of the monadic agent—and see itself confirmed as the structure of all valid worth-claims in the paradigms autonomously ordered to those conceptions. And because dialogic community requires these individualistic conceptions of public reason for its self-confirmation as law's theme, the frameworks they inform are now incorporated within a complex whole as particular examples of the one form of mutual recognition. Adequately understood, dialogic community is a name for this federation of paradigms. The mutual recognition of whole and part—the whole's respecting the part's autonomy, the part's acknowledging itself as part of a whole—is the archetypal reciprocity that each part evinces in its particular way.

Accordingly, the final step we must take is to show how the form of dialogic community—the mutual recognition of distinctive ends—is the latent theme of the paradigms of penal justice respectively ordered to formal agency, real autonomy, and political citizenship. This is to exhibit the structure of dialogic community in the penal law doctrines generated from these ideas.

4. Dialogic Community in the Paradigms

In formal right

To begin with, the form of dialogic community is visible in the standard of lawful liberty generated within the formal agency paradigm. My exercise of liberty is rightful only if consistent with an equal liberty for others, for only then can others recognize my action as valid without compromising the independence that qualifies them to give a validating recognition. So, for example, first acquisition does not confer a property binding others unless the things in one's possession are in principle available to all at a price that reflects the frustration of those who cannot have them; hence the common-law rules against restraints on alienation and against restraints on trade. Moreover, property in land use is never determined simply by one's subjective desires; for this would entail a duty on others to suffer the actions of a neighbour without any reciprocal deference to them. Rather, one has a property only in ordinary uses to which all are equally entitled, so that one's vulnerability to a neighbour's uses is matched by his symmetrical vulnerability to one's own. Similarly, the right to impose risks on others is limited to those ordinarily incidental to social interaction and that a self-respecting agent would consent to suffer as being consistent with an equal liberty for itself. A right to bind another to meet expectations he has raised by a promise crystallizes only if the promisee has reciprocally bound himself to the promisor. There is no need to multiply examples. The common-law criterion for enforceable claims to another's sufferance or service confirms dialogic community as the form of all valid right claims; and it does so out of the mouth of a monadic agent seeking confirmation for its own end-status.

Perhaps less obviously, however, the theme of dialogic community is also inscribed in formal right's theory of crime and punishment. Recall the account of punishment given by legal retributivism. A knowing interference with another's agency or a knowing breach of law involves an implicit claim of right to an unbounded liberty. Generalized, such a claim entails a negation of rights that leaves the claimant himself juridically defenceless against coercion. In manifesting this self-contradiction, punishment refutes the claim of right to an unbounded liberty and vindicates mutually recognized liberty—the common will—as the only framework of stable rights. But this logical movement itself manifests dialogic community in the following sense. The normative authority of the common will is validated out of the mouth of the very self who challenges it; and conversely, the dignity claim of the monadic agent is validated through the common will's deference to it (in requiring subjective fault for liability to punishment) as the vehicle for confirming its normative authority. Because retributive punishment involves the validation of the common will's normative authority by the adversary *qua* adversary, it is a punishment the adversary can rationally accept as making room for his self-authorship of his moral fate. Unlike the case with restorative justice, therefore, reconciliation leaves no unreconciled adversary who can delegitimate the norm.

It is true, of course, that in retributive justice the criminal's reconciliation to his punishment and to the rule of law is metaphysical rather than real. It is the thinking Agent in the criminal's shoes, not (necessarily) the criminal himself, who sees the error of its ways and whose devotion to law is won through law's including the agent in its realization. But that is a reason for supplementing retributive justice, not for abolishing it (see Conclusion). We can say that restorative and retributive justice, while sharing the form of dialogic community, are distinct manifestations, whose collapse into one or the other perverts the form. Thus, retributive justice without supplemental restorative institutions integrates the criminal ideally but not (necessarily) actually; restorative justice without institutions of retributive justice integrates the criminal actually, but since the alternative is legally unconstrained punishment, the integration is coercive.[14]

Further, the form of dialogic community is manifested in the grounds for non-justificatory exculpation generated by formal right. These grounds, recall, are involuntariness, mistake of fact, legal insanity, and colour of right, but not duress, necessity, or provocation. Why should the criminal law recognize the exculpatory force of blameworthy or pathological subjective states (for example extreme drunkenness, stupidity, sexist prejudice, schizophrenia, ignorance of law) when they negate volition or cause mistakes, but not honourable and healthy states when they do neither, as in the case of laudable love of life, love of family members, or justified anger, which at most excuse the culpable? The answer must be that law can recognize the exculpatory force of subjective states without loss to its authority only if the states to which it defers have manifested themselves in choices reciprocally respectful of law's authority. Thus subjective states exculpate when, regardless of their shamefulness, they negate a choice implying a denial of law's authority but not when, regardless of their respectability, they motivate such a choice.

The idea of dialogic community also reconciles the justificatory defences that allow certain kinds of reasons for action (self-defence, self-preservation) to exculpate with the irrelevance of motive to culpability. The point here is that both phenomena exhibit the structure of mutual recognition as the sole basis of valid claims to exculpation. Motive—one's subjective reason for choosing as one did—is irrelevant to culpability, because, whether noble or base, a motive acted upon drives a choice that, if the agent has knowingly interfered with another's agency, implies a challenge to the framework of mutual recognition that makes rights possible. To allow motive to exculpate because it reveals a decent character or because everyman would have acted upon it would mean that the standard of right has condescended to the individual subject without any reciprocal

---

[14] For the pitfalls of collapsing penal justice into an actual reconciliation between natural persons, see Annalise Acorn, *Compulsory Compassion: A Critique of Restorative Justice* (Vancouver: UBC Press, 2004), especially chs. 2 and 5.

recognition of the standard. Hence it would mean that the standard is not law; the agent chose to violate the standard, yet is proclaimed not guilty.

The same is true of justification. If the rightness of conduct depended on the actor's motives, the objectivity of rightness would break down. In a case of putative self-defence, the same transaction would be right from the viewpoint of the actor who acted reasonably from a motive of self-defence and wrong from the viewpoint of the one he mistook for an assailant. In a case of unknown justification, the same transaction would be wrong for the actor who repelled his attacker from a wicked motive and right from the perspective of the attacker. However, in recognizing self-defence as a justifying reason for coercion irrespective of motive, the norm defers to reasons for action without self-compromise, because the reasons are themselves objective. They are "guiding" rather than "explanatory" reasons, in Gardner's terminology; that is, they are reasons that apply generally to conduct rather than reasons that explain why one acted as one did.[15] Thus, the norm recognizes the justificatory force of a reason for acting only insofar as the reason reciprocally recognizes (or is compatible with) the objectivity of the norm.

We see the same structure in justificatory necessity. If someone destroys property to save his own, he is culpable for criminal mischief. But if someone takes property to avert death when no other choice is available, he is justified. In the former case, the law cannot accept the justificatory force of the defendant's reason without collapse, for the reason is a subjective motive rather than a guiding reason engaging the limit of property. In the latter case, the law can recognize the justificatory force of the defendant's reason (self-preservation) because his reason fits into a hierarchy of interests whose ranking is determined by the objective and universal needs of agency. Agency requires property, but whereas agency can survive the loss of an item of property, it cannot survive the loss of life. So property yields to the indispensable condition of agency as to the source of its own justification. Here again the legal standard admits a justifying reason for breaching it only insofar as doing so is consistent with recognition of the standard's authority.

The form of dialogic community is also the common theme of justifications against wrongdoers and justifications against innocents. Both types of justification confer on one agent an asymmetrical right to use force against another agent. How is this possible? How can a free agent apprehended by another as a threat assent to a law that demands he give up his liberty to defend himself against the force, and even against the lethal force, of an equal? How can a property owner who has no coercive duty to rescue a stranger assent to a law that requires him to forbear from defending his property against a needy interloper? The answer in both cases is a relation of mutual recognition between the law and the legally disadvantaged agent. Both the perceived threat and the property owner can recognize the law without loss to the end-status the law requires for validating assent only because the law reciprocally realizes their right no less than the other agent's.

---

[15] John Gardner, *Offences and Defences* (Oxford: Oxford University Press, 2007), 91.

The perceived threat surrenders his liberty to defend himself only to a realization of universal rights, not to another individual's interest in remaining safe from harm. That is to say, he gives up his liberty only if he *is* a wrongdoer voluntarily posing an imminent and unprovoked threat to another agent, and only if the force used against him keeps within the bounds of necessity and proportionality that makes it a realization of right. Likewise, the property owner gives up his right to defend his property, not to the interests of the interloper, but to a universal agency good whose superordination to private property preserves it as property and whose reciprocal subordination to property (reflected in the duty to compensate the owner) preserves it as *private* property. In both cases, then, the legally disadvantaged party is preserved and confirmed as an end in acknowledging the authority of law.

In real autonomy

We can also discern the form of dialogic community in the main features of the paradigm ordered to real autonomy. That framework generated a requirement that not only the incidence but also the measure of punishment be self-determined or derived from the criminal's own will. This means, first, that he can be punished only for those consequences of his wilful or reckless transgression that are connected in some degree to his agency (not for unforeseeable ones) and, second, that punishment must be ordinally proportionate both to the seriousness of the harm he caused and to the degree (intention, foresight, foreseeability) to which the harm is connected to his agency. But in the requirement that the criminal be subject to no penal fate he did not author, we again have an image of dialogic community. The punishing authority submits its claim of legitimacy to a test of self-imposability by the recipient, who can reciprocally recognize without self-abasement the authority of a punisher that defers to his rational assent.

Let us now consider the principles of justice applicable to public welfare offences. In Chapter 5, I tried to exhibit these principles as embodiments of the individual right of self-determination *vis-à-vis* the public authority. Now I want to exhibit them as examples of dialogic community *in* the embodiments of that right.

We saw that, within the sphere of public welfare offences, the justification of penal sanctions is purely instrumentalist. Their purpose is to deter with threats of disadvantage breaches of statutes that regulate the pursuit of satisfactions or that protect an agency good. Considerations of desert do not figure in the justification at all; for apart from a statute, one cannot will one's vulnerability to coercion by performing (omitting) the prohibited (mandated) actions. Still, this did not mean an absence of constraint on penalization. The state would cease to be a public order if it subordinated the public good of autonomy to the satisfaction of subjective preferences or if it secured the conditions of an autonomous life by means of liability rules that promote autonomy for some by denying it to others. Thus, the real autonomy paradigm generated two principles of justice applicable to public welfare penalties: the priority of autonomy over happiness pertaining to statutes regulating preference satisfaction, and the noncontradiction proviso applicable to statutes protecting agency goods. These principles mandated at least a due diligence (or reasonable mistake) excuse for breach of a statute, an excuse of reasonable ignorance of law, as well as a rule against imprisonment for negligent breaches. But these rules, too, instantiate the form of dialogic community. The agent submits to use by the state as a tool of deterrence only insofar as the state reciprocally respects the agent as an autonomous controller of its being so used.

Finally, the form of dialogic community is imprinted in the interaction between the formal agency and real autonomy frameworks. We saw this interaction in two places: in justificatory necessity and in mental disorder as both an exculpatory condition and a warrant for detaining the innocent.

The intriguing feature of justificatory necessity is that, while a negative right to exclude from one's property yields to a positive right to life, it does so without extinguishment, because the right to life reciprocally submits to an independent right to property. In emergencies, the right to what is essential to agency overrides rather than defines the property right, with the consequence that the override must limit the right only to the extent necessary to avert death. This mutual subordination of the paradigms is reflected in the law that, although the property owner cannot resist a taking to save a life, the taker has a duty to compensate him.[16] This, however, is an image of dialogic community. An individual right of monadic agency submits to a common good, which reciprocally submits to the autonomous ordering of a monadic conception of freedom.

The same form is visible in the law regarding the detention of the innocent insane. The latter are detainable after acquittal, not because they are nonagents lacking the capacity for free choice, but because (and to the extent that) they lack the deliberative and cognitive powers necessary to actualize the potential for self-determination their capacity for free choice carries. Because they lack the equipment for making self-determined choices, they command the diminished respect for their specific choices that is reflected in their detention for reasons of dangerousness alone or for their own good as others see it. Yet here too the liberty right based on the formal capacity for free choice is not submerged in concern for their good and that of others; rather, it maintains its force, so that only minimally impairing restrictions on choice are permissible. But this form of mutual subordination is the form of dialogic community.

In citizenship

I argued that morally blameless choices to commit unjustified wrongs in cases of necessity and duress afford the agent a complete excuse because they simulate formal right's conditions of nonjustificatory exculpation. Someone is exculpated if

[16] *Ploof v Putnam* 71A 188 (1908); *Vincent v Lake Erie Transport Co.* 124 NW 221 (1910).

he committed no wrong or if his trespass, because unwitting, implied no challenge to the authority of the legal norm delimiting stable rights. Someone is excused whose forbearance from wrong called for a saintly neutrality as between his and a stranger's life (or between doomed lives and saveable lives) and who, though he knowingly and unjustifiably coerced another, nonetheless lived up to the moral potential of an embodied agent bearing a proper name; for he did nothing to challenge the political community of which the legal norm is a part. His action was thus consistent with good citizenship. The connection between conformity to moral expectation and good citizenship may be drawn as follows.

Because judicial punishment is compatible with freedom only as capable of self-imposition by a notional agent in whom all are identical, the criteria of criminal culpability and responsibility are bloodlessly impersonal and objective. Grounded narrowly in external choice, they abstract from the full ethical character whose overall wellbeing lies in citizenship within a self-sufficient political community—that is, within a community directed, not solely to the protection of agency rights against interference (or agency goods against harm), but to the full satisfaction of dignitary needs, including familial love, cultural membership, fulfilling work, and civic participation. The perfection of the concrete, human individual in the citizen whose life is full brings in its train the virtues that are engaged in situations of necessity, duress, and provocation—a healthy valuation of one's life and that of loved ones, reasonable self-esteem, self-control, good judgment as to when self-preference or anger is appropriate. Accordingly, it is possible for an action to be one we would expect from a character whose ends are the role obligations comprising the dignified life and yet be culpable according to the criteria of guilt derived from abstract agency.

Excuses are tailored to this possibility. The agent is culpable before the legal norm but excused before the self-sufficient community. In this way, excuse preserves the authority of the legal norm while expressing the truth that the defendant has lived up to the ethical expectations of a political community of which the legal norm is only a particular expression. So understood, however, excuse, though peripheral to the penal law, is the best appearance of dialogic community within the penal law. This is so because, as the objectively confirmed form of valid worth-claims, dialogic community embraces all the manifestations of its form through which it is independently validated by an atomistic agent. It is the whole of which the manifestations are parts; and any concrete, reasonably self-sufficient political community (the United Kingdom, Canada, etc.) is the whole's body. Accordingly, in exonerating someone guilty before the abstract legal norm but blameless before the political community, the penal law expresses the subordination of the part to the authority of the whole. Yet, in excusing rather than exculpating the wrongdoer (that is, in treating excuse as an affirmative defence presupposing culpability), the penal law also expresses the whole's reciprocal respect for the jurisdiction of the part. The judgment of culpability is not set aside; it is superseded. Likewise does the law express the whole's respect for the part when it grounds excuse, not in a concession to weakness that is unrelated to the conditions of exculpation, but precisely in a simulation of those conditions—in conformity to public reason. But in the mutual recognition of whole and part, dialogic community appears, not simply through an image, but in person, as it were. What we see is not merely a type but the archetype itself.

5. Epilogue

If the paradigms of penal justice are particular manifestations of dialogic community, then it is logical for the overt principle of each paradigm to assert itself modestly rather than intransigently—that is, to assert itself only within bounds consistent with the distinctive ordering of the other principles; for each is now part of the whole rather than the whole itself. What is illogical is the hegemony of the part. This means that apparent contradictions and ostensibly *ad hoc* accommodations in the penal law conceal an underlying harmony and unity of principle.

For example, no compromise of principle is involved in viewing punishment as retributive in the sphere of crimes, as forward-looking in the sphere of public welfare offences, and as restorative overall. Punishment is retributive, not in the moral sense of requiting evil with the punishment it deserves, but in the legal and constitutional sense of visiting on the agent nothing but what is implied in the principle of its own action. Moreover, this is done, not for its own sake, but to actualize the human rights the criminal denied. By contrast, penalization is forward-looking where, though a law has been broken, no right denial is implicit in what the agent chose, and where the agent's autonomy is otherwise respected by affording him a defence of due diligence. Punishment is, finally, restorative insofar as the thinking Agent in the offender's shoes can accept its punishment as required by, and as consistent with, its right to liberty and self-determination and insofar as the empirical offender can be educated to the standpoint of the thinking one.

Because a plurality of theories of penal force can logically coexist in one penal system, it is not incoherent to say that penal coercion is properly constrained by desert in the sphere of crimes but by a "fair opportunity" to avoid liability in the sphere of regulatory offences. Nor does it compromise principle to require subjective *mens rea* as the fault threshold for crimes but to allow a negligence standard of fault for public welfare offences. Nor does it reflect ambivalence to require subjective *mens rea* for criminal culpability for wrongdoing but to allow objective foreseeability to count as a degree of criminal responsibility for consequential harms. Nor is it equivocation to say that harm-doing is irrelevant to punishability *simpliciter* but relevant to a just measure of punishment and to defence. Nor is it muddled thinking to have one theory of justification for self-defence, where the victim threatened a right protected by the formal agency model, and another for necessity and duress, where the victim is an innocent and justification must rest on the mutual subordination of rights and agency goods. Nor is it inconsistent to say that necessity justifies a taking but that the victim has a right to compensation, or that the insane have a right to stand trial (if they can understand the proceedings) and be judged under the same law applying to everyone else, but may be forcibly confined though acquitted. Nor does it reflect confusion to say that mistakes indicative of shameful qualities may exculpate, whereas honourable motives may only excuse. Nor to say that moral blamelessness excuses crime but not lawbreaking in the regulatory context, where due diligence warrants only a stay of prosecution. Nor is it contradictory to admit moral blamelessness as an excuse but not as a general theory of exculpation, even if this means saying that someone may be at once culpable and blameless.

All these accommodations between the paradigms now reflect not makeshift compromises between warring ideas, but mutual respect for principled boundaries. The penal law is neither a simple unity ordered to one idea nor a jumble of truce lines between competing ideas; rather, it is a unity of plural frameworks wherein one idea is diversely instantiated in subsystems ordered to formal agency, real autonomy, and political community, and wherein each constituent principle rules with a moderation befitting a part. Justice in the penal law is the good order of the whole, injustice the rule of what is properly constituent. Liberal penal law, we can say, is like the body of a complex organism. It is internally divided rather than simple; yet one pulse beats in all divisions.

Conclusion

Punishment and freedom

At last chapter's end I argued that the mutual accommodation of the three paradigms of penal justice is logically determined rather than merely pragmatically warranted because each forms part of a whole unified by the idea of dialogic community. Yet mutual accommodation is not only logically necessary; it is also essential to the reconciliation of punishment and freedom that distinguishes punishment from naked violence. This is so because, when a partial framework claims to tell the whole story about penal justice, the individual agent stands defenceless against state power when the prescriptions of the part run out. Inside the framework, there is some law to constrain state power; outside it, there is only the void.

For example, we saw that if the formalist paradigm is treated as exhaustive of penal justice, the agent will be liable to punishment only for a wilful interference with choice; but then it will be liable to a term of incapacitation reflecting all the unforeseeable consequences of its criminal wrong as well as to nonpunitive sanctions for unavoidable breaches of public welfare statutes. In both cases, the state's police power will be unconstrained by a requirement that the agent have control of its moral fate. Moreover, those forced by threats or circumstances to commit crimes will have no entitlement to an acquittal based on justification or excuse but will instead have to depend on the mercy of the judge or head of state. If, however, the real autonomy paradigm is treated as the whole, the agent will be subject to penal force only if it could have avoided liability; but it will be liable to criminal sanctions on the basis of negligence as well as to punishment for thoughts alone. Moreover, those incapable of self-determination will be vulnerable to legally untrammelled state power to protect the real autonomy of the capable. If communal solidarity is the sole framework of penal justice, the agent will be liable to extremely lenient treatment if it repents its crime but to unlimited punishment if it does not. In all cases, the agent will be subject to a public reason it can autonomously accept inside the framework but to private violence where the framework is silent.

The upshot is that judicial punishment is consistent with the freedom and inviolable worth of the individual agent only if it is subject to the constraints generated by all three frameworks in unison, each complementing the other. The whole is the ethical community sufficient for dignity—the community ordered to a public reason inclusive of all liberal conceptions thereof. Together, the constituent frameworks generate necessary and jointly sufficient conditions for distinguishing penal force from naked violence; for if the ethical community is sufficient for dignity, then we can say it is replete with law. There is no legal void in any space that human dignity requires centralized force to occupy. Accordingly, the penal force imposed by this community is force the thinking Agent could accept on the empirical agent's behalf, because it is throughout constrained by liability rules ensuring (a) that the force actualizes nothing but public reason and (b) that the empirical agent either implicitly authorized the force (that is, through the thinking Agent) by what it chose to do or, where it was impossible to authorize the force, could have avoided it.

Against this reconciliation of punishment and freedom, two objections might be raised. One is that the reconciliation is metaphysical rather than real. The other is that penal justice is inseparable from social justice, so that a theory of penal justice is valid only for a just society; it has no relevance to a society that distributes life advantages unfairly.[1]

Metaphysical and empirical reconciliation

One might object that the reconciliation of punishment and freedom embodied in the model penal law of a liberal legal order is metaphysical only—that the agent who is reconciled to penal force is only the thinking or reasonable Agent standing in the criminal's shoes, not the actual criminal himself. In the real world, one might argue, most offenders see in their punishment only the arbitrary violence of an establishment enforcing its interests as law; hence they are only worsened by punishment and, more often than not, return to crime. But (it will be argued) if crime control is part of the liberal state's duty to protect the real autonomy of its citizens, should not the focus of criminal law theory be on what will best work in the real world to socialize the selfish, the resentful, and the alienated? And should not that focus lead us to ask what institutional framework and liability rules will most likely induce flesh-and-blood criminals to take responsibility for their actions, to accept as fair the penal consequences of their crimes, and to mend their anti-social ways? Moreover, if the system modelled in the preceding pages fails to produce this result, why maintain it for the sake of the freedom of a nonexistent notional Agent?

This objection draws force from a distinction that necessarily opens up once we seek a theoretical justification of punishment. Such a justification must address itself not to empirical agents, who may be dull or bright, reasonable or stiff-necked, etc., but to the thinking and reasonable Agent. In this sense, a theory of penal justice must be metaphysical. It is quite true, moreover, that the metaphysical theory could not care less whether the empirical criminal is reconciled to his

---

[1] Alan Norrie, *Punishment, Responsibility, and Justice* (Oxford: Oxford University Press, 2000), 24–30, 98–102, 120–5.

punishment or not. As long as he *could* be if he saw clearly, his punishment is just, and with that the metaphysician is satisfied. Nevertheless, the empiricist's objection has force, not against the metaphysical enterprise as such, but only against one so self-absorbed as to forget the distinction between the metaphysical and the empirical, as Socrates was accused of doing by Aristophanes. Someone with his head in the clouds might persuade himself that the metaphysical solution to the ethical problem of punishment leaves nothing more to be accomplished.

Of course, no legal philosopher in his or her right mind would make such a claim. Much more remains to be done, but the remainder is the work, not of legal philosophers who explain, nor of lawyers who vivify, the framework justified by metaphysics, but of criminologists, social workers, and correctional officers whose specialized concern is with crime as a social problem for flesh-and-blood individuals. Theirs is the task of supplementing the institutions of criminal justice with those specifically designed to achieve the welfare goals of reduced victimization, victim reparation, and offender rehabilitation. And the success of those supplementary institutions—for example, special regimes for juvenile, aboriginal, and first-time offenders, a wide array of sentencing options—is properly measured by the reported degree of satisfaction of real people as well as by crime levels and rates of recidivism. On all these matters, the philosopher of criminal justice defers to the sociologist of crime.

However, the modesty of philosophers must be reciprocated by that of the empirically based professions. Justice is metaphysical and so the proper province of legal philosophy. To the extent that empiricism is self-absorbed, it blinds itself to the justificatory account of criminal justice institutions; and it persuades itself that those institutions must be judged solely by whether they effectively achieve the criminologist's aims. Since, however, the institutional framework is rationally ordered to the quite different function of metaphysical legitimation, it will inevitably fall short when measured against the criminologist's yardsticks of success; for does it not marginalize, and perpetuate the enmity between, victims and offenders in a process that represents them by adversarial proxies? And so criminologists, taking this as a sign of the system's dysfunction rather than of its alternative rationality, will be moved to replace it. The slogan of this movement might be "restorative, not retributive, justice".

Of course, the theorists of this movement are right to point out that the metaphysical reconciliation leaves physical people with little solace. Yet this is an argument not for dismantling the system justified by metaphysics, but for educating real criminals to the social basis of the worth they seek in isolation. Philosophers must respect this work even if they themselves have little to contribute to it. But equally, the empirical professions must respect the framework justified by metaphysics rather than seek to overturn it simply because an apparatus designed for their purposes would work better to achieve them. The framework we have is not a defective technique for accomplishing the criminologist's ends; it is the well adapted method of securing penal justice. Innovations to achieve the criminologist's aims must supplement this framework rather than replace it—for the sake of those very aims. For if the thinking Agent could not be reconciled to the system, any reconciliation of empirical agents would be an accommodation to their servility.

Penal justice and social justice

It may also be objected that the account of liberal penal justice offered here is of no relevance to actual penal systems, because it assumes away the social injustice that reduces state power to disguised private power, whether of economic class, gender, ethnicity, or whatever. Thus Jeffrie Murphy argues that, although retributive punishment is just in an ideally just society, it breaks down in an unjust one; for it presupposes conditions under which everyone benefits equally from the rule of law and so would rationally accept punishment for lawbreaking as necessary to that rule. Where the allocation of holdings is unjust, those unfairly disadvantaged cannot rationally view their punishment as serving their own rational interests; rather, they must perceive it is a tool of class oppression.[2] And so they will view crime, not as injustice, but as the justified rebellion of the oppressed.

It is very probably true that social injustice engenders crime. Poverty by itself can be blamed on luck or on oneself, but when poverty is linked to exploitation or discrimination, noble feelings can inspire unjust deeds. Still, one can reasonably claim that an account of penal justice is exclusively valid for a just society only if social injustice makes private violence or takings permissible (as distinct from understandable) and therefore makes punishment for these actions unjust. Yet, apart from the necessity case, for which the model law itself prescribes, it does not. Social injustice can neither justify nor completely excuse (if moral permissibility grounds excuse) an individual's violating rights that the perfectly just society would itself protect; and so it cannot be a reason for no longer deserving the punishment for an action one would otherwise deserve. Even if the social allocation of holdings is unjust and private property suspect, a private taking still violates a possessory right, which belongs even to a thief. And, of course, one has a right in one's person whether one lives in a just society or an unjust one. One can therefore speak of a class state that, in punishing only violations of rights that the just state would also protect, is at least just in the exercise of its penal power.

One might respond that, though the punishment of, say, an aboriginal person for an assault or theft he committed may be just, he will not experience it as just if it is imposed by a representative of the colonial oppressor and if the criminal justice system pervasively discriminates against aboriginals in meting out discretionary prison sentences. True. However, this is an argument, not against the validity

---

[2] J Murphy, 'Marxism and Retribution,' (1973) 2:3 *Philosophy and Public Affairs* 217–43 (Spring).

of a theory of penal justice for an unjust society, but for devolving sentencing to communities the aboriginal offender can trust.

Another version of the objection from social injustice might go like this. Social disadvantage for which one is not responsible affects one's abilities to conform to objective standards of care, foresight of consequences, and self-control; and yet if the penal law allowed these disabilities to diminish criminal responsibility, all its objective standards would collapse into individually customized ones (hence into no law at all), for the ability to overcome background disadvantages varies among individuals. And so the law cannot treat disabling social disadvantage as partially excusatory, with the result that the less responsible are punished as severely as the fully responsible. This suggests that a just penal law presupposes a just society wherein the only circumstances impairing one's ability to meet objective norms of conduct are those for which one can indeed be held responsible.

This objection may contain a kernel of truth. However, granting its force does not require accepting the point that a theory of penal justice is valid only for a just society. For, one can say that, as a matter of penal justice theory, the law should condescend *only* to disabilities for which the agent is not responsible. This principle is as valid for unjust societies as it is for just ones. One can also say that, as a matter of ideal theory, the penal law should treat as partially excusatory *all* disabilities beyond the agent's control. In an unjust society, this more demanding principle may have to be compromised for the sake of law's rule, but not necessarily. All that is certain is that, in the case of an unfairly disadvantaged offender, a court must experience a tension between its duty not to punish excessively and its duty to maintain objective standards of expected foresight and self-control. How it ought to resolve the tension is undetermined. At most, therefore, the difference between just and unjust societies is relevant to determining whether ideal penal justice theory can govern directly or through a diluted intermediary; it is not relevant to determining whether it can govern at all. Put otherwise, the objection from social injustice establishes only that unjust societies cannot have fully just penal systems because they cannot, consistently with the rule of law, take into account unjust disadvantage attenuating responsibility. It does not establish that a *theory* of penal justice cannot guide the penal systems of unjust societies toward the best approximation of the ideal of which they are capable.

Constitutional theory versus moral theory

A major theme of this book has been that a constitutional theory of the penal law's general part provides a more unified and ethically satisfying picture of it than any version of a moral theory. Whereas a moral theory sees the penal law's general part as embodying the principle that moral evil and only moral evil ought to be blamed and censured, a constitutional theory sees it as reconciling state coercion with the agent's inviolability. The best theory of the penal law's general part, I have argued, is a theory about when it is permissible for the state to coerce a free agent, not a theory about when it is appropriate for a community to blame and censure a member's moral character.

From the standpoint of a moral theory of the penal law, the main outlines of the positive law must seem perplexing. If the point of punishment is to give evil its due, what does or does not occur in the world as a result of chance should be irrelevant to criminal desert. Thus consequences should not affect the measure of punishment, and attempts and completed crimes should be punished equally. Conversely, bad character should be necessary for criminal desert and dangerously bad character sufficient. Thus mistakes attributable to blameworthy attitudes or intoxication should never exculpate, not even partially, whereas moral blamelessness should always exculpate, not simply excuse. Indeed, on the moral account, the law's distinction between exculpatory and completely excusing conditions should be abolished, for that account knows only one completely exonerating condition—blamelessness.

Yet these incongruities between moral theory and the penal law should tell us not that the penal law is a defective realization of morality, but that moral theory is not the medium through which the penal law becomes intelligible. To be sure, morality has a role to play in the sphere of excuse, but, as the concept of excuse implies, that role is peripheral to the main plot. The central story concerns the conditions under which liability to judicial coercion is consistent with freedom; and that story is rigorously nonmoral in the sense that its focus is exclusively on external choice insofar as the latter impinges on others' freedom. Thus, what matters is not what an external choice says about the inward self but what it implies for the existence of liberty rights and what degree of external connection exists between a right-denying choice and its harmful outcome. For a court, culpability consists in the public manifestation of a right denial, responsibility in the relative contribution of choice and chance to a right denial's harmful result. A character's wickedness is neither here nor there, and justly so; for it is incompatible with freedom for freedom to depend on others' opinions about what lies hidden in the soul. Indeed, it is just the law's one-sided focus on external choice as it impinges on others' freedom that explains why virtue must enter the penal law only through the back door of excuse.

Accordingly, in foregrounding external choices rather than inward states, the constitutional theory of the penal law gathers more of its object into a coherent narrative than its moral rival. Specifically, it can account for the penal relevance of outcomes (see Chapter 4), the general irrelevance of motive to culpability (Chapter 2), as well as the distinction between no-offence and excuse (Chapter 7). Moreover, it alone can make sense of the seemingly endless moral paradoxes in the penal law—for example, that the culpable can be morally blameless and the blameworthy nonculpable; and that an intentional killing motivated by compassion is a worse crime (murder) than an accidental killing through reckless indifference to life (manslaughter).

The reconciliation of external and internal standpoints

Because of their awkward fit with their object, moral theories of the penal law tend to be prescriptive *rather* than interpretive. That is, they prescribe for the penal law from a normative standpoint outside it rather than from one internal to the law itself. Thus their prescriptions, instead of holding the law to its own immanent reason, impose what to the lawyer appears as a foreign one. Moreover, the lawyer's sense of the moral philosopher's irrelevance to his enterprise is fully reciprocated. From the moralist's viewpoint, the internal interpretation of the penal law is given by the legal treatise, which, in holding the law only to its own rationality, stops short of questioning the law's internal norms. Accordingly, where critical theory is moral theory, we have a dichotomy between a critical standpoint whose prescriptions are alien to the law and an internal standpoint uncritical of law's immanent rationality.

What I have attempted in this book is a reconciliation of external and internal standpoints. Thus the internal point of view is given by a series of conceptions of freedom manifestly informing the penal law's various divisions: culpability for wrong, responsibility for harm, regulatory liability, justification, excuse. Far from being statically ordered to a fixed and unquestioned fundamental norm, the penal law is a process of self-criticism, as thin conceptions of freedom give way to more robust ones. Thus the critique of normative foundations is internal to the law itself. But, further, this internal critique is not the end of the story, because what is criticized is not discarded; it is rather demoted to a constituent member of a more inclusive system. And the inclusive idea unifying the whole—the idea compared with which the constituent conceptions are incomplete—is external to law in the sense that it orders the self-sufficient political community of which the administration of justice is only a part. And yet, though it is external to the penal law, the inclusive conception of public reason is not *alien* to the law; for, as we saw, the internal conceptions are so many partial instantiations of it. The norm of mutual recognition between ends is not one the legal philosopher imposes on the law; it is one acknowledged within the practice of law itself.

The constitutionalization of the general part

Because moral theories of the penal law are prescriptive without being interpretive, their prescriptions are justifiably viewed by those whose professional duty is to unfold the law from within as moral opinions. Now, of course, in a liberal democracy, moral opinions can acquire the force of law only if they are enacted into law by a parliamentary or congressional majority. On no account may judges hold common-law rules, still less penal legislation, answerable to nonlegislated moral opinions as to when it is appropriate to apply the penal sanction; for this would constitute a nonelected body's coercive imposition of its own moral views. As a consequence, where the only substantive normative guide for the penal law is moral philosophy, laws touching the general part will be immune from judicial review even in jurisdictions with a constitutionally entrenched bill of rights.

This is indeed the case in the United States and Israel, where judicial review of the penal law under constitutional norms has been mostly confined to the review of criminal procedures for fairness and of specific offences for permissible criminalization. Judicial scrutiny of rules touching the general part has been practically nonexistent.[3] Even in Canada, where substantive review of the general part has perhaps gone furthest, we see a general reluctance in courts to elevate common-law principles of substantive penal justice from defeasible presumptions guiding statutory interpretation to peremptory constitutional norms. Thus, for example, the common-law principle that subjective fault is required at the threshold of true crimes becomes the much diluted constitutional maxim that only crimes carrying the highest stigma require subjective fault.[4] There are, of course, many reasons for this phenomenon; but if moral philosophy were the only substantive normative beacon for the penal law, this is just what one would expect to find. Judges would be loath to elevate their moral opinions into the supreme law of the land, and they would be especially reluctant to hold the moral opinions of the democratic legislature answerable to their opinions. Indeed, it would be unconstitutional for them to do so.

By contrast, if the substantive guide for the penal law is a constitutional theory of the general part thematizing the reconciliation of penal force and freedom, then at least one impediment to the penal law's subjection to judicial review for substantive justice falls away. For now the constitutional entrenchment of a right not to be unjustly deprived of liberty by the state is the entrenchment of the general part as understood and revised by the best legal theory thereof. The common-law constitution weakly constraining the state's penal power can become part of the binding, written one without dilution. Many will no doubt have reservations about so expanded a scope for judicial review of penal legislation. But that is another subject.

---

[3] An exceptional case is *Robinson v California* 370 US 660 (1962).
[4] Compare *R v Pappajohn* [1980] 2 SCR 120 with *R v Martineau* [1990] 2 SCR 633.

Bibliography

Acorn, Annalise. *Compulsory Compassion: A Critique of Restorative Justice* (Vancouver: University of British Columbia Press, 2004).

Alexander, Larry. 'Insufficient Concern: A Unified Conception of Criminal Culpability,' (2000) 88 *California Law Review* 931.

——'Lesser Evils: A Closer Look at the Paradigmatic Justification,' (2005) 24 *Law and Philosophy* 611.

Aquinas, St Thomas. *Summa Theologica,* trans. Fathers of the English Dominican Province (New York: Benziger, 1947).

Aristotle. *Nicomachean Ethics*, in R. McKeon ed., *The Basic Works of Aristotle* (New York: Random House, 1941).

Ashworth, AJ. 'Sharpening the Subjective Element in Criminal Liability,' in RA Duff and NE Simmonds, eds, *Philosophy and the Criminal Law* (Wiesbaden, 1984).

—— 'Taking the Consequences,' in Stephen Shute, John Gardner, and Jeremy Horder, eds, *Action and Value in Criminal Law* (Oxford: Clarendon Press, 1993).

——'Responsibilities, Rights and Restorative Justice,' (2002) 42:3 *British Journal of Criminology*, 578–95.

——'A Change of Normative Position: Determining the Contours of Culpability in Criminal Law,' (2008) 11 *New Criminal Law Review* 232.

Austin, John. *Lectures on Jurisprudence*, 4th ed. (London: John Murray, 1879).

Beccaria, Cesare. *Of Crimes and Punishments,* trans. Jane Grigson (Oxford: Oxford University Press, 1964).

Bentham, Jeremy. *An Introduction to the Principles of Morals and Legislation* (Darien, Conn: Hafner, 1970).

Braithwaite, John. *Crime, Shame and Reintegration* (Cambridge: Cambridge University Press, 1989).

Braithwaite, John and Pettit, Philip. *Not Just Deserts* (Oxford: Clarendon Press, 1990).

Christie, Nils. 'Conflicts as Property,' (1977) 17(1) *British Journal of Criminology* (January).

Cragg, Wesley. *The Practice of Punishment: Towards a Theory of Restorative Justice* (London: Routledge, 1992).

Dan-Cohen, Meir. 'Decision Rules and Conduct Rules: On Acoustic Separation in Criminal Law,' (1984) 97 *Harvard Law Review* 625.

Dressler, Joshua. 'New Thoughts About the Concept of Justification in the Criminal Law: A Critique of Fletcher's Thinking and Rethinking,' (1984) 32 *UCLA Law Review* 61.

——'Exegesis of the Law of Duress: Justifying the Excuse and Searching for its Proper Limits,' (1989) 62 *Southern California Law Review* 1331.

Dubber, Markus. *Victims in the War on Crime* (New York: New York University Press, 2002).

Duff, RA. *Intention, Agency, and Criminal Liability* (Oxford: Blackwell, 1990).

—— *Criminal Attempts* (Oxford: Oxford University Press, 1996).

Duff, RA. *Punishment, Communication, and Community* (Oxford: Oxford University Press, 2001).
—— 'Rethinking Justifications,' (2004) 39 *Tulsa Law Review* 829.
—— *Answering for Crime* (Oxford: Hart, 2007).
Feinberg, Joel. *The Moral Limits to the Criminal Law*, vol. 1, *Harm to Others* (New York: Oxford University Press, 1984).
Fletcher, George. 'Proportionality and the Psychotic Aggressor,' (1973) 8 *Israel Law Review* 367–90.
—— *Rethinking Criminal Law* (Boston: Little, Brown, 1978).
—— 'The Right and the Reasonable,' (1985) *Harvard Law Review* 98 949.
—— 'Punishment and Self-Defense,' (1989) *Law and Philosophy* 8 207–8.
—— *The Grammar of Criminal Law* (Oxford: Oxford University Press, 2007).
Foot, Philippa. *Virtues and Vices and Other Essays in Moral Philosophy* (Oxford: Oxford University Press, 2002).
Gardner, John. 'On the General Part of the Criminal Law,' in Antony Duff, ed., *Philosophy and the Criminal Law* (Cambridge: Cambridge University Press, 1998).
—— *Offences and Defences* (Oxford: Oxford University Press, 2007).
Greenawalt, Kent. 'The Perplexing Borders of Justification and Excuse,' (1984) 84 *Columbia Law Review* 1897.
Grisez, Germain. 'Toward a Consistent Natural-Law Ethics of Killing,' (1970) 15 *American Journal of Jurisprudence* 64.
Gross, Hyman. *A Theory of Criminal Justice* (New York: Oxford University Press, 1979).
Hall, J. *General Principles of Criminal Law,* 2nd ed. (Indianapolis: Bobbs Merrill, 1960).
—— 'Negligent Behavior Should Be Excluded from Penal Liability,' (1963) 63 *Columbia Law Review* 632.
Hart, HLA. *Punishment and Responsibility* (Oxford: Clarendon Press, 1968).
Hart, HLA and Honoré, Tony. *Causation in the Law,* 2nd ed. (Oxford: Clarendon Press, 1985).
Hegel, GWF. *The Philosophy of History,* trans. J Sibree (New York: Dover, 1956).
—— *Philosophy of Right,* trans. TM Knox (Oxford: Oxford University Press, 1967).
Hobbes, Thomas. *Leviathan* (Oxford: Blackwell, 1957).
Horder, Jeremy. *Provocation and Responsibility* (Oxford: Clarendon Press, 1992).
—— 'Gross Negligence and Criminal Culpability,' (1997) 47 *University of Toronto Law Journal* 495.
—— 'Self-Defence, Necessity, and Duress; Understanding the Relationship,' (1998) 11 *Canadian Journal of Law and Jurisprudence* 146.
—— *Excusing Crime* (Oxford: Oxford University Press, 2004).
Hörnle, Tatjana. 'Hijacked Airplanes: May They Be Shot Down?' (2007) 10 *New Criminal Law Review* 582.
Hurd, Heidi M. 'Justification and Excuse, Wrongdoing and Culpability,' (1999) 74 *Notre Dame Law Review* 1551.
Husak, Douglas. *Philosophy of Criminal Law* (Totowa, NJ: Rowman & Littlefield, 1987).
—— 'Does Criminal Liability Require an Act?' in Antony Duff, ed., *Philosophy and the Criminal Law* (Cambridge: Cambridge University Press, 1998).

——'Strict Liability, Justice, Proportionality,' in AP Simester, ed., *Appraising Strict Liability* (Oxford: Oxford University Press, 2005), 93–99.
Kant, Immanuel. *Foundations of the Metaphysics of Morals,* trans. Lewis W Beck (Indianapolis: Bobbs Merrill, 1959).
——*The Metaphysics of Morals,* trans. Mary Gregor (Cambridge: Cambridge University Press, 1991).
Kadish, S. 'Excusing Crime' (1987) 75 *California Law Review* 257.
Klimchuk, Dennis. 'Necessity, Deterrence, and Standing,' (2002) 8 *Legal Theory* 339.
Lacey, Nicola. *State Punishment* (London: Routledge, 1988).
Llewellyn, Jennifer and Howse, Robert, 'Institutions for Restorative Justice: The South African Truth and Reconciliation Commission,' (1999) 49 *University of Toronto Law Journal.*
Mill, John Stuart. *On Liberty* (New York: Crofts, 1947).
Moore, Michael. *Act and Crime* (Oxford: Clarendon Press, 1993).
——*Placing Blame* (Oxford: Clarendon Press, 1997).
Moran, Mayo. *Rethinking the Reasonable Person* (Oxford: Oxford University Press, 2003).
Murphy, J. 'Marxism and Retribution,' (1973) 2:3 *Philosophy and Public Affairs* 217–43 (Spring).
Nagel, Thomas. *Mortal Questions* (Cambridge: Cambridge University Press, 1979).
Norrie, Alan. *Punishment, Responsibility, and Justice* (Oxford: Oxford University Press, 2000).
—— *Crime, Reason and History: A Critical Introduction to Criminal Law,* 2nd ed. (London: Butterworths, 2001).
Nozick, Robert. *Anarchy, State, and Utopia* (New York: Basic Books, 1974).
Posner, R. *Economic Analysis of Law,* 6th ed. (New York: Aspen, 2003).
Ripstein, Arthur. *Equality, Responsibility and the Law* (Cambridge: Cambridge University Press, 1999).
——'Authority and Coercion,' (2004) 32 *Philosophy and Public Affairs* 2.
——'In Extremis,' (2005) 2 *Ohio State Journal of Criminal Law* 415.
Robinson, Paul. 'A Theory of Justification: Societal Harm as a Prerequisite for Criminal Liability,' (1975) 23 *UCLA Law Review* 266.
——'Criminal Law Defenses: A Systematic Analysis' (1982) 82 *Columbia Law Review* 199.
——'Competing Theories of Justification: Deeds v Reasons,' in AP Simester and ATH Smith, eds, *Harm and Culpability* (Oxford: Clarendon Press, 1996), 45–70.
Robinson, Paul and Cahill, Michael. *Law Without Justice* (Oxford: Oxford University Press, 2006).
Shafer-Landau, Russ. 'The Failure of Retributivism,' in Joel Feinberg and Jules Coleman, eds, *Philosophy of Law,* 7th ed. (Belmont, Ca: Thomson, Wadsworth, 2004), 831–41.
Simester, AP. 'Is Strict Liability Always Wrong?' in AP Simester, ed., *Appraising Strict Liability* (Oxford: Oxford University Press, 2005), 21–50.
St Thomas Aquinas. *Summa Theologica,* trans. Fathers of the English Dominican Province (New York: Benziger, 1947).
Stewart, Hamish. 'The Role of Reasonableness in Self-Defence,' (2003) 16 *Canadian Journal of Law and Jurisprudence* 317.
Tadros, Victor. *Criminal Responsibility* (Oxford: Oxford University Press, 2005).

Thompson, Judith Jarvis. 'The Trolley Problem,' (1985) 94 *Yale Law Journal* 1395.
——'Self-Defense,' (1991) 20(4) *Philosophy and Public Affairs* (Autumn), 283–310.
Thorburn, Malcolm. 'Justifications, Powers, and Authority,' (2008) 117 *Yale Law Journal* 1070.
Uniacke, Suzanne. *Permissible Killing: The Self-Defence Justification of Homicide* (Cambridge: Cambridge University Press, 1994).
von Hirsch, Andrew and Ashworth, Andrew. *Proportionate Sentencing* (Oxford: Oxford University Press, 2005).
Williams, Glanville. *Criminal Law: The General Part,* 2nd ed. (London: Stevens, 1961).
Wilson, William. *Central Issues in Criminal Theory* (Oxford: Hart, 2002).
Woodward, J. 'Paternalism and Justification,' in W Cragg, ed., *Contemporary Moral Issues,* 3rd ed. (Toronto: McGraw-Hill Ryerson, 1992).

Index

actus reus see culpable action
agency goods 138–40, 172–3, 179, 184, 225, 229–30
Alexander, Larry 94
Aquinas, St Thomas 197–9, 201, 203
Aristotle 17, 19, 33, 228, 242, 248, 257–9
Ashworth, Andrew 17, 70, 133
attempts 115, 116, 121–8
Austin, John 101–8
automatism 273–5, 286–94

basic responsibility 30, 83–5
Bentham, Jeremy 25, 101–2, 106, 193–4, 241
blamelessness 183, 247–50, 254–62, 265–7, 317–20, 326
Bratty v Northern Ireland 274, 275, 292–3

Campbell and Bradley v Ward 123–4
causation 104, 133, 145–50, 158–65
character theory
    and criminal *actus* 65, 68
    of excuse 247–50, 254–62, 267–72, 318
    of *mens rea* 64–70
choice theory of *mens rea* 70–5
citizenship 6, 317–19
Coetzee, JM 311–12
common will 36, 167, 256, 259, 261, 318
communal solidarity (belonging) 5–8, 13, 307–12
comparative imputability 162–5
consent
    as authorizing punishment 2–5
    to bodily contact 89–92
    constructive 279–80
    monadic view of 89–92
    as negating wrong 219, 236
    relational view of 89–92
    unreasonable belief in, as exculpatory 89–92
conspiracy 121, 128–30
counselling 121, 128–30
culpable action 99–130, 302–3
culpable mind 59–97, 106–8, 116–17, 144, 230
criminal desert see desert
culpable wrong 37–41

desert
    legal and moral theory of, contrasted 15–20, 48–55

moral 167–8, 254–62, 317–18
proportionality 51–5, 147–9, 154–8, 167–8, 254–62, 317–18
in public welfare context 176–7, 188
of punishment simply 38–41, 76–7, 96–7, 116–17
detention after acquittal 273–94
dialogic community
    in communal solidarity 307–12
    in excuse 317–19
    form of 306–7, 312–19
    in formal right 313–16, 317
    in justificatory defences 314–17
    in political community 305–7
    public reason as 305–12
    in real autonomy paradigm 316–17
    in restorative justice 307–12, 314
    in retributivism 313–14
    in self-sufficient community 317–19
Dickson, Brian 242, 245–6, 248
disease of the mind 273–6, 283, 287, 289–94
double effect 197–205
DPP v Morgan 63, 92
due diligence 181, 182–5, 266–7, 302
Duff, Antony 17, 20, 30, 60, 62–3, 92–6, 154–7, 216
duress 75, 223–30, 238–40, 250, 317–19

entrapment 263–5
exculpatory conditions
    character theory of 64–7
    completely 11–12, 74–5, 81–5, 166, 236–7
    dialogic community in 314–15, 317–19
    legal retributivist theory of 81–5
    partially 267–72
excuse 2, 16, 233–72
    character theory of 64–70, 247–50, 270–2
    choice theory of 70–75
    as concession to human frailty 245–7, 269–70, 272
    and exculpation 235–7, 254–62, 267–72, 317–18
    as moral blamelessness 254–5, 262, 266–7, 320
    as moral involuntariness 241–5, 262
    parameters of 260–1
    partial 249–50, 267–72
    and political community 255–61
    and public reason 246–7, 261, 263, 266
    as staying state's sword 262–7

fault-undifferentiated crimes 150–8
Feinberg, Joel 9, 10
fitness to stand trial 285–6
Fletcher, George 15–16, 17, 79, 86, 103, 212, 235–6, 241
foreseeability 4, 56, 60–1, 80, 133–5, 143–51, 158–65
formal agency (formalist) paradigm 23–48
  and *actus reus* 100, 116–19
  dialogic community in 313–16
  interdependence with real autonomy 225–7, 297–300
  and justification against wrongdoers 57, 205–23
  limits of 55–8, 131–5, 224
  and *mens rea* 75–85
  and mental disorder 83–5, 276–7
  public reason in 23–8, 224
  and punishment 37–48
  and wrong 35–7
free choice
  and basic responsibility 30, 83–5, 283
  as capacity for rights 29–30, 276, 278–9
  and chance 133–5, 142–3, 147–50, 157–8, 162–5
  and desert 20, 38–41, 76–85
  and outcome responsibility 132–5, 146–58, 162–5, 241–5, 267–8
  protection of, as end of formalist paradigm 5, 23–35
  as theory of culpable mind 70–75

Gardner, John 17, 30, 215, 235–6, 241, 248–50, 315
general part ix, 23, 301, 325–6, 327–8
Grisez, Germain 199, 204
gross negligence 73, 78–9, 93, 94

Hall, Jerome 173–4
happiness 24–7, 38, 179–83, 317
harm 9–11, 31–2, 131–68
  to agency goods 138–40, 172, 179, 184
  for formalism 55–7, 131–2, 295, 301
  and lesser evil 194–5
  and measure of punishment 10, 32, 139, 319
  and public welfare offences 9–10, 139–40, 172, 179, 184
  and real autonomy 131–41, 295, 300–1
Hart, HLA 60–1, 71, 86, 100, 153, 156, 161–3, 188, 238, 302
Hegel, GWF 34–5, 45–8, 50, 147, 208, 231–2, 257
Hobbes, Thomas 50, 70, 201–3, 205, 211, 253, 298
Holmes, Oliver Wendell 86, 101–2
Honoré, Tony 161–3

Horder, Jeremy 17, 60, 95–6, 270
Hurd, Heidi 216
Husak, Douglas 109, 114–15, 303
Hyam v DPP 143, 151

ignorance of the law 86–7, 184–8
imaginary crimes 126–7
impossible attempts 125–8
imputability of results 132–5, 146–58, 162–5, 241–5, 267–8
inchoate crimes 107, 120–30
infancy 30–1, 81, 83, 87
innocence 7, 198, 223
  detention despite 273–94
  moral 254–62
  presumption of 292–3, 311
innocents 198, 223
  justification of force against 223–32, 315–16
insane automatism 273–7, 286–94
insanity (mental disorder) 30, 83–5, 97, 221–2
  burden of proof 282–3, 292
  as exculpatory 30, 83–5
  fitness to stand trial 285–6
  as justifying detention of innocent 273–94
intention
  and *actus reus* 102–4, 106–8
  as culpable mind 38–41, 60–3, 77–8, 176
  as grade of responsibility for harm 143–4, 147–50, 152–8, 163–5, 267–8
  and inchoate crime 120–8
  and public welfare offences 81, 177
internal and external viewpoints 12–15, 327
intervening events 158–65
intoxication 66–7, 68, 134–5, 267–8, 270–1
involuntary movements 101, 105–8, 161–2, 198, 206

justification
  double effect theory of 197–205
  impossibility of generalizing about 189–93
  lesser evil theory of 193–7
  of private force against innocents 223–32, 314–16
  of private force against wrong-doers 205–23, 314–16
  of punishment 1–5, 19–20, 38–55, 76–7, 116–17, 141–50
  putative 213–18, 229
  real 206–13
  unknown 219–23, 229

Kant, Immanuel 23, 26, 27, 29, 33–4, 42–5, 48, 50, 53, 67, 70, 141, 208, 224, 233, 241, 250–4, 257, 262–3

Index

legal retributivism 38–55
  as account of *actus reus* 116–17
  as account of culpable mind 76–81
  as account of exculpatory conditions 81–5
  contrasted with moral retributivism 19–20, 48–55
  dialogic community in 313–14
legal norm 36, 255–62, 318
lesser evil
  as justification 193–7, 231–2
  as excuse 260
Luftsicherheitsgesetz case 233–4, 239

Mill, JS 9, 10, 279–80
mistake
  of fact 73, 78, 82, 87–92, 97, 217, 229, 314
  of law 82–3, 86–92, 184–8
M'Naghten rules 83–4, 276–7, 283–7
Model Penal Code 74–5, 121, 151, 214
Moore, Michael 17, 18, 20, 60, 71, 101, 106, 109–18
moral blameworthiness
  as account of *actus* 108–15
  as account of *mens rea* 64–75, 92–4, 96–7
  legal culpability contrasted with 15–20, 33–5, 152–3, 157–8, 166–8, 255, 320, 326
  and public welfare offences 183
  and responsibility for harm 148–50, 152–8
  and unknown justification 219–21
moral involuntariness 241–5, 262
moral retributivism 19–20, 48–50, 108–15
moral theory 15–19, 325–6
Murphy, Jeffrie 324
mutual recognition 36–7, 46–7, 50, 76–7, 89, 210–11, 224–6, 227, 306–8, 312–20

Nagel, Thomas 142
necessity
  choice theory of 73
  dialogic community in 315–18
  double effect theory of 200, 204
  as excuse 233–62
  as justification 223–32
  lesser evil theory of 193–7
negligence
  civil 73–4
  as grade of responsibility for harm 132–5, 145–50
  gross 73, 78–9, 93, 94, 97
  and imprisonment 182, 183–4
  in public welfare context 178–88, 302
noncontradiction proviso 184–8
noncriminal penalties 21, 119–20, 139–40, 176–8
Norrie, Alan 79, 167
novus actus interveniens 158–65

officially-induced error 265–6
omissions 102, 105–6, 110–19, 130
outcome responsibility
  (see imputability of results)

Pagett v The Queen 165
partial exculpation 236–7, 249–50, 267–72
partial excuse 236–7, 249–50, 267–72
penal force, definition of 21
penal law as complex whole 8–12, 295–320, 321–2
People v Lewis 160, 162, 164
Perka v The Queen 241, 245–6, 248
political community 255–61, 305–7, 318
possession offences 119–20
practical indifference 92–6, 154–5
presumption of innocence 182–3, 292–3, 311
presumptive criminality
  (unequivocality) test 122–8
proportionality
  in excuse 260
  in justification 195–6, 212–13, 218, 221–2, 227–8, 230–2
  in punishment 51–5, 134–5, 147–58
provocation
  as justification for defensive force 201–3, 211, 237, 246, 250
  as partial excuse 268–72
public interest 21–2, 25
public reason
  appealed to by excuse 263–7
  as communal solidarity 307–12
  concept of 21–3
  as dialogic community 305–7, 312–20
  as formal agency 23–8, 224
  in public welfare context 179–88
  as real autonomy 131–7, 226
  of self-sufficient community 256–62, 318–19, 321–2
public welfare 138–9, 170, 184, 227–9, 256, 304
public welfare offences 9–10, 51, 57–8, 139–40, 169–88, 230, 316–17
punishment
  in formalist paradigm 37–48, 55–6, 303–4
  imprisonment 182, 184, 308
  point of 42–8
  proportionality 51–5, 134–5, 147–58
  punitive fines 177
  in real autonomy paradigm 301–4
  in solidarity paradigm 307–8

R v Barker 122, 128
R v Burgess 274
R v Caldwell 62–3
R v Cheshire 159, 160
R v Dudley and Stephens 237–9

R v Kemp 287, 290
R v Quick 288–90
R v Rabey 274–5, 289–90
R v Smith (1959) 159
R v Smith (2001) 269
R v Steane 152–3
R v Stone 274–5
R v Woolin 151–2, 154
Rawls, John 3–4
Raz, Joseph 237
real autonomy 5–6, 13, 28–9, 179–88, 226–8, 279, 282–94, 299–300
  dialogic community in 316–17
  paradigm of 131, 135–41, 227, 276–7, 295–6, 300–5, 321
  public reason as 131–7, 169, 226, 266–7
recklessness
  as culpability for wrong 64, 78–9, 92–6, 105, 118, 176
  as grade of responsibility for harm 62–3, 132, 134–5, 148–58, 164–5
  as practical indifference 93–6
regulatory offences *see* public welfare offences
rescues 110–14, 118–19
responsibility for harm 131–68
  and luck 136–7, 140–50
restorative justice 307–12, 314, 319
retributivism 19–20
  dialogic community in 313–14
  inapplicability to public welfare context 57–8, 80–1, 176–7
  legal 20, 38–41, 45–8, 50–5, 76–7, 81, 116–17, 133, 137, 302–3
  moral 20, 48–50, 108–15
right infringement (wrong) *see* transgression
Ripstein, Arthur 43–4, 60, 86–92

Robinson, Paul 194–6
rule of law 7, 57–8, 262–3, 304–5, 324

Salmond, Sir John 122–3, 128
sane automatism 273–6, 288–92, 294
self-defence 197–223, 281, 314–16
Simester, Andrew 175
Star Chamber, Court of 121, 129, 130
status offences 119–20
stay of penal proceedings 251–3, 262–7
strict liability
  for public welfare offences 178–9, 181–4, 186–7
  for results of culpable wrongs 131–5, 144–7
subjectivism 59–63, 76–97, 142, 144, 313, 314
  extreme 141–2
  and imprisonment 182, 184
  inapplicability to public welfare context 87, 173–8

Tadros, Victor 17, 60, 67–9
therapeutic detainability criteria 277–8, 283
thin-skull rule 56, 132, 146–7
Thomson, Judith 239
transgression (right infringement, wrong) 36–7, 106
  as justifying defensive force 206, 210
  punishment as 37–8
true crimes 8–12, 170–2

Uniacke, Suzanne 216

Welzel, Hans 102–3
wilful blindness 10, 60, 78–9
Williams, Glanville 123–5, 190–1, 197